East Asian Film Remakes

Screen Serialities

Series editors: Claire Perkins and Constantine Verevis

Series advisory board: Kim Akass, Glen Creeber, Shane Denson, Jennifer Forrest, Jonathan Gray, Julie Grossman, Daniel Herbert, Carolyn Jess-Cooke, Frank Kelleter, Amanda Ann Klein, Kathleen Loock, Jason Mittell, Sean O'Sullivan, Barton Palmer, Alisa Perren, Dana Polan, Iain Robert Smith, Shannon Wells-Lassagne, Linda Williams

Screen Serialities provides a forum for introducing, analysing and theorising a broad spectrum of serial screen formats – including franchises, series, serials, sequels and remakes.

Over and above individual texts that happen to be serialised, the book series takes a guiding focus on seriality as an aesthetic and industrial principle that has shaped the narrative logic, socio-cultural function and economic identity of screen texts across more than a century of cinema, television and 'new' media.

Titles in this series include:

Film Reboots
Edited by Daniel Herbert and Constantine Verevis

Reanimated: The Contemporary American Horror Remake
By Laura Mee

Gender and Seriality: Practices and Politics of Contemporary US Television
By Maria Sulimma

European Film Remakes
Edited by Eduard Cuelenaere, Gertjan Willems and Stijn Joye

Superhero Blockbusters: Seriality and Politics
By Felix Brinker

Hollywood Remakes of Iconic British Films: Class, Gender and Stardom
By Agnieszka Rasmus

East Asian Film Remakes
Edited by David Scott Diffrient and Kenneth Chan

East Asian Film Remakes

Edited by David Scott Diffrient and
Kenneth Chan

EDINBURGH
University Press

Edinburgh University Press is one of the leading university presses in the UK. We publish academic books and journals in our selected subject areas across the humanities and social sciences, combining cutting-edge scholarship with high editorial and production values to produce academic works of lasting importance. For more information visit our website: edinburghuniversitypress.com

© editorial matter and organisation David Scott Diffrient and Kenneth Chan 2023,2025
© the chapters their several authors 2023,2025

Edinburgh University Press Ltd
13 Infirmary Street
Edinburgh EH1 1LT

First published in hardback by Edinburgh University Press 2023

Typeset in 11/13 Ehrhardt MT by
IDSUK (DataConnection) Ltd

A CIP record for this book is available from the British Library

ISBN 978 1 3995 0816 2 (hardback)
ISBN 978 1 3995 0817 9 (paperback)
ISBN 978 1 3995 0818 6 (webready PDF)
ISBN 978 1 3995 0819 3 (epub)

The right of David Scott Diffrient and Kenneth Chan to be identified as the editors of this work has been asserted in accordance with the Copyright, Designs and Patents Act 1988, and the Copyright and Related Rights Regulations 2003 (SI No. 2498).

Contents

List of Illustrations vii
Foreword xi
Notes on Contributors xiii

Introduction: East Asian Film Remakes 1
David Scott Diffrient

Part I: Re-fleshing the Text: Sex, Seduction, Desire

1. How to Sell a Remake: The *Gate of Flesh* Media Franchise 27
   Irene González-López

2. Against Anaesthesia: *An Empty Dream*, Pleasurable Pain and the 'Illicit' Thrills of South Korea's Golden Age Remakes 49
   David Scott Diffrient

3. Two Faces of Seduction: Martial Heroines and Karmic Women in Chor Yuen's *Intimate Confessions of a Chinese Courtesan* and *Lust for Love of a Chinese Courtesan* 73
   Andrew Grossman

4. Japanese Self-Made Film Remakes as Self-Improvement: Professional Desires and DIY Fulfilment, from *Panic High School* to *Tetsuo* 92
   Mark Player

Part II: Serialising Ozu: The Enduring Legacy of a Cinematic 'Tofu Maker'

5. Definition and Progression: Ozu Yasujirō's 'Noriko Trilogy' 111
   Alastair Phillips

6. A Remake, But . . . : Media Infantility in Ozu Yasujirō's
   Good Morning 124
   Rea Amit

7. The Cinema of Serial Vitality: Ozu Yasujirō and Yamada Yoji 140
   Steve Choe

Part III: Revisiting Personal/Political Traumas in East Asian Action Films, Gangster Films and Westerns

8. Opting Out of History: Miike Takashi's *New Graveyard of Honor* 157
   Earl Jackson

9. The Promise of Hokkaidō: Trauma, Violence and the Legacy of the Imperial Frontier in Lee Sang-il's *Unforgiven* 182
   Lance Lomax

10. Benny Chan's *Connected* and the Hollywoodisation of Hong Kong Cinema 200
    Gary Bettinson

11. Vessels and Cargos: Spaces of Inclusion and Exclusion in Johnnie To's *Drug War* and Lee Hae-young's Korean Remake *Believer* 221
    Jinhee Choi

Part IV: Local Flavours and Transcultural Flows in East Asian Comedies, Dramas and Fantasies

12. The Power of Healing in *Little Forest*(s): Cross-Cultural Perspectives on Food, Friendship and Self-Identity, from Japan to South Korea 239
    Nam Lee

13. *More than Blue* and *Man in Love*: Transnational Korean-Taiwanese Film Remakes as a Facilitator for Taiwan Cinema 257
    Ting-Ying Lin

14. The Pan-Asian 'Miss Granny' Phenomenon 272
    Jennifer Coates, Hsin Hsieh, Sung-Ae Lee and Kate Taylor-Jones

15. Remaking in the Age of Chthulumedia: Stephen Chow's
    The Mermaid 291
    Kenneth Chan

Index 314

Illustrations

FIGURES

Figure 1.1	Osumi (Natori Yuko) takes her revenge on the sergeant who raped and killed her mother, in Gosha Hideo's *Gate of Flesh* (*Nikutai no mon*, 1988).	37
Figure 1.2	The cover art of the 2015 DVD release of Gosha Hideo's *Gate of Flesh* (*Nikutai no mon*, 1988), showing the character Sen sitting on the shoulders of an unidentified black man.	42
Figure 2.1	Painful dentist-office scenes in Yu Hyun-mok's *The Stray Bullet* (*Obaltan*, 1961) [top], the same director's *An Empty Dream* (*Chunmong*, 1965) [middle] and the latter film's Japanese-language source material *Daydream* (*Hakujitsumu*, 1964) [bottom], directed by Takechi Tetsuji.	62
Figure 2.2	As if standing before a mirror, the main characters in both *Daydream* (*Hakujitsumu*, 1964) and *An Empty Dream* (*Chunmong*, 1965) mimic each other's amorous actions, inside and outside a glass window that separates them.	67
Figure 3.1	Lady Chun and Ai Nu stand back-to-back during a brief interlude of the climactic swordfight in the wuxia classic *Intimate Confessions of a Chinese Courtesan* (*Ai Nu*, 1972).	82
Figure 3.2	Ai Nu luxuriates in a bed filled with ill-gotten jewels in Chor Yuen's *Lust for Love of a Chinese Courtesan* (*Ai Nu xin zhuan*, 1984), a remake of the same director's *Intimate Confessions of a Chinese Courtesan* (*Ai Nu*, 1972).	86

Figure 4.1	The student gunman goes in for the kill in *Panic High School* (*Kōkō dai panikku*, 1976) and its 1978 studio-produced remake.	99
Figure 4.2	A lurching camera moves the salaryman from side to side as he receives a phone call from the 'metal fetishist' in *The Phantom of Regular Size* (*Futsū saizu no kaijin*, 1986) and *Tetsuo* (1989).	103
Figure 5.1	Performative synergy in *Late Spring* (*Banshun*, 1949).	115
Figure 5.2	A trail of connections in *Early Summer* (*Bakushū*, 1951).	119
Figure 6.1	On the left side, a sign at the centre advertises Haraguchi Mitsue's services as a midwife in Ozu's *Good Morning* (*Ohayō*, 1959), and on the right side, a midwife sign is visible in his earlier film *I Was Born, But . . .* (*Otona no miru ehon: Umarete wa mita keredo*, 1932).	126
Figure 6.2	On the left side, Yoshii exercises by himself, using a stringed stretching device while appearing engulfed by electrical lines and clotheslines, and on the right side, the protagonists' neighbours are shown following the morning radio calisthenics, in these shots from *I Was Born, But. . .* (*Otona no miru ehon: Umarete wa mita keredo*, 1932).	134
Figure 7.1	One of several over-the-shoulder, shot-reverse shot sequences in Yamada Yōji's *Tokyo Family* (*Tōkyō kazoku*, 2013), illustrating this remake's stylistic divergence from its source material (*Ozu Yasujirō's Tokyo Story* [*Tōkyō monogatari*, 1953]).	145
Figure 8.1	In this shot from Miike Takashi's *New Graveyard of Honor* (*Shin jingi no hakaba*, 2002), during a sex act ice cubes spill onto the proclamation of a new Imperial Reign.	166
Figure 8.2	Ishikawa (Watari Tetsuya) and prostitute (Seri Meika) are strung out on heroin while an old man in the next cubicle prays in this moment from Fukasaku Kinji's *Graveyard of Honor* (*Jingi no hakaba*, 1975) (top), and in a corresponding scene from Miike Takashi's *New Graveyard of Honor* (*Shin jingi no hakaba*, 2002) (bottom), Ishimatsu (Kishitani Goro) leads Chieko (Arimori Narimi) into heroin addiction in a love hotel.	170
Figure 8.3	Sone Hideki as the figure of the would-be yakuza star, now murdered by the star of *New Graveyard of Honor* (top); Sone Harumi as Fukui, killed by Ishimatsu in *New Graveyard of Honor* (bottom).	176

Figure 9.1	Officers aim their weapons at Masaharu Kitaoji (Kunimura Jun), in this scene from Lee Sang-il's *Unforgiven* (*Yurusarezaru mono*, 2013), a remake of Clint Eastwood's *Unforgiven* (1992).	194
Figure 10.1	Bob (Louis Koo), the protagonist of Benny Chan's *Connected* (*Bochi tungwah*, 2008), dangles from a platform seconds before falling, in this Cantonese remake of the US action film *Cellular* (2004).	214
Figure 10.2	Bob's vehicle makes another type of 'connection' with a US cultural production – specifically, a truck full of Pepsi Max sodas – in this scene from *Connected* (*Bochi tungwah*, 2008).	216
Figure 11.1	Seo Yeong-rak (Ryu Jun-yeol) and two deaf-mute drug factory workers are staged geometrically as they play catchball in Lee Hae-young's *Believer* (2018), a remake of Johnnie To's *Drug War* (*Du zhan*, 2012) (top), and in a re-establishing shot, the three continue to play while their image and the factory are reflected on the water's surface (bottom).	228
Figure 11.2	Hong Kong gang members are geometrically arranged as they fire at the police in the final shoot-out scene from Johnnie To's *Drug War* (*Du zhan*, 2012).	231
Figure 12.1	A scene of food preparation in Yim Soon-rye's *Little Forest* (*Liteul Poleseuteu*, 2018), a Korean version of a Japanese film and manga series of the same title.	248
Figure 13.1	A well-known vocalist of Amis descent, A-lin (born Lisang Pacidal Koyouan), plays a singer in *More than Blue* (*Bi beishang geng beishang de gushi*, 2018), director Gavin Lin's Taiwanese remake of a South Korean film of the same title.	262
Figure 13.2	Stars Ivy Yi-han Chen and Jasper Liu bring a 'little freshness' to this Taiwanese version of the South Korean romantic drama *More Than Blue* (*Seulpeumboda deoseulpeun iyagi*, 2009).	265
Figure 13.3	In this early scene of *Man in Love* (*Dang nanren lianai shi*, 2021), A-cheng (Roy Chiu) appears dressed like a typical Taiwanese gangster and speaks Taiyu, putting a decidedly 'local' spin on the Korean-language original of the same title.	267

Figure 14.1 The mother of a new-born baby reacts negatively to the title character's comments while riding a subway, in this scene from Hwang Dong-hyuk's *Miss Granny* (*Susanghan Geunyeo*, a.k.a., *Suspicious Girl*, 2014), the Korean-language basis for several cinematic remakes across the East and Southeast Asian region. 281

Figure 15.1 The school of fish functions as a playful 3D transitional wipe in Stephen Chow's *The Mermaid* (*Meirenyu*, 2016). 302

Figure 15.2 An ancient painting depicts Mr Zheng and his mermaid lover in *The Mermaid* (*Meirenyu*, 2016). 308

TABLES

Table 1.1 The 'Gate of Flesh' franchise. 30

Table 8.1 Similarities and differences between plot points in *Graveyard of Honor* (1975) and *New Graveyard of Honor* (2002) 168

Foreword

Yiman Wang

With the birth of film came film remaking. In the age of mechanical (and digital) reproduction, filmmaking and remaking have been inherently intertwined. The long-running disparagement of remakes as merely pale imitations of the 'originals' is, therefore, best understood as symptomatic of the essentialist obsession with the 'first', which itself is nothing but a construct. The establishment of the field of film remakes studies over the past three decades has fundamentally challenged this original-copy hierarchy, underlining not only the socio-cultural-political contextualisation of film cultures and film remaking alike, but also the built-in intertextuality of the motion picture medium. Given the rhizomic nature of film industries and cultures across the world, remakes stand as the prime site for refuting Euro-American-centered film studies, while reckoning with the long-lasting ramifications of colonialism and coloniality, overlaid with global capitalism.

East Asian Film Remakes arrives on the scene to tackle precisely these overarching issues. Divided into four sections, the essays in this volume, magisterially edited by David Scott Diffrient and Kenneth Chan, collectively unfurl a kaleidoscopic landscape of expansive filmic and mediatic connections, some of which have been obscured and understudied; and their resurfacing through the contributors' rigorous research decisively reinforces the film medium's fundamental intertextuality and intermediality. Relatedly, the volume puts much-needed pressure on the very parameters of the object of study, namely, remakes. Highlighting the elasticity of the definition of remakes, the contributors demonstrate film remaking as part and parcel of filmmaking itself.

The volume's unique contribution, however, lies in its focus on East Asia (Mainland China, Hong Kong, Japan, Korea and Taiwan), a terrain rife with layered and convoluted contentions and connections both within and vis-à-vis other parts of the world. By foregrounding East Asian location-specific film remakes, this volume offers a fresh take on a multifaceted interactive filmic world that must be understood in terms of its own evolving ecology, rather than simply in reference to Euro-American cinema. It is energising to see East Asian, European, Australian and American scholars from diverse disciplines including Film and Media Studies, East Asian Studies and Cultural Studies collaborating on this critical project that charts out East Asian film remaking across history, space, politics, genres and aesthetics, inviting us to confront the pressing questions of what constitutes remaking in a medium that is predicated upon (digital) reproduction with differences; what do we gain by studying remakes in a world where connections go hand in hand with contentions, and, as co-editor Diffrient puts it, 'familiarity' and 'newness' become two sides of the same coin?

With the arrival of *East Asian Film Remakes*, we excitedly anticipate further transformations of the field of remake studies.

Notes on Contributors

Rea Amit is assistant professor in the Department of Modern Languages, Literatures and Linguistics at the University of Oklahoma. He holds a PhD in Film and Media Studies and East Asian Languages and Literatures from Yale University, and a master's in Aesthetics from Tokyo University of the Arts. He has published mainly on Asian media, aesthetics and theory in journals such as *Philosophy East and West*, *Positions*, *Participations* and *On_Culture*, as well as several book chapters in edited volumes.

Gary Bettinson is a senior lecturer in Film Studies at Lancaster University (UK), author of *The Sensuous Cinema of Wong Kar-wai* (Hong Kong University Press) and chief editor of the *Asian Cinema* journal (Intellect Press). He is editor (with Daniel Martin) of *Hong Kong Horror Cinema* (Edinburgh University Press) and (with James Udden) of *The Poetics of Chinese Cinema* (Palgrave Macmillan).

Kenneth Chan is Professor of English and Film Studies at the University of Northern Colorado. He is the author of *Remade in Hollywood: The Global Chinese Presence in Transnational Cinemas* (Hong Kong University Press, 2009) and *Yonfan's Bugis Street* (Hong Kong University Press, 2015). He is also co-editor of *Sino-Enchantment: The Fantastic in Contemporary Chinese Cinemas* (Edinburgh University Press, 2021).

Steve Choe is Associate Professor of Critical Studies in the School of Cinema at San Francisco State University. He is the author of *Afterlives: Allegories of Film and Mortality in Early Weimar Germany* (2014), *Sovereign Violence: Ethics and South Korean Cinema in the New Millennium* (2016) and *ReFocus: The Films of William Friedkin* (2021). Choe is also a co-editor of *Beyond Imperial Aesthetics: Theories of Art and Politics in East Asia* (2019) and the editor of *The Palgrave Handbook of Violence in Film and Media* (2022).

Jinhee Choi is Reader of Film Studies at King's College of London and the author of *The South Korean Film Renaissance: Local Hitmakers and Global Provocateurs* (2010) and the editor of *Reorienting Ozu: A Master and His Influence* (2018). She is currently completing her 'girl' book, tentatively titled *Forever Girls: Necrocinematics and Contemporary Korean Girlhood* (Oxford University Press). Her research areas include contemporary Korean films, urban space and cinema and philosophy of film, and her articles and book chapters have appeared in numerous journals and edited volumes, including: 'On a Lonely Planet, Feeling-in-Depth: Wong Kar-wai's *2046* and Chris Marker's *Sans Soleil*' appearing in *Deep Mediations: Thinking Space in Cinema and Digital Cultures* (University of Minnesota Press, 2021) and 'Home is Where the Kitchen Is: *Rinco's Restaurant* (2009) and *Little Forest* (2014, 2018)' in *Asian Cinema* (2020).

Jennifer Coates is Senior Lecturer in Japanese Studies at the School of East Asian Studies, University of Sheffield. She is the author of *Making Icons: Repetition and the Female Image in Japanese Cinema, 1945–1964* (Hong Kong University Press, 2016). Her current ethnographic research project focuses on early post-war film audiences in Japan.

David Scott Diffrient is Professor of Film and Media Studies in the Department of Communication Studies at Colorado State University. His articles have been published in several journals as well as edited collections about film and television topics. He is the co-editor of *Screwball Television: Critical Perspectives on Gilmore Girls* (Syracuse University Press, 2010) as well as the author of *M*A*S*H* (Wayne State University Press, 2008), *Omnibus Films: Theorizing Transauthorial Cinema* (Edinburgh University Press, 2014), *Comic Drunks, Crazy Cults, and Lovable Monsters: Bad Behavior on American Television* (Syracuse University Press, 2022), *Body Genre: Anatomy of the Horror Film* (University Press of Mississippi, 2023) and, with co-author Hye Seung Chung, *Movie Migrations: Transnational Genre Flows and South Korean Cinema* (Rutgers University Press, 2015) and *Movie Minorities: Transnational Rights Advocacy and South Korean Cinema* (Rutgers University Press, 2021).

Irene González-López is Lecturer in Japanese Studies at Birkbeck, University of London. Her research spans Japanese creative industries, with a special focus on post-war cinema and issues related to gender and sexuality, both in front of and behind the camera. Recent publications include '"Female Director": Discourses and Practices in Contemporary Japan' (co-authored, *A Companion to Japanese Cinema*, 2022); '*Red-Light Bases* (1953), a Cross-temporal Contact Zone' (*Handbook of Japanese Media*, 2022); *Tanaka Kinuyo: Nation, Stardom and Female Subjectivity* (co-edited, Edinburgh University Press, 2018) and 'Marketing the *Panpan*: Youth, Sexual Revolution, and Power' (*US-Japan Women's Journal*, 2018).

Andrew Grossman is a regular contributor to and editor of *Bright Lights Film Journal* and the editor of the anthology *Queer Asian Cinema: Shadows in the Shade* (Harrington Park Press). His recent publications include essays and book chapters in *The Routledge Handbook of Male Sex Work, Culture, and Society*; *Grief in Contemporary Horror Cinema* (Lexington); *A Critical Companion to Terry Gilliam* (Lexington); *Alice in Wonderland in Film and Popular Culture* (Palgrave); *The Encyclopedia of LGBTQIA+ Portrayals in American Film* (Rowman-Littlefield) and *Bloodstained Narratives: The Giallo Film in Italy and Abroad* (University of Mississippi Press).

Hsin Hsieh is a Ph.D. student and a sessional lecturer in the Department of Film, Theatre & Television at the University of Reading. She teaches theatre, film, short film and TV production. Her research interests include adaptation, media and cultural studies. Her recent adaptation-related papers include 'Intermediality in the Adaptation Process: The Role of (Live) Orchestra in Amadeus', presented at the University of Reading, and '"See" the Wind Sing: Male Narrative and Point-of-View in Murakami's *Hear the Wind Sing* (1982) Film Adaptation', presented at the Murakami Haruki International conference at Newcastle University.

Earl Jackson is Associate Professor Emeritus from the University of California, Santa Cruz, Professor Emeritus from National Chiao Tung University and currently Chair Professor at Asia University. He is the author of *Strategies of Deviance: Studies in Gay Male Representation* and numerous essays on Japanese and Korean cinemas, sexuality and New Narrative writers. He is the co-editor, with Victor Fan, of *The Scent of Boys* (*Nang* 7) and co-editor, with David Desser, of *The Films of Kinoshita Keisuke: Times of Joy and Sorrow* (forthcoming from Edinburgh University Press). Jackson is currently completing a monograph on crisis and signification in Japanese genre films.

Nam Lee is Associate Professor of Film and Media Studies at Chapman University's Dodge College of Film and Media Arts. Formerly a film critic and print journalist in Seoul, South Korea, she has published film reviews and articles on Korean cinema as well as scholarly articles focusing on the 1980s. She is the author of *The Films of Bong Joon Ho* (Rutgers University Press, 2020).

Sung-Ae Lee is a Lecturer in the Department of International Studies at Macquarie University, Sydney, Australia. Her major research focus is on fiction, film and television drama of East Asia, with particular attention given to Korea. Her research centres on relationships between cultural ideologies in Asian societies and representational strategies. Her work has appeared in *Adaptation, Asian Cinema, International Research in Children's Literature, Journal of Asian American Studies* and *Mosaic*, and in several essay collections, including *Subjectivity in Asian Children's Literature and Film* (Routledge, 2013), *Grimms' Tales Around the Globe* (Wayne State University Press, 2014), *Fairy Tale Films Beyond Disney* (Routledge, 2015), *Transmedia in Asia and the Pacific: Industry, Practice and Transcultural Dialogues* (Palgrave Macmillan, 2021) and *Orientalism and Reverse Orientalism in Literature and Film: Beyond East and West* (Routledge, 2021).

Ting-Ying Lin is an Assistant Professor in the Department of Information and Communication at Tamkang University, Taiwan. She received her Ph.D. in Media and Communications from Goldsmiths, University of London, UK. Her research focuses on Taiwan cinema, Hong Kong cinema, East Asian cinema and screen cultures. She has recently published in *Chung Wai Literary Quarterly* (2022), *Concentric: Literary and Cultural Studies* (2020), *Sport, Film and National Culture* (Routledge, 2020) and *Positioning Taiwan in a Global Context: Being and Becoming* (Routledge, 2019).

Lance Lomax is a Doctoral Candidate in the Department of English at Texas Tech University. His research foregrounds the intersections of Japan's visual culture, media industries, transnational exchange and moments of crisis that developed around paradigms of conflict and peace, modernisation and imperialism and disaster and recovery. His research seeks to contribute to studies of media ecologies, popular cultural exports and modes of production, distribution and reception framed through a constellation of mediated representations and responses that have and continue to serve myriad interests within and beyond Japan's physical and ideological borders. His work has previously appeared in the *Journal of Film and Video* and is forthcoming on topics such as non-Western approaches to teaching silent cinema and Asian representation in 1960s Hollywood and American television.

Alastair Phillips is Professor of Film Studies at the University of Warwick, UK. He is the author of a BFI Film Classic on *Tokyo Story* (BFI/Bloomsbury Publishing, 2022) and the co-editor (with Hideaki Fujiki) of *The Japanese Cinema Book* (BFI/Bloomsbury Publishing, 2020). He is an editor of *Screen*.

Mark Player is a writer and researcher who specialises in Japanese cinema and media. He holds a Ph.D. in Film from the University of Reading. His research has been featured in journals such as *Japan Forum* and *Punk & Post-Punk*, and in edited volumes such as *Punk Identities, Punk Utopias: Global Punk and Media* (Intellect, 2021) and *Fifty Key Figures in Cyberpunk Culture* (Routledge, 2022). He is currently working on his first monograph, which is about Japanese cinema and punk.

Kate Taylor-Jones is Professor of East Asian Cinema at the University of Sheffield. She has published on topics including colonial Japanese and Korean cinema, cinema and landscape in East Asia and domestic violence and the sex trade. She is author of *Divine Work: Japanese Colonial Cinema and its Legacy*. Her current project – *Ninagawa Mika, Miyake Kyoto and Ando Momoko: Shōjo Dreams and Unruly Idols* will be published by Edinburgh University Press. She is co-editor of *International Cinema and the Girl: Local Issues, Transnational Contexts* and *Prostitution and Sex Work in Global Cinema: New Takes on Fallen Women*.

Yiman Wang is Professor of Film & Digital Media at the University of California, Santa Cruz. She is the author of *Remaking Chinese Cinema: Through the Prism of Shanghai, Hong Kong and Hollywood* (2013). She was a NEH (National Endowment for Humanities) awardee in 2019–20. She has guest-edited a special issue for *Feminist Media Histories* on Asian feminist media (2019) and has published numerous articles in journals and edited volumes on the topics of Chinese cinema studies, independent documentary, star studies, ecocinema, race and gender in early cinema and film remakes and adaptation.

Introduction: East Asian Film Remakes

David Scott Diffrient

Over the past three decades, the subject of cinematic remakes has emerged as a major subdiscipline in film studies, giving rise to a host of critical, philosophical and theoretical approaches that highlight the historical significance of iterative storytelling within and across different national contexts. Thanks to the ongoing efforts of Daniel Herbert, Thomas Leitch, Kathleen Loock, Lucy Mazdon, Claire Perkins, Constantine Verevis and several other scholars who are drawn to the remake's contradictory appeals and intertextual complexities, this long-disparaged category of filmmaking – once brushed off by critics as little more than a derivative copy or pale imitation of an original text – is now recognised as a legitimate cultural form in its own right, one that aesthetically reframes the distant or recent past while providing a paradoxically nostalgic vantage on modern-day issues. Indeed, with so many published studies of remakes currently available, it would seem that very little remains to be said about a topic that is already brimming with taxonomies and terminology unique to this most bankable and pervasive type of cultural production.

Despite a proliferation of books and articles about remakes, however, a regional survey of representative films produced in East Asia is only just now – with this publication – coming to fruition. This volume seeks to fill a significant gap in the history of remakes by bringing together original contributions from experts in Chinese, Hong Kong, Japanese, South Korean and Taiwanese cinemas, thereby providing fresh perspectives on a subject that has largely been confined to North American and European contexts. It builds upon a few important publications, including Yiman Wang's *Remaking Chinese Cinema: Through the Prism of Shanghai, Hong Kong and Hollywood* (2013) and Sarah Woodland's *Remaking Gender and the Family: Perspectives on Contemporary Chinese-Language Film Remakes* (2018), which have been instrumental in securing a place for what Wang refers to as 'peripheral and subaltern' remakes in US, British and other academic arenas where Sinophone studies now sits comfortably alongside film studies. However, as an edited collection of fifteen chapters (including a roundtable discussion about the pan-Asian 'Miss Granny' phenomenon that began in 2014 with the Korean-language *Suspicious Girl* [*Susanghan geunyeo*] and has so far resulted in seven remakes across East and Southeast Asia), this book does not focus exclusively on any one nation's cinematic output. Instead, motion pictures produced throughout the region will be analysed and contextualised in relation to the industrial and sociopolitical factors that either facilitate or hinder artistic and commercial enterprises in mainland China, Hong Kong, Japan, South Korea and Taiwan.

With a growing number of multinational coproduction agreements and collaborative partnerships uniting talent from each of these five areas comes the recognition that remakes play a pivotal role in breaking down barriers and building up a sense of shared history. Of course, unresolved territorial disputes and the lingering traumas of previous decades' armed conflicts, including Japan's military incursions into its neighbouring countries throughout the motion picture medium's first forty years (from around the turn of the twentieth century leading up to the Second World War), dampen any such overly optimistic appraisals of a filmmaking category that is chiefly undertaken for economic, rather than ideological, reasons. Nevertheless, it is hoped that a more fully developed picture of East Asia as a cultural sphere will come into view through the exploration of classic and contemporary films that are at once 'familiar' and 'foreign', or rather steeped in the combined similarities and differences that make the remake such a fascinating hermeneutic object. Cross-cultural remakes in particular evoke a combined feeling of familiarity and strangeness that is itself deserving of in-depth analysis. Indeed, their 'uncanniness' – as recognisably similar yet distinct takes on stories that have stood the test of time and are literally translated for different linguistic communities across national borders – necessitates a liminal type of spectatorship if their situationally derived meanings are to be gleaned.

Fittingly, many of the contributors to this volume adopt a fluid, mobile, border-crossing perspective on remakes that have been produced in cultural contexts far removed from those of their originating texts and, in some cases, have been disseminated around the world through unofficial channels (via bootleg videos, illegal downloading/filesharing sites, etc.). In doing so, our authors are able to frame the strangely familiar scenarios at the heart of such disparate films as Lee Sang-il's *Unforgiven* (*Yurusarezaru mono*, 2013), a Japanese remake of Clint Eastwood's Western of the same title, and Stephen Chow's *The Mermaid* (*Meirenyu*, 2016), a Chinese slapstick reimagining of Walt Disney's *The Little Mermaid* (1989) and Hans Christian Andersen's 1837 fairy tale, within the conceptual parameters established by the scholars cited above while going beyond existing interpretative paradigms in pursuit of a language well suited to the spatiotemporal and geopolitical contingencies unique to East Asia. This volume, therefore, seeks to supplement the pioneering work of Herbert, Leitch, Loock, Mazdon, Perkins, Verevis and other theorists not only in its global repositioning of the subject but also through its contributing authors' fashioning of a new critical vocabulary befitting classic and contemporary Chinese, Hong Kong, Japanese, South Korean and Taiwanese remakes. Ironically, the vague sensation of having 'been there, done that', which this particular mode of cinematic praxis tends to inspire in viewers (even when they have not actually seen the film upon which a remake is based), is offset by the sheer novelty of this book's regional focus, not to mention the unexpected detours that our authors make when chasing down a text's elusive, culturally specific meanings.

Much of this book's instrumentality to the field of cinema studies will be found in the case studies themselves, several of which remain relatively unknown to non-specialists despite ongoing efforts to shine a spotlight on them through film festival retrospectives, university screenings, conference panels and other media-related gatherings. For example, the Taiwanese female spy thriller *The Best Secret Agent* (*Tianzi Diyihao*, 1964), director Zhang Yin's recently 'rediscovered', digitally restored remake of a Shanghai film produced nearly twenty years earlier, is significant not simply as a cross-cultural take on the 007-James Bond phenomenon of the 1960s, but also as a showcase for the kind of bricolage-like borrowing for which many contemporary filmmakers are famous (and which had been part of their forerunners' creative arsenal dating back several generations). Like a few of the other motion pictures discussed in this volume, Zhang's commercially successful *taiyupian*, with its focus on a seductive undercover agent known simply as '001' (or 'Heavenly Writ No. 1' [*Tianzi diyi haowho*]) who undertakes sabotage efforts against the colonial government during the Sino-Japanese War, localises globally recognisable signifiers (in this case, those related to British espionage and Cold War paranoia) for several obvious reasons, not the least of which is the profit-earning potential of a cultural export that would have been familiar to most audiences in Taiwan. But this and other remakes' enduring significance is also related to their revisionist perspective on previous decades' national traumas – their ability to proffer narrative 'solutions' to unresolved conflicts of the past.

This latter idea is taken up by several of this volume's contributors, who note the special salience of the word 'remake' throughout the East Asian region (where urban environments, national governments and the notion of civil society itself have undergone subtle and seismic changes since the turn of the twentieth century). Propelled by the twin engines of industrialisation and modernisation and achieved at an incalculable human cost (on the backs of blue-collar labourers, peasants, migrants and other exploited members of the working class), the many transformations that have occurred in China, Hong Kong, Japan, South Korea and Taiwan over the last 100-plus years might seem far removed from the topic of cinematic remakes. However, few cultural forms are as evocative as the remake in conjuring the paradoxical need to 'wipe the slate clean' while retaining something of the past – namely, those traditions that carry over into the contemporary moment like ghostly palimpsests of a time when, depending on one's perspective, things were either 'better' or 'worse' than the current state of affairs. I will broach this topic toward the end of this Introduction, through a brief discussion of the appropriately titled Korean action film *A Better Tomorrow* (*Mujeokja*, 2010), which some readers will recognise as a remake of John Woo's hugely influential work of the same title from 1986 (and which, by most critical accounts, is believed to have been 'beaten' by its 'better' Cantonese-language forerunner despite director Song Hae-sung's best efforts to improve upon the original). By taking up this particular case study as an illustration of the cross-cultural remake's capacity to engage serious sociopolitical issues, I ask what it means for a seemingly derivative motion picture to shift thematic focus from counterfeiting and other criminal activities in the Hong Kong underworld (as depicted in Woo's film) to illegal arms trafficking and the lingering pain of national division (which director Song's film foregrounds through the antagonistic relationship between North Korean defectors and sympathisers who, unlike their predecessors from the original, die in the end).

Moreover, recent remakes like *Going by the Book* (*Bareuge saljaare*, 2007), a Korean version of the Japanese crime-comedy *Bang!* (*Asobi no jikan wa owaranai*, 1991) that humorously pivots on a simulated bank heist and other police training exercises designed to highlight the artifice of 'cops-and-robbers' scenarios, are symptomatic of the complexities and ambiguities that characterise a condition that has been described as 'postmodern'. After postmodernism and its attendant descent into moral relativism had led to a questioning of 'grand narratives' beginning in the 1980s, epistemic uncertainty came to define those cultural productions of the ensuing decades that, though nostalgically 'stuck in the past', anticipated a future time when intertextual referentiality would become an even more deeply engrained aesthetic feature. Today, it is not uncommon to see renowned auteurs, studio filmmakers and purveyors of cinematic 'trash' adopt a mode of playful self-consciousness in their parodic, pastiche-filled homages to – or heist-like pilferings of – previous generations' motion pictures; nor is it unusual for spectators to experience both confusion and a sense of déjà vu when watching a film that seems paradoxically empty and full – a textual void filled with polysemic potential, bursting at the seams with meanings that are only accessible when one is able to ascertain a film's intertextual references. This book aims to help viewers sort through the intertextual layers of this profoundly citational form of cinema and to move East Asian filmmaking from the periphery to the centre of remake studies.

Over four interlocking sections, the contributing authors of this volume collectively cover a wide range of topics, touching on everything from auteurism to censorship debates and the promotional discourses surrounding cinematic remakes, film franchises, serialised stories, trilogies and other intertextually connected bodies of work. The English-language title of Benny Chan's *Connected* (*Bochi tungwah*, 2008), a Cantonese remake of the American action film *Cellular* (2004) that contributing author Gary Bettinson discusses in a chapter about the Hollywoodisation of Hong Kong cinema, is certainly apt; not only as a metaphor for the bond that exists between a prior work and its offshoot(s) or descendent(s), but also insofar as this book brings disparate texts and various critical perspectives together with the goal of further connecting East Asian film studies to a broader body of scholarship concerning remakes. Although readers might detect a temporal order behind the arrangement of the chapters, the book's organisation does not hew to a strictly chronological series of case studies. Instead, chapters are grouped according to particular themes, topics and methodologies, with the goal of having the contributors' words amplify the arguments put forth by other authors within their sections while, in certain cases, revealing that what is sometimes believed to be 'unique' to one cultural setting or film industry (for instance, that of Japan) can also be detected in neighbouring areas (for instance, that of South Korea). Importantly, the very idea of the 'remake' as a fluid category of cultural production – one that is open to interpretation and prone to revisionist conceptualisation (owing to its own revisionist tendencies relative to previously produced motion pictures) – is brought to the fore by a gathering of minds which are not always of the same mind when it comes to the main subject of this volume. Such discursivity and debate – not to say disagreement – confirms our belief that remakes 'matter' precisely because they encourage different ways of looking at the world as well as alternative approaches to telling stories that, though frequently trivialised by reviewers, can have a lasting impact on humanity.

Under the heading 'Re-fleshing the Text: Sex, Seduction, Desire', the first section of this book gathers together chapters that highlight the sensual and corporeal appeals of the medium. Relatedly, this section's authors discuss some of the ways that cinematic remakes, including button-pushing films made over a half-century ago, have been financed, marketed and sold to a public whose voracious appetite for the boldly new yet comfortably familiar dovetails with the loosening of social mores and the relaxing of industrial restrictions concerning salacious onscreen content. Irene González-López kicks things off with a sweeping tour through the '*Gate of Flesh*' (*Nikutai no mon*) media franchise that was launched in Japan in the immediate aftermath of the Second World War, and which would eventually encompass eight versions of Tamura

Taijirō's 1947 novel *Gate of Flesh* (including a stage play, an erotic show, a telefilm and five feature-length movies). Although many readers will be familiar with Suzuki Seijun's 1964 version, González-López shows us why the other cultural productions that preceded or followed it are also deserving of consideration for the way that they facilitated crosspollination across Japan's media industries over the franchise's sixty-year timespan and played a vital role in prompting the nation's citizenry to reimagine their modern history. Moreover, what might at first seem like *adaptations* of Tamura's novel – an example of the 'literature of the flesh' (*nikutai bungaku*) phenomenon that prompted new carnal imaginings of subjectivity in the post-war period – are really *remakes* to the extent that they call back to particular scenes or characters that are found not in the literary text but rather in the previous films that are based on the novelist's work.[1] González-López supports this argument through careful textual and paratextual analysis as well as an abundant supply of critical and industrial discourse. She looks not only at key moments within the individual narratives (which are often repeated with significant variation, text-to-text) but also at movie posters, DVD covers and other promotional materials that, taken together, amount to a more comprehensive picture of the meaning-making process; one in which meanings, as she states, are 'plural and contested rather than unequivocal or completely under control'.

'Control' is at the heart of my own contribution to this volume, and the question I broach (relative to the burgeoning film industry of South Korea during the 1950s and 1960s, leading up to and encompassing its 'Golden Age') is how much power its creative personnel had over work that fell under the purview of government officials and which was held to a seemingly arbitrary set of moral standards with regard to political and sexual content. Taking the relatively little-known yet notorious film *An Empty Dream* (*Chunmong*, 1965) as my main case study, but extending my analysis to other unofficial remakes of Japanese films produced during that politically contentious period, I argue that two types of 'illicit' activity converged around the time of its belated theatrical release. One had to do with the remaking process itself, as several Korean filmmakers (including *An Empty Dream*'s producer, Wu Gi-dong, and its director, Yu Hyun-mok) were taking Japanese films as their source material out of professional necessity as much as convenience (owing to the steep production quotas that the newly enacted Motion Picture Law placed on local companies annually) and despite their country's ban on cultural artefacts from the former coloniser. Another suggestion of illicitness concerns the explicit nature of this film's representations, including scenes of carnal lust, libidinal desire and exposed flesh that went far beyond any previous big-screen offerings in South Korea, but which owed their existence to a pioneering 'pink film' (*pinku-eiga*) made one year earlier in Japan: Takechi Tetsuji's *Daydream* (*Hakujitsumu*, 1964). Like Takechi's film, Yu's *An Empty Dream* features shots of writhing, perspiration-soaked bodies that upset censors when it was finally shown in Seoul (only to be quickly removed from theatres) and which resulted in the director being charged with breaking the nation's obscenity laws. Drawing upon archival documents, including interoffice memos between producer Wu and representatives of the Ministry of Public Information, I argue that this controversial remake of a Japanese production, which has been referred to by some critics as a 'plagiarism' of that earlier work, marks a decisive moment in the history of South Korean filmmaking, when commercial artists with a predilection for narrative experimentation were testing the limits of what was permissible and venturing into uncharted waters even as they were relying upon pre-tested material that had proven successful elsewhere.

A similar sort of boundary-pushing and representational excess can be found in Hong Kong movies from that same period and just thereafter, including a series of bawdy sex comedies modelled on British 'Carry On' films and a steady supply of steamy potboilers produced at the Shaw Brothers' Movietown studio (including transplanted Japanese director Nakahira Kō's *Summer Heat* [*Kuang lian shi*, 1968] and *Diary of a Lady-Killer* [*Lie ren*, 1969], based on his own risqué films made in Japan, *Crazed Fruit* [*Kurutta kajitsu*, 1956] and *The Hunter's Diary* [*Ryojin nikki*, 1964], respectively). Taking the Shaws' sexploitative wuxia classic *Intimate Confessions of a Chinese Courtesan* (*Ai Nu*, 1972) as a leaping-off point to discuss its softcore-style remake *Lust for Love of a Chinese Courtesan* (*Ai Nu xin zhuan*, 1984), Andrew Grossman looks at how filmmaker Chor Yuen – the writer and director of both motion pictures – drew from Ming-era erotic literature as well as contemporaneous films made in the United States and Europe (everything from women-in-prison flicks like *The Big Doll House* [1971] and *The Big Bird Cage* [1972] to 'the lesbian-themed vampire outings of Hammer Studios and French filmmaker Jean Rollin') to challenge patriarchal assumptions of women's place in traditional costume dramas and in society more generally. The original film's Chinese title refers to the nickname of the female protagonist, who is made into a 'love slave' when she flies into the orbit of a cruel brothel-keeper and proceeds to exact ass-kicking revenge against the men who raped her. As a kind of 'martial concubine', Ai Nu embodies the transformative function of remakes, which tend to adopt certain characteristics of previous films but also adapt them in sometimes socially or politically significant ways. According to Grossman, *Lust for Love of a Chinese Courtesan*, which largely strips away the feminine swordplay of Chor's earlier costume drama but leaves its lesbian subplot intact, locates power not in any one character's martial prowess but in the 'financial mechanisms of the brothel' (which serves a masculine clientele, including corrupt officials, and promises pleasure to a heterosexual male gaze, diegetically and extradiegetically). As he states, 'the remake's cynical revisions undoubtedly reflect the hypercapitalist mood of mid-1980s Hong Kong, when so many local films envisioned acquiescence to commercialism as a fait accompli'.

Of course, Chor Yuen was not the first or only filmmaker to remake his own films. Indeed, the history of the medium is chock-full of what some scholars call 'self-remaking'. Famous examples of this phenomenon produced outside of East Asia include Alfred Hitchcock's *The Man Who Knew Too Much* (1934/1956), Michael Haneke's *Funny Games* (1997/2007), George Sluizer's *The Vanishing* (1988/1993) and, most recently, David Cronenberg's *Crimes of the Future* (1970/2022), although the last one is less a straightforward remake of the Canadian provocateur's early-career sci-fi film than a late-career rekindling of his mid-career thematic fixations (body horror, polymorphous perversity, etc.). Although it has hardly been mentioned in previous studies of the subject, an even greater number of East Asian directors have remade their previous efforts – an enduring facet of each nation's film industry dating back to the first Asian 'talkies' of the 1930s. For instance, Bu Wancang, a prolific Chinese filmmaker based in Shanghai until he moved to Hong Kong for political reasons in 1948, directed *Love and Duty* (*Lian'ai yu yiwu*, 1938) seven years after the release of his silent film of the same English title (although with a different Chinese title: *Qing tian xuelei*); a once-lost but recently discovered classic of China's 'Golden Age' starring the legendary actress Ruan Lingyu (whose suicide, at the age of 24, 'made the new film especially poignant') (Harris 2013: 56). Bu's compatriot, Wu Yonggang, similarly turned his silent directorial debut *The Goddess* (*Shennü*, 1934) into a sound version with the 1938 release of *Rouge Tears* (*Yanzhi lei*) (Wang 2013: 18–47). A more recent illustration of this tendency occurred in 2001, when the Vietnamese-born Hong Kong auteur Tsui Hark brought his supernatural wuxia film *Zu: Warriors from the Magic Mountain* (*Xin shushan jianke*, 1983) into the digital age with the subtly retitled *Legend of Zu* (*Shushan zheng zhuan*, 2001). Referred to by one critic as less a remake than a 'problematic addendum' to the original film, this box-office disappointment was based on the same fondly remembered source material (Huanzhulouzhu's 1932 novel *Legend of the Swordsmen of the Mountains of Shu*), but was graced with a few too many cheesy CGI effects to put it on equal footing with Tsui's critically adored precursor (Schroeder 2004, 83).

Tsui Hark's adopted home of Hong Kong has long been a favoured outpost for cinematic wayfarers to ply their trade in an industry that might bear some resemblance to the ones they left behind, but which is distinguished by its unabashed commitment to commercialisation and reliance on proven formulas for success. There are, of course, other elements that mark Hong Kong cinema as a distinctly hybridised cultural enterprise, from its highly developed studio system and star system (which recalls Hollywood's own from the 1930s and 1940s) to its embrace of 'scandalous', sensationalistic content (as early as the 1950s and 1960s), its mix of competing languages (with a 'Cantonese comeback' sparked by the 1973 release of Chor Yuen's *The House of 72 Tenants* [*Chat sup yee ga fong hak*], a profitable remake of a Mandarin-language film of the same title made ten years earlier), and its networked connections with other Anglophone and Sinophone communities, beyond those of Taiwan, Singapore and Malaysia (during the boom years of the 1980s and 1990s). But few other locations in the region seemed to attract filmmakers so intensely as Hong Kong did during its first 'Golden Age', which saw Nakahira Kō, Inoue Umetsugu and other creative personnel from Japan assimilate into a stratified mode of production where a certain amount of artistic freedom was granted to contract directors, and where 'novelty' could ironically be found in pre-existing material (simply by having those directors remake their earlier Japanese-language films).

Back in Japan, the major studios at that time – Daiei, Nikkatsu, Shōchiku, Tōei and Tōhō – also encouraged self-remaking on the part of directors who had delivered commercially successful motion pictures in the past, or whose artistic imprimatur had been widely accepted as a benchmark of quality that might further burnish the reputation of the financially struggling companies with which they worked. Having started as a director at Shōchiku in the late 1930s before signing a multi-year contract with Nikkatsu in the mid-1950s, Nishikawa Katsumi typified the first of those two rationales, as someone who helmed profitable youth films and crowd-pleasing romantic dramas throughout the 1960s before being given the opportunity to remake his 1963 hit *The Dancing Girl of Izu* (*Izu no odoriko*) ten years later (only this time for Tōhō). During the mid-1970s, around the same time Nishikawa was making his second adaptation of Nobel prize-winning author Kawabata Yasunari's 1926 novel *The Dancing Girl of Izu*, thousands of high-school and college students began making films of their own, harnessing relatively cheap equipment (including 8mm cameras) and eventually attracting the attention of studio representatives through their outrageous creations, which made up in ingenuity what they lacked in production values. In his chapter, Mark Player focuses on this largely unexplored facet of 1970s and 1980s Japanese cinema, narrowing the lens on two young autodidacts from that generation – Ishii Gakuryū (a.k.a. Ishii Sōgo) and Tsukamoto Shin'ya – who led the way toward a 'self-made' film revolution. As Player explains, the experimental and narrative-fiction shorts made by Ishii, Tsukamoto and other amateur filmmakers, who wore their influences on their sleeves and tried to emulate the American and Japanese movies that they loved (albeit on shoestring budgets, casting fellow students in lead and supporting roles), exude energy and a punk, DIY aesthetic, which companies like Nikkatsu were seeking out amidst an industrial crisis. This resulted in Ishii and Tsukamoto being given the opportunity to remake their earlier shorts as feature-length studio productions: *Panic High School* (*Kōkō dai panikku*, 1978) and *Tetsuo: The Iron Man* (1989) respectively. Such films, which depart from both Japanese mainstream and arthouse traditions, demonstrate how an aura of authenticity can enhalo even the most imitative of works so long as the 'desire-fulfilment dialectic', which Player skilfully unpacks, remains intact from the formative stages of those artists' careers to their transition to professional work as directors worthy of imitation themselves.

It has been said, by no less a wit than Oscar Wilde, that 'Imitation is the sincerest form of flattery that mediocrity can pay to greatness'. However, few among us would describe Claire Denis, Hou Hsiao-Hsien, Jim Jarmusch, Aki Kaurismaki, Abbas Kiarostami, Koreeda Hirokazu, Stanley Kwan and Wim Wenders – just a few of the many international auteurs to pay imitative homage to the Japanese filmmaker Ozu Yasujirō – as 'mediocre' talents dependent on the artistically 'superior' output of someone who (by his own admission) was prone to repeat elements from past work. The fact that these and countless other creative artists have found inspiration in Ozu's quiet, introspective family dramas (*shōshimin-eiga*), a genre that tends to emphasise the everyday lives of 'common people' and which became his forte in the years leading up to and following the Second Sino-Japanese War (after he had dabbled in comedies, crime films, gangster films and social problem films during the late 1920s and early 1930s), speaks to the enduring appeal of a filmmaker who famously described himself as a 'tofu-maker' (Joo 2017, 155; Choi 2018, 5). That oft-quoted expression has typically been understood as Ozu's modest, if not entirely self-deprecating, way of explaining his choice to repeatedly return to the same seemingly banal scenarios and themes (often involving small, intergenerational crises and the expectation of marriage that many parents have for their grown children), from film to film; as well as his preference for an idiosyncratic style that is simple and unadorned yet complex and deep in its plumbing of the melancholic surface of the world.

Although numerous essays, articles and books have been devoted to Ozu's 'Ozu-isms', his minimalist yet rigorous approach to filmmaking and the contemplative quality of his work continue to reward careful study. Indeed, no wide-ranging exploration of remaking practices in the East Asian context would be complete without a consideration of the ways that the Japanese director not only reworked earlier material but also inspired subsequent filmmakers to 'ape' or 'parrot' his signature style, including those from his own country, ever since his passing in 1963. As such, this volume brings together three chapters that delve into the profundities of Ozu's remakes – remakes of his own earlier films as well as those that are subtly or obviously indebted to non-Japanese productions – while further diversifying the range of conceptual approaches to the book's main subject. Leading off that series of auteuristic investigations is Alastair Phillips's analysis of *Late Spring* (*Banshun*, 1949), *Early Summer* (*Bakushū*, 1951) and *Tokyo Story* (*Tōkyō monogatari*, 1953), three films whose dark subtexts sometimes get lost behind the bright, beaming smile of star Hara Setsuko. Referred to by cultural historians as 'the Garbo of Japan', the actress – a symbol of screen virtue during her country's cinematic 'Golden Age' of the 1950s – is as much a staple of Ozu's classic period of filmmaking as his palette-cleansing 'pillow shots' and low-level 'tatami-mat shots' are. Before withdrawing from the spotlight 'after her final screen appearance at the age of 42' (Ishii 2020), Hara had appeared in six of the director's films; most memorably his 'Noriko Trilogy', named after the marriageable character she plays in *Late Spring*, *Early Summer* and *Tokyo Story*. In his chapter, Phillips considers the ontological question of what it means to call this group of films a 'trilogy' and probes the aesthetic and political consequences of using a recurring character played by a legendary icon as a rationale for that critical serialisation of the texts. Phillips is drawn to the patterns of repetition and difference that litter Ozu's body of work, but the methods that he employs to suss out their possible meanings textually and contextually – investigating the literal and figurative movement or 'progression' of Hara's character Noriko from one film to the next – differ from those of other contributors. As such, this section of the book, with each Ozu-inspired chapter offering a variation on a core set of ideas, could be likened to the director's lauded remakes.

Pivoting from the trio of films comprising Ozu Yasujirō's 'Noriko Trilogy' to a much earlier black-and-white production, *I Was Born, But. . .* (*Otona no miru ehon: Umarete wa mita keredo*, 1932) and its loose remake from 1959, the colour production *Good Morning* (*Ohayō*), Rea Amit presents a compelling argument about a different kind of movement, one of regression rather than progression. Tracking the emergence of television as a potentially emancipatory form of mid-century mass communication, he notes that *Good Morning*, though an 'updated version' of its thematically similar forerunner (which likewise focuses on two precocious boys), dwells on 'dysfunctional forms of communication and archaic modes of media consumption'. Indeed, its characters' media illiteracy and infantility are stressed in a way that not only offers a unique perspective on contemporaneous anxieties about the purported 'dumbing down' effects of otherwise innocuous broadcast programming (including televised sumo wrestling and quiz shows), but also recalibrates the reversal of parental authority over children that occurs in *I Was Born, But. . .*. If that silent film could be said to present a gently satirical view of Japanese 'de-mediation' through humorous scenes of miscommunication, then the continuation of that theme in its television-age remake, punctuated with funny-sounding farts and meaningless phrases spoken by kids in suburban Tokyo, could be interpreted as Ozu's and cowriter Noda Kōgo's combined authorial commentary on the prolonged effects of technological as well as familial incompetency on the larger social body.

Bringing our Ozu section to an end, Steve Choe shifts this volume's historical orientation away from classics of the past toward contemporary debates about the questionable motives given by filmmakers for remakes that, in the eyes of some critics, do not justify their existence or which seem superfluous next to an understated masterpiece like *Tokyo Story*. The latter film, frequently cited as one of the greatest motion pictures ever made, served as the basis for Yamada Yōji's *Tokyo Family* (*Tōkyō kazoku*, 2013), a remake which solicited predictably unfavourable comparisons from reviewers who might otherwise have judged it differently had it been based on a less canonical work. In his chapter about Yamada's seemingly 'pointless' or 'unnecessary' remake, Choe highlights *Tokyo Family*'s subtle poeticism and explains its significance as a gateway to its creator's larger body of work, including Yamada's 'A Class to Remember' (*Gakkō*) series (1993–2000) and his 'What a Wonderful Family!' (*Kazoku wa tsurai yo*) series (2016–2018). Those series, encompassing four and three feature-length films respectively, showcase the talents of the same seasoned performers who appear in the remake of Ozu's *Tokyo Story* (including Hashizume Isao and Yoshiyuki Kazuko, who play the elderly couple Shūkichi and Tomiko Hirayama, previously played by Ryū Chishū and Higashiyama Chieko). This 'serial vitality', according to Choe, 'passes through discursive binaries that typically separate actors from their roles 'through the image of a human being that is bound by the experience of aging'. Films, too, age. They also become more vital through the passage of time and the memories they trigger in audiences who witness versions of their own 'flickering lives' – flickering between past, present and future – as shadowy projections on a screen. Far from being heedless to such metaphysics, the quiet domestic dramas of Ozu and Yamada, which recast the same actors and retell the same stories (to such an extent that the 'conventional binaries between the original and the copy' no longer hold), tap into the medium's latent capacity to mirror the physical world and momentarily slow the ceaseless flow of time.

Speaking of temporality: It is noteworthy that the running time of Yamada's *Tokyo Family* (146 minutes) is longer than that of Ozu's *Tokyo Story* (136 minutes) by ten minutes. Such a discrepancy, though not as large as that between other remakes and the films that inspired them, hints at differences in the pacing and organisation of narrative material that furthermore belies the idea that one is little more than a 'shot-for-shot' facsimile of the other. An even bigger durational difference can be seen, or rather 'felt', in the running times of Fukasaku Kinji's *Graveyard of Honor* (*Jingi no hakaba*, 1975), which clocks in at 94 minutes, and Miike Takashi's *New Graveyard of Honor* (*Shin jingi no hakaba*, 2002), which clocks in at 131 minutes. Earl Jackson explores both films in his chapter, which makes the case that Miike's remake conjures the spirit of real-world yakuza kingpin Ishikawa Rikio (who is played by Watari Tetsuya in Fukasaku's original) through the fictional character of Ishimatsu Rikuo (Kishitani Goro), but nevertheless 'opts out of history'. It does this in part by refusing to abide by the once-unshakable belief that Japan is a homogenous nation of consensus rather than internal strife and social division. Unlike its predecessor, the remake begins at the end: it depicts the death-by-suicide of its sociopathic protagonist, a former dishwasher-turned-mobster-turned-prisoner who is posthumously shown climbing the ranks of Tokyo's criminal underworld yet plummeting into a moral abyss with each violent blow delivered or heroin injection received. Though lacking the biographical and historical details of the 1975 original, which is rooted to the then-fashionable subgenre of *jitsuroku* or 'true record' films (distinguished by their gritty, 'frenetic, pseudo-documentary style') (Sharp 2011, 65), *New Graveyard of Honor*, which is set in the 'Lost Decade' of the 1990s, makes telling allusions to the doomsday cult Aum Shinrikyō (which carried out a deadly subway sarin attack mid-decade) and to the bursting of Japan's economic bubble (which contributed to widespread pessimism and a growing distrust of discredited bureaucrats and government institutions). Those two national traumas, Jackson emphasises, cannot be easily reduced to explanatory narratives, though Miike 'gestures toward a historical consciousness whose own failure nevertheless constitutes a historical record of the zeitgeist' that the remake 'both addresses and reflects'.

Significantly, Fukasaku's *Graveyard of Honor*, which focalises the 'psychic desolation of early post-war Japan' from the perspective of its main character Ishikawa (thus allowing us to read the country's 'macro-historical changes' through his micro-historical or biographical details as a member of the yakuza), furthermore gestures toward the problems faced by Taiwanese, Chinese and Korean minority residents (pejoratively referred to as the *sangokujin*) in police-raid scenes that illustrate how the authorities relied upon their underworld proxies – something that is not present in Miike's remake *New Graveyard of Honor*. Another, more recent Japanese genre film that registers the violent inequalities endured by ethnic minorities is Lee-Sang-il's *Unforgiven* (*Yurusarezaru mono*, 2013), a remake of Clint Eastwood's revisionist Western *Unforgiven* (1992). As discussed by Lance Lomax, colonial legacies and the issue of indigeneity undergird Lee's jidaigeki Western, which is set during Japan's Meiji-era imperial expansion into the island of Hokkaidō and revolves around the efforts of a former samurai, Kamata Jubei (Watanabe Ken, stepping into the boots of Eastwood's William Munny), to help a former comrade claim a bounty on the men who have disfigured a prostitute named Natsume (Kutsuna Shiori). Viewers who are familiar with the source material will see the obvious parallels between it and the remake, helmed by a director whose experiences as a Zainichi Korean living in Japan surely inform his complicated relationship to the story, which is subtly recast to accommodate questions of nationhood and identity – including that of Hokkaidō's indigenous Ainu people (dispossessed of their land by Japanese settlers expanding the frontier to the north) – not found in the original. In his chapter, Lomax calls attention to the lack of justice accorded to Natsume, whose attacker was himself a former samurai, albeit someone who (unlike Jubei) has powerful friends. This, he argues, is just one illustration in the remake that 'inequalities and social stratification . . . remained intact despite promises of a new and modern Japan under the Meiji Restoration'. As such, *Unforgiven* contributes to 'the ongoing "remaking" of Japan's cultural imaginary and rethinking of its history problem'.

Redirecting our focus from Japan to Hong Kong and then to South Korea, the chapters that follow Lomax's contribution continue his interrogation of historical consciousness, albeit through case studies which are distantly removed from the geopolitical setting of that jidaigeki Western. Gary Bettinson uses the career of Kowloon-born Hong Kong director Benny Chan Muk-sing as a barometer of the transformations that have occurred in the local industry and in society at large after the 1997 Asian financial crisis and that same year's transfer of sovereignty from the United Kingdom to the People's Republic of China. Rather than simply advocate for Chan's status as an auteur whose corpus of films – mainly high-octane action-thrillers and star-driven comedies – display stylistic and thematic consistency, Bettinson elaborates a more expansive view of the filmmaker's place in commercial Hong Kong cinema, which has partnered with Mainland Chinese companies and implemented several significant changes in recent years. If a 'voracious appetite for imitation' really is, as Patricia Aufderheide maintained twenty-five years ago, a 'distinctive and long-standing feature of Hong Kong film' (1998, 192), then the persistence of that appetite in post-handover cinema could be taken to suggest that a certain stability and continuity further characterise the local industry, despite what are perceived to be seismic shifts as a result of local industry leaders' strengthening political ties with PRC government officials. Chan is certainly not alone in habitually recycling elements from previous productions, though his 2008 film *Connected* – an authorised remake of David R. Ellis's 2004 thriller *Cellular* – has been hailed as the first of its kind: a multinational coproduction between Hollywood, Hong Kong and Mainland companies (Emperor Motion Pictures, China Film Group, Warner China Film HG, Armor Entertainment and Sirius Pictures International) that legally purchased remake rights (as opposed to the 'remaking-by-stealth' practices that typified earlier generations). What makes *Connected* especially fascinating, though, is the fact that it essentially 'Hollywoodises' a Hollywood film, one that had adopted several of the 'aesthetic features more typical of 1980s Hong Kong cinema than of Hollywood storytelling in the early 2000s', thus restoring principles of traditional dramaturgy (e.g., narrative causality, clearly defined and convincingly motivated character goals, etc.) and revealing Chan's knack for innovating existing materials in ways that are gratifying to him yet financially sound at a time of economic uncertainty.

Another innovative Hong Kong director, Johnnie To, takes centre stage in Jinhee Choi's contribution to this volume. Or, rather, the prolific director of *Drug War* (*Du zhan*, 2012) and dozens of other action-filled crime films shares that stage with Lee Hae-young, the Korean director of *Drug War*'s remake *Believer* (*Dokjeon*, 2018), which the author analyses with an eye to its allegorically resonant departures from its source material (To's first coproduction with the PRC). By and large, Lee's remake sticks to the labyrinthine plot of the Hong Kong-Mainland coproduction, which is set in the city of Jinhai and portrays the procedural work of a police inspector, Captain Zhang Lei (Sun Honglei), who enjoins an amphetamine manufacturer to help him take down a drug-dealing operation while undercover. As Choi discusses, the remake puts more emphasis on the male rivalry between the chief of police in the narcotics division, Won-ho (Cho Jin-woong), and a mysterious drug lord whose true identity is withheld until the ending. Moreover, in accordance with other Korean gangster movies and crime film conventions (on view in such box-office hits as *A Bittersweet Life* [*Dalcomhan insaeng*, 2005] and *A Dirty Carnival* [*Biyeolhan geori*, 2006]), *Believer* depicts a hierarchical, corporate-like structure of the male-dominated criminal syndicate, in which gangsters – like post-IMF salarymen – are each addressed in a manner befitting a legitimate company (e.g., as 'Associate Director', as 'Assistant Manager', etc.) and power-hungry middlemen fail to scale the social ladder owing to a 'premature fall'. That sudden descent, the result of some 'transgression' on their part, typically leads to death or some other punitive form of narrative retribution, and the insistence on their elimination is one of the ways that the Korean remake distinguishes itself from its cinematic precursor.

Besides *Believer*, a host of other action films from the past two decades, including remakes based on non-Korean productions (such as *City of Damnation* [*Yoogamseureowoon dosi*, 2009], *Cold Eyes* [*Gamsijadeul*, 2013], *The Target* [*Pyojeok*, 2014], *Luck Key* [*Leokki*, 2016]) and *The Beast* [*Biseuteu*, 2019]), have earned plaudits for their stylish takes on police procedurals, crime dramas and detective thrillers if not for their originality as 'derivative' works lacking the narrative inventiveness of their Japanese, Hong Kong and French predecessors. Often, these films have been critically disparaged as being inherently 'inferior' to the motion pictures that inspired them, though increasingly fans of South Korean cinema have vocally thrown their support behind these localised, stylistically 'superior' spins on stories about the antagonistic relationship between law breakers and police officers or private detectives. The fact that the urban action film hinges primarily if not entirely on that dichotomy, which is typically staged as a battle for supremacy involving representatives from opposing factions on the streets of Seoul, Busan and other cities, makes the genre especially useful as a means of addressing critics' tendency to discuss remakes in strictly adversarial terms. Indeed, the many physical altercations and dramatic confrontations that occur in the above films can be allegorically linked to the pitting of an original production and its remake against one another, with one side (usually the former) emerging as the 'better' of the two competing films.

Consider, for instance, director Song Hae-sung's 2010 remake of John Woo's landmark action film *A Better Tomorrow* (*Ying hung boon sik*, 1986), itself a work inspired by the earlier Hong Kong films *The Story of a Discharged Prisoner* (*Ying xiong ben se*, 1967) and *The Brothers* (*Long hu xiong di*, 1979). For most critics, the 'better' of the two *Better Tomorrows* is clearly the one directed by Woo, although his role as an executive producer on Song's version complicates efforts to separate the two antagonistically. In fact, the critical application of superlatives to the original film only intensified in the wake of the remake's 2010 theatrical release. Notably, both Woo and Song defended the remake as a decidedly 'localised' film, one that was not a pale imitation of the original text, which is famous for sparking a cultish degree of devotion among fans – young men in particular – not just across East Asia but around the world. In a joint press conference with Song in Seoul on September 9, 2010 (one week before its domestic theatrical release), Woo confessed that he cried while watching the Korean version, which he sees as a 'new movie' that is considerably different from its precursor, with its own unique storyline concerning two brothers who escaped from North Korea. Likewise, Song described his remake as a 'reconstituted movie' overflowing with sentiments that would resonate perhaps more strongly with his countrymen than with global audiences, owing to the emphasis that he and writer Jo Chang-ho placed on brotherly love and betrayal, something that shifted the narrative away from action toward drama. The South Korean remake's prioritising of intensely emotional dramatic conflicts over lengthy gunfight sequences was not received favourably by local commentators, however. For example, pop culture critic Jeong Deok-hyeon complained that Song's film failed as both an action film and a social commentary on the North Korean defector problem due to its director's conflicting impulses of, on the one hand, reviving the cross-cultural allure of Hong Kong neo-noir or 'heroic bloodshed tropes' (popularised in Woo's films of the 1980s and 1990s) and, on the other hand, crafting an original drama.

Limited space prevents me from saying much about the original *A Better Tomorrow*, which was theatrically released in 1986, two years after the Sino-British joint declaration officialised Hong Kong's handover to mainland China effective 1 July 1997. Readers who are familiar with the film might recall that it begins with a nightmare sequence reminiscent of a similarly disorienting moment in Alfred Hitchcock's *Vertigo* (1958). Starting with a close-up of a sleeping man's head, shown in profile, Woo cuts to a black-and-white long shot of a younger man being shot in the back on the street. Another combination of the same two images follows: that of the sleeping man suddenly gasping in horror followed by a monochromatic rendering of the dream that has startled him awake, and which shows the injured man falling to the ground. A jump cut to three successively repeating shots (from different angles) of the sleeper bolting up from his bed in a start is capped by a concluding close-up of his eye slowly closing, perspiration beading on his forehead and dripping down his face. As the next scene opens after the film title, the camera slowly tilts down the façade of a white skyscraper to focus on a different character, Chow Yun-fat's Mark Lee, who – cigarette dangling from his lips and dark sunglasses hiding his eyes – is dressed in roguish business attire, including the loose-fitting duster jacket for which this iconic figure is known by fans. While Mark grabs a quick bite to eat from a street food vendor, a Rolls-Royce drives up to the curb and the man from the previous scene (a character named Sung Tse-Ho [Ti Lung]) opens the door, inviting him to hop in. Against the film's opening credits and an upbeat electronic score, the lawbreaking duo, smiling from ear-to-ear, can be seen entering a modern office building and taking the elevator up to a scientific research laboratory, where several professionals wearing white lab coats are busy producing flawless counterfeit US currency ($50 and $100 bills).

The opening minutes of the South Korean remake display vastly different aesthetic sensibilities and cultural politics. Whereas the character Ho's nightmare in the Hong Kong original is an imaginary event that externalises a guilt-ridden gangster's fear of losing his younger sibling (Leslie Cheung's character Kit) as the price of his involvement in organised crime, his Korean counterpart Hye-ok (Ju Jin-mo) relives his painful past in a flashback-dream. The first shot of Song's film is a close-up of two men's hands locked together against a nondescript natural backdrop at night. A subsequent image of their hands being separated is accompanied by a distant yelling, the word 'brother' ('hyeong') reverberating to the accompaniment of sombre string music on the soundtrack. The nightmare ends with a point-of-view shot of Hye-ok hiding behind a bush and witnessing his mother and younger brother being captured by North Korean border guards. A frontal shot of rifle fire intercuts with a low-angle close-up of Hye-ok waking up, drenched in sweat, and lifting his half-naked body from bed. Melancholic music plays over the crosscut images, which show close-ups of Hye-ok's scarred back and a reed bracelet (a memento hinting at his fraternal bond with the separated family member). This opening scene in Song's *A Better Tomorrow* attests to the fact that the nightmare is a realistic flashback to the past rather than an expressionistic abstraction of some future anxiety, as in Woo's original. While Woo's style is clearly in line with Ackbar Abbas's notion of *déjà disparu* (or the 'already disappeared'), owing to the fact that the Hong Kong director's action film aesthetics and manipulation of speed, time and movement (in the form of jump cuts and slow-motion effects, for instance) work to divert one's attention from pressing geopolitical matters, Song's style is firmly grounded in more conventional continuity editing and focalised, affective storytelling aimed at contextualising the epistemic present in relation to a presumably known past and situating a personal/familial tragedy within the larger narrative of national politics.

Another recent South Korean remake of a non-Korean film – director Yim Soon-rye's *Little Forest* (*Liteul Poleseuteu*, 2018), based on a two-part film of the same title by Mori Junichi (which was adapted from Igarashi Daisuke's manga series *Ritoru Foresuto* [2002–2005]) – is the subject of Nam Lee's contribution to this volume. As the lead-off chapter to the book's final section, devoted to the 'localising' strategies adopted by contemporary cultural producers who remake well-known films from other countries, Lee's study sheds light on the challenges involved in catering to local audiences while capitalising on thematic elements and other textual features that attracted those filmmakers to the projects in the first place. Like Ting-Ying Lin, whose chapter on two Taiwanese remakes of South Korean crowd-pleasers (*More than Blue* [*Bi beishang geng beishang de gushi*, 2018] and *Man in Love* [*Dang nanren lianai shi*, 2021]) paints an equally optimistic picture of transnational coproductions and cross-cultural exchange, Lee problematises the tendency to essentialise national attributes (as distinctly 'Taiwanese' or 'Korean' features, for instance) that can only be understood by residents born and raised in the countries where those narratives are set. But she also recognises the need to add more than a dash of culturally resonant ingredients as part of the 're-flavouring' of a movie from one context to another; a necessity literalised in *Little Forest*, which not coincidentally concerns the preparation and cooking of aesthetically appetising dishes. Although the many tastefully composed yet tantalising shots of the main character's culinary concoctions (including fairly standard items like *sirruteok*, *sujebi* and *baechu jeon*, as well as unusual ones like fried acacia flower fritters) might seem like 'food porn' to the casual observer, they serve as visual reminders of the need to ground Korean cultural productions in the semantic soil of their own homegrown predecessors – something that Yim's film succeeds at doing through its further foregrounding of the female protagonist's complicated relationship to her mother (a staple of local works, past and present, but one that is not nearly as pronounced in the Japanese version of *Little Forest*).

With the exception of the tellingly titled Italian comedy-drama *Perfect Strangers* (*Perfetti sconosciuti*, 2016), which has been remade nearly two-dozen times in countries around the world (from Mexico to Greece and a few Asian locations, including China, Japan, South Korea and Vietnam), no film in recent memory has captured the imagination of so many international audiences and sparked so many remakes as Korean director Hwang Dong-hyuk's *Miss Granny* (*Susanghan Geunyeo*, literally translated as 'Suspicious Girl', 2014). If not entirely unprecedented, the 'Miss Granny phenomenon' is remarkable as a manifestation of transcultural flows across the East and Southeast Asian regions, where a total of seven remakes have been produced, not to mention multi-episode television adaptations (and not counting features either made or about to be made in non-Asian contexts). Because of the wide cultural range of these remakes, we find it propitious that four scholars with backgrounds in Chinese, Japanese and Korean cultural histories – Jennifer Coates, Hsin Hsieh, Sung-Ae Lee and Kate Taylor-Jones – agreed to a cowritten chapter that operates more like a collaborative roundtable, with multiple perspectives being offered to explain what about the original film made it such a translatable or adaptable text. Individually and collectively, the authors take stock of the central narrative premise – a free-spirited yet heavy-hearted septuagenarian, set in her ways and partially to blame for her extended family's woes, magically transforms into a twenty-year-old who becomes a singing sensation before sacrificing her newfound youthfulness to save her grandson – and consider whether it is best suited to one national context over all the others. They furthermore echo Nam Lee's inquiries into representations of motherhood while bringing the topic of gendered ageism into the equation.

In a way, 'Miss Granny' can be understood as a 'universal' story to the extent that no one particular setting necessarily alters it or accentuates its underlying themes better than any of the other settings. Nevertheless, the places and spaces on view in each version of the film – the specific metropolitan locations though which the female protagonist moves – are important not just as diegetic settings but also as a means of placing the story into different historical contexts, where certain buildings, streets or other parts of the urban landscape stand out as a result of their extradiegetic significance. In keeping with previous chapters in this book, a question emerges as to how the three films made in the East Asian region – the Korean-language original as well as the versions produced in neighbouring China (*20 Once Again* [*Chóng făn èrshí suì*, 2015]) and Japan (*Sing My Life* [*Ayashii Kanojo*, 2016]) – incorporate historical referents, particularly those that formed the social backdrop of the main character's adolescent coming-of-age as a young girl who was exposed to economic and familial hardships decades ago. Viewers who have seen only one or two of these films might wonder if wartime and/or post-war experiences are conveyed either directly or indirectly in the other remakes (including those produced in Vietnam, Thailand, Indonesia and the Philippines), and if so through which means.

Importantly, as a seventy-something woman inhabiting the body of a twenty-something woman, the protagonist of each film (for instance, Mal-soon in the Korean original, played by Shim Eun-kyung as her young self and Na Moon-hee as her older self) personifies the remake as a unique type of cultural production that is simultaneously 'old' and 'new'. In the same way that she gives the people around her a 'strange' or 'creepy' feeling, owing to her uncanniness as a liminal figure stuck between past and present (something that most of her family members remain oblivious to, at least until narrative's end), the remake is 'haunted' by the presence of its earlier self, or rather an original ghostly 'other' that cannot be shaken off or completely exorcised from the minds of audiences who have seen that earlier version. This is suggested in variations of a line spoken by her older male companion, a long-time friend who laments that he cannot forget the missing woman's smile. Readers who find themselves sufficiently interested in the many films comprising 'Miss Granny' as a transnational phenomenon will be left to question whether one version of its story stresses this aspect of the title character – her literal embodiment of the remake's uncanny conflation of oldness and newness (or 'then-ness' and 'now-ness') – more emphatically than do the others.

The seemingly contradictory dyad of 'familiarity' and 'newness' has been a heavily promoted feature of East Asian film remakes for decades, going back to the some of the earliest instances of cinematic remaking in Hong Kong, including Yang Gongliang's *New White Golden Dragon* (*Xin baijin long*, 1947) and Hu Peng's *New Sister Flowers* (*Xin zimei hua*, 1962), and becoming even more pronounced in recent years. Like the original title of *New Love without End* (*Xin bu liao qíng*, 1993), a remake of the classic tearjerker *Love without End* (*Bu liao qing*, 1961) that was given the grammatically incorrect French title *C'est la vie, mon Cherie* upon its international release, the global fandom for Hong Kong films since the 1990s has often been predicated on their freshness and vitality – the seemingly endless ways that familiar scenarios and generic conventions can be creatively repackaged or made 'strange'. And that newness, at the levels of both creative enterprise and critical reception, continues to inform our understanding of Hong Kong cinema as an ever-evolving space of cultural hybridity relative to Mainland China as well as other nations beyond the Pacific Rim. Stephen Chow's *The New King of Comedy* (*Xin xiju zhi wang*, 2019), a sequel-like reboot of the same director's *The King of Comedy* (*Xiju zhi wang*, 1999), is only the latest example of that fresh yet familiar 'strange-making' on the part of a homegrown talent who has continually remade himself and his career in accordance with broader social and industrial changes.

Notably, in his review of *The New King of Comedy* for the Asian film, media and culture website VCinema, Daniel Kratky dwells upon the *newness* of Chow's latest offering, remarking that the aging filmmaker has managed to stay 'relevant' as a genre deconstructionist by finding unconventional ways of delivering his trademark visual jokes (2019). Whereas the Hong Kong humourist had previously depended on short takes and fast cutting rates (in cinematic spoofs such as *From Beijing with Love* [*Gwok chaan Ling Ling Chat*, 1994] and *Shaolin Soccer* [*Siu Lam juk kau*, 2001]), this remake of *The King of Comedy* gave him the opportunity to compose shots and edit scenes differently, through sophisticated staging, mobile framing and long takes. Posing the rhetorical question, 'How is it possible for a fast-paced Cantonese comedian to make a funny film [through such slow means]?', Kratky concludes that Chow 'adapts new techniques . . . to reinforce the important aspect of his poetics, humour', and that stylistically this indicates a move away 'from the Cantonese norm' (Ibid.). Ironically, the reviewer's commentary recalls Victor Fan's description of a much earlier remake, the aforementioned *New White Golden Dragon*, which likewise distinguished itself through the director's penchant for long takes, fluid camera pans and carefully choreographed dolly shots over traditional shot-reverse-shots and other formal devices – a stylistic choice that not only maintains the spatiotemporal unity of scenes but effectively transforms a familiar narrative into 'a series of acts informed by the changing dynamic of the human relationships' (Fan 2015). The point is that Stephen Chow's 'brand-new style' (to use Kratky's expression) is nearly as old as Hong Kong cinema itself.

I cannot help but note that the reviewer – clearly appreciative of Chow's filmmaking prowess (in contrast to the many disappointed critics who have called *The New King of Comedy* a 'pointless remake that fails to reinvent or expand on the original' and which 'shouldn't have been made') (Shaw 2019) – does not mention the thing that most sets this film apart from the director's earlier works, including the movie that inspired it in the first place. Unlike *The King of Comedy*, which was shot in Hong Kong, the remake is a Mainland production that was filmed in Zhuhai and Beijing. At first glance, it would seem to provide further evidence of the special administrative region's cultural 'disappearance' (to borrow Ackbar Abbas's theory) following its 1997 handover to China. Gary Bettinson maintains that the 'Mainlandisation' thesis, when applied to Hong Kong cinema in the age of recent coproduction agreements, exaggerates the degree to which local filmmakers are stymied artistically and the craft practices involved in making motion pictures are disrupted by 'Mainland modes of production' (i.e., more 'fastidious' work protocols and bureaucratic hoops to jump through that put a damper on the previous system's 'freewheeling spontaneity' and 'piecemeal plotting') (2020, 18–19). Rather than witnessing 'traditional Hong Kong aesthetics and routines of film practice' being effaced by 'a brand-new, distinctly Sinicized' style and mode of moviemaking, he argues, we are seeing filmmakers like Stephen Chow, Benny Chan, Gordan Chan and Peter Chan adapt in real time to incremental rather than seismic industrial changes with the same ingenuity that their screenwriters have brought to the adaptation process (essentially 'remaking' literary properties into cinematic works). Singling out Chow as someone who, 'now firmly embedded in Mainland culture', remains as zany as he was when he started his directorial career just prior to the 1997 handover, Bettinson believes that 'the local industry's proud heritage of formal experimentation, stylistic exuberance, and creative free expression' has been enhanced, rather than diminished, through the current arrangement (formalised in 2003, when Hong Kong and Mainland China entered into a bilateral trade agreement, known by its English acronym CEPA: Closer Economic Partnership Arrangement).

Another Chow-directed visual extravaganza, *The Mermaid*, is the subject of this book's final chapter, written by co-editor Kenneth Chan. As a quirky reworking of a 'transnational fantasy subgenre, the mermaid film' (which, as Chan notes, was popularised through director Ron Howard's *Splash* [1984] and given local 'flavouring' through Hong Kong productions ranging from Kao Li's *The Mermaid* [*Yu meiren*, 1965] to Norman Law's *Mermaid Got Married* [*Renyu chuanshuo*, 1994]), Chow's box-office juggernaut in its country of origin did not drum up similar levels of commercial success when it was sent abroad beginning in 2016, and the reason for that disparity might have something to do with 'the innovative and counter-intuitive ways with which [Chow's] humour becomes entwined with and connected to the ethical and ideological core of the film and its message'. Oscillating between text and sociopolitical context but going beyond his main case study to speculate on the global iconicity of the mermaid as an ecocritical figure of increased significance in the digital age, Chan's elastic, wide-ranging analysis tracks the presence of aquatic beings across a panoply of cinematic and non-cinematic works (gesturing, for instance, toward a 1904 short film made by Georges Méliès as well as ancient and modern Chinese oral and literary traditions which remind us that 'what Chow has concocted here is . . . not new'). In doing so, he demonstrates how the liquid spaces that serve as placeless homes to underwater denizens – including the title character of *The Mermaid* (a seductive creature who seeks revenge against the man whose company has wreaked havoc on her oceanic community) – might also be metaphorically inhabitable by media scholars with a vested interest in de-territorialising East Asian studies or uprooting traditional (West-oriented) approaches to the transnational.

In that respect, Chan's chapter, like the 'Miss Granny' roundtable co-authored by Jennifer Coates, Hsin Hsieh, Sung-Ae Lee and Kate Taylor-Jones, is a mise-en-abyme of the book as a whole, which provides a fluid accounting – rather than a static snapshot – of the remake as a profoundly consequential type of cultural production and creative praxis; one that can move us beyond engrained notions of the national and the transnational as (falsely) agreed-upon terms that are nevertheless central to East Asian studies. It is hoped that the current volume sparks renewed interest in cinematic remaking beyond the case studies assembled by its contributing authors, and beyond the arbitrarily defined confines – the literal and figurative borders – of the imagined communities that comprise each comfortably familiar yet strangely unfamiliar film's 'home'.

NOTE

1. The question of whether a remake is *really* an adaptation of a non-cinematic text (for instance, a novel or a short story) has longed vexed movie critics, adding yet another wrinkle to the task of unpacking a given film's intertextual references or its point of progenitive contact to one particular text over any number of others. Within the East Asian context alone, there are countless examples of motion pictures that are part of a long line of adaptations, but which were made by creative personnel who not only watched but took elements from other films based on the same literary work. For instance, in a bid for greater respectability, Ikeda Toshiharu, a Japanese director best known for making cheaply shot 'pink films' and exploitative horror films (many of them released directly to video) in the 1980s, turned to author Tanizaki Jun'ichirō's novel *The Key* (*Kagi*) as the foundation for a slightly more 'elevated' erotic drama than what he had helmed during the first decade of his career; and in 1997 his version of that well-known

text, also titled *The Key*, achieved notoriety as 'the first theatrically released film to portray full-frontal nudity' in Japan) (Harper 2008,:30). But it is not inconceivable that Ikeda also drew inspiration from previous adaptations of Tanizaki's novel, including Wakamatsu Kōji's earlier pink film *The Key* (*Kagi*, 1983), Kumashiro Tatsumi's slightly more expensive yet unsuccessful Roman Pornu production for Nikkatsu likewise titled *The Key* (*Kagi*, 1974), and Ichikawa Kon's more critically esteemed yet oddly titled *Odd Obsession* (*Kagi*, 1959). The latter film especially seems to have been on the mind of Ikeda, who set his version of Tanizaki's story in 1959, the year that Ichikawa's was released, and who adopted 'artful' framings of a middle-aged couple's lovemaking that are similar to those composed by legendary cinematographer Miyagawa Kazuo (despite the earlier film being shot in black-and-white rather than colour).

REFERENCES

Bettinson, Gary. 2020. 'Yesterday Once More: Hong Kong-China Coproductions and the Myth of Mainlandization.' *Journal of Chinese Cinemas* 14, no. 1: 16–31.
Choi, Jinhee. 2018. 'Introduction.' In *Reorienting Ozu: A Master and His Influence*. Edited by Jinhee Choi. New York: Oxford University Press.
Fan, Victor. 2015. *Cinema Approaching Reality: Locating Chinese Film Theory*. Minneapolis: University of Minnesota Press.
Feeley, Jennifer. 2014. 'Mandarin Pop Meets Tokyo Jazz: Gender and Popular Youth Culture in Late 1960s Hong Kong Musicals.' In *Sinophone Cinemas*. Edited by Audrey Yue and Olivia Khoo, 101–19. New York: Palgrave Macmillan.
Harper, Jim. 2008. *Flowers from Hell: The Modern Japanese Horror Film*. Hereford: Noir Publishing, 30.
Harris, Kristine. 2013. 'Ombres Chinoises: Split Screens and Parallel Lives in *Love and Duty*.' In *The Oxford Handbook of Chinese Cinemas*. Edited by Carlos Rojas and Eileen Chow, 39–61. New York: Oxford University Press.
Herbert, Daniel, ed. 2017. *Film Remakes and Franchises*. New Brunswick: Rutgers University Press.
Ishii, Taeko. 2020. '*The Truth About Hara Setsuko*: Behind the Legend of the Golden Age Film Star.' Nippon.com, 10 June. https://www.nippon.com/en/japan-topics/bg900161/. Accessed 5 June 2022.
Joo, Woojeong. 2017. *Cinema of Ozu Yasujiro: Histories of the Everyday*. Edinburgh: Edinburgh University Press.
Kratky, Daniel. 2019. '*The New King of Comedy*: The Unexpected Shape-Shifting of Stephen Chow.' *VCinema*, 24 March. http://www.vcinemashow.com/the-new-king-of-comedy-china-2019-the-unexpected-shape-shifting-of-stephen-chow/. Accessed 17 September 2021.
Loock, Kathleen and Constantine Verevis, eds. 2012. *Film Remakes, Adaptations and Fan Productions: Remake-Remodel*. Basingstoke: Palgrave-Macmillan.
Mazdon, Lucy. 2000. *Encore Hollywood: Remaking French Cinema*. London: British Film Institute.
Raine, Michael. 2014. 'Adaptation as "Transcultural Mimesis" in Japanese Cinema.' In *The Oxford Handbook of Japanese Cinema*. Edited by Daisuke Miyao, 101–23. Oxford: Oxford University Press.
Schroeder, Andrew. 2004. *Tsui Hark's Zu: Warriors from the Magic Mountain*. Hong Kong: Hong Kong University Press.

Sharp, Jasper. 2011. *Historical Dictionary of Japanese Cinema*. Lanham: Scarecrow Press.
Verevis, Constantine. 2006. *Film Remakes*. Edinburgh: Edinburgh University Press.
Wang, Yiman. 2013. *Remaking Chinese Cinema: Through the Prism of Shanghai, Hong Kong, and Hollywood*. Honolulu: University of Hawai'i Press.
Woodland, Sarah. 2018. *Remaking Gender and the Family: Perspectives on Contemporary Chinese-Language Film Remakes*. Leiden: Brill.

Part I
Re-fleshing the Text: Sex, Seduction, Desire

CHAPTER I

How to Sell a Remake: The *Gate of Flesh* Media Franchise

Irene González-López

From Noh theatre and ukiyo-e woodblocks to radio dramas, cinema and manga, adaptations and remakes have been prevalent in the creative and cultural industries of Japan for centuries. The sheer amount of transmedial texts bears witness to the pleasure and benefits that Japanese audiences and producers have traditionally found in the repetition of familiar stories, scenarios and character types.[1] From the early post-war era going forward, creative and cultural industries expanded at an unprecedented pace, leading to a greater crosspollination among different media outlets (film, radio, television, etc.); an increase in the number of media-literate audiences; and the consolidation of a rich tradition of criticism in print. Examining the Japanese 'Gate of Flesh' (*Nikutai no mon*) media franchise that was launched two years after the end of the Second World War and which was based on and inspired by Tamura Taijirō's novel *Gate of Flesh* (1947), this chapter explores the industrial contexts, textual features and critical discourses that shape the intricate relations among its iterations. Approaching remakes as a powerful means for a nation to come to (cultural) terms with its past, I hope to shed light on the cultural image of this franchise and its role over several decades in shaping the popular memory of this tumultuous historical period along gendered narratives.

As the basis for eight adaptations and remakes, including theatrically released motion pictures, a telefilm and a stage play, Tamura's original text from the immediate post-war period is regarded as a progenitive work in the cultural imagination of Japan in the aftermath of defeat. Alongside the literary output of writers such as Noma Hiroshi, Dazai Osamu and Sakaguchi Ango, Tamura's novel is representative of the 'literature of the flesh' (*nikutai bungaku*) that depicted the liberated carnal body as the gate to a new, autonomous subjectivity in opposition to the national body (*kokutai*) of the pre-war militarist regime that systematically repressed corporeal desires. Despite the relevance of Tamura's work and the large number of iterations it has germinated, thus far no attempt has been made to critically unpack the potential of 'Gate of Flesh' to further our understanding of how adaptations and remakes both capitalise on and encourage the crosspollination of cultural and creative industries in Japan, while playing an important role in the continuous remembering and reimagining of national history.

In recent decades, scholarship on adaptations and remakes has overcome the limited focus on comparative textual analyses that tended to prioritise the 'original' text, a critical practice which previously dominated the discipline. Building upon yet departing from traditional approaches to the subject in his influential book *Film Remakes* (2005), Constantine Verevis proposes an analytical model sensitive to three interconnected layers of significance, conceptualising remaking as:

1) an industrial category (with attention paid to authors, stars, cycles and commerce);
2) a textual category (focusing on plot, narrative and genre); and
3) a critical category (acknowledging the important role that reception and institutional discourses play).

Applying Verevis's approach to Japan's pre-war studio system productions, Kinoshita Chika underscores the importance of historicising remakes and adaptations to identify the 'intertextual, intermedial, and inter-networking connections in the industry' (2017, 88). Inspired by Verevis's and Kinoshita's work, this chapter examines historically specific, interrelated practices of industry, critics, audiences and the state to deepen our understanding of how meaning is created, shaped and disseminated within and across each iteration. In further exploring a great variety of materials that surround each text, meaning is often revealed to be plural and contested rather than unequivocal or completely under control.

Verevis argues that 'remakes are "pre-sold" to their audience because viewers are assumed to . . . at least possess a "narrative image" of the original story' (2005, 3). In the case of a franchise like 'Gate of Flesh', with eight recognised iterations proliferating over sixty years across literature, theatre, cinema and television, I would suggest that the narrative image of the adapted work is partially superseded by that of the franchise, which functions as a cumulative text that capitalises on the prestige and accessibility of certain later versions and which allows for synergies, overlaps and discrepancies. Because 'we often know many texts only at the paratextual level' (Gray 2010, 26), promotional materials and critical discourses are particularly important in such a media-saturated landscape as that of post-war Japan. Drawing on

Gérard Genette, Robert Stam defines paratexts as 'the accessory messages and commentaries that come to surround the text and at times become virtually indistinguishable from it' (2000, 65). These include, according to Jonathan Gray, trailers, interviews with creative personnel, Internet discussions, entertainment news, reviews, fan creations, posters, DVDs, CDs and spinoffs, amongst others (2010, 1). Paratexts allow us to examine how a story is sold, consumed and discussed but, as Gray argues, they are not merely accessories; instead, 'they create texts, they manage them, and they fill them with many of the meanings that we associate with them' (Ibid., 6). In fact, as this chapter demonstrates, promotional paratexts may even differ in content or tone from the film text. Following Gray, I approach each iteration as only a part of the extended presence of audio and visual proliferations that give meaning to the 'text', which can be understood as an encompassing entity.

Catherine Grant argues that acknowledged adaptations and their surrounding discourses are expected to 'recall the adapted work, or the cultural memory of it' (2002, 57). While Grant seems to refer to something very similar to what Verevis calls 'narrative image', the term 'cultural memory' draws attention to the shared yet heterogeneous, endlessly shifting and fragmented discursive practices involved in the collective imagining of an original text and its perceived enduring relevance. A long-standing media phenomenon such as 'Gate of Flesh' allows us to identify those elements that, despite variations, remain constant throughout the franchise, making up the core of the urtext's cultural memory that impacts the production, promotion and reception of its offshoots. I argue that these core elements enable us to reveal the ideological discourses that the urtext, reworked and reinvigorated through its iterations, contributes to the popular memory of Occupied Japan. Moreover, in conjuring up the cultural memory of Tamura's *Gate of Flesh*, subsequent iterations seek to legitimise their own 'remade' vision of this crucial period in Japanese history.

The first section of this chapter maps the franchise to chart overlaps and discrepancies among the many versions of 'Gate of Flesh'. In locating each of them against its specific historical and industrial context, I hope to shed light on various factors that impacted production, including censorship, stardom and ideological trends. The aim is not to provide an exhaustive textual analysis but to highlight a number of narrative and aesthetic elements that call into question any linear and hierarchised relation between the urtext and its iterations. The second section explores how 'Gate of Flesh' has been marketed and assessed. It examines a wide range of paratexts to analyse how they converge, clash and diverge, granting value and identity to each iteration and the franchise in emotional, cultural, political and economic terms. Grounded on the historical specificity of Japanese media industries, the following analysis seeks to offer new perspectives from which to rethink remakes as an enthralling platform for cultural dialogue.

MAPPING THE 'GATE OF FLESH' FRANCHISE

Table 1.1 shows the nine recognised versions of 'Gate of Flesh' to date. Just five months after the publication of Tamura's novel in 1947, the story was adapted into a provocative, commercially successful stage play, directed by Ozaki Masafusa. The first cinematic version, directed by Makino Masahiro and Ozaki Masafusa, was produced in 1948 under the censorship of the Allied Occupation. In 1964, three more adaptive works were produced: choreographer and producer Fukai Toshihiko, who operated primarily in striptease shows, staged a version at Osaka's Nishigeki Music Hall; Suzuki Seijun made the film version probably best known to foreign audiences; and Onchi Hideo directed a film that recounted the reunion of the characters twenty years later. In 1977, Nikkatsu Roman Porno released a soft-porn version directed by Nishimura Shōgorō, and it was followed in 1988 by another adaptation by Gosha Hideo for Tōei studio. Finally, a telefilm produced by TV Asahi and Tōei studio and directed by Inohara Tatsuzō was broadcast in 2008. The recurrent presence of Tōhō, Nikkatsu and Tōei suggests their intention to maximise the literary property which they have paid for. Most versions are difficult to access, especially outside Japan, and the majority have not been previously analysed in English-language scholarly publications. While all of the iterations of 'Gate of Flesh' exclusively credit Tamura's novel as their

Table 1.1 The 'Gate of Flesh' franchise

YEAR	TITLE	FORMAT	AUTHOR /DIRECTOR	PRODUCTION /PUBLISHER
1947	*Gate of Flesh* (*Nikutai no mon*)	Novel	Tamura Taijirō	*Gunzō*
1947	*Gate of Flesh*	Stage play	Ozaki Masafusa	Kukiza (Tōhō Theatrical Company involved)
1948	*Gate of Flesh*	Film	Ozaki M. and Makino Masahiro	Yoshimoto Productions (distribution: Tōhō)
1964	*Gate of Flesh*	Erotic show	Fukai Toshihiko	Unknown. Staged at Nishigeki Music Hall
1964	*Gate of Flesh*	Film	Suzuki Seijun	Nikkatsu
1964	*The Call of Flesh* (*Jotai*)	Film	Onchi Hideo	Tōhō
1977	*Gate of Flesh*	Film	Nishimura Shōgorō	Nikkatsu Roman Porno
1988	*Gate of Flesh*	Film	Gosha Hideo	Tōei
2008	*Gate of Flesh*	Telefilm	Inohara Tatsuzō	TV Asahi and Tōei studio

source, this section demonstrates that the film versions incorporate important elements from previous ones, and in some cases could be categorised as remakes of those earlier texts rather than adaptations of the novel.

Tamura wrote *Gate of Flesh* upon his return to Japan after more than five years at the war front in China. Set in Tokyo in the aftermath of war, it tells the story of a gang of five *panpan* (streetwalkers often catering to American GIs) who live in a burnt-out building under a strict code of behaviour and whose encounter with a war veteran named Ibuki Shintarō shatters the balance of their community. The novel was first published in March 1947 in the recently established literature periodical *Gunzō* (*Gathering Images*). Tamura was catapulted to fame as the publication 'heated up the public opinion' and triggered a fad of 'flesh novels' (*nikutai shōsetsu*) (Okuno 1958, 221). By 1983, at the time of Tamura's death, it had sold 700,000 copies (*Asahi* 1983, 161). Writing again for *Gunzō* in 1961, Tamura recalled his experience of creating *Gate of Flesh*. Tokyo was devastated and people's biggest daily concern was finding food. As a result, there was yet very little literary activity, but Tamura, 'after experiencing war', felt as if 'nothing could scare [him]' (1961, 252). The city was changing quickly with the spread of what John Dower calls the 'subcultures of defeat', where the *panpan*, the black market and the '*kasutori* culture' demimonde[2] overlapped as 'shocking yet mesmerizing symbols of the collapse of the old order and the emergence of a new spirit of iconoclasm and self-reliance' (1999, 122). Tamura transposed their provocative themes into the respectable literary sphere that *Gunzō* aimed to represent (Nakamura 1978). He recalls being captivated by the *panpan* catering to American GIs. 'Perhaps I felt some kind of empathy towards these women, because I had also led for many years a life of confronting the world with flesh and bone' (1961, 253). While a shared struggle for survival and extreme physical experiences made Tamura identify with the *panpan*, he also introduced the character of returned soldier Ibuki as his alter ego. The novel expressed the conflicted emotions that past and present triggered in Tamura and probably many others in Japan: 'When I finished writing [*Gate of Flesh*], I felt as if I had vomited something that had been stuck in my stomach . . . I have never felt anything like that before or after' (Tamura 1961, 253).

Taking advantage of the novel's momentum, in August 1947 the theatrical troupe Kukiza, which had been established one year earlier, adapted the story into a stage play, scripted by Ozawa Fujio and directed by Ozaki Masafusa. The project was instigated by Hata Toyokichi, an entrepreneur who saw business opportunities in the relaxations of censorship on nudity and sexual representations. Working with Tōhō Theatrical Company, Hata sought to make the Teitoza theatre of Shinjuku the epicentre of the '*ryoki* culture' (literally 'seeking the bizarre') in synergy with the *kasutori*. At Teitoza he produced the first 'picture-frame nude show' (*gakubuchi nūdo shō* – a static precursor of the strip show that featured scantily dressed women posing inside large-scale picture frames) and had Kukiza's *Gate of Flesh* premiere there too. The play became a sensational hit, largely due to the provocative costumes and sexual references, and with a climactic scene depicting the stripping and beating of one of the female characters (Okuno 1958, 220). By December 1947, the stage play had become the most-performed theatrical work since the end of the war (Nakae 1947, 36). It was performed more than 1,200 times over three years – 700 times in Tokyo alone (Kamiya 2009, 154), with three sessions a day, upped to four on Sundays and bank holidays (Nakae 1947, 36; *Yomiuri* 1947, 2; *Asahi* 1983, 161).

The fad for 'flesh novels' initiated by Tamura, amplified by the *kasutori* culture and the erotic show business, triggered a short-lived cycle of '*panpan* films' – director Mizoguchi Kenji's *Women of the Night* (*Yoru no onnatachi*, 1948) being the first to be released. According to director Ozaki from Kukiza, the project for the cinematic adaptation had already begun in September 1947, but due to issues with the script and the cast, the film was not released until August 1948 (*Shineiga* 1948, 22; Kamiya 2009, 157, 177). Produced by Yoshimoto Productions and distributed by Tōhō, the film was directed by Ozaki together with legendary director Makino Masahiro, scripted again by Ozawa Fujio to follow closely his play and featuring many Kukiza actors. It became a great box-office success (Kamiya 2009, 157). The film's depiction of sexuality and violence is more restrained than in the previous texts because censorship in cinema was much stricter than in other creative industries, with pre- and postproduction censorship undertaken by the Civil Information and Education Section (CIE) and the Civil Censorship Detachment (CDD). Films had to demonstrate that 'crime does not pay' and, in the case of *Gate of Flesh*, the CIE stipulated that the producers should 'tone down the cynicism of streetwalkers and useless emphasis on money in the revised script' (Hirano 1992, 74–5, 283).

The impact of these first two iterations on subsequent versions cannot be overstated; plot elements and characters introduced by Ozaki and Ozawa, and not present in Tamura's novel, resurface in later remakes. For instance, Maya is presented as a naïve newcomer instead of the co-leader of the gang as portrayed in the novel; a shift which is replicated in Suzuki's and Nishimura's films (1964 and 1977 respectively). The stage play also introduced two new characters who feature in the film: a policewoman who befriends *panpan* Sen, and a priest who attempts to 'save' the *panpan* and receives greater prominence in the 1948 film, appearing to stand in for the Occupation (or its censorship) by representing the victory of order and morality against Ibuki's seemingly outdated values. The priest re-emerged in Suzuki's version, albeit leading to a tragic fate as the character (played by Chico Lourant) commits suicide after being seduced by *panpan* Maya (Nogawa Yumiko). Director Inohara Tatsuzō's 2008 telefilm merges both into a policeman (Naitō Takashi), who acts as a moral compass and builds a close relationship with Sen (Mizuki Arisa). Moreover, the 1948 film's central music piece, *Hoshi no nagare ni* ('In the Flow of the Stars', 1947),³ became another prominent intertextual element in the franchise. This hit song about a *panpan* who wonders 'who has made me this kind of woman?' (*konna onna ni dare ga shita*) features seven times in the 1948 film, and later in Suzuki's, Nishimura's and Gosha's versions.

The year 1964 saw the release of three further iterations. While official discourses sought to globally exhibit Japan's successful modernisation at the Tokyo Olympics, interest in the 'literature of the flesh' resurged, driven by political discourses critically revisiting the 'success' of post-war Japan and by the relaxation of censorship that triggered a 'nudity boom' (*hadaka būmu*) in the cultural industries (Sawa 1964, 233). After Fukai's erotic stage version premiered in February, Nikkatsu released Suzuki's *Gate of Flesh* in May. This 'adult film' (*seijin-eiga*) is representative of the exploitative strategy major studios pursued in the 1960s to confront the crisis of mainstream cinema and compete with the rapidly expanding *pinku* market of independent erotic productions.⁴ For instance, Maya and Ibuki's sexual intercourse is explicitly depicted but the screen is partially blurred and darkened to hide the lower part of the naked bodies – a technique common in pink films known as *bokashi* (blurring). The depiction of *panpan* gang fights becomes an excuse for an exploitative representation of women-on-women violence that all subsequent versions echo. Suzuki's film revived the eroticism and shock value of Tamura's novel and Kukiza's stage play by going 'further than any major studio production had gone before in terms of putting sex and sadism on the big screen' (Sharp 2008, 58).

As noted earlier, several elements introduced by Ozaki, such as the characterisation of Maya as a newcomer and the featuring of 'In the Flow of the Stars', appear in Suzuki's and other later versions. It is, therefore, difficult to determine from which version later films would take these elements, but the impact of Suzuki's version is undeniable; especially in its depiction of the Occupation and its gender politics. While the 1948 film could only hint at the US-led military Occupation of Japan by, for instance, showing signs in the streets written in Latin alphabet, Suzuki was able to introduce for the first time American GIs to the story. In filling in the gap forced by previous political censorship, the film re-frames the plot as a gendered narrative of post-war Japan as a woman violated by the Occupying power, echoed in all subsequent versions where sexual violence perpetrated by GIs abounds. In Suzuki's film, for example, Maya is gang raped by a group of GIs offscreen, but Nishimura's 1977 version explicitly depicts the aggression in the film's opening. This sense of foreign attack is further highlighted by framing the *panpan* as agents of national resistance. Suzuki's film chose to characterise the protagonists as *wapan* (*panpan* catering exclusively to Japanese men) in open conflict with *yōpan* gangs (sex workers specialising in foreigners). All subsequent films, except Gosha's 1988 version, follow this pattern, one that suggests an intention to make the *panpan* characters more sympathetic to Japanese audiences as icons of subversive resistance.

In September 1964, Tōhō released the 'adult film' *The Call of Flesh* (*Jotai*), written and directed by Onchi Hideo. Aware of Suzuki's competing project, Onchi's adaptation combined *Gate of Flesh* with another of Tamura's novels, *The Terracotta Woman* (*Haniwa no onna*, 1961). In doing so, *The Call of Flesh* depicts the reunion of *panpan* Sen (Kusunoki Yūko) and Maya (Dan Reiko) with Ibuki (Nanbara Kōji) twenty years later, and the plot takes us back and forth in time as their reencounter triggers memories of the early post-war. The scarce explanations about characters and events of the past indicate an assumption by the filmmakers that audiences are familiar with Tamura's novel and perhaps with Suzuki's version. Both films evoke a certain nostalgia toward the early post-war years which, although chaotic and dangerous, seemed full of vital energy. As in the novel, the aftermath of defeat is depicted as a time when destruction also meant a new beginning; when, in being pressed against the law of survival, one could break free from societal rules. Both films also connect the early post-war to contemporary concerns but do so in very different ways. In Suzuki's version, Joe Shishido, playing Ibuki, resembles Tamura's character as a powerful masculine force driven by unrestrained desires. Scantily dressed for most of the film, the tanned muscular body of Shishido, to whom all women surrender, functions as a narcissistic, homoerotic fantasy for the male spectator. Maya ends empowered by her awakening to love and desire, and Sen (Kasai Satoko) remains proud and strong leading the trade. All three impudently defy the GIs. Onchi's version, on the other hand, exposes the futility of Tamura's and Suzuki's fantasy of masculinity by morphing Ibuki in the 1960s into a drug addict living on Sen's income (now the madam of a club). Sen regrets being unable to integrate into 'respectable' society, while Maya is a fulltime housewife, trapped in a marriage that ensures social and economic stability. Whereas Suzuki's film celebrates chaotic freedom and connects the characters' rebellious spirit to anti-American feelings effervescing in Japan in the 1960s, Onchi's version criticises the alleged comforts of contemporary society as underpinned by the uninterrupted commodification of sexuality.

The Call of Flesh is the first iteration to provide historical contextualisation to the story, drawing attention to the role that long-standing franchises like 'Gate of Flesh' play in shaping popular memory. Whether inspired by Onchi's film or through coincidence, all subsequent iterations include similar introductory scenes. In Onchi's version, the first flashback is introduced by a lengthy montage sequence of striking images, including the atomic bomb, wounded and crippled people, General Douglas MacArthur descending from a plane, the war trial of General Tōjō Hideki, children in ruined schools, and Military

Police patrolling the streets. This montage sequence bears witness to the ways in which the memories of defeat and Occupation were already visually codified and emotionally charged by the mid-1960s. Both Nishimura's 1977 version and the telefilm begin with shorter montage sequences that include images of the atomic bomb; and Gosha's film (1988) opens with onscreen text explaining Japan's destruction in quantitative terms (for example, '92 cities attacked during the war'; '1,500,000 dead'; 'Tokyo indiscriminately bombed 130 times'). The desire to provide a historical frame for younger audiences who do not have direct memories of past events or who lack extensive historical knowledge is also evident in promotional paratexts, as will be discussed later. But this kind of contextualisation also amplifies the emotional and political impact of the story, feeding into the victimisation discourse that makes the atomic bomb and the Tokyo bombings the beginning of the (hi)story, decontextualised from Japan's previous war actions. Over six decades, the 'Gate of Flesh' franchise helped to reproduce, albeit with significant variations, the narrative of a feminised Japan suffering the consequences of a war framed as an abstract entity with no antecedents or accountable leaders.

In 1977 Nishimura Shōgorō directed another version for Nikkatsu studio, which had shifted all of its production to softcore porn six years earlier under the brand Roman Porno to stave off bankruptcy. The trailer promotes this iteration as a 'mega-production' (*chōdaisaku*) (Nikkatsu 1977), a term denoting particularly expensive Roman Porno films that were often adaptations of canonical literary works (like those by Tanizaki Jun'ichirō and Edogawa Ranpo) and occasionally reusing properties for which Nikkatsu had already acquired rights, as in the case of *Gate of Flesh*. Those 'mega-productions' allowed Nikkatsu to exhibit its technical prowess and sophisticated studio sets, differentiating itself from the low-budget pink industry. The film shares many narrative elements with Suzuki's version and exacerbates the eroticisation of Ibuki (Endō Seiji), featuring, for instance, his naked body in the shower while all the *panpan* stare at him with desire. Here the homoerotic fantasy of domination and rebellion articulated for the male viewer is further connected to nationalistic pride because, whereas in other versions Ibuki gets injured when stealing money or products, here it is in a fight where he stabs a GI for spitting and stepping on the Japanese flag.

The casting of Miyashita Junko, one of the most legendary icons of Roman Porno, illustrates the importance of stars as intertexts (Verevis 2005, 8). In Roman Porno, female stars were tightly linked to distinct 'types' of women and, in the case of Miyashita, that was a romantic, irrational woman often involved in masochistic relationships (such as in director Kumashiro Tatsumi's *Street of Joy* [*Akasen Tamanoi nukeraremasu*, 1974]). In casting Miyashita in the role of Machiko, the *panpan* who gives herself to passionate love and is brutally punished by others for it, Nikkatsu heavily relied on her star image to create a grounded character, while simultaneously endowing the film with her prestige. This was particularly useful from a commercial perspective, because the rest of the female cast were newcomers who had yet to develop a solid star image in the studio.

A similar use of stars connected to character types, film cycles or auteurs can be found in other iterations. Suzuki's version capitalises on Shishido's star persona as eccentric maverick, which the director had contributed to in films such as *Youth of the Beast* (*Yaju no seishun*, 1963). Moreover, the critically acclaimed debut of Nogawa Yumiko as Maya likely led Suzuki to cast her the following year as a sex worker in love with a Japanese soldier in another adaptation of Tamura's literature, *Story of a Prostitute* (*Shunpuden*, 1965). Finally, in the telefilm, the radical transformation of Sen's character relies on Mizuki Arisa's star persona as a rational and outspoken woman with a strong sense of justice (reflected, for instance, in the drama *Saitō san* [Kubota Mitsuru, Iwamoto Hitoshi and Honma Miyuki, 2008]). The effectiveness of this intertextual referentiality depends, of course, on the knowledge of audiences. But it is frequently enhanced by the extratextual referentiality that is produced by critics and which circulates in cultural commentaries. For instance, a review of Gosha's version underscores the similar roles Katase Rino (Sen in the film) and Natori Yuko (playing Osumi, the leader of another *panpan* gang) had played in 1987 in the same director's critically acclaimed *Tokyo Bordello* (*Yoshiwara enjo*, 1987), a film adaptation scripted again by Kasahara Kazuo depicting prostitutes in the Meiji period (1868–1912). Drawing attention to character types, explicit sex scenes and other narrative and cinematographic aspects, the review uses the connections between the films to legitimise Gosha's approach to the sex industry and his depiction of sex and violence in *Gate of Flesh* (Takahashi 1988).

The telefilm, directed by Inohara Tatsuzō, was produced by TV Asahi and Tōei studio and was broadcast on 27 December 2008 as a 'special drama' (*supesharu dorama*). It offers a very liberal adaptation of the novel, but one that is not as original as it might seem, because it draws heavily on plot twists and key scenes from Gosha's 1988 version. The plotline in the telefilm of Sen being driven by revenge, seeking to find the GI who raped both her and her mother, appears in Gosha's film through the character of Osumi. In both of these more recent films, Sen's gang is saving money to establish a business and quit sex work, Machiko is the newcomer (played by Nishikawa Mineko in 1988, and by Miura Rieko in 2008) and the strength of women's communities is underscored. This entails an important shift from the centrality of masculinity and male-centred sexuality embedded in Tamura's novel and reproduced in Suzuki's and Nishimura's versions, and instead returns to the 1948 film's focus on women's relationships. Consequently, the telefilm capitalises on the popularity of the franchise, while

Figure 1.1 Osumi (Natori Yuko) takes her revenge on the American sergeant who raped and killed her mother, in Gosha Hideo's *Gate of Flesh* (*Nikutai no mon*, 1988).

distancing itself from its exploitative trappings in an attempt to broaden its audience.

In the preceding section, I have sought to demonstrate that Tamura's novel does not consistently function as the primary source text in 'Gate of Flesh'. Although some iterations remain difficult to access for general audiences, significant overlaps suggest that filmmakers did engage with previous scripts, if not with the films themselves, when working on a new version. Nevertheless, the story greatly changes from one iteration to the next and only a few general settings and scenes remain consistent across the franchise; the beating of Machiko and Maya's affair with Ibuki being the two most significant. These episodes are important vehicles for the depiction of violence and eroticism, which stand out as the core of the 'Gate of Flesh' narrative image, as reflected also in the preference for 'adult'-oriented genres in many iterations. But violence and eroticism operate as containers for different narrative, aesthetic and ideological meanings in each version. Historical, political and industrial factors, such as censorship and the post-war boom of erotica and its revival in the 1960s, also significantly affect the remakes. Relatedly, stardom, authorship and creative talent – what Kinoshita refers to as 'inter-networking connections' – provide crucial intertextual and intermedial references beyond the urtext. As analysed in the following pages, all these elements are further mobilised in the promotion and reception of the texts, enriching and complicating the meaning created in and across each iteration.

SEEING THE NARRATIVE IMAGE OF 'GATE OF FLESH' THROUGH ITS PARATEXTS

This section examines a wide range of paratexts to elucidate how producers and audiences justify and assess each iteration. Shedding light on the recurrent and contradictory discourses found across these materials, we continue to chart, from a different perspective, the shifting narrative image of the franchise.

Virtually all of the promotional materials that I have consulted mention Tamura Taijirō, reflecting legal requirements and the status of his literary property; or, rather, the shadow that it casts upon its iterations. In the trailers of Suzuki's, Nishimura's and Gosha's versions, Tamura's name appears even before that of the film's director, establishing a hierarchy of authorship and prestige. The VHS box of Nishimura's Roman Porno film further highlights Tamura in connection to the 'literature of the flesh', which suggests the greater importance of the endorsement of the literary canon for softcore productions that seek to be evaluated beyond their erotic value. In stark contrast, the two early iterations of 1948 disregard Tamura's authorship. A small advertisement for the stage play in the *Yomiuri* newspaper (1947a) does not mention Tamura or Ozaki, but calls attention to the Kukiza troupe, and two other small advertisements for the 1948 film also highlight Kukiza while failing to credit Tamura, with only one mentioning directors Makino and Ozaki (*Yomiuri* 1948a, 1948b). This hints at potential differences in copyright legislation according to industries and the format of the advertisement, since the poster of the 1948 film does credit Tamura. In any case, it seems that the continuity of the director, scriptwriter and cast between the two texts allowed the downplaying of the novel as 'original' and highlighted the stage play as equal if not even above it as source material for the film (*Kindai eiga* 1948; *Shineiga* 1948). This is visually reinforced by the choice of publicity stills that depict the priest and the policewoman, characters added to the story in the stage play (*Kindai eiga* 1948).

An examination of promotional paratexts further corroborates the notion that the franchise's narrative image is one of eroticism and violence, shifting between sensationalism and political critique. Except for the telefilm, promotional materials for all other iterations highlight the story's status as a 'problematic work' (*mondai saku* – which, in Japanese, can refer to both a text dealing with a relevant social problem and one provoking controversies) that had become a 'hot topic' (*wadai ni natta*) in public opinion. Although transgressive eroticism is a major selling point, promotional materials sometimes used images more titillating than anything shown in the films themselves. For instance, publicity stills for the 1948 film feature Sen (Todoroki Yukiko) lying on the floor wearing a top with a wide neckline that accentuates the cleavage and Maya (Tsukioka Chiaki) topless, although her breasts are partly hidden (*Kinema junpō* 1948).

These images were certainly used on promotional materials to arouse viewers' expectations by building on the controversial stage play and the thriving *kasutori* culture where images of *panpan* abounded, even though the actual film is much demurer. Similarly, it is said that in promoting the play, producer Hata endlessly recounted in the media the widely publicised incident of a woman who committed suicide from Teitoza's roof after watching the play two nights in a row, underlining that the play must have moved her to that decision in some way or another (Nakae 1947, 39). Relatedly, *The Call of Flesh* was occasionally promoted under the logline: 'Woman's unrestrained instincts! Seize her in the raw as sex triggers a revolution in the woman's body!' (Sawa 1964, 228), which reduces Onchi's complex historical analysis of power dynamics to sexploitation. Paratexts like these amplify the shock value of the iterations, challenging the viewers to dare to watch a 'problematic work'.

In addition to *auteurist* endorsement and the appeal of shock value, the remakes of *Gate of Flesh* are often expected to fulfil a socio-cultural function. Although the focus shifts with time, both promotional materials and reviews underscore the relevance of historical authenticity as a means of enlightening the audiences. In the case of early iterations, the veracity of the depiction of the *panpan* was upheld as a selling point (*Shineiga* 1948) and echoed in the reviews as later examined. In the 1960s, however, the concern with authenticity was applied not to the *panpan* but to the depiction of the spirit of defeated Japan; and in the twenty-first century promotional allegations of veracity are rearticulated in terms of historical education. In a press conference, Mizuki Arisa stated that, for her, the central aim of this remake was to make 'today's people' aware 'that there was such a period in Japanese history' (Rising Productions 2011). Similarly, Griseldis Kirsch, in analysing the media franchise of 'I Want to Be a Shellfish' (*Watashi wa kai ni naritai*), notes that the promotion of the 1994 television drama version read: 'Do you know the truth about the war?' (2009, 91). By addressing those who lack first-hand knowledge, these television productions capitalise on renowned literary works to position themselves as fulfilling a cultural need by narrating the historical 'truth'.

Inconsistency among paratexts is common because it allows promotional agents to appeal to various audiences. For example, in contrast to the above-discussed titillating publicity stills of the 1948 film, another promotional piece finds director Ozaki lauding cinema's moral imperative. According to him, the film's ending includes several scenes absent in the novel that draw attention to Sen's fate, inspire sympathy towards her and deliver a 'clear resolution' that satisfies 'the morality akin to film' (*eigateki moraru*) (*Shineiga* 1948, 22). The film, therefore, was simultaneously presented in Ozaki's words as embracing cinema's moral responsibility, and hence welcoming censorship, and in images as a sensationalistic spectacle pushing the boundaries of what could be shown on screen. By referencing the 'memory of a work' – as Grant would have it (2002, 57) – but not actually delivering it, contradictory publicity complicates or multiplies the core image of an iteration. The case of the telefilm evidences the level of ideological and narrative contradiction that paratexts allow, encouraging audiences to decode actively those surrounding materials in combination with their own knowledge about the film, the franchise and its numerous intertexts. The main publicity still features six *panpan* looking straight into the camera with a defiant, proud expression on their faces, underscoring the idea of strong women also verbally stressed in the telefilm's entry on Tōei's website (2008) and in Mizuki's press conference (Rising Productions 2011). In contrast, the trailer incorporates erotic and violent images that assert the remake's connection to the franchise but primarily focuses on melodramatic scenes accompanied by the subtitle: 'Sorrowful women who lived in a sorrowful era', emphasising the vulnerability and suffering of the *panpan*. However, in yet another twist, Tōei's website reads: 'The subject of the best seller written by Tamura Taijirō after the war is "the liberation of the flesh". But this film shifts the focus to "motherhood"', which the entry connects to comforting memories of one's mother in difficult times, women's nurturing relationships and the realisation of a woman whose instinct of motherhood is awakened (Tōei 2008). While the maternal instinct is similarly depicted in the telefilm tainted with conservative tones, it does not come across as the central theme. Combining ideas of women's empowerment with images of melodramatic victimisation, and sexploitation with images of woman as essentially mother, the telefilm maximises its potential audiences.

Discrepancies among promotional paratexts at the time of the text's release also facilitate the 'adaptation' of its narrative image across the years to accommodate shifting sensibilities. The promotional image for Gosha's film published in the *Yomiuri* newspaper (1988b, 20) pictures a titillating close-up of Sen's legs (recognisable as such thanks to her tattoo) and another woman in bondage underneath her, while the logline reads: 'Embracing them incautiously is dangerous.' While, like previous iterations, the film is publicised as pushing the boundaries of what was permissible for a 'regular film' (*ippan gekieiga*), other paratexts stressed the centrality of independent women. In an article in *Yomiuri* newspaper, Katase (Sen in the film) is quoted as stating: 'I empathise with these women who earnestly sought to move forward in life . . . Women nowadays are strong because they choose to be so, but in that period men were no good and women had no choice but to be strong. It is a different meaning of strength. I would like young women to see this aspect of the film' (*Yomiuri* 1988a, 15). Katase addresses female spectators and justifies the film in emotional and cultural terms appealing to current and historical matters affecting women. Similar to the paratextual framing of the 1948 film, promotional images are connected to exploitation while promotional written texts focus on more noble or profound appeals. The fact that both paratexts were published on the same day in the same newspaper suggests that they are not necessarily targeting different audiences. But approximately ten years later the VHS box cover attached to the 1999 home video release did not use the poster image advertised at the time of the film's release. Instead, the VHS and DVD covers, attached to the 1999 and 2015 home video releases, respectively, feature Sen on the shoulders of an unidentified black man, looking into the camera smiling, and surrounded by images of other women, who also exude joy and self-confidence. In this way, they shift the spotlight from images of eroticism and violence to the positive depiction of empowered women (returning to Katase's approach) to appeal to new audiences and sensibilities. Moreover, since no black actor features in Gosha's film, the VHS and DVD covers appear to reference Suzuki's version, now an established cult film, which featured Lourant in the role of the black priest.

Finally, the promotion of Suzuki's version in other countries offers insights into paratexts beyond the control of the filmmakers. Contemporaneous foreign posters do not mention Tamura and downplay Suzuki because, presumably, they would not be meaningful references to audiences. The film is rather blatantly promoted as Orientalist sexploitation of high technical quality guaranteed by colour cinemascope. An American poster reads 'Lusty Onas and 50,000 GIs' and defines 'onas' (probably from the Japanese *onna*, meaning 'woman') as 'Beautiful Japanese women', suggesting in contradiction to the actual film that the *panpan* characters cater to foreigners. The film is endorsed by the famous producer-distributor Jack H. Harris and a review in the *L.A. Times* describing it as 'the boldest ever', stressing quality referents familiar to American audiences while appealing to shock value. Relatedly, an Italian poster for Suzuki's film *Le Professioniste dell'Amore* highlights the presence of GIs and erotic women with orientalist physical traits and includes illustrations of Japanese temples, although no temples appear in the film. It is furthermore intriguing that, despite the Orientalist tones, the female figures in other foreign posters of Suzuki's film rather resemble Caucasian women in their physical traits. In this way, the fantasy of subjugation combines familiarity and 'othering' to appeal to a presupposed white male viewer, offering Japanese women as easily consumable objects. In contrast, later paratexts (such as the Criterion Collection DVD cover) have clearly shifted to revolve around Suzuki as auteur; although one could argue that shock value is part of his director persona and thus it remains a selling point without needing to be foregrounded.

Turning to the texts' reception, I shall explore the role of critics and other professionals from the creative industries in establishing the framework within which the iterations were to be read and assessed. While Kitamura Kyōhei notes that theory on remakes in Japan has been scarce until recently (2017, 25), I propose that media criticism offers a compelling alternative to scholarly

Figure 1.2 The cover art of the 2015 DVD release of Gosha Hideo's *Gate of Flesh* (*Nikutai no mon*, 1988), showing the character Sen sitting on the shoulders of an unidentified black man.

discourses to explore how the practice and merit of remakes and adaptations are theorised in Japan. My examination of reviews of the franchise proves most critics agree that fidelity to the original is not a priority. Instead, they demand that the remake offers some additional value, frequently in ethical or ideological terms. In reviewing Ozaki's stage play, for instance, theatre director Nakae Ryusuke criticises Tamura's novel for idealising Ibuki, who is 'a victim of war but also reckless criminal with no borders' and constitutes a 'man of a period of transition between two eras' with an 'old vision of the accomplished individual' (1947, 38). The stage play, Nakae contends, reaffirms the lifestyle of Ibuki and fails to expose that his old-fashioned conception of the flesh cannot liberate the individual subjectivity:

> The theatrical adaptation of a novel should never be made to please the author of the original. One must first immerse oneself in the world of the original work without reserve, there one must feel and perceive everything, and by grasping the momentum of the raising vision of the development of a correct future, one must demolish the work's boundaries and bring a new life to the author's voice based on today's environment (Ibid.).

Nakae demands a critical stance that breaks through the limitations of the urtext to revitalise the story according to the new author's vision of a 'correct future'. Being truthful to the novel becomes, in this case, the failure of the adaptation. Interestingly, he underlines the 'today' when discussing a text adapted only five months after its publication. In doing so, he presupposes a contemporary moral standard that must be incorporated into the adaptation, regardless of whether the source text exhibited it or not. The fact that Ozaki and Ozawa may have engaged in a similar critical process but arrived at another vision of a correct future seems to escape Nakae.

Reviewing Suzuki's version, critic Oshikawa Yoshiyuki exposes the potential conflict between the economic and ethical value of a remake. Oshikawa renders Suzuki's film as an exploitative revival of the *ero-guro* aesthetic (erotic and grotesque) full of excessive images that would be unthinkable to show on television; this being the only reason for its notable box-office success. This remake is, Oshikawa argues, unjustified because it 'offered nothing new' and failed to reflect on the tragedy of these women (1964, 80–1). Oshikawa does not define what this novelty should be, but underscores, like Nakae, the ethical responsibility of an adaptation, even if Suzuki's exploitative depiction may be more truthful to the urtext. To offer another example, critic Nakamura Muneo, in his devastating review of Nishimura's version, stated that 'film adaptation is always a kind of criticism (*hihyō*)' (1978, 168). Like Nakae, Nakamura demands that an adaptation grasp the core of the work to offer a personal, critical perspective on it; but, unlike Nakae, he expects the filmmaker to convey the zeitgeist of the adapted work, not of the remake. Nakamura regrets that Nishimura 'misread' the original work, creating a film full of 'contemporary sentimentality' that fails to depict the energy of the early post-war and engage with the profound questions Tamura addressed throughout the story: 'What is a human being? What is to live? What is the meaning of fear? Of insecurity? Of solitude? Of joy? Of redemption?' (Ibid.).

The preceding examples illustrate how most Japanese reviews of 'Gate of Flesh' focus on a critical comparison with the urtext in ideological and aesthetic terms. This tendency, I argue, is determined by the controversial subject of the novel and the enduring debates about the merit and legacy of the Occupation. It is thus not necessarily representative of critical discussions around media franchises in Japan in general. The status of Tamura made discussions concentrate not only on his *Gate of Flesh* but also on his idiosyncrasy and the philosophy of the 'literature of the flesh'. Often disregarding the exploitative and misogynistic traits of this literary school, many reviews include extensive explanations and critical revisions of Tamura's ideas that allowed critics to exhibit their knowledge of the literary canon and uphold the value of cinema (and of film criticism) by making films accountable for articulating transcendental discussions about the meaning of human existence (for example, Nakae 1947; Nakamura 1978; Takahashi 1988).

As noted earlier, reviews in the early post-war period emphasised the importance of the remake's veracity in its depiction of social reality, which often entered into conflict with the prescriptive idea of films as upholding moral values. A piece published in a 1950 issue of *Fujin kōron* (*Women's Review*) – arguably Japan's most important women's journal and a major advocate of anti-prostitution discourses – retrospectively praised Ozaki and Makino's film for its realistic depiction of the *panpan* and their 'short temper and terrorism' (*terorizumu*) (Tairamura and Nakano 1950, 35). According to Tamura, however, his intention was never to provide a truthful social portrayal but to use the *panpan* as an allegory: 'I became absorbed in writing about my image of these women . . . There are no real facts. It was all imagined by me' (1961, 253). Nevertheless, the article from *Women's Review* reflects how early *panpan* films were referenced as documenting the sex trade while simultaneously being held accountable for their impact on sexual mores (Hirano 1992, 74–5; González-López 2018, 42–4). Relatedly, in a newspaper article published in April 1949, the author decries the fact that children in Tokyo have recently taken to playing a game called 'gate of flesh' (*nikutai no mon*). 'Whether influenced by the novel or the play', the game consists of a girl being tied up by her hands and stripped of some of her clothes while the boys play Ibuki and pretend to beat her up (*Asahi* 1949, 2). Stressing the shared concerns of PTA groups and some scholars, the author claims that 'something needs to be done' because 'children copy everything they see' (*Asahi* 1949, 2).

Considering that in neither the novel, the stage play or the 1948 film does Ibuki participate in any beating, this gender violence constitutes another 'adaptation' of 'Gate of Flesh' that bears witness to the rhizomatic creative potential of a text's narrative image. On the other hand, regardless of the writer's intention, this article would contribute to the amplification of audiences' curiosity, just like Hata's morbid recounting of the suicide incident.

To conclude, it is important to draw attention to the contrast between the numerous negative reviews written by professional critics and the great box-office results several of the iterations achieved. Reviews by members of the audience, moreover, do not necessarily echo the selling points highlighted by filmmakers and thus prove audiences' active and selective reading of paratexts. In the case of the telefilm, reviews by spectators published in major newspapers focus on the actors' performances and the emotional appeal of the story, often praising the engaging depiction of strong women; in contrast, Ibuki's character and the writer Tamura are sometimes not even mentioned (for example, *Yomiuri* 2008; *Yomiuri* 2009). Virtually all reviews, amateur and otherwise, refer to the *panpan* as 'vigorous' (*takumashii*), using the same term as Mizuki in the press conference and Tōei on the website. This coincidence reflects the intertextual and intermedial circulation of key words and evidences the franchise's successful shift from a masculine focus to a feminine one, as the exact same term is used in the trailer for Suzuki's film but applied to Ibuki: 'A man, vigorous reverence and desire' (Nikkatsu 1964). While spectators of the telefilm appear drawn to certain elements found in promotional discourses, none of the reviews analysed here mention motherhood, historical knowledge or the 'literature of the flesh'. Although any generalisation is problematic, these reviews suggest that for contemporary television audiences, articulating Tamura's philosophy is no longer a priority. Yet, 'Gate of Flesh' is still appealing for reimagining occupied Japan according to shifting sensibilities.

CONCLUSION

With its politicised subject and its transgressive aesthetics expanding over nine versions across sixty years, the media franchise of 'Gate of Flesh' offers a fascinating opportunity to experiment with a methodology grounded in the historically specific conditions of post-war Japan and its media economies. Examining the interrelated roles and practices of the creative industries, critics, audiences and the state reveals the complexity of adaptation and remakes as well as their great potential to enhance our understanding of the workings of popular culture.

The franchise functions as a cumulative text where the themes of suffering, survival and personal awakening that make up the narrative image of 'Gate of

Flesh' are incessantly reworked. Charting differences and overlaps among the iterations sheds light on the network of intertextual and extratextual referentialities – suggesting limitless hermeneutic potentialities – that feed meaning into each iteration, while reworking the cultural memory of Tamura's story. Paratexts play a crucial role in establishing the framework in which each iteration is meant to be read, but discrepancies abound. These contradictions, however, can be extremely productive as they allow the narrative image of the franchise to take on a life of its own, beyond the control of filmmakers, resulting in the expansion of readings and audiences, multiplying the places each iteration and the franchise as a whole occupy in popular culture and its memory. The novel is not always the primary reference, which complicates the distinction between adaptation and remake, but the few scenes that remain a consistent presence across the franchise are seen as encapsulating the violence and passion of early post-war Japan. While the plot and ideas of Tamura's novel are often very freely reworked in the iterations, his prestige legitimises the franchise's depiction of Japan in the aftermath of defeat, infusing transgressive images with political meaning and a sense of historical authenticity. The texts' narrative image is consequently equated to the cultural memory of Occupied Japan, as a specific space and time. Each iteration offers a different understanding of this historical period and its gender politics, and of the lessons that contemporaneous Japan can learn from its past.

ACKNOWLEDGEMENTS

I would like to thank Kerstin Fooken and Laurence Green for their assistance during the pandemic in accessing primary materials used in this research.

NOTES

1. Recent studies of these subjects include the works of Nakamura (2016), Coates (2016), Kitamura et al. (2017), Kirsch (2019), Denison (2020) and Wroot (2021).
2. The *kasutori* culture was articulated through myriads of short-lived, cheap publications that, in addressing primarily male audiences, dealt with erotica, sensationalistic crimes, exposés and fictional stories.
3. The music is composed by Tone Ichirō, the lyrics are by Shimizu Minoru and the song was first performed by Kikuchi Akiko.
4. After film attendance reached its pinnacle in 1959, audiences and box-office returns began to rapidly decrease in Japan. The crisis of the studio system can be attributed to various factors, including the inflexible block-booking system, the failure of the double-bill programmes, the rise of television and other entertainment industries, and the mass exodus to the suburbs that partially led to the loss of female audiences. While major studios were faced with a dire financial situation by the mid-1960s, imported films and domestic independent productions, especially erotic ones, were on the rise.

REFERENCES

Asahi. 1949. 'Nikutai no mon.' 4 April, 2.
Asahi. 1983. 'Tensei jingo.' 5 November, 161.
Coates, Jennifer. 2017. *Making Icons: Repetition and the Female Image in Japanese Cinema, 1945–1964*. Hong Kong: Hong Kong University Press.
Denison, Rayna. 2020. 'Manga at the Movies: Adaptation and Intertextuality.' In *The Japan Cinema Book*. Edited by Hideaki Fujiki and Alastair Phillips, 203–13. London: Bloomsbury.
Dower, John W. 1999. *Embracing Defeat: Japan in the Aftermath of World War II*. London: Penguin.
González-López, Irene. 2018. 'Marketing the *Panpan* in Japanese Popular Culture: Youth, Sexuality, and Power.' *U.S.-Japan Women's Journal* 54: 29–51.
Grant, Catherine. 2002. 'Recognising Billy Budd in *Beau Travail*: Epistemology and Hermeneutics of an Auteurist "Free" Adaptation.' *Screen* 43, no. 1: 57–73.
Gray, Jonathan. 2010. *Show Sold Separately: Promos, Spoilers, and Other Media Paratexts*. New York: New York University Press.
Hirano, Kyoko. 1992. *Mr. Smith Goes to Tokyo: The Japanese Cinema under the American Occupation, 1945–1952*. Washington, DC: Smithsonian Institute.
Kamiya, Makiko. 2009. 'Senryōki 'panpan eiga' no poritikkusu – 1948 nen no kikai shikake no kami.' In *Senryōka no eiga – kaihō to ken'etsu*. Edited by Iwamoto Kenji, 151–86. Tokyo: Shinwasha.
Kindai eiga. 1948. 'Nikutai no mon.' July, n.p.
Kinema junpō. 1948. 'Nikutai no mon.' Early July, n.p.
Kinoshita, Chika. 2017. 'Sainō to shisutemu – 1950 nendai Daiei ni okeru Mizoguchi Kenji, rimeiku, janru keisei.' In *Rimeiku eiga no sōzōryoku*. Edited by Kitamura Kyōhei, Shimura Miyoko, Ogawa Sawako, Kawasaki Kōhei, Washitani Hana and Watanabe Daisuke, 75–108. Tokyo: Suiseisha.
Kirsch, Griseldis. 2019. 'Recreating Memory? The Drama *Watashi wa Kai ni Naritai* and its Remakes.' In *Persistently Postwar: Media and the Politics of Memory in Japan*. Edited by Blai Guarné, Artur Lozano-Méndez and Dolores P. Martinez, 85–102. New York: Berghahn.
Kitamura, Kyōhei. 2017. 'Rimeiku eigaron josetsu.' In *Rimeiku eiga no sōzōryoku*. Edited by Kyōhei Kitamura, Shimura Miyoko, Ogawa Sawako, Kawasaki Kōhei, Washitani Hana and Watanabe Daisuke, 9–37. Tokyo: Suiseisha.
Kitamura, Kyōhei, Shimura Miyoko, Ogawa Sawako, Kawasaki Kōhei, Washitani Hana and Watanabe Daisuke, eds. 2017. *Rimeiku eiga no sōzōryoku*. Tokyo: Suiseisha.
Nakae, Ryusuke. 1947. 'Kukiza no mon.' *Teatoro* 80: 36–9.
Nakamura, Miharu. 2016. *Eiga to bungaku: kōkyō suru sōzōryoku*. Tokyo: Shinwasha.
Nakamura, Muneo. 1978. 'Nikutai no mon.' *Kinema junpō*. February, 168–9.
Nikkatsu. 1964. *Nikutai no mon* (Suzuki). Official Japanese trailer. https://mubi.com/films/gate-of-flesh. Accessed 1 March 2022.
Nikkatsu. 1977. *Nikutai no mon* (Nishimura). Official trailer. https://www.videomarket.jp/title/192781/sA192781002999H01. Accessed 1 March 2022.
Okuno, Tatsuo. 1958. 'Kaisetsu.' In *Nikutai no mon, Nikutai no akuma*, 220–8. Tokyo: Shinchō.
Oshikawa, Yoshiyuki. 1964. 'Nikutai no mon.' *Kinema junpō*. Late July, 80–1.
Rising Productions. 2011. Press Conference by Mizuki Arisa, held on 9 December 2008. https://www.youtube.com/watch?v=WC5gy2PImWY. Accessed 1 March 2022.
Sawa, Kōzō. 1964. 'Hadaka ni saseta sutā no kimochi.' *Fujin kōron*. October: 226–33.
Sharp, Jasper. 2008. *Behind the Pink Curtain: The Complete History of Japanese Sex Cinema*. Godalming: FAB.

Shineiga. 1948. 'Nikutai no mon wo kataru.' July, 22–3.
Stam, Robert. 2000. 'Beyond Fidelity: The Dialogics of Adaptation.' In *Film Adaptation*. Edited by James Naremore, 54–76. New Brunswick: Rutgers University Press.
Takahashi. 1988. 'Nikutai no mon.' *Kinema junpō*. May, 170.
Tamura, Taijirō. 1961. 'Nikutai no mon wo kaita koro.' *Gunzō*. October, 252–3.
Tairamura, Taiko and Nakano Yoshio. 1950. 'Tōkyō no 25 ji.' *Fujin kōron*, November, 30–9.
Tōei. 2008. 'Nikutai no mon.' (Inohara). https://www.toei.co.jp/tv/special/nikutai.html. Accessed 1 March 2022.
Verevis, Constantine. 2005. *Film Remakes*. Edinburgh: Edinburgh University Press.
Wroot, Jonathan. 2021. *The Paths of Zatoichi: The Global Influence of the Blind Swordsman*. Lanham: Lexington Books.
Yomiuri. 1947a. 'Shinharu no goraku.' 26 December, 2.
Yomiuri. 1947b. Advertisement *Nikutai no mon* (Ozaki). 13 October, 2.
Yomiuri. 1948a. Advertisement *Nikutai no mon* (Ozaki and Makino). 4 August, 2.
Yomiuri. 1948b. Advertisement *Nikutai no mon* (Ozaki and Makino). 8 August, 3.
Yomiuri. 1988a. 'Katase Rino ga taiatari engi – Katsushuen no Tōei *Nikutai no mon*.' 8 April, 15.
Yomiuri. 1988b. 'Nikutai no mon' (Gosha). Advertisement, 8 April, 20.
Yomiuri. 2008. 'Dorama supesharu *Nikutai no mon*.' 27 December, 32.
Yomiuri. 2009. 'Eiga no yōna jūkōkan.' 19 January, 25.

CHAPTER 2

Against Anaesthesia: *An Empty Dream*, Pleasurable Pain and the 'Illicit' Thrills of South Korea's Golden Age Remakes

David Scott Diffrient

During South Korea's cinematic Golden Age of the 1960s, motion picture remakes – especially those that were based on non-Korean productions – could be called 'illicit' in either one of two ways. As exemplified by director Kim Ki-duk's notorious 1964 release *Barefoot Youth* (*Maenbaleui cheongchun*), 'illicitness' might refer to unlawfulness, or the legal complications that arise when movie producers do not follow the proper channels of copyright clearance or other protocols involved in making near-replicas of existing works (Yecies and Shim 2016, 82, 94–5). In this case, Kim's controversial youth romance about a pair of star-crossed lovers from opposite sides of the track, financed by Geukdong Heungeop (a film company that the director had co-founded five years earlier) and written by Seo Yoon-seong (who would later re-team with Kim to concoct the endearingly cheesy *Godzilla* knockoff *Yongary, Monster from the Deep* [*Taekoesu Yonggary*, 1967]), copied the screenplay of Nakahira Kō's *Mud-Spattered Purity* (*Dorodarake no junjō*, 1963) without seeking permission to do so from the author of the original novel (Fujiwara Shinji), the Japanese filmmaker or the studio for which Kō worked (Nikkatsu). As archival scholar Chung Chonghwa elucidates, however, a license to produce *Barefoot Youth* had been obtained from the original film's screenwriter, Baba Masaru, though as the 'adapter' of the novel he was falsely referenced as the sole arbiter on the issue of remake rights, which was made more complicated by the fact that 'the Republic of Korea (ROK) was not then a party to the Universal Copyright Convention' (Chung 2016, 15).

A side-by-side comparison of the two films – each of which was shot in anamorphic widescreen (although the Japanese original was photographed in colour and features a running time of 91 minutes encompassing 126 scenes, whereas the Korean remake was photographed in black-and-white and features a running time of 117 minutes encompassing 122 scenes) – reveals significant thematic, tonal and visual differences (Chung 2016, 11–24; Chung 2017, 68). Nevertheless, despite those textual disparities and the now-verified belief (supported by archival evidence) that approval had been given (albeit in an unconventional, unofficial manner), *Barefoot Youth* was and still is commonly referred to by journalists and cultural historians as not just an inferior copy or pale imitation but an outright 'plagiarism' (*pyojeol*) of the original (Lee 2002, 71; Chung 2017, 68; Klein 2020, 120). As such, this most 'iconic' and 'quintessential' coming-of-age film from that period (Chung 2014, 227n62; An 2018, 84), itself responsible for a string of knockoffs starring handsome leading man Shin Seong-il (for example, *The Youth Are Thirsty* [*Cheongchuneun mokmaleuda*, 1964], *Student Couple* [*Haksaeng bubu*, 1964] and *Dangerous Youth* [*Uiheomhan cheongchun*, 1966]), has often been held up as a demonstration of the pitfalls involved in remaking a work from a neighbouring yet distant cultural context. It has also been used as evidence of unscrupulous industrial practices or individual creative choices that reflect poorly on a nation that has itself been accused of emulating its colonial and neocolonial 'masters' to the point where traditionally Korean customs have all but disappeared and local productions have been stripped of the things that once set them apart from Japanese and US films.

As if diegetically anticipating this unauthorised remake's perceived violation of industrial norms, the film's plot hinges on the theme of transgression, embodied in the physically and emotionally entangled persons of the rebellious young couple – local gangster Du-su (Shin Seong-il) and wealthy ambassador's daughter Johanna (Um Aing-ran) – whose different class affiliations and familial upbringings all but guarantee a tragic ending to their socially prohibited romance. Their union, in other words, is as ill-fated as that between the two countries whose forced commingling through the remaking (or 'plagiarising') process brings to a head those political factors that made 'normalisation' such a hotly contested idea around the time of *Barefoot Youth*'s release (in the lead up to the Treaty on Basic Relations between Japan and the ROK, signed into law the following year, in the summer of 1965). Tellingly, fierce protests, led by the nation's youth (mainly students from Seoul National University and other institutions of higher learning who were dissatisfied with the Park Chung-hee administration's handling of diplomatic negotiations), broke out a few months after this film's February premiere. Such factors remind us of the way that cultural productions, even those that were pre-emptively censored by the government, could reflect that era's volatile mix of progressive and regressive sensibilities while galvanising audiences outside movie theatres. Better known as the June 3 Resistance Movement, that series of hunger-strikes and street demonstrations prompted President Park to harness the power of his military regime and declare martial law, which would eventually be terminated nearly two months later (on July 29, 1964) (Lee 1985, 50). Using an expression that would not be out of place in mid-1960s cultural commentaries about contemporaneous youth films (*cheongchun yeonghwa*), bursting at the seams with images of gangland street violence as well as lustfully eruptive moments when young, hormonally revved-up men and women engage in illicit activities, historian Chong-Sik Lee describes the sentiments of those caught up in the June 3 movement as an 'emotional explosion' (Ibid.).

This latter connotation of 'illicitness' hints at the other way that a Korean-language remake from that period might have raised the eyebrows of audiences who were gradually acclimating themselves not only to a nascent youth movement within the culture at large (giving rise to dozens more Japanese-inspired coming-of-age films throughout the mid-1960s) but also to a boldly experimental brand of avant-garde cinema that was as daring in its rejection of traditional narrative formulas as it was immodest in its display of licentious behaviour. Theatrically released one year after *Barefoot Youth* had set box-office records (drawing approximately 150,000 moviegoers to Seoul's Academy Cinema by the early spring of 1964) (Chung 2016, 12), director Yu Hyun-mok's *An Empty Dream* (*Chunmong*, 1965) was one such illicit remake. However, in this instance, Yu and the film's producer, Wu Gi-dong, had sought permission from the creator of its source material – Japanese filmmaker Takechi Tetsuji's *Daydream* (*Hakujitsumu*, 1964) – before the Korean director stepped behind the camera and transformed a sexually explicit tale of a dental check-up gone horribly wrong into a meditation on the medium's ability to alter one's perception of the world through hallucinatory imagery. At once expressionistic and surrealistic, Yu's black-and-white film draws upon the visual syntax of much earlier European and American landmarks, including Robert Wiene's *The Cabinet of Dr. Caligari* (1920) and Alfred Hitchcock's *Spellbound* (1945), while paving the way for future productions that would similarly exploit salacious subject matter and titillating views of semi-naked bodies to compete against American imports at the box office. And it does so by taking a similar, if slightly different, approach than that of *Barefoot Youth* and other commercial hits, using a Japanese film as its basis but being transparent about its intertextual indebtedness in a legally responsible way that, ironically, freed Yu to pursue his own artistic ambitions without fear of (inevitable) commercial failure.

Notably, the 1964 production helmed by Takechi (who had started out as a theatre critic and rose to prominence as a producer of experimental kabuki plays before entering the motion picture industry) was infamous in its own right as Japan's first widely distributed, independently made 'pink film' (*pinku-eiga*), paving the way for subsequent softcore pornographic releases just as Yu's film would do in South Korea, albeit belatedly (once the government relaxed its policies toward screen content, if not political free speech, a few years later). And, in a similar manner to that faced by the Korean filmmaker, who was 'dragged through the courts' following the release of *An Empty Dream*, the Japanese filmmaker would soon be arrested on indecency charges before emerging victorious in a 'public battle over censorship' (unlike Yu, who ultimately lost his suit and was asked to pay a small fine for breaking his country's obscenity laws) (Yecies and Shim 2016, 51; Park 2019, 226). As such, *Daydream* is as deserving of critical evaluation as Yu's film is. However, for the purposes of underscoring the power of remakes to unmake the past allegorically (which, in South Korea, is associated with Japanese imperialism) while foregrounding the pain that had become so widespread following former army general Park's 1961 coup and his administration's concessionist stance toward the former coloniser, this chapter concerns itself primarily with a Korean-language case study whose English-language title (a subtle departure from its literal translation: 'A Spring Dream') connotes the combined feelings of hopefulness and fruitlessness associated with the nation's rebellious youth movements of the 1960s.

Although big-screen entertainment along with other popular amusements (including the then-emerging medium of television) might be thought of as mildly diverting forms of cultural 'anaesthesia', easing the hearts and minds of audiences who might otherwise have experienced anxiety amidst such political turmoil, *An Empty Dream* reveals the extent to which pain had seeped into the semantic terrain of many genre films, including those that were ostensibly concerned with the libidinal pleasures of the flesh. Such metaphors begin to make rhetorical sense in light of this film's main setting: an otherwise unassuming dentist's clinic where people writhe suggestively in perspiration-soaked pain and where actual anaesthesia is administered to patients like Jae-ho (played, not coincidentally, by the same actor who had starred in *Barefoot Youth*, Shin Seong-il). Nursing a sore tooth, Jae-ho seeks relief from the mounting discomfort that will only worsen over the course of the episodic narrative, once the medication takes effect and his daydreams become nightmares. Through an analysis of *An Empty Dream* that moves from context to text and that builds upon archival materials as well as the historically grounded scholarship of Brian Yecies and Aegyung Shim (whose book *The Changing Face of Korean Cinema* offers a rare look at Yu's film), I hope to show how this and other 'illicit' remakes of South Korea's Golden Age form a postcolonial critique by transgressing literal and figurative boundaries. Before exploring the textual transgressions of *An Empty Dream*, a brief consideration of the film's context – its production history, its connections to Yu's more highly respected films from that period, and the controversies surrounding its 3 July 1965 theatrical release (in Myeongbo Theater) – will clarify why it is representative of the challenges faced by commercial artists forced to abide by the nation's Motion Picture Law (MPL: Yeonghwabeop) enacted in January 1962, but also wholly unique as a piece of perversely subversive art that dared to depict unprecedented levels of wanton lust on the silver screen.

(PRE)PRODUCTION CONTEXTS AND PRECEDING TEXTS

Although the actual shooting of *An Empty Dream* was completed in a relatively short period of time following the Ministry of Public Information (MPI)'s approval of its production (in May of 1965), the lead-up to that stage was drawn out over a few months as a result of the ministry's concerns about the script's sexual suggestiveness and 'vulgarity' (*bisok*). Wu Gi-dong, a seasoned producer-distributor at Segi Corporation (Segisangsa, or the Century Trading Company) whose resumé includes authorised remakes such as *Wife's Confession* (*Anaeneun gobaekhanda*, 1964), cross-cultural adaptations of literary works such as *The Count of Monte Cristo* (*Amgolwang*, 1968) and controversial foreign film imports such as the American teen pic *Blackboard Jungle* (1955) and the British teenpic *Beat Girl* (1960), had been in contact with the ministry's Motion Picture Division near the end of 1964, filing an official application to adapt Takechi Tetsuji's film on 31 December of that year. As Alexander Zahlten points out in his discussion of the plagiarism debates swirling around this and other mid-1960s Korean productions, Wu likely acquired a copy of the Japanese script, which had been published in the magazine *Shinario* (*Scenario*), from an unnamed contact in Japan, a 'common practice in the Korean film industry' at that time (2012, 44–5). Indeed, with the banning of Japanese popular culture after the 1945 liberation, Korean film industry personnel were often forced to rely surreptitiously on overseas contacts and 'travelling businessmen as well as students studying in Japan' for materials that might help them not only keep pace with other motion picture industries within the region but also meet mandatory annual production quotas (in order to maintain their companies' registration status under the MPL) (Yecies and Shim 2016, 91). As an 'open secret' known by practically everyone in the industry and even lampooned in the pages of the popular movie magazine *Silver Screen*, Korean filmmakers' tendency to borrow storylines from Japanese motion pictures, which, with few exceptions, could not be legally exhibited outside of film festivals, was born out of necessity – a tactical means for them to continue operations under the strict guidelines set by the government.

Given state regulatory prohibitions against what was colloquially known as 'Japanese colour' (*waesaek*), related to a film's cast, themes and other elements, as well as Hollywood imports, Wu Gi-dong's attempts to adapt two Japanese films in the 1960s – the producer had earlier overseen the Yu Hyun-mok-directed courtroom drama *Wife's Confession*, an official remake of Masumura Yasuzō's *A Wife Confesses* (*Tsuma wa kokuhaku suru*, 1961) – is somewhat extraordinary in and of itself. The Korean Film Archive (KOFA)'s collection of MPI film censorship documents provides primary evidence that sheds light on contrasting reactions from state regulators on *Wife's Confession* and *An Empty Dream*. While the earlier film sailed through censorship review with minimal intervention (the MPI requested a reduction of just one love scene), *An Empty Dream*'s production plans were met with strong headwinds from the onset. After receiving official notice (on 21 January 1965) that his application for production (then titled *Daydream*) had been denied on the basis that the scenario was too similar to that of the Japanese film, he submitted another request a few weeks later (on 15 February) with a new title, after he had drawn director Yu Hyun-mok to the project and asked for changes to the scenario's content from scripter Kim Han-il. In a memorandum dated 22 April 1965, Park Su-hyeon, writing on behalf of the ministry's Motion Picture Division, informed the Segi Corporation president that his latest request had likewise been rejected, not only because the planned film's scenario was still too much like the story of *Daydream* (albeit under a different title), but also due to the writer's 'sensational' (*seonjeongjeok*) treatment of the subject matter – human lust – that, from the perspective of state regulators, was too salacious in its current form (Park of MPI 1965, MPI files). Specifically, the proposed production, based on the scenario that had been submitted, violated the MPL's exhibition permit enforcement regulations (*sihaenggyuchi'ik*) as codified in two subitems of a clause concerning the excitation or provocation of audiences' 'sexual urges' and the depiction of naked bodies or obscene physical contact (ranging from heterosexual intercourse to men and women bathing together).

In a remarkably lengthy response that was sent to the MPI two days later (on 24 April), the producer elaborated his and director Yu's intentions and attempted to explain why partial nudity was necessary as a means of symbolically representing the film's main theme: the confrontation between good and evil. As Wu Gi-dong stated in his letter, rather than seeking to violate public standards of moral decency, he and Yu were endeavouring to reveal, in the 'purest' yet most abstract way possible (in the form of an avowedly avant-garde film), the spiritual conflicts that arise when humans are driven by their desires (Wu 1965, MPI files). Noting that the 'zenith' of creative achievement in the sculptural arts was reached centuries earlier, in an ancient Greek culture that celebrated rather than shied away from the nude as the 'consummation of divine principles', the producer went further than most people in his line of work to rationalise a representational mode that could be seen as being merely exploitative: one that was designed to cater to base spectatorial urges rather than to the high-minded philosophical leanings of the Korean intelligentsia. In gesturing toward the more warmly receptive attitudes surrounding classic Greek sculptures and other objects of antiquity made on the other side of the world, and in emphasising the need to call out the hypocrisy of humankind while also acknowledging its inherent goodness (despite its susceptibility to corruption or vice), Wu made sweeping rhetorical moves that were in excess of what other motion picture producers at that time were doing in their own responses to the

MPI. Indeed, he appeared to want nothing less than to 'foster a creative spirit in our industry and suggest new dimensions of film art through experimental artistic intentions' (Wu 1965, MPI files) – something that his chosen director, Yu Hyun-mok (whose motto, according to the producer, was 'Art First'), had longed to do ever since helming *The Stray Bullet* (*Obaltan*, 1961), a critically praised, now-canonical work of socially relevant cinema that established the filmmaker as the preeminent auteur of his generation (Yu 1995, 150–1).

Significantly, *The Stray Bullet* was produced in the wake of the momentous 19 April 1960 student uprising – a truly revolutionary movement to oust Syngman Rhee (the autocratic president of South Korea's First Republic: 1948–1960) and bring about democratic change after a prolonged period of US-backed authoritarian rule. Like the temporary relaxation of state censorship under the parliamentary-style civilian government of Prime Minister Chang Myon, the Second Republic was short-lived. It lasted little more than a year before being brought to a precipitous end by the Park Chung-hee-led coup d'état of 16 May 1961. But it was a fertile period for talented industrial personnel such as Yu Hyun-mok, whose newfound freedom of political expression made it possible for him to bring to light the harsh social realities of post-war Korea during that brief interim. Hence, he was able to make *The Stray Bullet*, a gloomy look at the impoverished lives of a family beset by financial hardships, torn apart by personal tragedies, and desperate to escape a cramped shantytown in Seoul that has been their home ever since they fled the North at end of the Korean War. There in the ironically named 'Liberation Village' (Haebangchon), the family's woes are verbally summed up by the seemingly senile, emotionally traumatised matriarch, who repeatedly cries, 'Let's get out of here!' ('Kaja!'). They are also physically manifest in the person of her eldest son, the nominal head of the family (in the absence of his dead father), who is suffering from a severe toothache that requires medical attention. Notably, Cheol-ho (Kim Jin-kyu), an underpaid accountant whose battle-scarred war-veteran brother is arrested by the police after a foiled bank robbery; whose sister is romantically attached to a disabled ex-soldier boyfriend but prostitutes herself with American GIs; and whose pregnant, malnourished wife eventually dies during childbirth, is shown clutching his jaw throughout much of the film. Over time, his palpable dental pain registers as a symptom of some deeper problem afflicting Korean society. To paraphrase film historian Hyangjin Lee, the male protagonist's teeth are rotten because society itself is rotten (2000, 17). The fact that Cheol-ho's mouth continues to hurt even after he finally visits a dentist's clinic (paid for with the 'dirty money' earned by his sister) suggests how the general 'sickness' associated with the corrupt Syngman Rhee administration would continue to spread even after his retreat into exile, infecting contemporaneous attempts to build a better world for future generations.

Given the film's overwhelmingly pessimistic, literally biting depiction of what Lee calls 'the agonies of [a] people who have to live in such an "abnormal" society' (2000, 17), it is not surprising that *The Stray Bullet* would be removed from public exhibition two months after the 16 May coup (Chung 2021, 190), as if it were an unsightly wisdom tooth necessitating immediate extraction in order for the newly empowered Park regime to exert control over cultural productions that would be held to a more rigorous set of regulations beginning in the summer of 1961. Knowledge of such contextualising factors, including the ROK government's renewed efforts to weed out politically subversive elements (both in front of and behind the camera), makes it possible for film historians to trace a trajectory of state censorship that would place considerably larger obstacles before Yu Hyun-mok in the lead up to his 1965 production of *An Empty Dream* than what he faced five years earlier, at the beginning of the decade. But even at the textual level, in terms of *The Stray Bullet*'s meandering plot and the prolonged pain experienced by the beleaguered bank clerk Cheol-ho, one can see how this undisputed masterpiece of Korean cinema anticipates Yu's subsequent works; none more so than the main case study of this chapter, which tellingly begins where that earlier production left off. Indeed, though *An Empty Dream* is most obviously indebted to Takechi's *Daydream* insofar as it shares with that Japanese-language source material a rather unusual main setting that foregrounds its status as a cross-cultural remake (specifically, the dentist's office, which appears in its lengthy opening and closing sequences), the film is also iteratively linked to the director's previous work by virtue of extending *The Stray Bullet*'s toothache-as-metaphor social commentary into new, previously untested waters. One can only speculate if the filmmaker intuited this transformative potential when Wu Gi-dong presented him with the opportunity to direct a doubly 'illicit' version of the Japanese film. Was Yu drawn to the project because he discerned a connection between what he had achieved during the relatively unrestrained if economically constrained period of creative freedom between Rhee's First Republic and Park's military junta rule and what he was hoping to do as an established auteur around the middle of the decade (someone who, in the words of the Korean producer, had long nurtured an interest in making an 'experimental [*silheomjeok*] art film')?

It is telling that a replica of Auguste Rodin's instantly recognisable bronze sculpture *Le Penseur* ('The Thinker') – either a full-size plaster cast or a miniature version carved from clay – appears during the opening title sequence of *The Stray Bullet*. This nude male figure, sitting at an angled profile relative to the camera and framed against an expressionistic backdrop that is at odds with the film's neorealist aesthetics, harkens back to the French sculptor's original piece (created in 1904 and exhibited at Paris's Musée Rodin) rather than to the ancient works of Greek statuary that producer Wu Gi-dong referenced in his 24 April 1965 letter to the MPI. Nevertheless, a parallel between Wu's rhetorical framing of *An Empty Dream* as an experimental film project worthy of the same respect given to classical works of art and this inexplicable visual reference to a neoclassical sculpture in the earlier film is discernible. Factors such as these help to explain why he might have resorted to such unusual claims when making the case for a motion picture that could be seen as being merely 'derivative' or 'unoriginal', not unlike the poor copy of *Le Penseur* that Yu placed at the beginning of *The Stray Bullet*.

Importantly, the latter film concludes with shots that call back to that sculptural symbol of deep mental contemplation yet resist its fixity – its immovability – by showing Cheol-ho becoming as 'aimless' in his nocturnal drifting as a stray bullet. Sweating profusely and spitting up blood after a trip to the dentist's office has failed to remedy his pain, the protagonist even describes himself as such while slumped in the back of a taxi. A liminal figure lacking direction and muttering to himself that he is an 'obaltan' ('stray bullet'), Cheol-ho tells the cabbie to drive him back to 'Liberation Village' and then immediately shifts his destination to the university hospital before he changes his mind once again and asks to be dropped off at the Jungbu police station where his brother is being detained. 'Kaja!' he finally wails, echoing his demented mother's ravings and making a spectacle of his abject suffering. Shot in the dead of night, the film's bookending scenes thus bracket this depressing tale of 'a mild-mannered man defeated by the overwhelming circumstances of his present life' as a gruelling process of both 'remaking' and 'unmaking' the past (Jeong 2011, 92). Just as the opening scene's mock version of *Le Penseur* alludes to an 'original' work of art that preceded it (albeit one that, by design, was intended to spawn multiple versions or knockoffs), so too does the final scene and its night-time images of a taxicab snaking along roadways with no obvious target gesture toward a tragic past that is not unique to this refugee family: a perpetually uprooted existence that has turned them and millions of other Koreans into strangers in their own land.

The Stray Bullet's unrelentingly bleak tone, on top of the political suggestiveness of the crazed older woman's mantra 'Kaja!', made it a tough sell for local audiences and put it at the forefront of national debates involving several state agencies that regulated motion picture production and exhibition during the early years of the Park Chung-hee administration (Chung 2021, 190). As Hye Seung Chung has shown in her revisionist take on film censorship during South Korea's Golden Age, the MPI along with the Security Bureau of the Ministry of the Interior, the Ministry of Education and the KCIA brought different agendas ('including, but not limited to, national security, public morality, suppression of obscenity, protection of children, and market demands') to bear on productions that were expected to evoke a 'relatively "cheerful" attitude' (Ibid.). In other words, 'national uplift' and bright, healthy modes of living rather than dark, satirical commentary on the 'social malaise' that had spread throughout South Korea was encouraged by government bodies with a vested interest in pacifying the masses and giving moviegoers something to feel good about. This is most apparent in the many 'tacked-on optimistic endings' that would become more conspicuous as the decade wore on, but which fulfilled a much earlier mandate (found in the Ministry of Education's 1958 performance art permit guidelines) 'to show the pleasure of the free world through pure artistic catharsis and entertainment' (Chung 2022, 24). Of course, the 'pleasure' that the Ministry of Education and other national organisations had in mind was not the kind of libidinal enticement that was discernible in *An Empty Dream* even before cameras started rolling in May of 1965 (based on information contained within its scenario and screenplay) and which perturbed the representatives from the MPI with whom Wu Gi-dong maintained frequent contact throughout the first half of that year. And therein lies the primary source of resistance, above and beyond the Korean production's indebtedness to a Japanese film, among government officials who were themselves acting on behalf of a presidential administration committed to building amicable relations with the country's former coloniser (on the way to signing a normalisation treaty on 22 June 1965). In other words, the licentiousness of the proposed project, more than its plagiaristic reliance on an existing work, became the main source of consternation and deliberation in the letters between Wu and the MPI throughout the spring of 1965.

In the aforementioned letter to the ministry's Motion Picture Division (dated 24 April), the producer described in detail his and director Yu's plans for revisions to the film's treatment, indicating specific scenes that would either be deleted or drastically altered in order to scale back on potentially offensive, 'vulgar' moments (including 'sensual' shots of bare breasts, images of a woman's 'eyes burning with lust' and an erotically provocative musical number involving a seductive female dancer) (Wu 1965, MPI files). Scenes in the screenplay that depicted members of the opposite sex locked in heated confrontation, he promised, would be retooled so as 'to symbolise the conflict between good and evil' (and not to play up the scenario's kinky, sadomasochistic underpinnings). When one male character embraces a female character from the back, Wu Gi-dong noted, it would be filmed in such a way as 'to symbolise modern humanity's conflicting morals in which evil takes good as hostage', and the man's beastly behaviour (tearing her dress, binding her in rope, etc.), as well as the 'mixture of pain and ecstasy' expressed by the woman, would be sensitively transcribed to the screen without exploiting the duo's 'abnormal personalities' (Ibid.). Wrapping up his lengthy missive with a statement to the effect that he and director Yu would exercise caution during the shooting of *An Empty Dream* so as not to violate the rules for exhibition permit, Wu demonstrated a willingness to comply with the industry's regulatory standards and vowed to act as a self-censoring producer as committed to the MPI's strict moral guidelines as he was supportive of the artistic aspirations of the filmmaker. Such split allegiances hint at the predicament in which many South Korean film industry personnel found themselves during the 1960s.

Three days later (on 27 April), the producer sent the ministry a revised scenario attached to the production application, indicating the changes that he had promised. The MPI officially accepted his application on 13 May 1965, giving their approval of the production and highlighting the fact that it was, indeed, the moral vexations surrounding onscreen images that might provoke or excite audiences' 'sexual urges' (rather than the problem of borrowing too heavily from a Japanese production) that had to be dealt with before the cameras could begin rolling. Upon notification that their production application had finally been approved, principal photography began almost immediately, and the entire production would wrap up before the end of May (a speedy shoot, in part because the lead and supporting roles had already been cast and most of the sets had been designed and assembled in advance). Additional problems would present themselves after a print of the finished film as well as its trailer were sent to the KCIA, a national intelligence service (established four years earlier, on 20 May 1961) that served in an advisory role, intervening whenever political matters took precedence. As revealed in a series of interagency memos throughout June of 1965 (in advance of *An Empty Dream*'s planned theatrical debut), the filmmakers were suddenly forced to lower their expectations for a wide release only to witness their work being used as an excuse to go after the director, who was believed to have violated obscenity laws and would soon face prosecution. Before examining the KCIA's harsh reaction to the film, which was ultimately deemed 'pornographic' (*eumhwa*) and injurious to the 'wholesome sexual morals of citizens through portrayals of masochistic perversion' (Park of KCIA 1965, MPI files), I wish to turn to the cinematic text itself and highlight particular scenes that might have led government officials to suspend *An Empty Dream*'s exhibition permit almost as soon as it had been granted.

'A MIXTURE OF PAIN AND ECSTASY': INTERPRETING *AN EMPTY DREAM*

Although a dentist's clinic serves as the main setting for the film's frame narrative, *An Empty Dream* actually begins with a two-and-a-half-minute pre-credits sequence in which three young children – a small girl wearing a billowing white dress and two equally diminutive boys competing for her hand (one dressed in top hat and tuxedo, the other a beret-wearing artist decked out in bohemian black) – appear on a dark, sparsely decorated theatrical stage and act out an abbreviated, 'family-friendly' version of the narrative that will follow. Set to Johann Strauss's 'Blue Danube' waltz (a graceful musical composition recently featured in Hwang Dong-hyuk's Netflix hit *Squid Game* (*Ojingeo geim* [2021–present]), this opening sequence stands outside the story proper yet anticipates the film's main themes, albeit with a trio of prepubescent performers dancing onstage and presenting the viewer with a 'clean' version of the ensuing story: two men (boys) clash over their love of a woman (girl), who ultimately falls into the arms of the wealthy, tux-wearing impresario after the other suitor has been dealt with. In one sense, this autonomous sequence harkens back to the past, recalling not the Japanese original, *Daydream* (which begins with close-up shots of white paint squirting, or 'ejaculating', onto a canvas to the accompaniment of an offscreen woman's orgasmic moans), but rather an earlier crime film/romantic drama directed by Yu Hyun-mok. That film, *Forever with You* (*Geudaewa yeongwonhi*, 1958), begins with an image of three kids playing together in the mud alongside a brick wall that separates a city street from a prison on the other side (a space revealed by the camera in an arching crane shot). On the other hand, this opening of *An Empty Dream* points ahead, readying the audience for what is to come in the narrative, as if it were a miniaturised, theatricalised version of a very adult story concerning sexual desire. Given the kids' small stature, it literally plays out in 'miniature' the plot of the larger film while metatexually staging the act of cinematic remaking as an iterative process rooted to the phenomenon of repetition.

Any suggestion that this film might be suitable for all ages is quickly squashed by the ensuing scene, the first of the story proper, which begins with the sudden crashing of a cymbal. Against a primal drumbeat, close-up shots showing medical equipment inside a dentist's clinic are ghoulishly inserted: sharp metal tools as well as dental moulds and skulls that hint at the horrors to come. While *An Empty Dream* can be categorised as an experimental art film-cum-psychosexual fantasy (one that foregrounds male desire for a frequently fetishised female object of the scopophilic gaze), its intertextual nods to Robert Wiene's landmark work of German Expressionism *The Cabinet of Dr. Caligari* and to Roger Corman's low-budget American independent production *The Little Shop of Horrors* (1960), which likewise features a weirdly unnerving scene set in a dentist's office, make it possible to conceive of this remake as a horror film of sorts; one that lingers on bodily fluids and gaping orifices as much as it does on the heaving breasts, parted lips and orgasmic gasps of a female patient (played by Park Su-jeong) whose combined pleasure and pain at having her teeth operated on establishes a discombobulating tone early on in the narrative. Apart from a series of graphic matches, in which close-up shots of phallic dental instruments, including a Novocain needle, are intercut with images of tools inside a machine shop or at a construction site (for example, bandsaws, drills, a jackhammer and metal cutters), the first scene of the film following its Strauss-scored pre-credits sequence contains copious views of the woman either leaning forward or lying back in her chair, spitting milky saliva into the sink and exposing her cleavage while being manhandled by the groping dentist (played by Park Am).

Privy to all of this is the film's male protagonist, Jae-ho (Shin Seong-il), who, like her (and like Cheol-ho from the aforementioned *The Stray Bullet*), is receiving treatment for a toothache in the clinic. Even before it is his turn to see the dentist, while waiting in the lobby Jae-ho is shown thumbing through a book of photos of couples embracing, his eyes settling on one particularly salacious image of a woman's bare bottom. This establishes him as a media consumer, a spectator drawn to lurid material whose attraction to the smartly dressed woman (who enters the waiting room at the very moment when he flips to the page with the bare bottom) is instantaneous and appears to be driven by physical lust. The protagonist's interest in her only increases once his name is called and he begins to receive his dental treatment. Seated to the side, Jae-ho watches silently as the woman passes out from pain and is carried to a bed in the same room, where the dentist and his female assistant, after putting smelling salts up to her nose, proceed to open her blouse, unzip her skirt, roll down her stockings, and rub her sweaty chest before giving her stomach a deep massage. When viewed today, the dentist's behaviour, coupled with the male protagonist's compulsion to silently spy upon the other man's actions while remaining (un)comfortably seated in his chair, are problematic to say the least: a form of sexual and spectatorial predation/violation that plays upon the audience's presumed desire to witness something taboo in a motion picture that, at the time of its production, was unprecedented in the annals of South Korean film history. Indeed, for all of producer Wu Gi-dong's stated commitment to reducing the amount of obscenity in the screenplay before cameras had started rolling, what director Yu Hyun-mok actually shot – especially much of the footage featuring Park Su-jeong (a new actress who was cast opposite the industry's biggest star, Shin Seong-il, winning the role over hundreds of other women) – 'verged on the pornographic' and is nearly as suggestive as any of the scenes in the Japanese 'pink film' *Daydream* (Zahlten 2012, 48; Kim 2019, 182).

The two films' lengthy opening scenes (running sixteen minutes in the Japanese original and fourteen minutes in the Korean remake) are remarkably similar. Nevertheless, stylistic discrepancies hint at slightly different thematic preoccupations on the part of directors who use that clinical setting as a comfortably familiar yet repulsively creepy entryway into a nightmarish dream world. The frightening dental tools that appear in *An Empty Dream* are shot in much the same way that Takechi and his cinematographer, Takeda Akira, visually frame them, though their film features a more freewheeling use of handheld camera, which tilts, spirals and flips upside down to evoke a heightened sense of unbridled sexual energy. *Daydream* also includes more point-of-view shots, from both the dentist's and the patients' perspectives, which put the spectator into physically or morally compromised positions. In contrast,

62   DAVID SCOTT DIFFRIENT

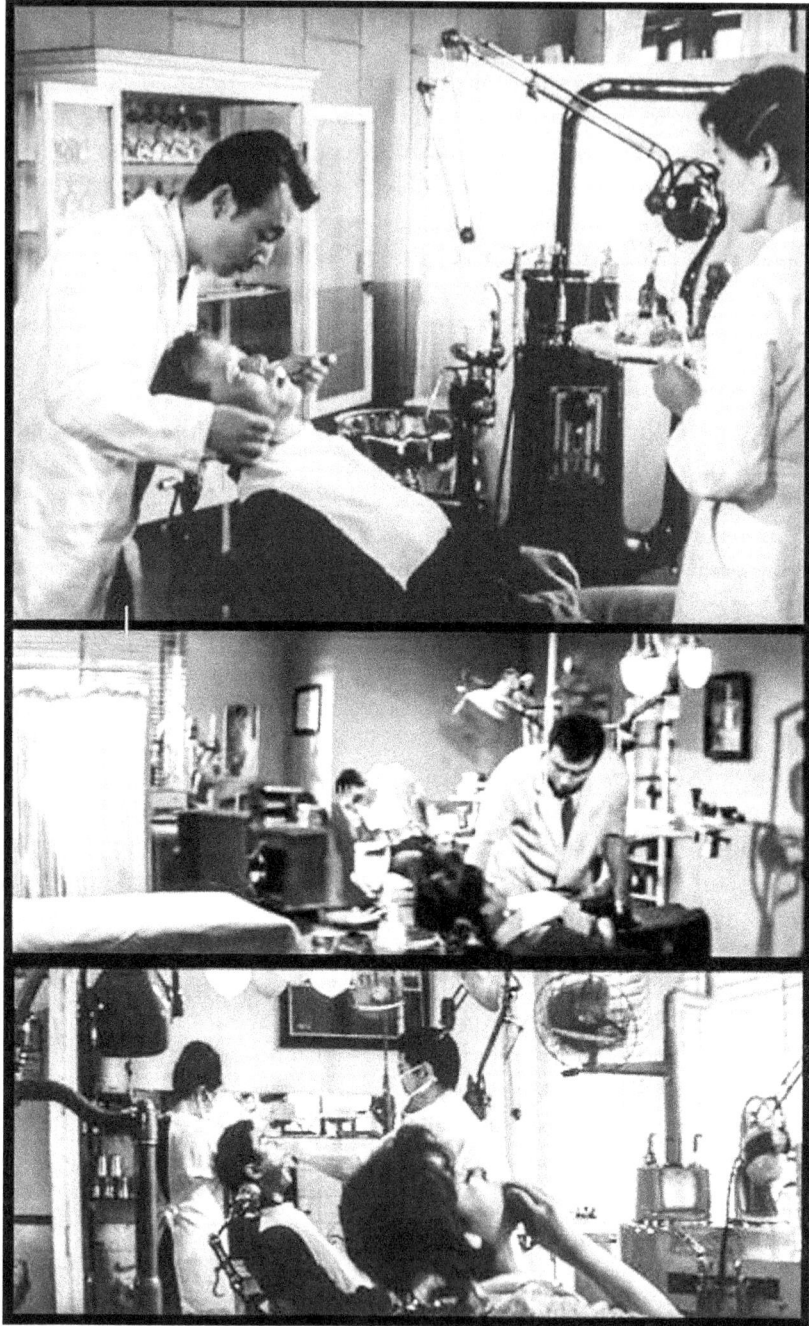

Figure 2.1 Painful dentist-office scenes in Yu Hyun-mok's *The Stray Bullet* (*Obaltan*, 1961) [top], the same director's *An Empty Dream* (*Chunmong*, 1965) [middle] and the latter film's Japanese-language source material *Daydream* (*Hakujitsumu*, 1964) [bottom], directed by Takechi Tetsuji.

Yu Hyun-mok's film distinguishes itself through its incorporation of odd cutaways – the aforementioned graphic matches as well as seemingly random insert shots of a cat, a rabbit, flowers and an airplane's whirling propellers – that reveal it to be as indebted to the 1920s Soviet school of dialectical montage as it is to that decade's German Expressionism. Extreme close-ups of the dentist's eyes and his patients' open mouths appear almost as frequently in the Korean film as they do in the Japanese one, but the expressions on those characters' faces suggest subtly different emotions, with the latter film featuring more sadistically menacing or terrified looks than the former (an effect intensified by Takechi's use of experimental music, a high-pitched metallic drone coupled with the eerie plucking of shamisen that differs considerably from the jazzy, percussive sounds that accompany the first scene of Yu's film).

The most glaring point of divergence between the two motion pictures concerns their fetishistic framing of the seemingly unconscious woman's body: whereas Park Su-jeong's character Mun-ja is groped in bits and pieces to the point that she appears to take pleasure in her predicament (with close-ups of her heaving, bra-covered chest followed by shots of her legs crossing and her lips curling into a smile, all while keeping her eyes closed), the female patient played by Michi Kanako (who would go on to appear in several other sexploitation films directed by *pinku-eiga* specialist Wakamatsu Kōji) is kissed and then bitten above her breasts, which are fully exposed once the dentist lowers her undergarment. Obviously, no such shots could appear in the South Korean film, owing to restrictions placed on cinematic depictions of nudity at that time. Nevertheless, Yu pushes the limits of permissiveness by placing so much emphasis on innuendo-filled images of Mun-ja pleasurably partaking in her own debasement at the hands of a man whose professional responsibility is to alleviate, rather than aggravate, his patients' pain.

In both films, the dentist's office scene sets up the rest of the narrative, which is an extended dream sequence that slowly fades up following a close-up shot of the heavily anesthetised male protagonist's eyes, glazed over from the nitrous oxide. It begins with a highly stylised musical number, which – in the Korean version – echoes the pre-credits scene involving the three kids. However, now there is only one adult performer, Mun-ja. Dressed in an elegant evening gown, she steps onto the stage of a shadowy, sparsely populated nightclub, empty save for a group of silent, stone-faced waiters standing motionless around the room. A few seconds into her cabaret song (Toni Arden's 1958 version of 'Padre'), which Mun-ja lip-syncs in English, Jae-ho enters the Art Deco-themed nightclub. Carrying an oversized abstract painting rendered in a Cubist style, he injects yet another art-historical aesthetic tradition into the proceedings. The protagonist is soon joined by the Svengali-like dentist, who – as the manager of the nightclub – has traded in his medical scrubs for a black tailcoat, top hat, cane and beard (a look that is visually reminiscent not only of Werner Krauss's mysterious Doctor Caligari but also of José Mojica Marins's undertaker character 'Coffin Joe' in the Brazilian horror film *At Midnight I'll Take Your Soul* [*À Meia-Noite Levarei Sua Alma*, 1964]).

With this piling up of intertextual allusions (on top of its references to the Japanese original, which notably does not foreground such features), *An Empty Dream* is ironically very 'full', stuffed with so many cross-cultural signifiers – so many conspicuous signposts directing our attention outside the text – that it might seem to contain little in the way of authentically 'Korean' elements. However, as I have argued elsewhere, South Korean films are partially distinguished by their profusion of ostensibly 'non-Korean' signifiers, a seemingly disproportionate level of cultural appropriation that is in keeping with the nation's modern history of syncretic fusion (resulting from Japanese colonisation, US neocolonialism and the embeddedness of East Asian and Euro-American texts in the popular imaginary). More recently stereotyped as a 'Copywood' problem (in journalistic accounts of the mainstream motion picture industry, which at times appears to emulate Hollywood productions), the tendency among Korean filmmakers to borrow from other works made outside the country was even more pronounced in the 1960s (Diffrient 2009, 105–6). Pilfering material from European and Japanese films as well as American cultural products, *An Empty Dream* is, on the one hand, representative of the combinational and citational density of motion pictures made during that time. On the other hand, this 1965 film stands as an exceptional work of exploitation art whose capacity to blend the traditional markers of 'high' and 'low' – mixing elevated philosophical musings about the nature of good and evil with base bodily urges and libidinal desires – is matched only by its deftness in chaining together multiple intertextual references across a stream-of-consciousness narrative that, at first glance, appears to be 'structureless'.

Film critic Jasper Sharp uses that latter word in his description of the Japanese original, suggesting that its 'succession of sexy set-pieces revolving around a series of fantasies in a dentist's waiting room' lacks the organisational logic of more traditionally plotted motion pictures (2001). However, it would be inaccurate to say that it and the Korean remake do not have a structure. Their narratives, while episodic, are organised around the central dilemma faced by the male protagonist, whose attraction to and pursuit of a woman he has just met are consistently thwarted by a man of higher social standing. Along the way, the main character is confronted by literal obstacles in the form of physical barriers, including a windowpane and (in the Korean version) a barbwire fence, which prevent him from claiming the largely silent woman as his own. As an 'obscure object of desire', she seems desperate for his help but remains elusive throughout the first half of the film, evading his grasp right when he nears her. In Yu's film (the more narratively adventurous of the two), she frequently disappears and reappears as if part of a magic act, becoming a moving target until he finally catches up with her in yet another theatrical setting, this time one that is dressed to look like a barren desert. When he finds Mun-ju – a parched victim of heatstroke – passed out on the sand, he digs into the ground in search of water or some other miracle that might save her, only to come up 'empty' (in keeping with the English-language title of the film). With all other options exhausted, Jae-ho resorts to prayer, closing his eyes, putting his palms together and sending a silent message up to the heavens. His prayers are answered, as an oasis suddenly appears in the distance. He drags her sarong-wrapped body to a group of fake palm trees, where he proceeds to pour coconut milk into her mouth. Recalling the earlier scene set in the dentist's office, the white liquid, shown dripping down her chin in extreme close-up, is meant 'to suggest fellatio' (Kim 2020, 90). While this scene, occurring around the 45-minute mark and scored to lounge-like jazz music, might suggest that Jae-ho has finally overcome his impotence and attained his goal, the couple's sweaty embrace in the sand is cut short once the bearded man reappears and – pointing his pistol at the sun – shoots the lights out. Here, as before, the structural logic of *An Empty Dream* is apparent, with the hero's carnal desire once again being thwarted by a rival for the woman's affections, who is now in possession of that most phallic of instruments: a gun.

Tellingly, this seven-minute-long desert scene does not occur in the Japanese film, which instead shows the male protagonist, Kurahashi (Ishihama Akira), grabbing Cheiko (Michi Kanako) by her pearl necklace – a kind of dehumanising dog leash – as they move through an abandoned rooftop children's playground. That desert scene's inclusion in *An Empty Dream* is doubly significant, insofar as it attests to the Korean director's eagerness to creatively depart from his source material even as it draws attention to other motion pictures featuring similar iconography and musical scores, including a cycle of nihilistic youth films produced in Japan in the years leading up to its 1965 theatrical release. Specifically, the shots of the Korean couple writhing in the sand, their bodies entangled and wet with perspiration, recall not only Teshigahara Hiroshi's New Wave classic *Woman in the Dunes* (*Suna no Onna*, 1964) but also the teenaged lovemaking and heavy petting on view in the so-called 'Sun Tribe' (*Taiyouzoku*) films inspired by Furukawa Takumi's *Season of the Sun* (*Taiyō no kisetsu*, 1956) and Nakahira Kō's *Crazed Fruit* (*Kurutta kajitsu*, 1956) (Desser 1988, 40–1; Kelso-Marsh 2020, 52). Examples of that cycle, noted for their on-location shooting, modern jazz soundtracks, and tendency to objectify young women (who are frequently turned into sexual playthings by disillusioned, hypermasculine young men), include Ōshima Nagisa's *The Sun's Burial* (*Taiyō no Hakaba*, 1960) and Nakahira Kō's *That Guy and I* (*Aitsu to watashi*, 1961). As film historian Chung Chonghwa notes, the latter motion picture is one of two adaptations of Ishizaka Yōjirō's best-selling novels produced at the Nikkatsu Film Company (the other being Tasaka Tomotaka's *A Slope in the Sun* [*Hi no ataru sakamichi*, 1958]) that were remade by Korean filmmakers during the early 1960s (both starring the soon-to-be-wed acting duo Shin Seong-il and Um Aing-ran): Kim Ki-duk's *Private Tutor* (*Gajeong gyosa*, 1963) and Kim Su-yong's *Classroom of Youth* (*Cheongchun gyosil*, 1963). According to Chung, *Classroom of Youth*, though rooted to the conventions of the family drama, marked the advent of rebellious youth movies in South Korea, and was even advertised to the public as the country's first 'sex film' (*seong yeonghwa*), one that would drive audiences 'wild with excitement' (or so claimed the film's promotional ad copy) (2017, 78).[1] The shot of Park Am's tuxedoed villain pointing his gun at the sun in *An Empty Dream* could be seen as taking aim at Japanese 'Sun Tribe' films as well as their Korean knockoffs. Significantly, by shooting out the light, he plunges the main character, his only nemesis, into darkness once again, repeating a motivic element of the film that belies its status as a 'structureless' narrative.

Eventually, like those in *Daydream*, the trio of characters at the heart of *An Empty Dream* find themselves inside an ornate department store at night, where the woman eventually tries to flee the more aggressive of the two men by running down an escalator moving in the opposite direction and shedding articles of her clothing in the process. Alone save for the living mannequins that model black underwear and stand motionless around the hyperstylised set, the three characters reprise the same conflict that has been a central component of the film's narrative since its pre-credits dance number involving children. From its opening minutes until its penultimate scene, this story of a man confronted by his own metaphorical 'lack' and a woman torn between two rivals for her affections has foregrounded an aesthetics of theatrical presentation or display, and the film's episodic structure (borrowed from the Japanese original) endows those themes with a serialised mode of salacious engagement, as if the audience were seated before a burlesque show or vaudeville performance. In fact, the department store mannequins, as much as the female contortionist who performed a risqué acrobatic dance on the nightclub stage following Mun-ja's 'Padre' number, bring this aspect of *An Empty Dream* to the fore and link motion picture spectatorship with the embodied sensation of standing in front of a shop window display and watching an oddly static striptease.

Tellingly, an earlier scene of the film – certainly its kinkiest, though not as rough as the corresponding moment of S&M in the Japanese original – hinges upon Jae-ho's inability to breach the physical barrier between himself and the woman, whom he views from outside the villain's luxury apartment. Standing before a window looking in, he witnesses her being bound by rope and eventually hooked up to an electrical current apparatus as part of a cruel game of torture. And yet each rotation of the voltage dial seems to increase her pleasure. During a break between the bondage and the electrical nerve stimulation, the other man steps away momentarily, leaving Mun-ja to approach the window. After explaining to Jae-ho that she is enduring this 'humiliation' for his sake (so that his life might be spared from her torturer's deadly jealousy), she plants a kiss upon the glass. He reciprocates and mimics kissing her. For a brief moment they appear to be as one even as they remain separated by the window, and their temporary union brings together the inside and outside spaces of this strangely built environment. As suggested above, this is one of many instances when the strangers-turned-lovers share a fleeting physical and emotional connection with each other only to be torn apart and forced to contend with yet another impediment to their peaceful coexistence and the happy ending that potentially awaits them as a couple.

Nevertheless, that traditional form of narrative closure eventually comes during the film's final scene, one that returns us to the dentist's office (where Jae-ho awakes from his drug-induced sleep) and shows Mun-ja leaving behind her handkerchief (which he dutifully delivers to her outside the clinic). Seated in her car, she offers him a ride, at which point the couple drives off not into the sunset but down a busy city street. Significantly, this shot of the metropolis fades to black and is soon replaced by images of flowering trees in some unspecified nature area, a decidedly romantic conclusion to an otherwise provocative account of libidinal desire.

Figure 2.2 As if standing before a mirror, the main characters in both *Daydream* (*Hakujitsumu*, 1964) and *An Empty Dream* (*Chunmong*, 1965) mimic each other's amorous actions, inside and outside a glass window that separates them.

A HAPPY ENDING?

No such happy ending seemed to await Yu Hyun-mok following his film's limited theatrical release during the first two weeks of July 1965, when newspaper ads attempted to whet the public's appetite for *An Empty Dream*'s salacious content (Yecies and Shim 2016, 51). In fact, the film was almost prevented from being exhibited in local theatres once members of the KCIA received a print for review one month earlier. An official letter from the KCIA to the Motion Picture Division of the MPI, dated 5 June 1965, indicated that the national intelligence service took umbrage at the 'masochistic perversion' of the film, which could 'inflict injuries on the wholesome morality of citizens' (Park of KCIA 1965, MPI files). So 'injurious' was the motion picture that it was accused of violating the nation's obscenity law, and the KCIA urged the MPI to move the case to the Ministry of Justice for prosecution. In response, the MPI – an organisation that was generally concerned with the economic wellbeing of the film industry and sought to protect its creative personnel from unwarranted attacks – urged for censorship of the print rather than prosecution, and thereafter communicated with Segi Corporation about the need to bring *An Empty Dream* into alignment with motion picture enforcement regulations (by making cuts to any scenes showing women's exposed breasts) (Lee 1965, MPI files). An exhibition permit, conditional upon the producer's willingness to make the necessary changes, was finally given at the end of June, one that would have allowed *An Empty Dream* to be theatrically shown within a two-year window. That permit was eventually suspended, however, and the film, which did not earn much at the box office, was likely not shown in theatres after its initial two-week run.[2]

One reason that Yu Hyun-mok faced such resistance to his film from government officials, including those who were typically more concerned with political matters and foreign relations than with the potentially harmful effects of sexually explicit screen content, is that three months prior to its theatrical release he had delivered a public speech on the topic of freedom of expression at the International Conference for Cultural Freedom (Segye Munhwa Jayu Hoeui). As Brian Yecies and Aegyung Shim elaborate, his seminar presentation in March of 1965 drew attention to the plight of fellow filmmaker Lee Man-hee (2016, 54). One month earlier, Lee had released his latest production, *Seven Female POWs* (*Chilinui yeoporo*, 1965), only to see its exhibition permit be suspended by the KCIA, which called for his arrest for violating the National Security Act (which, among other things, made communism illegal in South Korea). Although he 'was eventually cleared of violating [his country's] anticommunist laws', Lee was effectively 'graylisted' and scapegoated by the government, and a similar fate awaited Yu once he boldly gave his speech in support of his controversy-courting colleague (Ibid., 41). In other words, the

KCIA's concern over *An Empty Dream*, while perhaps justified (given its brazen foregrounding of sexual desire), was likely a form of retaliation against the filmmaker (Zahlten 2012, 49). Its brief theatrical release thus gave lead prosecutor Choi Dae-hyeon, who (according to Yecies and Shim) 'was infamous for his hardline anticommunist stance', a convenient pretext to interrogate and eventually indict Yu (2016, 54).

Nearly two years later, in March of 1967 (after seeing his case finally go to trial, at the Seoul Criminal District Court), Yu Hyun-mok and his film were once again thrust into the spotlight when the judge's ruling was reported in newspapers. An article in *Dong-a Ilbo* dated 15 March indicated that the filmmaker had been found 'not guilty' of the first charge (violation of anticommunist law) and 'guilty' of the second charge (obscenity). Although the prosecution had sought a prison term of one-and-a-half years and a license suspension for the same period of time, Judge Kim Cheong-hyeon ultimately did away with the sentencing and reduced the penalty to a 30,000 won fine. This largely symbolic fine amounted to a slap on the wrist, and as the prosecution initiated appeals the judge took to noting how deeply Western culture had seeped into Korean cinema, bringing with it 'significant changes' with regards to the 'sexual ethics' of onscreen representations ('Ruling on Movie' 1967, 3). During an interview that appeared in the pages of *Hanguk Ilbo* four days later, the director expressed sadness at seeing his film being labelled as 'obscene', and found it especially absurd that so much controversy surrounded its depiction of female nudity since actress Park Su-jeong had been covered in a flesh-coloured nylon body stocking throughout the shooting of a scene singled out by the judge (the one inside the department store where she flees her attacker – a 'sex pervert', according to the court official – on an escalator) ('Sunday Interview' 1967, 7; 'Talk of the Film Industry' 1967, 5). Moreover, the offending shot, which was only three seconds long, had been cut out of prints and therefore posed no 'risk' to the delicate sensibilities of audiences (based on the legal opinions offered up by three lawyers interviewed by *Chosun Ilbo* on 31 March) ('*An Empty Dream* Controversy' 1967, 5). Asking his interviewer the rhetorical question of why nude models are not just tolerated but 'deified' within the world of art yet are the basis for criminal prosecution within the world of cinema, Yu then reiterated a claim that his producer, Wu Gi-dong, had made on his behalf two years earlier: that *An Empty Dream* is 'not an entertainment film' but an 'experimental film' that attempts to demonstrate the artistic value of the medium. Taking a page from his own film (which ironically features the kind of 'happy ending' that was mandated by the government's ministries), he concluded the interview on an optimistic note, saying that the 'not guilty' verdict on the anticommunism charge had renewed his hope for democracy in his country ('Sunday Interview' 1967, 7).

Ultimately, Yu Hyun-mok, who passed away in 2009 (at the age of eighty-three), would live long enough to see *An Empty Dream* be redeemed, thereby earning the 'happy ending' that it had been denied for so many years. In 2004, at the 8th Bucheon International Fantastic Film Festival, a partially restored print of his film (featuring fourteen minutes of previously lost sound) was featured in a Korean cinema retrospective (Zahlten 2012, 45). Two years later, researchers at the Korean Film Archive in Seoul ranked *An Empty Dream* as the 37th most significant domestic motion picture 'produced and released between 1936 and 1996' (Yecies and Shim 2016, 55). As Brian Yecies and Aegyung Shim note, 'After a wait lasting four decades', Yu was finally 'given credit for his innovative exploration of themes and aesthetics that had proved so provocative in the mid-1960s' (Ibid.). Occurring nearly a decade after Japanese motion pictures could be legally distributed and commercially exhibited in South Korea (with the dropping of a fifty-year import barrier in 1998), this conclusion to the contextual story surrounding his once-shunned, now-revered cinematic text was perhaps more bittersweet than happy; for it came in such a belated way and failed to fully alleviate the pain that he had earlier felt when *An Empty Dream* was labelled by government officials and cultural commentators as both 'pornography' and a 'plagiarized' version of Takechi Tetsuji's *Daydream*. Having endured an exhausting trial that 'lasted for more than 18 months' in the mid-1960s, and having seen his glory days as the preeminent auteur of his generation fade during the 1970s and 1980s (when, amidst industrial downsizing, a younger generation of equally brash filmmakers, such as Bae Chang-ho, Lee Jang-ho and Jang Sun-woo, rose to prominence), he was understandably circumspect about the effects that archival restoration and critical reevaluation would have – on him or his larger body of work – near the end of his life in the mid-2000s. Still, the late-career reframing of a controversial, commercially unsuccessful remake as something deserving of respect – a goal that the director and the film's producer, Wu Gi-dong, had tirelessly pursued in their attempts to raise cinema's reputation to the level of other art forms – attests to the need to expand historical frameworks when exploring adaptive works whose meanings are necessarily contextual and in constant flux.

NOTES

1. When compared to *An Empty Dream*, Kim's *Classroom of Youth* seems almost puritanical, though it does build toward a passionate kiss between Shin and Um during a night-time thunderstorm that results in their characters seeking shelter from the rain inside a bedroom (where they bring their lovemaking to a head atop the bed before the scene fades out).
2. According to Yu, who described himself as 'by nature . . . a director who is far from eroticism', *An Empty Dream* failed commercially 'because it was not an easy film for mass audiences to understand' (1995, 150–1). Suspension did not occur strictly because this

Korean-language remake too closely mimicked the content of its Japanese source material. Nevertheless, around that same time (on 29 June 1965), *Daehan Ilbo* published an article that 'warned openly about the legalization of film from Japan and the possible "flood of sex films"', something that Alexander Zahlten notes in his exploration of the 'plagiarism' debates swirling around this and other productions of 1965. According to Zahlten, that year began with the Korean Filmworker's Guild promising that it was 'voluntarily cancelling production plans for 44 "remakes" of Japanese films (out of an eventual annual production of around 200 films)' (2012, 50, 52).

REFERENCES

Anon. 1967. 'The Talk of the Film Industry [Yeounghwage hwaje],' *Sina Ilbo*, 7 February, 5.
Anon. 1967. 'Ruling on the Movie *An Empty Dream*'s Obscenity Charge [Yeonghwa *Chunmong* eumhwa pangyeol].' *Dong-a Ilbo*, 15 March, 3.
Anon. 1967. 'Sunday Interview [Ilyo inteobyu].' *Hanguk Ilbo*, 19 March, 7.
Anon. 1967. 'Movie *An Empty Dream* Controversy about Application of Law [Yeonghwa *Chunmong* byeopjeokyongsibi].' *Chosun Ilbo*, 21 March, 5.
Chung, Chonghwa. 2016. 'The Topography of 1960s Korean Youth Film: Between Plagiarism and Adaptation.' *Journal of Japanese and Korean Cinema* 8, no. 1: 11–24.
Chung, Chonghwa. 2017. 'Mode of Cinematic Plagiarism and Adaptation: How Ishizaka Yojiro's Novels Launched Korean Youth Film.' *Korea Journal* 57, no. 3: 56–82.
Chung, Hye Seung. 2021. 'Archive Revisionisms: Reevaluating South Korea's State Film Censorship of the Cold War Era.' In *The Cold War and Asian Cinemas*. Edited by Poshek Fu and Man-Fung Yip, 174–93. New York: Routledge.
Chung, Hye Seung. 2022. 'Fending off Darkness, Uplifting National Cinema: Korean Film Censorship and The Stray Bullet.' Unpublished conference paper, Korean Film Workshop, University of California, Berkeley, 4–5 August.
Desser, David. 1988. *Eros Plus Massacre: An Introduction to the Japanese New Wave Cinema*. Bloomington: Indiana University Press.
Diffrient, David Scott. 2009. '*Over That Hill*: Cinematic Adaptations and Cross-Cultural Remakes, from Depression-Era America to Post-war Korea.' *Journal of Japanese and Korean Cinema* 1, no. 2,: 105–27.
Jeong, Kelly Y. 2011. *Crisis of Gender and the Nation in Korean Literature and Cinema: Modernity Arrives Again*. Lanham: Lexington Books.
Kelso-Marsh, Caleb. 2020. 'East Asian Noir: Transnational Film Noir in Japan, Korea, and Hong Kong.' In *Renegotiating Film Genres in East Asian Cinemas and Beyond*. Edited by Lin Feng and James Aston, 41–68. Cham: Palgrave Macmillan.
Kim, Chung-kang. 2019. 'Mist (1967): "Art Cinema" under Dictatorship.' In *Rediscovering Korean Cinema*. Edited by Sangjoon Lee, 173–86. Ann Arbor: University of Michigan Press.
Kim, Chung-kang. 2020. 'A Female-Dressed Man Sings a National Epic: The Film *Male Kisaeng* and the Politics of Gender and Sexuality in 1960s South Korea.' In *Queer Korea*. Edited by Todd Henry, 175–204. Durham: Duke University Press.
Lee, Chong-Sik. 1985. *Japan and Korea: The Political Dimension*. Stanford: Stanford University Press.
Lee, Dal-hyeong. 1965. 'Exhibition Permit for Korean Film *An Empty Dream* Guksanyeonghwa *Chunmong* sangyeongheoga].' 30 June, Ministry of Public Information (MPI) Film Censorship Files, Korean Film Archive (KOFA).

Lee, Hyangjin. 2000. *Contemporary Korean Cinema: Culture, Identity and Politics*. Manchester: Manchester University Press.

Lee, Sang Dawn. 2002. *Big Brother, Little Brother: The American Influence on Korean Culture in the Lyndon B. Johnson Years*. Lanham: Lexington Books.

Lee, Sangjoon. 2014. 'The Emergence of the Asian Film Festival: Cold War Asia and Japan's Reentrance to the Regional Film Industry in the 1950s.' In *The Oxford Handbook of Japanese Cinema*. Edited by Daisuke Miyao. Oxford: Oxford University Press.

Min, Eung-jun, Jinsook Joo and Han Ju Kwak. 2003. *Korean Film: History, Resistance, and Democratic Imagination*. Westport: Praeger.

Park, No-min of KCIA. 1965. 'Notice of Film Recensorship Opinion [Yeonghwajaesim euigyeontongbo].' 5 June, MPI files, KOFA.

Park, Su-hweon of MPI. 1965. 'Notice of Feature Film *Empty Dream* Production Application Acceptance [Geukyeonghwa *Chunmong* jejaksingosuritongbo].' 22 April, *An Empty Dream*, MPI files, KOFA.

Sharp, Jasper. 2001. '*Daydream*.', *Midnight Eye*, 20 March. http://www.midnighteye.com/reviews/daydream/. Accessed 9 May 2022.

Wu, Gi-dong. 1965. 'Suggestions for Feature Film Empty Dream Production [Geukyeonghwa *Chunmong* jejakaegwanhangeunuiseo].' 24 April, *An Empty Dream*, MPI files, KOFA.

Yecies, Brian and Aegyung Shim. 2016. *The Changing Face of Korean Cinema: 1960 to 2015*. New York: Routledge.

Yu, Hyun-mok. 1995. *Film Life* [*Yŏnghwa insaeng*]. Seoul: Hyehwadang.

Zahlten, Alexander. 2012. '*Daydreams*.' In *Place and Space in Japanese Cinema*. Edited by M. Downing Roberts, 43–55. Tokyo: University of Tokyo Center for Philosophy.

CHAPTER 3

Two Faces of Seduction: Martial Heroines and Karmic Women in Chor Yuen's *Intimate Confessions of a Chinese Courtesan* and *Lust for Love of a Chinese Courtesan*

Andrew Grossman

INTRODUCTION: THE PARADOX OF THE MARTIAL CONCUBINE

In Hollywood action cinema, as in Western culture at large, heroism and masculinity are more or less interchangeable. Even today, the rare female-centred Hollywood action film is prefaced by apologetic advance publicity, as if to prepare audiences for 'empowered' images of heroic women. Chinese literature and film, of course, have long valorised martial women, presenting them as equals to their male counterparts. Countless short stories, novels, stage dramas and operas have presented swordswomen as forces that potentially complicate or destabilise Confucian standards of patriarchal power. In his study of China's literary swordswomen, Roland Altenburger identifies the Tang heroine Nie Yinniang as an archetypal heroine who 'radically subverts the conventional [Confucian] system of gender roles' (2009, 75). According to Altenburger, Ming writer Hu Rujia's tale *Lady Wei Eleven* represented a further advance in this tradition, as the titular heroine expressly defines herself as a 'sword knight (jianxia)' who roams beyond the domestic sphere (2009, 138). Lu Hsun's *A Brief History of Chinese Fiction* cites the Qing novel *The Gallant Maid* – filmed by Li Han-hsiang as *The Adventure of the 13th Sister* (*Ernü yingxiong chuan*, 1959) – as a new turning point in the modern, secular portrayal of the swordswoman. Here, the martial woman is an 'artificial' ideal, combining 'heroism and the traditional feminine virtues' without any of the mythological trappings of the *Journey to the West* tradition (Lu Hsun 1959, 339).

While centuries of swordswomen have challenged Confucian gender roles, it is important to recall that the wuxia genre itself violates much of Confucian morality. Granted, martial arts films dealing with Wong Fei-hung or Shaolin monks generally espouse conservative, male-dominated Confucian norms. Wuxia heroes are usually wanderers exiled from family units and governmental institutions, for they embody the societal detachment of Daoism more than the obligatory relations of Confucianism. As James J. Y. Liu observes in *The Chinese Knight-Errant*, the wuxia hero pledges loyalty and devotion to strangers as well as friends – a notion that radically violates Confucian social norms (Liu 1967, 7). In his egalitarianism, the nomadic wuxia hero personifies Mozi's ideas of 'love without discrimination' and corrective 'knight-errantry', values that seek to redress Confucian systems that only pretend to order and harmony (Shek 1995, 135). As wuxia heroes 'take justice into their own hands' and do 'more than required by common standards of morality', they break away from Confucian moderation and 'right' relations (Liu 1967, 4). The itinerant hero's detachment perhaps explains the unceremoniously abrupt endings of so many Shaw Brothers wuxia films, which usually picture victorious heroes walking into artificial, set-bound sunsets: the narrative of the un-Confucian wanderer knows no closure or homecoming.

As it deviated from strict Confucian expectations, the wuxia narrative simultaneously opened the door to active female participation – but with implicit conditions attached. Generally speaking, the swordswomen of traditional wuxia cinema, exemplified by Shaw Brothers productions of the mid- and late-1960s, positioned the heroine's martial prowess against her sexual agency. Swordswomen could move powerfully through the martial arts world as long as they suppressed their sexualities, whether through strategies of self-denial or through opportunistic cross-dressing charades. The examples are too numerous to recount, but consider Chang Pei-pei in Lo Wei's *The Golden Sword* (*Long men jin jian*, 1969): she first appears cross-dressed as a martial youth who ruthlessly dispatches villains at an inn. When she subsequently lets down her guard (and garb) to reveal a beautiful femininity, she never again engages in such a supreme martial display. When she later marries a swordsman, she refuses even conjugal sex on their wedding night, as if her martial powers would be depleted by sexual exertion (an old trope in Daoist mysticism). At other times, the daring yet suppressed swordswoman is contrasted with the sexually loose but disempowered commoner. In the prologue of Chang Cheh's *The Flying Dagger* (*Fei dao shou*, 1969), for instance, a young peasant woman is sexually assaulted by a rogue and then rescued by a chaste swordswoman, again played by Chang Pei-pei. Though she remains feminised in her subsequent encounters with an invincible hero, played by Lo Lieh, she spurns his amorous advances and balks at the prospect of crossing anything more than swords. In the end, she remains unspoiled, while sexual activity is relegated to the passive body of the prologue's rape victim.

Feminine passivity reaches a zenith in the figure of the concubine, whose politically circumscribed sexuality became the root of a tragic aesthetic, if we see the story of Yang Guifei as exemplary.[1] Admittedly, there also exists the archetype of the scheming, upwardly mobile concubine, such as Golden Lotus in the Ming novel *Jin Ping Mei* or the competitive consorts of Zhang Yimou's *Raise the Red Lantern* (*Da hong deng long gao gao gua*, 1992) and Hou Hsiao-Hsien's *Flowers of Shanghai* (*Hai shang hua*, 1998). The ladders of social mobility for such women, however, offer only so many rungs. No matter their scheming, these female characters remain trapped within a closed patriarchal system. The binaristic formula that separated martial, politically active women from domestic concubines went largely unchallenged until Chor Yuen (Chu Yuan)'s *Intimate Confessions of a Chinese Courtesan* (*Ai Nu*, 1972) was theatrically released. Generally considered the first Chinese film with overt lesbian themes, the film flagrantly (homo)eroticises the chaste wuxia swordswoman while also martialising the passive concubine. Notably, it is difficult to recall a Shaw Brothers wuxia production of the era that allowed male heroes to cross their own typological boundaries, for Chinese literary traditions had likewise divided male protagonists into abstemious swordsmen and licentious scholars. Perhaps director Chor Yuen, through a male-gazing lens, saw the female body as an object that could combine the erotic id and the martial superego in an experimental yet socially acceptable manner. Obviously, envisioning a same-sex male wuxia couple would have been commercially untenable in 1972.

As a tale of two courtesans-cum-swordswomen who violently oppose patriarchal orders, *Intimate Confessions* reimagines martial women as licentious and often amoral, a startling break from wuxia norms. The film's story concerns Ai Nu (Lily Ho), a girl kidnapped into servitude by Lady Chun (Betty Pei Ti), a cruel brothel-keeper and brilliant swordswoman. Rather than remain a passive victim, like so many literary concubines, Ai Nu accrues martial power, exacts revenge against her male exploiters and surreptitiously plots revenge against her female captor. The film's fusion of the martial and the erotic hinges upon a lesbian eros between Ai Nu and Lady Chun, who adopts the role normally reserved for a promiscuous patriarch in the standard concubine narrative. As a lesbian couple, Ai Nu and Lady Chun are positioned both outside and against the patriarchy under which Lady Chun's brothel ostensibly operates. Chun's brothel, a tool of literally torturous exploitation, ultimately becomes an obstacle to the women's jointly proposed freedom. In the climax, the two women join forces to destroy patriarchal officials, an army of soldiers and the brothel in the process. But the brothel's treacherous economy corrupts them to a point no eros can repair and catalyses their tragic fates. Like the wuxia hero, the women 'take justice into their own hands', but like the concubine, they must suffer fatally for their impetuous transgressions.

Chor Yuen pursued a different narrative trajectory in his 1984 remake, *Lust for Love of a Chinese Courtesan* (*Ai nu xin zhuan*, literally 'The New Story of Ai Nu'). Not a needless repetition of *Intimate Confessions*, *Lust for Love* retains the first film's sexploitative tone but substantially undoes (or transgresses) much of the original's transgressions. While *Intimate Confessions* ends with Ai Nu instigating the brothel's downfall, the remake sees her usurping Lady Chun's position as the brothel's new mistress. Ai Nu thus no longer subverts the system but coldly acquiesces to its temptations. Notably, *Lust for Love* robs Lady Chun of her martial power, as she outsources her violence to a male agent. The remake reimagines 'power' as foremost the financial mechanisms of the brothel, intertwined with the evildoings of corrupt officials, while martial power is demythologised and demoted to the status of hired labour. The remake's cynical revisions undoubtedly reflect the hypercapitalist mood of mid-1980s Hong Kong, when so many local films envisioned acquiescence to commercialism as a fait accompli.[2]

THE INFLUENCE OF MING EROTIC LITERATURE

Released in 1972, *Intimate Confessions* absorbed a number of transnational trends that exploited lesbian themes for presumed male spectators, from Roger Corman's women-in-prison cycle of the early 1970s to the lesbian-themed vampire outings of Hammer Studios and French filmmaker Jean Rollin. These sexploitation influences are tangential, however. Chor Yuen's themes, tone and imagery are principally derived from Ming erotic literature, famous for its depictions of depravity and licentiousness. In the first volume of his *History of Sexuality*, Michel Foucault attempts a rather broad distinction between the *ars scientifica* of the West, which produces sexuality through scientific and institutional norms, and the *ars erotica* of the East, which draws truth 'from pleasure itself' and is 'not considered in relation to an absolute law of the permitted and the forbidden, nor by reference to a criterion of utility, but first and foremost in relation to itself' (1978, 57). Apart from Daoist or Tantric sex manuals, which might exist beyond doctrinaire regimes of power, Foucault's attempt at a grand dichotomy seems ill-informed. Although it is true that Chinese philosophy generally treats sexuality as an ethical concern, not a pseudoscientific one, the erotic novels of the Ming reveal precisely the webs of institutional power that Foucault sees as endemic to Western modernity. From the *Jin Ping Mei* to Li Yu's *The Carnal Prayer Mat* (written in 1657, published in 1693) – and by extension to *Intimate Confessions* – Chinese concubines are hardly free from 'criteria of utility'. Though more decadent than her Western counterparts, the Chinese concubine is always positioned as a commodity within phallocratic feudal economies, and her value rises or falls according to personal loyalties and courtly happenstance.

In Ming erotica, these power relations often translate into narratives of gendered determinism: male libertines enjoy possibilities for redemption while wanton, irredeemable women are left dejected or dead. This gender inequity comes to the fore – with a touch of absurdism – in Li Yu's controversial masterpiece of Chinese literature *The Carnal Prayer Mat*, best known to global audiences through Michael Mak's somewhat watered-down erotic comedy *Sex and Zen* (*Yu pu tuan zhi: Tou qing bao jian*, 1991). After many debauched episodes, the libertine hero, Vesperus, discovers the wife he abandoned has been sold to a brothel. Rather than allow Vesperus to learn of her sad fate, she hangs herself – at which point Vesperus, wracked with guilt, slices off his greatest treasure, a monstrous, alchemically enhanced penis. After he takes the tonsure and retreats to a Buddhist temple, his two young daughters die of illness, their lives fatalistically sacrificed for his egoistic excesses. Vesperus is not simply let off the hook for his carnal wrongdoings: his wife and daughters become the price of his redemption.

In their study of Ming erotica, Wu Cuncun and Mark Stevenson argue that such gendered determinism is little more than a 'karmic cliché' that perpetuates misogyny through Buddhistic pretexts (Wu and Stevenson 2011, 475). Perhaps Wu and Stevenson slightly overstate their case, as a few Ming works focus on female libertines and dispense with tropes of Buddhistic retribution. Most noteworthy in this regard is *The Lord of Perfect Satisfaction*, an anonymously authored, early seventeenth-century Ming novella that predates *The Carnal Prayer Mat* by several years. The novella unapologetically details Empress Wu-Zetian's dalliances with various male consorts (including the phallically gifted youth of the title) through her septuagenarian years. The work's indulgent depiction of the dowager's insatiable sexual appetites makes it remarkably modern, even by twenty-first-century standards. But just as the story does not punish her carnal excess, neither does it provide any approbation or closure. In the end, she is left spiritually and morally empty after a lifetime of royal dissolution. The Ming novel *The Tale of a Foolish Woman* (*Chipozi zhuan*) similarly centres on a female wanton left spiritually barren by decadent pursuits. Slightly varying the sexist formula of the 'karmic cliché', the titular woman 'is left to reflect on the cold and loveless years she has lived alone, taking solace in Buddhist prayers' (Wu and Stevenson 2011, 487), yet never finding the officially sanctioned, institutional redemption afforded Vesperus in *The Carnal Prayer Mat*.

While *Intimate Confessions* and *Lust for Love* draw their themes and imageries from Chinese literary erotica, they do so only to violate that tradition's gendered assumptions. The films' heroic (or antiheroic, depending on one's perspective) women are not simply passive vessels open to patriarchal manipulation or cyphers that facilitate stale Buddhist symbolisms. Though *Intimate Confessions*, which ends tragically, does not entirely abandon the karmic cliché, its heroines fight against the patriarchy through which gendered determinism arises. As they battle corrupt male officials on multiple fronts, the film's heroic concubines subvert and pervert the ways in which wuxia heroes 'take the law into their own hands' and exceed 'common standards of morality', to use Liu's phrases above. Whereas the standard (male) hero exceeds Confucian morality only to achieve higher, more altruistic forms of justice, the heroines of *Intimate Confessions* embark on a mission as self-serving as it is sympathetic.

MARTIAL POWER IN *INTIMATE CONFESSIONS OF A CHINESE COURTESAN*

A brief synopsis of *Intimate Confessions*' plot will help to accentuate the film's themes. Set during an unspecified period of the Qing dynasty (1644–1912), the story begins with the peasant girl Ai Nu being abducted by the powerful lesbian brothel-keeper Lady Chun, who proves herself a formidable villain from the outset. Inspecting her recent captives, Lady Chun realises one girl's hymen is no longer intact and demands to know who deflowered her. When the girl refuses to name her lover, the older woman elicits a confession by vaginally torturing her with a massive candle. Lady Chun then dispatches the deflowerer, proving herself an expert in martial arts. When beautiful Ai Nu demonstrates a more rebellious spirit, Lady Chun attempts to whip her into submission – literally. When her violence fails, she realises Ai Nu's powerful will and inner strength. Switching strategies, Lady Chun tries to seduce Ai Nu, knowing that, once acquiescent, she will become the brothel's star attraction.

As part of her initiation, Ai Nu is pimped out to four powerful, perverted members of the gentry, each of whom rapes her. After her ordeals (including torture in one villain's customised iron dungeon), she attempts suicide, only to be rescued by Lady Chun's pitiable slave, Yan Shunzhi (Wan Chung-Shan), who swears to help Ai Nu exact revenge. Unfortunately, Yan Shunzhi's kung fu proves no match for Lady Chun and her phalanx of guards, and he is shortly killed in a failed plot. Realising that she cannot depend on a male saviour, Ai Nu mobilises the seductive power of her body, acting the part of the perfect concubine and becoming Lady Chun's lover, yet secretly plotting revenge all the while. As Lady Chun's new favourite, Ai Nu accrues political power, learns kung fu and becomes wily enough to murder, in ways ingenious, her four abusive 'clients' one by one, all in rape-revenge fashion. Hopelessly smitten with Ai Nu but not blind to her murders, Lady Chun becomes sexually aroused by Ai Nu's appetite for revenge. Yet, she fears that Ai Nu will eventually turn against her. When Lady Chun confronts her, Ai Nu confesses to killing one of her abusers but insists that her vengeance and her love are intertwined: 'I think

I'm becoming like you, hating men . . . That's why I sought revenge . . . but this could mean that I'll love you more.'

Meanwhile, a local constable hounds Ai Nu after her abusers start mysteriously disappearing. Ai Nu is too clever, however, to leave behind any definitive evidence. Though the constable nominally adopts the role of a detective, we are given no reason to side with him. Not a righteous arbiter of justice, the constable facilitates the rule of a corrupt officialdom and never considers the plight of poor girls abducted into slavery. In a climactic, cathartic bloodbath, the constable finally turns the tables on Ai Nu, but Lady Chun, still blinded by love, prevents him from taking her into custody. At that point, the two women unite their swords, slaughtering scores of the constable's men and Lady Chun's own rebellious guardsmen. In the aftermath, as they stand over a mountain of corpses, Ai Nu reveals that her love for Lady Chun has been only the vehicle of her revenge. Now mortally wounded and missing an arm, Lady Chun whispers in despair, 'I never imagined you could be more vicious than I.' But Ai Nu is foiled by a final act of sentimentality: granting Lady Chun a farewell kiss, Ai Nu falls victim to the treacherous woman's poisoned lips.

We've said previously that Chinese erotic literature often absolves men and punishes women for their respective excesses, if we take *The Carnal Prayer Mat* as exemplary. At first, *Intimate Confessions* seems no exception, as the women's anarchical affronts to masculine law (represented by the constable) yield karmic reckonings. But Ai Nu and Lady Chun are not sacrificed for the welfare of a male protagonist. Indeed, *Intimate Confessions* lacks a heroic male subject whose sins can be redeemed by women predestined for tragedy. The film's male figures are generally immoral (the lecherous officials) or amoral (the constable who enforces an unjust order). The only ethical man is the slave, Yan Shunzhi, but he enters the film already emasculated and impuissant, and thus without a hubris to be redeemed. If we consider Ai Nu and Lady Chun individually, not simply as an antipatriarchal 'unit', we might say that Lady Chun's demise is karmically appropriate, since she is a villainous exploiter of women, even if she becomes sympathetic in the final act. Yet, Ai Nu is from the outset a victim, not a villain, and her trail of revenge is justified within the film's own ostensible schema, as there are no legitimate authorities to whom she can turn.

We can only conclude that Ai Nu's death recuperates the masculinist wuxia genre itself, which here allows Ai Nu a 'limited' period of rebellious autonomy before pulling the rug out from under her. Her sin is neither licentiousness (for concubines should be licentious) nor the translation of that licentiousness into lesbianism (a ubiquitous theme in Chinese erotica). Her transgression, rather, is that she has broached – or confused – two traditionally discrete arenas: passive feminine eroticism and active feminine martiality. By taking the law into her own hands, she threatens to weaponise her sexuality, levelling it unilaterally against her rapists and conflictedly against Lady Chun. By delimiting Ai Nu's agency through karmic tropes, the film expands the genre without transcending it, visualising a new, hybridised protagonist – the courtesan-avenger – only to kill her off, thwarting her attempts at boundary-crossing. That *Intimate Confessions* reverts to karmic clichés does not mean, however, that it should be sacrificed on the altar of progressive politics. The film offered intrepid images of lesbian heroines long before it was fashionable to do so. Only when the two women finally unite to slaughter a slew of villains does the film envision any pair of empowered and inspired lovers. The women's courage, in turn, exposes a phallocratic society so wholly vicious that it – unlike Vesperus in *The Carnal Prayer Mat* – can never be redeemed.

THE SWORDSWOMAN AS NEO-FEMME FATALE

Before examining Chor Yuen's 1984 remake, *Lust for Love of a Chinese Courtesan*,[3] we should reflect further on the two axes of male spectatorship assumed by *Intimate Confessions*: the masculinist assumptions of the wuxia and the male gazing of kitschy sexploitation. Even if we were to put aside the issue of karmic sexism, we cannot ignore the fact that Ai Nu and Lady Chun's lesbian adventure is ensconced within a film and a genre produced by (and aimed primarily at) heterosexual men. The women may fight against patriarchy within the film, but their violence is reframed by an overriding male spectatorship that designates women's bodies as expendable sexual vessels, not persevering revolutionary agents. Simply put, the film cannot imagine Ai Nu and Lady Chun as wuxia heroines who ride off into the sunset – as do standard Shaw Brothers protagonists – while retaining their active, nonheteronormative sexuality. Nor can it imagine a more ethical resolution in which Ai Nu rides off alone, after having defeated Lady Chun at her own games. The audience is left with a quixotic, doomed rebellion without clearly articulated goals or a foreseeable endgame. The women's fateful death becomes a *fait accompli*.

Whether one sees Lady Chun and Ai Nu succumbing to Buddhistic fates or, as I have suggested, the masculinist limits of the era's wuxia, they are ensnared within a generic misogyny that frames women's sexuality as equally titillating and threatening. In cinema, this type (or archetype) of misogyny is seen most clearly in film noir's femme fatale, who reembodies the temptation of Eve. On view in Hollywood and Poverty Row studio productions such as *Murder, My Sweet* (1944), *Double Indemnity* (1944), *Detour* (1945) and *Out of the Past* (1947), the femme fatale represents an object of desire that must remain a disposable object – that is, she should never become an active subject that truly threatens the integrities of noir heroes, much as the concubines of *Intimate Confessions* must be contained by karma. Analysing the misogyny of Hollywood's noir era, Mary Anne Doane suggests that masculinist genres present female sexuality as 'indecipherable' because it 'is always in excess – even if it is simply the desire to desire, the striving for an access to a desiring subjectivity' (1987, 122). In noir and even in the 'woman's film' of classical Hollywood, uncontrolled feminine desire usually threatens or brings destruction – to the male hero, the traditional family and/or the woman herself. The karmic clichés that inform *Intimate Confessions* may not differ substantially from deterministic noir storylines that, as Doane says, kill off dangerously sexualised women 'to insure closure for the narrative'[4] (Ibid.). In a novel twist, *Intimate Confessions* effects this closure by positing two femme fatales who, acting as protagonists, try to access the kind of active subjectivity noir reserves for male heroes. But because they are embroiled in a plot that pits their 'desiring subjectivities' against one another, Ai Nu and Lady Chun cancel each other out, disintegrating the joint threat their lesbianism might pose to patriarchal orders.

Despite the film's reputation as sexploitation, Lily Ho and Betty Pei Ti reveal precious little flesh – the bulk of the film's female nudity is delegated to supernumeraries (there is no male nudity). Like the censored, buttoned-up women of noir, the heroines mainly signify eroticism through seductive posturing and sensuous couture. In their bedroom scenes, they wear flowing gowns, pose under layers of makeup and lounge amidst decorative chinoiserie, framed and lit for maximum allure. As fabric substitutes for flesh, the film's heroines reembody the overproduced, over-accessorised male fantasy of the femme fatale. This re-embodiment carries with it a sense of frustration, however. Because the evil, Eve-like woman of noir inhabited an immaculately censored Hollywood, her iconicity arose from necessary strategies of concealment and mystification (in addition to the celebrity discourse of the actress). That *Intimate Confessions* has its two leads repeat this outmoded strategy, while farming out the nudity to extras, misdirects the male gaze without repudiating it. The result is an elaborate tease that rebuffs the 'modern' (circa 1972) demand for nudity and harkens to premodern traditions of Chinese figure-drawing that signify feminine sensuality and liveliness through billowing attire, not naked flesh. Throughout the history of Chinese art, Mary Bittner Wiseman suggests, the liveliness of female figures has been represented through 'free-flowing' gestures and garments. In the absence of nudity, Chinese artists have portrayed the 'path of . . . energy [and] life force' of female figures through the 'folds and curves of their robes and sleeves' (2011, 128). In the film's bloody climax, when the heroines' garments encompass the flow of their swords, this sensuous 'life force' takes a deadly turn. Only when they are mortally wounded do their clothes come apart at the seams, oozing the Shaw Brothers' patently artificial yet strangely erotic stage blood.

Figure 3.1 Lady Chun and Ai Nu stand back-to-back during a brief interlude of the climactic swordfight in the wuxia classic *Intimate Confessions of a Chinese Courtesan* (*Ai Nu*, 1972).

While parallels exist between noir's fatal women and the heroines of *Intimate Confessions*, Doane's notion of the transgressive woman's 'excess' (derived from Lacanian psychoanalysis) does function differently within a culturally Chinese – and sexploitative – context. As concubines, Ai Nu and Lady Chun project not 'excessive' desire per se but the absence of anything but desire. As it privileges the concubine's tragedy over her potential rebellion, *Intimate Confessions* makes Ai Nu's autonomy – not her sexuality – unrepresentable within the limits of the narrative. Nevertheless, Ai Nu attempts to rebel in ways the femme fatale does not or cannot. A prisoner to and victim of unregulated desire, the traditional femme fatale corrupts men, but rarely (if ever) transcends noir's masculinist logic. She is integral to the genre rather than a threat to it. Because her petty, self-interested schemes only reflect misogynist stereotypes, her actions cannot amount to genuine social rebellion. Of course, any true rebellion was 'unrepresentable' within the postlapsarian morality of the Hays Code. In *Double Indemnity*, Barbara Stanwyck's manipulative character Phyllis Dietrichson might successfully seduce Fred MacMurray's insurance salesman Walter Neff, but the claims adjuster played by Edward G. Robinson finally doles out moral order and Hollywood's Catholic version of karmic retribution. In *Intimate Confessions*, Chor Yuen moves the disruptive force from the level of content (that is, the plot) to that of form (that is, the genre through which the plot unfolds). Not content to have the characters seduce or betray one another, *Intimate Confessions* rather tempts the audience with the tantalising possibility that Ai Nu might successfully transgress the limits of the wuxia – quite a real possibility, given that the wuxia's integrity is here compromised by the spirit of the concubine narrative. Indeed, the lesbian lovers seem to be on the brink of exceeding the concubine's usual lifespan up until the final scene, when their 'excess' – initially sexual, immanently political – is curtailed by a film that pulls the rug out from under them.

Chor Yuen's 1984 remake *Lust for Love of a Chinese Courtesan* sees Ai Nu escape karmic retribution only to embrace her own commodification as a source of 'entrepreneurial' power. A noirish vixen rather than a martial warrior, the 'new' Ai Nu reflects the cynicism of its decade. Like the urban sex workers who pervade so many Hong Kong melodramas of the 1980s, she must either accede to and master the game of capitalism or get trampled underfoot.

ECONOMIC POWER IN *LUST FOR LOVE OF A CHINESE COURTESAN*

Made a year before the Shaw Brothers shuttered their regular production schedule, *Lust for Love of a Chinese Courtesan* is less a rigid remake of *Intimate Confessions* than a series of variations on its themes. *Lust for Love* retains the original's basic story: young Ai Nu is captured, abused and seduced by Lady Chun, and initiated into the cruel ways of Chun's brothel. But *Lust for Love*'s deviations are more significant. Partially dropping the karmic cliché, the remake sees Lady Chun suffer a tragic yet sympathetic end. Meanwhile, a calculating, upwardly mobile Ai Nu schemes not to ruin the brothel but to replace the older woman as its proprietress (metatextually suggesting how the remake, as the younger of two texts, is sometimes said to substitute for the original work). Reimagining Ai Nu as a cutthroat opportunist, not a passive victim, the film echoes the worldview of much of 1980s Hong Kong cinema, which – besides committing itself to churning out remakes – embraced the era's capitalist boom with a mixture of wild-eyed enthusiasm and cynical resignation.

If *Intimate Confessions* merged the heroines' eroticism with their martial power, *Lust for Love* makes their eroticism tantamount to economic power. As part of this postfeminist bargain, Lady Chun (Yu An-an) and Ai Nu (Hu Kuan-chen) no longer act as martial heroines. As such, the film casts off wuxia garb and retreats into the concubine genre. Yet, the heroines' 'de-martialisation' now signifies the modernisation of their power. Like the boss of a crime syndicate, the Lady Chun of the 1980s plays the role of a respectable businessperson, colluding with politicians and rarely dirtying her hands with violence. When enemies threaten her enterprise, she outsources assassinations to a male underling, Xiao Yei (Chang Kuo-Chu). (In one scene, Lady Chun slices off the arm of a miscreant, but only after Xiao Yei has subdued him.) Although he is Lady Chun's childhood protector and present lover, Xiao Yei lives exiled from her wealth and privilege, relegated to a ramshackle hut at the outskirts of her estate. The film returns martial and erotic identities to male and female roles, respectively, in accordance with a 'modern' division of labour. Lady Chun is elevated to a purely managerial position, while the flying swordsman, Xiao Yei, is demoted to the role of alienated employee. The brothel's economy becomes the real seat of power, and Xiao Yei's martial arts are merely a means to an end.

In this unheroic, capitalistic schema, Ai Nu not only acquiesces (eventually) to her own commodification, but she also foregoes the rape-revenge strategy of the first film. Her initial rape in this film – by four officials, as in *Intimate Confessions* – instils a trauma that renders her hysterical for much of the film's first half. Though she castrates another rapist and kills an elderly official who attempts to molest her, these are frenzied acts of self-defence, not parts of a premeditated revenge plot. Realising that local magistrates and officials are in Lady Chun's pocket, Ai Nu plots a purely economic revenge, manipulating the older woman's affections not to ruin the brothel, as in the first film, but to enact a hostile takeover. Whereas *Intimate Confessions* offers outsized protagonists with little connection to recognisable humanity, *Lust for Love* provides its characters with psychologising backstories. Through flashbacks, we learn that Ai Nu, Lady Chun and Xiao Yei all grew up in dire poverty. Chun, an orphan, was herself inducted into the brothel as an adolescent and eventually usurped the role of proprietress, a pattern Ai Nu will replicate. The trio's economic backgrounds have made them hardened, not empathetic, however. As Lady Chun tells Ai Nu after her backstory unfolds: 'No man will ever marry a prostitute . . . never cry or ask for help'. Throughout the film's second half, Ai Nu takes the advice too much to heart, especially after Chun forces Ai Nu to witness Xiao Yei assassinate their enemies. By the film's end, Ai Nu will have surpassed the mercenary ambitions of Lady Chun, who becomes a sentimental figure pining for the youthfulness that Ai Nu represents.

Xiao Yei, meanwhile, resigns himself to his own form of prostitution. Once Chun's valiant protector, he now sells his sword and resents his servitude. The transformation of his character is revealed through two complementary montages. Stressing his phallic potency, the first montage intercuts his intercourse with Lady Chun and his impalement of an enemy, such that his sword seems to pierce Chun at the point of orgasm. The second montage occurs in the film's final third, when Lady Chun has prioritised her new relationship with Ai Nu over her old one with Xiao Yei, now dejected and pathetic. Here, the two women's tender lovemaking is intercut with a masturbating Xiao Yei, furiously grasping the hilt of his sword. His relative impotence is shared by the film's other sympathetic male character, Lin Yun (Alex Man), an inspector who investigates Ai Nu's killings. Unlike the corrupt constable in *Intimate Confessions*, he actually upholds Confucianist virtues – his name literally translates as 'Soul'. Yet, he is not an analogue to the character of Yan Shunzhi, the self-sacrificing slave of *Intimate Confessions*. Unlike Yan Shunzhi, who gives his life for Ai Nu without a second thought, Lin Yun possesses merely conventional virtues that go no further than legal or 'right' relations. Though he provides a starving Ai Nu with a blanket in the opening scene, his character exists mainly so that she, in a gesture of both amorality and autonomy, can reject him and his Confucian 'soul' in the denouement.

Where *Intimate Confessions* offered a cathartically bloody finale, *Lust for Love* offers a bittersweet anti-climax. In the film's second half, Ai Nu seduces Xiao Yei as part of her plan to strip away Lady Chun's power. Meanwhile, Lady Chun laments that life has forced her to prioritise easily acquired lucre over ever-elusive love. Jealous of Ai Nu's growing relationship with an embittered Xiao Yei, Lady Chun sleeps with him one last time before trying to kill him while his back is turned. Reacting instinctively, Xiao Yei mortally wounds his attacker, not knowing it is Lady Chun. After Xiao Yei dies from his wounds, Chun, herself at death's door, asks Ai Nu for a final kiss – this time without poisoned lips. As observed in an earlier section of this chapter, the plot of *Intimate Confessions* sees Lady Chun and Ai Nu cancelling each other out, effectively visiting karma upon one another for their transgressions against the wuxia genre itself. But *Lust for Love*, which demotes the power and status of martial arts, is not a real wuxia. Here the karmic force is transferred to a heterosexual couple, who atone not for formal transgressions but for the sins they commit on the level of plot (that is, their mercenary ambitions). After Chun dies, Ai Nu rebuffs the judgmental gaze of an onlooking Lin Yun and retreats to her brothel, where she luxuriates among ill-gotten jewels as the end credits roll. She has not renounced the world. By this point, the world likely has renounced her. If history repeats itself, one day Ai Nu might find herself challenged by a new upstart (a satirist might see *Lust for Love* as a concubine's version of *All About Eve* [Joseph L. Mankiewicz, 1950]). Or perhaps Ai Nu, less sentimental than Lady Chun, would become like the Wu-Zetian of *The Lord of Perfect Satisfaction*, insatiable and grasping until the very end.

I previously remarked that *Intimate Confessions* could not imagine its heroines overcoming karma and riding off into the sunset, as do male wuxia heroes. *Lust for Love* avoids this issue by repositing Ai Nu and Lady Chun as unmartial femme fatales, unburdened by pretentions to heroism. If *Intimate Confessions* intersects with the wuxia, *Lust for Love* more firmly belongs to the Ming erotic tradition, its brief, perfunctory martial arts sequences notwithstanding. Wholly missing in *Lust for Love*, however, is the daring wit of an author like Li Yu. The film's tone is dreamy and languorous, and Chor Yuen presents his unsubtle commentary on self-commodification solemnly, even though he offers no solutions to the problem. Though Xiao Yei and Lady Chun become the dualised recipients of karmic retribution, Ai Nu's perseverance becomes 'tragic' in a political sense. The Ai Nu of *Intimate Confessions* at least had the righteous cause of vengeance against her rapists; the Ai Nu of the 1980s aims only to reproduce a system of economic exploitation and finds solace in

Figure 3.2 Ai Nu luxuriates in a bed filled with ill-gotten jewels in Chor Yuen's *Lust for Love of a Chinese Courtesan* (*Ai Nu xin zhuan*, 1984), a remake of the same director's *Intimate Confessions of a Chinese Courtesan* (*Ai Nu*, 1972).

conspicuous consumption. The final image of Ai Nu luxuriating in ill-gotten jewels hammers this point home. As the courtesan's upward mobility acquires a capitalist rationale, her sexual excess becomes an economic excess. Further, she becomes masculinised not through martial chivalry, as does the swordswoman, but through the sort of ruthlessly capitalistic narrative more typical of the gangster film.

MODERN CONCUBINES AND THE PROBLEM OF AUTONOMY

'The desire for autonomy is at the heart of what it means to be human', says the philosopher Michael Davis, 'and yet the desire for autonomy is not autonomy' but something much more limited: 'a hatred of being ruled' (1988, 3). Hatred, perhaps the most universal of feelings, paves treacherous paths to emancipation. In *Lust for Love*, Ai Nu's desire for autonomy, born of hatred, only makes her a prisoner of the damning materialism that overwhelms her. Tragically, she embraces what the world makes her become. Of course, Ai Nu's entrapments in both films are the symptoms of her politico-historical milieu. Because she is distilled from traditions marked by karma and prearranged gender roles, her autonomy is not a generic likelihood. A premodern heroine with pretentions to modern autonomy will risk tragedy of some kind, even if *Intimate Confessions* teases us with the prospect of Ai Nu's rebellion.

Whereas *Intimate Confessions* is a romantic tragedy, *Lust for Love* is something of a gangster film in disguise. Though enacted in period costume, *Lust for Love*'s cynical – if still sentimental – commentary on upward mobility and sexual commodification makes it a quintessentially modern Hong Kong film. Without altering his themes, Chor Yuen could have set *Lust for Love* within the urban slums of 1984, turning Lady Chun into a scheming madam, Ai Nu into a victim of sex trafficking, the corrupt officials into corrupt policemen, and Xiao Yei into a gangster with a heart of gold. Whether in period costuming or modern dress, Ai Nu's successful social climbing inverts the downbeat formula of Hong Kong's numerous 1980s sex work dramas, which share with *Lust for Love* a bitter commentary on women's sexual and bodily autonomy. In films such as *Lonely Fifteen* (*Jing mei zai*, 1982), *Midnight Girls* (*Wu ye li ren*, 1986) and *Girls without Tomorrow* (*Ying zhao nü lang*, 1988), the slavery of the concubine becomes the indentured servitude of uneducated club girls, and unregulated capitalism effectively reproduces systems of feudal subservience. The upper limit of the modern prostitute's mobility is not autonomy but lower-middle class dignity. In *Midnight Girls*, for instance, the sorry fate of a prostitute is juxtaposed with friends who find respectable – but dead-end – employment as secretaries. Of course, 'realistic' stories about club girls cannot restage the fantastic mobility of Ai Nu, who magically seizes martial or economic power after only a few scene changes. Karma, or its residue, only glosses the modern prostitute's sad fate: club girl dramas clearly villainise not licentious women but a system that discards women past the conventional age of wanton lust.

All genre filmmaking, whether set in premodern or modern times, proposes a contest between the individualistic consciousness a hero projects and what that consciousness can accomplish within the bounds – sometimes fixed, sometimes elastic – of generic norms. The notion that heroes actually can accomplish something is essential to the narrative illusion. Supposedly agentic characters accomplish only what genre filmmakers contrive and only what they believe mass audiences, at particular sociohistorical moments, will condone or tolerate. But even genre films that provide characters with opportunities for mock-agentic choice-making usually deny them political consciousnesses. This political lack, notably and primarily, debilitates male action heroes, who rarely espouse clear, holistic philosophies of justice. Instead, the flamboyant heroism with which they defeat generic villains is falsely conflated with an articulated fight for structural change.[5] In Hollywood spectacles, we assume – rightly or wrongly – that female heroes needn't explicitly espouse a political agenda because some sort of feminism supposedly inheres in their cause, even if they do nothing more than commit acts of violence against boorish men. But with Chinese cinema, we cannot venture casually feminist assumptions. Though the traditional swordswoman casts off domesticity, her agencies are tightly circumscribed by her sexual expression. Chor Yuen's duology at first liberates the swordswoman by melding her with the concubine, but then delimits that freedom with narrow, self-interested revenge plots. While Ai Nu transgresses the swordswoman's orthodox limits, her lesbian transgression does not yield a feminist consciousness any more than her amorality sparks a political awakening. It is therefore difficult to claim that she represents anything more than a caricatured feminism. This point theoretically extends to any number of 'girl power' action films that define power only as personalised physical force. For instance, Hong Kong *policiers* such as *Yes, Madam!* (*Huang jia shi jie*, 1985), *Royal Warriors* (*Huang jia zhan shi*, 1986) and *Righting Wrongs* (*Zhi fa xian feng*, 1986) ask us to overlook the fact that the high-kicking skills of colonial policewomen (as portrayed by Cynthia Rothrock and Michelle Yeoh) do nothing to solve social inequities. Arguably, the problem is endemic to many action-film genres that historically have used purely technical innovations (that is, visual effects) to camouflage their lack of moral innovations.

The temptation to interpret Ai Nu's disruption of heteronormative patriarchy as implicitly feminist surely remains. Yet, we also have the right to ask what potentially lies beyond karmically and generically forestalled conclusions. What might Ai Nu and Lady Chun have accomplished had they lived? Neither woman seems to care much about exploited women at large. Had they overcome karma and emerged victorious in *Intimate Confessions*, we cannot envision them liberating the brothel's prostitutes or continuing an antipatriarchal crusade on more altruistic fronts. *Lust for Love* forestalls feminist possibilities by providing Ai Nu with a vulgar, greedy endgame, and the camera scorns her amorality in the final scene, in case audiences miss the point.

To avoid ending this chapter on a pessimistic note, I would like to conclude by briefly comparing Chor Yuen's duology with Patrick Lung Kong's *The Call Girls* (*Ying zhao nu lang*, 1973), a modern sex work film that rejects karmic-generic designs and instead moves moral contentions to the explicit level of text. Although critic Law Kar rightly points out that *The Call Girls* 'exploit[s] social realism as titillation' and sensationalises 'the commodification of women' (2010, 4), the film's socially conscious liberalism was novel for 1973 and exerted much influence on the pseudo-realism of Hong Kong's new wave. Unlike *Intimate Confessions* and Lung Kong's previous *Teddy Girls* (*Fei nu zheng zhuan*, 1969), a juvenile delinquency melodrama, *The Call Girls* features no violent revenge plotline. Like *Lust for Love*, it instead traces the attempted upward mobility of female sex workers as they seek entrée into monied circles (in this case, by marrying wealthy urban professionals). We needn't entertain a detailed synopsis of the film, a melodrama that follows 'five ladies of pleasure', as the director put it, through a series of humiliations and tragedies, culminating in suicides, poisonings, gangland killings and so on (Shing 2010, 33). A metatextual conceit prevents us from reducing these human tragedies to fate, however. Included among the film's characters is an investigative journalist who, as part of his controversial television program, conducts interviews about sexual morality and the legalisation of prostitution.

These interviews reflect and implicitly comment on incidents in the plot. In the context of Chinese-language cinemas circa 1973, this was a fairly bold conceit. To question the social mores that underlie the very acts that transpire in the film is to abjure karma and instigate an ethical understanding of human action. The film thus encourages us to understand the girls' tragedies as socially constructed rather than karmic. In one scene, a middle-aged social scientist – previously seen patronising a call girl – appears on the journalist's television show to advocate for the legalisation of sex work, calling prostitution a 'social good'. At the film's climax, the heroine, after suffering numerous humiliations, is spurned by her fiancée after he and his whoring father discover her background in sex work. She then turns to her ex-fiancée and in flat, ironic monotone mouths the words of the social scientist she has seen on television: 'Prostitution is a social good . . .' The irony is more subtle than it initially seems. Throughout the film, we witness the horrors that attend sex work, but these horrors are the results of illegal and stigmatised sex work, precisely what the social scientist has decried. Had sex work been destigmatised from the beginning, would such tragedies ever have occurred? After all, laws, unlike karma, can be changed to comport with modern notions of justice.

At the time, Lung Kong's moderately progressive social dramas, as Law Kar observes, were commercially overwhelmed by the monopolising fantasies of the Shaw Brothers (2010, 6). Only belatedly did the Shaw Brothers finally join the new wave realism bandwagon with *Hong Kong, Hong Kong* (*Nán yǔ nǚ*, 1983) and *The Illegal Immigrant* (*Fei fa yi min*, 1985), films ironically prepared by Lung Kong's legacy. To risk a crude simile, we might say that the Shaw Brothers' costumed fantasies are like concubines themselves – luxurious, ornate, and seductive, yet demanding from customers a fixed fee. The Shaw Brothers' standard price was the ubiquitous karmic conclusion, the films' 'strong' female characters notwithstanding. The problem with generic filmmaking is not that it claims freedom is impossible, for we know that in reality, freedom is an ideal necessarily defined, qualified and reformulated into social contracts. The problem, rather, is that generic or 'karmic' filmmaking does not see freedom as either aspirational or desirable. We may wonder why an age professing ill-defined 'freedom' at all costs continues to cling to genre filmmaking's morally prearranged fantasies. This problem becomes far less paradoxical if audiences only claim to desire freedom and in fact prefer safe, familiar or reactionary outcomes to anxiously uncharted paths. While contemporary action films might freight themselves with joking ironies, pretended self-deprecation cannot substitute for a transformative critique, something that *The Call Girls*, for all its old-fashioned melodrama, does attempt. Without such a critique, we remain trapped between the alternate positions of Ai Nu in *Intimate Confessions* and *Lust for Love*, either acquiescing to received fates or reproducing the very systems that entrap us.

NOTES

1. Jing Sun's masterful *The Peach Blossom Fan* (*Tao Hua Shan*, 1963) provides a notable exception to the 'passive concubine' formula. Derived from a Qing-era play by Kong Shangren, the film features a courtesan who performs in the presence of corrupt officials an opera that ironically deals with hypocrisy and corruption. Through the use of irony, the courtesan becomes willful yet remains nonviolent.
2. Acquiescence to capitalist lifestyles is a common theme in Hong Kong cinema of the 1980s, though some films, such as Michael Hui's *Chicken and Duck Talk* (*Jī tóng yā jiǎng*, 1988), take a cynical view of corporate commercialism. More typical are the numerous gangster films that, following *A Better Tomorrow* (*Yīngxióng běnsè*, 1986), glorified signs of conspicuous consumption (expensive cars, flowing champagne, etc.). The trend toward commercialism is also evident in the style of Hong Kong cinema of the mid-1980s, when the glossy, marketable productions of Cinema City and D&B Films supplanted the grittier, more realistic films that marked the early Hong Kong new wave.
3. The convoluted English title presumably refers only to Lady Chun, who 'lusts' after love; Ai Nu only lusts for power and money.
4. Doane hedges a bit on Hollywood karma, suggesting that transgressive women, though doomed, can nevertheless 'flaunt . . . their excess. . . . for a moment of cinematic time'. Doane's subsequent comment, 'And one sometimes gets the sense, from the love story, that "anybody could've been her"', is far less convincing, considering that Hollywood's fantasies are blatantly unrelatable (1987, 122).
5. Admittedly, there are some exceptions, particularly tropes that involve a cynical mercenary developing a political consciousness after realising that he is fighting for the wrong side. In Hollywood, the trope usually has the mercenary fighting overseas in a developing nation – his politically conscious gaze is rarely directed at America.

REFERENCES

Altenburger, Roland. 2009. *The Sword or the Needle: The Female Knight-Errant in Traditional Chinese Narrative*. Berlin: Peter Lang.
Davis, Michael. 1988. *Ancient Tragedy and the Origins of Modern Science*. Carbondale: Southern Illinois University Press.
Doane, Mary Ann. 1987. *The Desire to Desire: The Woman's Film of the 1940s*. Bloomington: Indiana University Press.
The Fountainhead of Chinese Erotica: The Lord of Perfect Satisfaction. 2003. Translated by Charles R. Stone. Honolulu: University of Hawai'i Press.
Foucault, Michel. 1978. *The History of Sexuality, Volume 1: An Introduction*. Translated by Robert Hurley. New York: Pantheon Books.
Law, Kar. 2010. 'Lung Kong in Our Time.' *Director Lung Kong: Oral History Series 6*. CD-ROM, Hong Kong: Hong Kong Film Archive.
Liu, James J. Y. 1967. *The Chinese Knight-Errant*. London: Routledge and Kegan Paul.
Lu, Hsun. 1959. *A Brief History of Chinese Fiction*. Translated by Yang Hsien-Yi and Gladys Yang. Peking: Foreign Language Press.
Shek, Richard H. 1995. 'Tan Sitong.' In *Great Thinkers of the Eastern World*. Edited by Ian P. McGreal. New York: Harper Collins, 138.

Shing, Angel. 2010. 'Oral History Interview: Patrick Lung Kong.' In *Director Lung Kong: Oral History Series 6*. Edited by Patrick Lung Kong. CD-ROM, Hong Kong: Hong Kong Film Archive.

Wiseman, Mary Bittner. 2011. 'Gendered Bodies in Contemporary Chinese Art.' In *Subversive Strategies in Contemporary Chinese Art*. Edited by Mary Bittner Wiseman and Liu Yuedi, 125–46. Boston: Brill.

Wu, Cuncun and Mark Stevenson. 2011. 'Karmic Retribution and Moral Didacticism in Erotic Fiction from the Late Ming to the Early Qing.' *Ming Qing Studies*, 467–86.

CHAPTER 4

Japanese Self-Made Film Remakes as Self-Improvement: Professional Desires and DIY Fulfilment, from *Panic High School* to *Tetsuo*

Mark Player

In *Film Remakes as Ritual and Disguise*, Anat Zanger writes, 'The relationship between original and version [of a film] encapsulates the dialectic of repetition, the dialectic between old and new, before and after, desire and fulfilment' (2006, 9). Such 'dialectics' are especially palpable when directors decide to remake one of their own films, bringing the filmmaker's motivation to retrace or return to past work into metareferential focus. For David Desser, 'directors remaking their own film within the same broad national context' represent 'cases that move beyond the typical auteur who persistently works in the same idiom or with the same motifs' (2017, 164). Constantine Verevis notes that this phenomenon 'might be located in a filmmaker's desire to repeatedly express and modify a particular aesthetic sensibility and world view in light of new developments and interests' (2006, 60).

The extensive history of Japanese cinema features numerous examples of high-profile directors evoking or directly returning to past work. As discussed in other chapters within this volume, Ozu Yasujirō was prone to revisiting and reshaping past ideas. Perhaps the most obvious example of this was his late-career classic *Floating Weeds* (*Ukikusa*, 1959): a colour remake of his earlier silent *A Story of Floating Weeds* (*Ukikusa monogatari*, 1934). To give another example, Ichikawa Kon returned to one of his most famous films, the humanist anti-war drama *The Burmese Harp* (*Biruma no tategoto*, 1956), and remade it as a sweeping colour version in 1985.[1] In both cases, the gap between 'original' and 'remake' is vast (25 and 29 years respectively), spanning numerous technological and industrial changes that have reshaped film aesthetics and production practices (including changing preferences towards synchronised sound, colour film stock and aspect ratios). They perhaps also fulfil the promise of film remakes as '*industrial products*' that 'are "pre-sold" to their audience because viewers are assumed to have some prior experience, or at least possess a "narrative image", of the original story' (Verevis 2006, 3, original emphasis). This arrangement satisfied their director's desire to return to past material (whether that be for financial or artistic reasons, or to re-imagine older works with newer technologies), while also providing commercial benefit to the studios that produced them, allowing them to court new generations of audience with pre-existing scenarios.

The phenomenon of filmmakers remaking their own films is discernible not only throughout the history of Japan's mainstream motion picture industry (driven by the commercial interests of executives and producers at Daiei, Nikkatsu, Shōchiku, Tōei, Tōhō and other major production companies), but also among amateur modes of film production within more condensed timeframes. This was the case for those operating within the heyday of Japan's *jishu-eiga* ('self-made film') scene during the 1970s and 1980s, when thousands of young people self-produced short and feature-length narrative films by (mostly) using accessible 8mm cameras. However, for some of these self-made filmmakers, the act of remaking one's own film came with the prospect of launching a professional career in film directing. Using Japan's self-made filmmaking scene from this era as a case study, this chapter builds on Zanger's and Verevis's comments about remaking in particular to consider a different kind of motivation: one that sees the Japanese film remake as a mode of professional development and advancement for amateur or early-career filmmakers. This process gave new talent much-needed experience, as well as the chance to test, refine and expand upon ideas and improve their technical skills, with the ultimate goal of drawing the industry's attention to their potential as professional filmmakers who could be trusted to handle larger projects. This chapter also highlights how that generation of Japanese filmmakers was especially susceptible to this kind of motivation as their understanding of film production was largely informed by patterns of emulation, in which aspiring filmmakers tried remaking the conventions of films they were seeing in cinemas and on television within their early 8mm work, as was the case with Ōmori Kazuki, Kurosawa Kiyoshi, Nagasaki Shun'ichi and Anno Hideaki, among many others. However, I argue that this practice of DIY (do-it-yourself) remaking challenges 'the vast majority of critical accounts of film remakes which understands remaking as a one-way process: a movement from authenticity to imitation' (Verevis 2006, 58). Instead, it points toward what Verevis refers to as a 'wider and more open-ended intertextuality' that recasts remaking in broader terms, 'ranging from practices of allusion and quotation to patterns of repetition (and variation)' (2006, 59).

After introducing Japan's self-made filmmaking scene and situating it as an alternative method for filmmaker development during a period in Japanese cinema when new talent was largely neglected by a struggling film industry,

I will focus on two interconnected cases that bookend this era of self-made filmmaking. Occurring a decade apart, both involve aspiring filmmakers producing a short narrative film on 8mm and then quickly remaking it as a feature. The first case focuses on Ishii Gakuryū (then going by, and henceforth referred to as, Ishii Sōgo), who was given the unprecedented opportunity to co-direct a feature-length remake of his first 8mm short *Panic High School* (*Kōkō dai panikku*, 1976) for the venerable studio Nikkatsu, released in 1978. The second case focuses on Tsukamoto Shin'ya, whose legendary cult feature *Tetsuo: The Iron Man* (1989), which features complex handmade practical and stop-motion animation effects, had been previously rehearsed in his 8mm short *The Phantom of Regular Size* (*Futsū saizu no kaijin*, 1986). This chapter analyses the production contexts of both pairs of films to demonstrate that the act of quickly remaking one's short amateur film into a feature-length work speaks to the dialectic of 'desire and fulfilment' identified by Zanger, albeit along professionalised lines. In both cases, I argue that this desire-fulfilment dialectic is a way to orientate and help contextualise the motives behind Ishii's and Tsukamoto's early filmmaking practices, which oscillated between authentic and imitative expression as they transitioned from amateur to professional status.

JAPAN'S SELF-MADE FILM SCENE AND ITS PROFESSIONAL DESIRES

In Japan, self-made film (*jishu-eiga*) refers to a mode of DIY film that is 'self-financed and produced outside of the industry and screened predominantly in noncommercial venues' (Sharp 2011, 111). Mainly practiced by students, self-made filmmaking reached a cultural zenith during the 1970s and 1980s due to a confluence of factors. To highlight two: first, Kodak introduced Super 8 film capable of recording synchronised sound in 1973 (Ektasound), making it easier than ever for amateur filmmakers to shoot narrative films containing dialogue. In 1975, 8mm camera and projector sales reached an all-time high (Dew 2020, 219) as many manufacturers put out their own sync-sound cameras in response to growing demand; Chinon offered a range of 'Direct Sound' camera models that proved popular, for example. Second, a semi-organised grassroots network of self-made film production and exhibition began to coalesce throughout major Japanese cities and their universities (for example, Tokyo universities with active self-made film circles included Nihon, Waseda, Meiji, Hosei and Rikkyo), eventually bringing the phenomenon to both the industry's and public's attention. This culminated in the creation of what is known today as the Pia Film Festival in 1977, which continues to dedicate itself to the exhibition and promotion of self-made films (Player 2021).

As such, the turn of the 1980s signalled a major shift in the perception of what could easily be written off as 'amateur movies' or 'home movies', as self-made filmmaking became an exciting frontier for new talent and ideas to emerge, such as those of Ishii and, a little later, Tsukamoto. Self-made filmmakers typically drew upon their immediate surroundings and circumstances for subjects, including but not limited to: the high school/university experience; issues of romance and sexuality; identity, both national and generational (or lack thereof); and their interests in media, particularly music (including Japan's then-burgeoning punk scene) and, as I shall go on to discuss further, cinema.

However, while self-made filmmaking activities encompassed a range of subjects and styles (ranging from ambitious genre recreations to personal self-reflexivity), something that united many participants was an overt desire to become professional filmmakers. Indeed, a major reason for young people turning to self-made filmmaking in the first place was that the Japanese film industry was unable to reliably support new talent. The deterioration of Japan's studio system throughout the 1960s and 70s curtailed the apprenticeship opportunities that new filmmakers had previously relied upon to forge a career in film. Traditionally, new filmmakers joined a major studio as an apprentice, learned the craft from more experienced personnel and worked up to the role of 'director' over several years (as had been the case for the previously mentioned directors Ozu and Ichikawa). However, these apprenticeship pathways had mostly disappeared by the 1970s as studios either downsized, declared bankruptcy (like Daiei did in 1971) or prioritised distribution instead. As such, '[the] main sites for relevant training were moved out of the film industry [. . .] and into adjacent industries and alternative cultural spaces – into soft-porn production and jishu-eiga [. . .], as well as the TV advertising industry' (Tezuka 2013, 171).[2] Something that self-made filmmaking offered over other alternatives, such as soft-porn (known in Japan as *pinku-eiga* or pink film) and TV advertising, was the instantaneity and accessibility promised by the new sound Super 8 format, which had simplified the technicalities of the medium to the point where almost anybody could use film as a means of self-expression without the need for extensive training or an expensive studio infrastructure.

As such, rather than turn to the film industry for training and development opportunities, many self-made filmmakers instead turned to cinema itself, absorbing the conventions of their favourite and newly discovered films, directors and genres. Many self-made filmmakers who operated in the 1970s and 1980s tended to be highly cine-literate, partly fuelled by them having greater access to a broader range of films than had previous generations. Television and a nascent home-video market provided ancillary options for movie-viewing beyond regular cinemas, and the Art Theatre Guild, as well as a growing number of independently operated *meigaza* (repertory cinemas) and *minishiatā* (mini theatres), promulgated a diverse film culture that also screened non-Japanese productions. To navigate this plethora of viewing options, those in Japan's largest cities used information magazines to find out which films were playing and where. For example: Tokyo had *Pia* and *City Road*, Osaka had *Play Guide Journal* and Nagoya had the unrelated *Nagoya Play Guide Journal*. All of these began publication in the early 1970s and were essential for circulating screening information in the pre-internet era.

Therefore, many embryonic efforts by self-made filmmakers during this time tended to be imitative of their cinematic tastes, be it foreign or domestic, studio or independent, arthouse or grindhouse. The early films of Ōmori Kazuki, whose much-admired 8mm works from the turn of the 1970s helped lay the groundwork for Japan's self-made film scene, reportedly 'displayed the influence of Jean-Luc Godard' (Jacoby 2008, 237), with Ōmori himself singling out Godard's *2 or 3 Things I Know About Her* (*Deux ou trois choses que je sais d'elle*, 1967) as the film that began his obsession with the filmmaker (1978, 9). Conversely, Tsukamoto Shin'ya's earliest 8mm short, *Mr. Primitive* (*Genshi-san*, 1974), made when he was just fourteen years old, was effectively an homage to the *daikaijū-eiga* (giant monster films) of his childhood (including the *Godzilla* and *Gamera* film series), showing a giant caveman (played by Tsukamoto's school friend) wreaking havoc on a (model) city (Mes 2005a, 21). Early self-made works by Kurosawa Kiyoshi (five years Tsukamoto's senior and then a university student) were shaped by contemporary American films such as director Don Seigel's *Dirty Harry* (1971). This applies to films such as Kurosawa's early 8mm short *Teacher of Violence: Massacre in Broad Daylight* (*Bōryoku kyōshi: Harachū daisatsuriku*, 1975), about a group of delinquent students attempting an armed takeover of their university campus that, in the director's words, took place in a 'Dirty Harry world' (Kurosawa 2006, 16–17).[3] In a 2006 interview, Nagasaki Shun'ichi acknowledged that many of his early self-made films were him 'imitating films that I liked' (Stephens and Mes 2006), which included the rough-and-ready action/exploitation films produced by Nikkatsu and Tōei, such as Itō Shun'ya's *Female Prisoner 701: Scorpion* (*Joshū Nana-maru-ichi Gō / Sasori*, 1972). There were also cases of self-made filmmakers producing unabashed fan films. The long-running *tokusatsu* (special effects) TV property *Ultraman* was an especially popular target of homage for aspiring filmmakers. A young Ichisei Takashige (now an accomplished film producer) made *Ultra Q No. 29 – The Darkness is Coming* (*Urutorakyū No. 29 'yami ga kuru!'*, 1979), an unauthorised twenty-ninth 'episode' of the twenty-eight-episode long TV series *Ultra Q* (1966), shot on 8mm. Elsewhere, a young Anno Hideaki wrote, directed and starred in *Return of Ultraman* (*Kaettekita Utoraman*, 1983), a short 8mm fan film based on *Ultra Q*'s follow-up series *Ultraman* (1966–1967).[4]

In many ways, this process of imitation represents its own form of DIY film remaking – one in which young, inexperienced filmmakers professed their filmmaking desires by attempting their own version of a piece of professional media.[5] While such imitation could be considered derivative, this process helped self-made filmmakers get a handle on conventional cinematic strategies (such as genre tropes and particular camera techniques). In other words, while self-made filmmaking represented a new form of authentic and direct filmmaking expression (a mode wherein filmmakers could pick up an easy-to-use 8mm camera and just 'do it yourself'), the tendency of many filmmakers toward imitation not only fed into their expression but ultimately became beneficial for their professional development as the industry began to take notice. In the case of Ishii Sōgo, this process of remaking the conventions of professional films in his first self-made short *Panic High School* led to the unique opportunity of remaking it for a major studio. In doing so, it became instructive to other self-made filmmakers also looking to make the same jump into professional film production.

ISHII SŌGO'S *PANIC HIGH SCHOOL*: FROM SELF-MADE TO REMADE

Born in Fukuoka in 1957, Ishii was a teenager when sync-sound Super 8 cameras changed what was possible for self-made filmmaking during the mid-1970s. He recalled: 'When I was in my third year of high school, Japan's 8mm equipment greatly advanced, and that innovation gave me hope that maybe I could use it to film movies' (Damiani 2020). In 1976, Ishii enrolled at the film department of Tokyo's Nihon University College of Art (abbreviated as Nichigei), which gave him access to filmmaking equipment. He also formed a self-made filmmaking club with former high school classmate Ōya Ryūji (who enrolled at Meiji University), calling it Kyōeisha (roughly meaning 'crazy film group'). According to Ishii, the name was meant as a pun on the film studio Tōei (Murakami 2007, 29). Like fellow Nichigei student Nagasaki Shun'ichi, Ishii was similarly drawn to Tōei's contemporary action cinema, particularly yakuza films such as Fukusaku Kinji's *Street Mobster* (*Gendai Yakuza: Hitokiri Yota*, 1972) and *Battles Without Honor and Humanity* (*Jingi Naki Tatakai*, 1973). He also had an interest in New Hollywood, with Dennis Hopper's *Easy Rider* (1969), Sam Peckinpah's *The Wild Bunch* (1969) and William Friedkin's *The French Connection* (1971), among several others, regarded as being particularly influential on his early filmmaking sensibilities (Tanano and Kobayashi 2006, 55–62). When asked why he wanted to make 8mm films that were similar to films playing in theatres, Ishii jokingly replied, 'I didn't expect to make the same thing. I was trying to make something more interesting than that!' (Murakami 2007, 30).

Panic High School was Kyōeisha's first self-made film production, which was shot in a Fukuoka high school during summer vacation. A short work of around sixteen minutes, the narrative is driven by visual action, leaning into the filmmakers' financial and technological limitations: a disgruntled student turns up to class with a rifle and shoots his maths teacher dead. The school is then evacuated as police pursue the student through empty corridors and classrooms, leading to an exchange of gunfire and, finally, a tense standoff involving some remaining students as hostages. The protagonist is finally apprehended and taken away by police. Although exposition is sparse, the film serves as something of an indictment on the pressures faced by Japanese students while preparing for strenuous university entrance exams – an experience that was still fresh in Ishii's and Ōya's minds. Ishii recalled: 'I was talking with my classmate Ōya Ryūji: "Let's make an 8mm movie about the madness of trying to get into university"' (Murakami 2007, 29). However, in a director's statement for the film, Ishii stresses that '*Panic High School* is, first and foremost, an entertainment film' (Ishii 1977).

Panic High School caused a sensation within self-made film circles. It gained wider public and media interest after it participated in a self-made filmmaking competition hosted by *Maeda's Young Up* (*Maeda no yangu appu*, 1972–1977), a youth variety show featured on NET (now TV Asahi). The film was featured on the show in November 1976 (Tanano and Kobayashi 2006, 17), followed by a 'NET Young Up' screening event at the newly opened Image Forum cinematheque in February 1977, screening with eight other self-made films (including Kurosawa's above-mentioned *Teacher of Violence*). *Panic High School* was also a regular fixture at further *jishu jōei* (self-screening) events organised by Kyōeisha. As such, the film became something of an incendiary calling card not just for Ishii's talents as an aspiring director, but the talents of the self-made filmmaking scene at large.

However, what made *Panic High School* especially remarkable was its makers' earnest desire for professionalism. The film features dozens of actors, who play students and police officers (sourcing actors from amateur theatre troupes was a common tactic among self-made filmmakers). Kyōeisha also managed to acquire two real police uniforms to use as costumes (Anon. 2006), as well as a small camera dolly system to film tracking shots of students quietly working at their desks before the pandemonium of the shooting ensues. When asked about the dolly, Ishii responded, 'I saw it in a movie and thought about using it. I had watched at least a thousand movies since my third year of high school. It was as if how to make a film had entered me completely' (Murakami 2007, 30).

Despite its rickety 8mm presentation (such as imprecise camerawork, jerky frame rate, soft focus, blunt editing and indistinct on-location audio), Kyōeisha's attempt at making what was ostensibly a mini version of a professional action film was not lost on executives at Nikkatsu. Executives soon approached Ishii (then a 20-year-old, second-year university student) with a proposition that seems unthinkable today let alone in 1977: to remake *Panic High School* as a studio feature. For the past few years, Nikkatsu had mostly produced *roman porno* (ostensibly soft-porn/pink films made with studio-level resources) and was looking to re-enter mainstream film production, with a particular eye for youth movies (something the studio had excelled at in previous decades). As such, not only was *Panic High School* an early instance of self-made filmmakers transitioning into studio film production, but it also represents the first clear-cut example of a major studio seeking to co-opt talent from the self-made film community and re-enter mainstream film production with a 'pre-sold' narrative. As noted by Alexander Zahlten, 'What attracted Nikkatsu to Ishii's film was a kind of brand name. *Panic High School* was a film that had created a sensation that could be utilized by switching to a different mode of production and dissemination in order to capitalize on the youth audience' (2011, 85).

In an effort to recapture some of the self-made authenticity that made the 8mm film appealing in the first place, Nikkatsu envisioned its remake of *Panic High School* as a collaborative venture between Kyōeisha and the studio. Ishii was given the opportunity to co-direct the film, with Nikkatsu partnering him up with Sawada Yukihiro (one of the studio's veteran directors), and Ōya was appointed as one of the film's producers. Studio screenwriter Kōnami Fumio drafted a new script, one that gave the protagonist a clearer and more sympathetic motivation (his actions are now in response to the school's lack of compassion when a classmate commits suicide over exam pressures). Other Kyōeisha members were also invited to join the production, including Matsui Yoshihiko as an assistant director and Itō Toshiaki as part of the camera team. The group as a whole received the credit of 'Seisaku Kyōryoku' ('Production Co-operation'), as seen during the film's end credits. Promotional literature for the remake also stressed the collaborative nature of its production. Sawada's director's statement for the film's promotional pamphlet warmly speaks of how the partnership between Nikkatsu and Kyōeisha 'bridges the gap' between the studio and Japan's youth, adding that 'the young talent of Ishii and Ōya from Kyōeisha give strength to the film and is the key to its success' (Sawada 1978).

Figure 4.1 The student gunman goes in for the kill in *Panic High School* (*Kōkō dai panikku*, 1976) and its 1978 studio-produced remake.

However, the reality of this collaboration was far from harmonious, with numerous clashes reported to have occurred on set between Kyōeisha's members and Nikkatsu's crew (Tanano and Kobayashi 2006, 18). Matsui recalled that Ishii was only allowed to direct certain scenes,[6] with Sawada handling the bulk of directing himself. Most of the original film's rough DIY energy was smoothed out by homogenised professional studio practice, although a scene in which terrified students rush down a stairwell as the armed protagonist fights his way up evokes the visual chaos of the 8mm version as the camera is placed in the thick of the action – 'It's one of the few scenes in the [remake] that I like', Ishii recalled (Mes 2005b). Ultimately, the project demonstrated that while self-made filmmakers were often infatuated with the results of professional studio production – to the point of attempting to remake its conventions within their own work – they were not so inclined when it came to its systemised procedures, finding it difficult to reconcile their autodidactic methods with that of an industrial production context. Ishii reflected:

> I thought watching a professional production would be helpful for my future. But instead I found it painful. Sawada Yukihiro was very kind in explaining how to use a professional film studio, but to be frank, I didn't think it was necessary. It's inexcusable, I know, but I just wasn't interested in such a forced system. I will do things my own way to the last (Murakami 2007, 31–2).

Returning to Zanger's dialectic of desire and fulfilment between a remake and its original, the original 8mm *Panic High School* represents a clear desire on the part of Ishii (and its crew of self-made filmmakers) to carve out a successful career in film production, evidenced by the fact that not only did its making display great ambition, but those ambitions were realised by imitating the conventions of studio-produced genre films. However, its remake proved insufficient in terms of fulfilling those desires. While it gave Ishii the opportunity to engage with genre conventions within its typical, studio-bound production context, the professional reality of studio film production clashed with the expectations created by his amateur attempt at professionalisation when making the original self-made film.

Ishii subsequently disowned the remake of *Panic High School*, despite it being a perfectly serviceable studio feature (he does not list the film on his official website, for example).[7] However, this experience did prove strangely motivating for him, as he recalled: 'I was so angry at the Nikkatsu producers for essentially pushing me out of my own film, that I wanted to show them what I was capable of on my own' (Mes 2005b). This resulted in the feature-length self-made film *Crazy Thunder Road* (*Kuruizaki Sandā Rōdo*, 1980). Originally intended as Ishii's Nichigei graduation film, Kyōeisha managed to secure some funding from a *meigaza* called the Kamiita Tōei Cinema (Domenig 2005, 15). This allowed Ishii to shoot on 16mm, a format that was suitable for theatrical projection. The film is about *bōsōzoku* biker-gangs, culminating in a spectacular showdown between the protagonist and a coalition of bikers that have turned against him. Like the original *Panic High School*, the DIY spectacle of *Crazy Thunder Road* immediately drew interest when Kyōeisha began showing it at various self-organised screening events. It soon attracted the attention of another studio, Tōei, which offered to buy the film, blow it up to 35mm and give it a nationwide release. When asked whether he was hesitant about working with another studio, Ishii remarked, '*Crazy Thunder Road* was a different case. I made it entirely the way I wanted to make it, so if Tōei wanted to distribute the film, I was very happy to have them do so' (Mes 2005b). In doing so, Tōei preserved the authentic aesthetics of Ishii's micro-budget self-made filmmaking instead of trying to studio-ize them like Nikkatsu had done with its *Panic High School* remake.

This situation, then, presented the fulfilment that had not been directly attained during the remaking of *Panic High School*, allowing Ishii to showcase his DIY filmmaking skills without interference while also being able to utilise the distribution and marketing apparatus of a major studio. Despite its origins as a student film, *Crazy Thunder Road* was both a critical and commercial success, paving the way for Ishii to direct further features with major companies, including *Burst City* (*Bakuretsu toshi*, 1982) (funded and distributed by Tōei) and *The Crazy Family* (*Gyaku funsha kazoku*, 1984) (co-produced by the Art Theatre Guild). Ishii 'graduating from underground 8mm filmmaking to the professional film industry', a process that began with him remaking *Panic High School*, set a 'precedent that would be followed by numerous young directors in the two decades that followed' (Mes and Sharp 2005, 68), thus demonstrating that their professional desires could be fulfilled regardless of the seemingly disadvantageous state of the film industry. Yamamoto Masashi, another self-made filmmaker, once stated, 'I thought: Ishii is a fool. But if he could get a movie out like that – I could too. I could do it better' (Hunter 1998, 190).

Another one of those young directors was Tsukamoto Shin'ya, who was a first-year Nichigei student when the *Panic High School* remake was released in 1978. Tsukamoto recalled that Ishii's leap from amateur to professional filmmaker garnered 'fame and admiration' among his fellow students (Mes 2005a, 40). Having made several 8mm films since 1974, and recognising the 'tremendous flow from self-made films to theatrical films' that had been galvanised by Ishii's efforts (Tsukamoto quoted in Lindy Hop Studios 2006, 53), Tsukamoto embarked upon a similar process that eventually resulted in what arguably remains his most famous work, *Tetsuo: The Iron Man*. This process was defined by a similar desire-fulfilment dialectic between *Tetsuo* and Tsukamoto's earlier, lesser-known 8mm film *The Phantom of Regular Size*.

TSUKAMOTO SHIN'YA'S *TETSUO: THE IRON MAN* AND ITS *PHANTOM* PRECURSOR

Tetsuo: The Iron Man (1989) is something of a landmark in the annals of Japanese film history, taking the international film world by surprise after it won Best Film at the 1989 FantaFestival (a genre film festival held in Rome since 1981). *Tetsuo* is a surreal, low-budget body horror film about a salaryman (Taguchi Tomorowo) who transforms into a grotesque scrap metal monster (becoming the 'Tetsuo' – meaning 'iron man' – of the film's title). He inadvertently kills his girlfriend (Fujiwara Kei) with his mechanised penis, which has transformed into a power drill, referred to by Tsukamoto as '*chin chin doriru*', or 'penis drill' (Eater Editorial Department 2002, 55). He then clashes with a superpowered 'metal fetishist' (played by Tsukamoto), who is revealed to be the orchestrator of his metamorphosis. The film ends with them assimilating into a large biomechanical vehicle that sets off to create a 'new world' in their image.

Tetsuo's striking use of handmade practical and costume effects, together with erratic pixilation (stop-motion animation of human subjects) that allows its cyborg characters to glide along desolate Tokyo streets at high velocities, and pounding industrial music made it one of the most original films to emerge from Japan in many years, while also evoking North American cult and horror cinema such as Sam Raimi's *The Evil Dead* (1981) and David Cronenberg's *Videodrome* (1983) and *The Fly* (1986). Shot on grainy 16mm monochrome film, its production was lengthy, arduous and entirely self-funded, with Tsukamoto investing five million yen of his personal savings to make it (Japan Home Video later supplied about eight million yen in completion funds) (Persons 1993, 51–2). In doing so, the film was not a compromised product of the old studio system in the same way that Ishii's remake of *Panic High School* had been. As noted by Tom Mes, 'Rather than being built on the remnants of the past, [*Tetsuo*] gave Japanese cinema a future. As such, we can safely call the film a watershed' (2005a, 10).

However, what many did not realise at the time was that *Tetsuo*'s scenario of man-machine assimilation, as well as some of its most striking DIY filmmaking techniques, had been explored earlier by Tsukamoto in a short film called *The Phantom of Regular Size* (1986) (henceforth *Phantom*), which features the same basic storyline as *Tetsuo*. Like *Tetsuo*, *Phantom* features a transforming salaryman who kills his girlfriend, again with his 'penis drill', and is then tormented by an antagonist with whom he finally assimilates. The film features the same main cast, with Taguchi, Fujiwara and Tsukamoto playing the same characters they went on to play in *Tetsuo*. Tsukamoto once described the two films as being part of 'one idea' (Eater Editorial Department 2002, 55).

These similarities seemingly mark *Tetsuo* out as a feature-length remake of *Phantom*. However, unlike Ishii's original *Panic High School*, *Phantom* had not been widely seen. It was one of 611 self-made films submitted to the 1987 Pia Film Festival, but was not selected. As such, *Phantom*'s obscurity meant that *Tetsuo* was not perceived as a 'pre-sold' narrative when it was unleashed on audiences, especially those outside Japan, who would have been mostly oblivious to self-made film culture. The only time the two films had been put into any kind of dialogue by that point was when Tsukamoto's next (and last) 8mm film *The Adventure of Denchu Kozo* (*Denchū kozō no bōken*, 1987; henceforth *Denchu Kozo*) won the Grand Prix at the 1988 Pia Film Festival. Pia's subsequent public screenings of *Denchu Kozo* included *Phantom* as a supporting short and a trailer for *Tetsuo*, which Tsukamoto had just completed (Mes 2005a, 46).

A direct comparison between *Phantom* and *Tetsuo* reveals a similar dialectic of desire and fulfilment previously discussed in relation to Ishii's *Panic High School* films. While *Phantom*'s quickly produced, experimental nature means that it plays out more like a collection of loose visual ideas rather than a coherent narrative, certain elements are replicated wholesale in *Tetsuo*, most notably a scene in which the salaryman (now mostly transformed) is taunted by Tsukamoto's antagonist character over the phone. In both films this is shot in medium close-up. The camera repeatedly jolts left and right, throwing Taguchi's tormented (and heavily made-up) face from one side of the frame to the other as he holds the receiver to his ear.

There are also elements in *Phantom* that are not only replicated in *Tetsuo* but 'improved', especially in terms of the visceral excesses for which *Tetsuo* would become infamous. This includes *Tetsuo*'s most gruesome scene: Fujiwara being killed by the salaryman's 'penis drill'. After passing out from a stab wound inflicted by Fujiwara in self-defence, the salaryman wakes up to find her riding his 'penis drill', with copious amounts of blood (rendered a glistening black by the monochrome film stock) spraying up the curtains behind

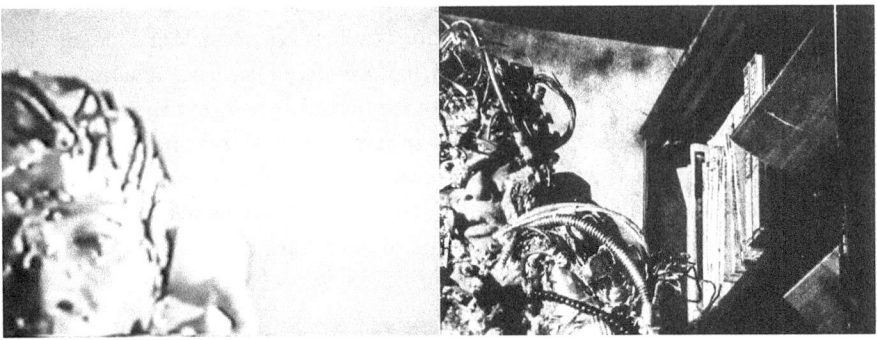

Figure 4.2 A lurching camera moves the salaryman from side to side as he receives a phone call from the 'metal fetishist' in *The Phantom of Regular Size* (*Futsū saizu no kaijin*, 1986) and *Tetsuo* (1989).

her. According to Tsukamoto, the extreme goriness of this scene was a direct response to its counterpart scene in *Phantom*, which plays out with minimal blood due to disorganisation during the shoot (Eater Editorial Department 2002, 55). As such, the desires expressed by the making of *Phantom* are thus fulfilled by the making of *Tetsuo*, giving Tsukamoto another chance to realise his ambitions with a little more experience and better production value afforded by the larger film format, more sophisticated costumes and props (albeit still handmade), more fake blood and a longer shoot. Principal photography for *Tetsuo* lasted four months (Persons 1993, 52). *Phantom*, by contrast, was shot in 'four or five days, maybe less' (Tsukamoto quoted in Mes 2005a: 39).

However, by delving a little deeper into Tsukamoto's rationale for making both films, I argue that the desire-fulfilment dialectic of self-made film remakes can also manifest in reverse. Tsukamoto intended *Tetsuo* as an 'entertainment film' (quoted in Lindy Hop Studios 2006, 55) (echoing Ishii's feelings toward the 8mm version of *Panic High School*), despite the film's subsequent reputation as a gruesome cult classic. This partly influenced his decision to shoot the film on 16mm rather than 8mm, for, as he recalled, 'if I made a 16mm film, it would be fit for theatrical screening. To all intents and purposes, I could call it a real movie. It was a step up from self-made independent films' (Mes 2005a, 49). However, when Tsukamoto began devising the 'iron man' concept that eventually became *Tetsuo*, he had not directed a self-made film for several years. Instead, his interests had turned to staging amateur theatre productions via his own theatre troupe Kaijū Shiatā (Sea Monster Theatre), which included Taguchi and Fujiwara. Since graduating from Nichigei in 1982, he had also gained employment in the advertising industry. Shooting TV commercials for numerous brands, Tsukamoto began experimenting with faster, discontinuous editing styles. This included jump cuts and a rudimentary stop-motion animation effect that later developed into the volatile pixilation technique used in *Tetsuo*. Tsukamoto's iteration of pixilation differed somewhat from past filmmakers who had popularised the technique (such as Norman McLaren and Jan Švankmajer) in that his was achieved with a non-fixed camera: an actor stands in the street and a single frame is photographed. As the actor moves forward and reposes, the camera also moves a similar distance and another frame is then taken. The process is repeated over and over, resulting in a frenetic visual effect that Tsukamoto describes in the Japanese documentary *Basic Tsukamoto* (2003) as 'like riding a rollercoaster'. This was in stark contrast to the style of his earlier 8mm films, which he also describes in *Basic Tsukamoto* as being 'very static' and 'one scene with one cut'.

The new techniques developed by Tsukamoto with his advertising work rekindled his interest in filmmaking, leading him to quit his job in 1986. As Tsukamoto explains, 'At first, I wanted to experiment with stop motion, but it was a mess because I hadn't practiced [filmmaking] for a while' (Eater Editorial Department 2002, 54–5). Therefore, rather than launch straight into making a 'real movie', Tsukamoto returned to the world of 8mm self-made films and began work on *Phantom*, referring to it as an 'experiment' and 'practice' for *Tetsuo* (Eater Editorial Department 2002, 55). As such, this was not just an opportunity for him to experiment with story ideas for his 'iron man' film concept, many of which were then reused in *Tetsuo*, but to revive and update his existing filmmaking skills. The pixilation technique seen in *Tetsuo* was utilised in *Phantom* for the first time. While the disjointed frame-by-frame effect appears fully formed, there is uncertainty as to its role within the internal logic of the film's narrative. It is most notably used to depict the salaryman (prior to any visible transformation) being chased by a mysterious woman with a cybernetic hand (Kanaoka Nobu, another actor from Tsukamoto's theatre troupe), implying that the early stages of metallic transformation give characters the ability to move like superhuman vehicles. However, *Phantom* also uses pixilation to animate time-lapse-style shots of the Japanese general public, which presumably do not have the same locomotive powers as Taguchi's and Kanaoka's characters. Parts of their chase take place on busy streets, resulting in dozens of pixilated bodies on screen at times, creating further visual confusion. 'I wasn't really trying to clearly express an idea or a viewpoint with *Phantom*', Tsukamoto admitted, 'the exercise and the experimentation aspect were more important to me when I made it' (Mes 2005a, 40). In *Tetsuo*, this ambiguity of narrative purpose has been rectified, with Tsukamoto limiting pixilation to moments of travel and transformation involving metallic characters, such as Taguchi's salaryman, Kanaoka's 'Woman in Glasses' (reprising her role from *Phantom*) and Tsukamoto's 'metal fetishist'. To avoid confusion, their chase scenes are shot in empty streets within the industrial and suburban sprawls of Tokyo. As such, pixilation in *Tetsuo* became a low-cost yet visually spectacular way to demonstrate the superhuman abilities of these posthuman characters, which became a selling point for the film upon its release as well as a recurring talking point for critics (for an overview of the film's UK critical reaction, see Conrich 2005, 97–8).

This reading of the two films allows for a reversal of the desire-fulfilment dialectic. For Tsukamoto, the desire was to make *Tetsuo* – a 'real movie' – from the outset, after having shot numerous self-made 8mm films during the 1970s and having then moved on to work in other media (theatre and TV advertising). However, lacking the necessary experience to execute the DIY special effects sequences necessary for his 'iron man' story, he returned to self-made filmmaking to produce what was ostensibly a 'test film' in the form of *Phantom*, with many of its elements then repeated in *Tetsuo*. In doing so, making *Phantom* brought about the fulfilment of skills and confidence necessary to then make *Tetsuo*, a production that came at great personal financial risk for Tsukamoto.

As such, the desire-fulfilment dialectic found within self-made films and their remakes is not necessarily a linear process in which desire precedes fulfilment. Likewise, the relationship between *Tetsuo* and its *Phantom* precursor also subverts the 'one-way process' that, as previously noted by Verevis, is typically ascribed to remakes: a process that moves 'from authenticity to imitation' (2006, 58). This one-way process can be applied to Ishii's *Panic High School* films, whereby a studio sought to capture the authenticity of the original 8mm film only to result in a professional imitation that Ishii no longer recognised as his own work, although this is complicated somewhat by the first *Panic High School* also being an imitation of studio films (including those made by Hollywood directors). In Tsukamoto's case, *Tetsuo* is not so much an imitation of *Phantom* but rather *Phantom* imitates the desires Tsukamoto had for *Tetsuo*, which points towards a 'more open-ended intertextuality' also mentioned by Verevis. This open-endedness is possible because Tsukamoto had complete control over the making of both films (whereas Ishii did not), allowing for a more natural dialogue to occur between them. This can also be seen in the other *Tetsuo* films Tsukamoto went on to produce, including *Tetsuo II: Body Hammer* (1992), which is viewed more as a 'continuous growth of an idea begun in the first film' (Conrich 2005, 98) rather than an outright sequel, and a belated *Tetsuo: The Bullet Man* (2009), which operates along similar lines to *Body Hammer* in this respect. All three films (four including *Phantom*) chart a gradual evolution of repeated narratives and aesthetic variations, again made possible by Tsukamoto's continued status as an independent within the Japanese film industry.

To conclude, both cases highlighted in this chapter demonstrate the ways in which self-made filmmakers during the 1970s and 80s operated within a dialectic of desire and fulfilment. First, they orientated their amateur film practice by ostensibly remaking the conventions of professional films; and, second – in the cases of Ishii and Tsukamoto – they remade their own films to gain a foothold within the Japanese film industry. This process bore mixed results for Ishii, who felt unfulfilled by his professional remake of *Panic High School* but whose example fuelled the professional desires of many other self-made filmmakers; and positive results for Tsukamoto, whose *Tetsuo*, made possible by previous 8mm experiments, exposed this generation of Japanese filmmaking to an international audience. These cases also demonstrate that this dialectic of desire and fulfilment can occur in parallax: in Ishii's case, professional desire led to DIY fulfilment (eventually achieved with the making of *Crazy Thunder Road*, which had been spurred on by his negative experience remaking *Panic High School*); in Tsukamoto's case, DIY fulfilment acts as a springboard to realising professional desires. As such, a malleable back and forth exists between these two positions within Japanese self-made filmmakers, especially those on the cusp of professionalisation, seemingly operating in a continuous feedback loop of desire, fulfilment, authenticity and imitation in both their amateur and early professional films.

NOTES

1. Ichikawa's final film, *The Inugamis* (*Inugami-ke no Ichizoku*, 2006), was also a self-remake – a reworking of his own production of the same title from 1976 (given the slightly different English title *The Inugami Family* upon its international release).
2. There was also the Yokohama Academy of Film and Broadcasting (Yokohama Hōsō Eiga Senmon Gakuin) – now known as the Japan Institute of the Moving Image (Nihon Eiga Daigaku) – which began in 1975. However, places were expensive and limited.
3. This, and all quotations from Japanese sources, have been translated into English by the author.
4. Anno went on to write and produce *Shin Ultraman* (2022), directed by Higuchi Shinji: a modern live-action blockbuster reimaging of the classic *Ultraman* TV show.
5. The phenomenon of fan productions has long been included in the ever-widening field of film remakes. See Loock and Verevis (2012).
6. This was communicated to me by Matsui Yoshihiko via an email exchange on 16 December 2018.
7. Ishii Sōgo's official website can be found at www.ishiisogo-gakuryu.com (last accessed 25 January 2023).

REFERENCES

Anon. 2006. 'Special Feature for Panic High School.' *Sōgo Ishii Sakuhin-shū DVD BOX 1— PUNK YEARS 1976–1983* [*Sōgo Ishii Collected Works DVD-BOX 1: PUNK YEARS 1976–1983*] [DVD supplements]. Tokyo: Transformer.
Conrich, Ian. 2005. 'Metal-Morphosis: Post-Industrial Crisis and the Tormented Body in the *Tetsuo* Films.' In *Japanese Horror Cinema*. Edited by Jay McRoy, 95–106. Edinburgh: Edinburgh University Press.
Damiani, Matteo. 2020. 'Interview with Gakuryū Ishii (Sogo Ishii).' *Retrofuturisto*, 25 August. https://retrofuturista.com/interview-with-gakuryu-ishii-sogo-ishii. Accessed 25 January 2023.
Desser, David. 2017. '"Crazed Heat": Nakahira Kō and the Transnational Self-Remake.' In *Transnational Film Remakes*. Edited by Iain Robert Smith and Constantine Verevis, 164–76. Edinburgh: Edinburgh University Press.
Dew, Oliver. 2020. 'The Archive. Screening Locality: Japanese Home Movies and the Politics of Place.' In *The Japanese Cinema Book*. Edited by Hideaki Fujiki and Alastair Phillips, 214–27. London: British Film Institute.
Domenig, Roland. 2005. 'A Brief History of Independent Cinema in Japan and the Role of the Art Theatre Guild.' *MINIKOMI: Austrian Journal of Japanese Studies* 70: 6–16.
Eater Editorial Department, eds. 2002. *Mūbī pankusu* [*Movie Punks*]. Tokyo: Telegraph Factory.
Hunter, Jack. 1998. *Eros in Hell: Sex, Blood and Madness in Japanese Cinema*. London: Creation Books.

Ishii, Sōgo. 1977. 'Kantoku kara.' ['From the Director.'] In *Kyōeisha hataage jōeikai* [*Kyōeisha Launch Screening*] [screening booklet]. Fukuoka: Kyōeisha, not paginated. Text reprinted in Tanano, Naoto and Kobayashi Ginti, (eds. 2006. 'Age of Rage.' In *Sōgo Ishii Sakuhin-shū DVD-BOX 1—PUNK YEARS 1976–1983* [*Sōgo Ishii Collected Works DVD-BOX 1: PUNK YEARS 1976–1983*]. DVD booklet, Tokyo: Transformer, 53.

Jacoby, Alexander. 2008. *A Critical Handbook of Japanese Film Directors: From the Silent Era to the Present Day*. Berkeley: Stonebridge Press.

Kurosawa, Kiyoshi. 2006. *The Film Art of Kurosawa Kiyoshi* [*Kurosawa Kiyoshi no eigajutsu*]. Tokyo: Shinchōsha.

Lindy Hop Studios, eds. 2006. *Alternative Movies in Japan: Nihon eiga no panku jidai 1975–1987* [*Alternative Movies in Japan: Japanese Film from the Punk Era, 1975–1987*]. Tokyo: Aiko Co., Ltd.

Loock, Kathleen and Constantine Verevis. eds. 2012. *Film Remakes, Adaptations and Fan Productions*. Basingstoke: Palgrave Macmillan.

Mes, Tom. 2005a. *Iron Man: The Cinema of Shinya Tsukamoto*. Guilford: FAB Press.

Mes, Tom. 2005b. 'Sogo Ishii.' *Midnight Eye*, 15 June. http://www.midnighteye.com/interviews/sogo-ishii-2. Accessed 25 January 2023.

Mes, Tom and Jasper Sharp. 2005. *The Midnight Eye Guide to New Japanese Film*. Berkeley: Stonebridge Press.

Murakami, Kenji. 2007. 'Ishii Sōgo intabyū' ['Ishii Sōgo Interview']. In *Hotwax: Nihon no eiga to rokku to kayōkyoku Vol. 7* [*Hotwax: Japanese Films, Rock and Pop Songs, vol. 7*]. Edited by Maeda Masahiro and Saotome Masako. Tokyo: Ultra Vibe, 28–37.

Ōmori, Kazuki. 1978. *Making of Orenji rōdo kyūkō* [*The Making of Orange Road Express*]. Tokyo: Pia Books.

Persons, Dan. 1993. 'Tetsuo: The Iron Man.' *Cinefantastique* 23, no. 5: 51–2.

Player, Mark. 2021. 'Uto*Pia*: An Early History of Pia and its Role in Japan's "Self-Made" Film Culture.' *Japan Forum*, DOI: 10.1080/09555803.2021.1895283.

Sawada, Yukihiro. 1978. Untitled director's statement, in *Kōkō dai panniku* [*Panic High School*]. Film pamphlet, Tokyo: Nikkatsu, not paginated.

Sharp, Jasper. 2011. *Historical Dictionary of Japanese Cinema*. Lanham: Scarecrow Press.

Stephens, Chuck and Tom Mes. 2006. 'Shunichi Nagasaki.' *Midnight Eye*, 8 June. http://www.midnighteye.com/interviews/shunichi-nagasaki-2/. Accessed 25 January 2023.

Tanano, Naoto and Kobayashi Ginti, (eds. 2006. 'Age of Rage.' In *Sōgo Ishii Sakuhin-shū DVD-BOX 1—PUNK YEARS 1976–1983* [*Sogo Ishii Collected Works DVD-BOX 1: PUNK YEARS 1976–1983*]. DVD booklet, Tokyo: Transformer.

Tezuka, Yoshiharu. 2013. 'Dynamics of the Cultures of Discontent: How Is Globalization Transforming the Training of Filmmakers in Japan?' In *The Education of the Filmmaker in Europe, Australia and Asia*. Edited by Mette Hjort, 171–88. Basingstoke: Palgrave Macmillan.

Verevis, Constantine. 2006. *Film Remakes*. Edinburgh: Edinburgh University Press.

Zahlten, Alexander. 2011. 'Free-Floating Intensity, Attraction and Failure: Ishii Sōgo/Gakuryū at the Shifting Center of the Film Industry of Japan.' *Cineforum* 13: 79–95.

Zanger, Anat. 2006. *Film Remakes as Ritual and Disguise: From Carmen to Ripley*. Amsterdam: Amsterdam University Press.

Part II
Serialising Ozu: The Enduring Legacy of a Cinematic 'Tofu Maker'

CHAPTER 5

Definition and Progression: Ozu Yasujirō's 'Noriko Trilogy'

Alastair Phillips

In his influential discussion of 'the Noriko Trilogy', a sequence of post-war films directed by Ozu Yasujirō and starring Hara Setsuko as the trilogy's eponymous female lead, Robin Wood argues that what unites the otherwise loose affiliation of *Late Spring* (*Banshun*, 1949), *Early Summer* (*Bakushū*, 1951) and *Tokyo Story* (*Tōkyō monogatari*, 1953) is the notion of any 'resistance to definition' (1998, 94). For Wood, the idea of 'definition' refers uniquely to the issue of the films' complex projection of Noriko's subjectivity and the articulation of female desire within a generic structure that ultimately denies her full agency. This chapter pursues the matter of Ozu's projection of feminine agency across the three films, but also returns to a more foundational question concerning 'definition'. What does it mean precisely to define these films retrospectively as a 'trilogy'? What are the aesthetic and political consequences of considering this set of films in sole relation to the recurring name of a character played by their central female star? Is it possible to read the films in relation to each other in other mutually informing ways that continue to be critically meaningful in the context of recent scholarship on the politics of film trilogies? By opening up these issues, especially in relation to the subject of mobility on both a textual and contextual level, this chapter thus aims to shed new light on the complex ways in which Ozu's interest in pattern, repetition and difference operated at this transitional moment in popular Japanese cinema.

Of course, the very notion of a screen trilogy is in itself a mobile concept and, to this extent, Wood's definition of a screen trilogy, at least to some degree, matches one of the variations proposed by Claire Perkins and Constantine Verevis in their foundational work on the topic. Perkins and Verevis's notion of 'authorial remaking' argues for a specific form of attention 'to the repetition of themes, settings, styles, characters, and actors' that may occur across a set of three films directed by a single director in ways that can be said to typically constitute an 'authorial vision' (2012, 12). Ozu's work fits the bill on a number of levels, not least because his singular filmmaking method involves such a visibly recognisable set of distinctive stylistic attributes that his mode of looking is visible in every single frame of the films in question.[1] The issue of mobility here is, therefore, less one of whether Ozu moves his camera or not – he rarely does in the trilogy – but what his gaze specifically enables. For Wood, the central thematic or narrative concern of the films – what he calls 'the mainspring of the first two' and 'of secondary but increasing importance in *Tokyo Story*' – lies in 'the pressures put on Noriko to marry (or in *Tokyo Story* to remarry, and her resistance to this)' (1998, 114). This predicament is articulated across the three films in such a consistently fluid and dynamic fashion that it not only becomes possible to read each film in terms of their singular presentation of three different women with the same name played by the same actress, but also in terms of the evolution of an authorial 'value system' that Wood suggests actually 'invite[s] us . . . to become the Noriko of *Tokyo Story*' (Ibid., 112).

Putting aside the problematic question of spectatorial engagement at this level, Wood's emphasis on progression has enormous significance for how we may wish to proceed in terms of reading these three films as constituent parts of a trilogy. In the first two films, Noriko is a young single woman – twenty-seven years old and twenty-eight years old, respectively – living at home in Kita Kamakura, the northern middle-class neighbourhood of the coastal town of Kamakura, once briefly the capital of Japan. In *Late Spring*, she lives alone with her elderly father Professor Somiya (Ryū Chishū) and spends her time socialising with friends, visiting Tokyo (an hour or so away) and generally tending to her parents' domestic requirements in a lively, warm-hearted and solicitous fashion. She has no independent income, and the film ends with her decision to yield to her father and aunt's slightly furtive machinations to get her to marry a suitor prepared for her. The nexus of the family house is intensified in *Early Summer*; this time there are more family members living together, including Noriko's grandparents and her brother, his wife and their two boys. Importantly, at the same time, Noriko's own social sphere is also extended to include a wider circle of female friends and a male office boss in central Tokyo. Her decision to marry is seen as more assertive, but nonetheless constraining, as the controversial choice she makes out of her two opposing suitors – a businessman in his forties and a widower with a young daughter – also results in the dissipation of a family network previously dependent on her salary. By the time of *Tokyo Story*, Noriko is working and living alone in the capital; she is also cut off from any blood ties as all the family members within the narrative of the film, including the visiting parents from the distant coastal town of Onomichi, are related to her husband, who was killed in the war. She firmly, if silently, rebuts the feeling offered by her in-laws that she should now consider remarrying.

The expansion of Noriko's social and geographical horizons within the narrative structure the trilogy, and the greater degree of spatial (and affective) mobility this enables also serves as a counterpart to a wider sense of the character's emerging agency. If Wood is right in stating that, despite variations in terms of age, family structure, marital status, employment and domestic arrangements, 'Noriko remains essentially the same character throughout', it is also possible to see the trilogy moving forward from 'the unqualified tragedy of *Late Spring*' (1998: 115) to the more hopeful and potentially enabling conclusion of *Tokyo Story*. Here, Noriko's burgeoning relationship with her unmarried sister-in-law, Kyōko (Kagawa Kyōko), articulates a more open-ended and progressive embodiment of Japan's post-war modernity, one in which the character of the younger, provincial schoolteacher is linked to the more worldly urban experience of her older female relative on various levels, including the motif of the train journey. Noriko's ability to adjust her emotional bearing when it comes to the requirements of both the older and younger generations in the film, seen in conjunction with her independent freedom of movement across rooms, neighbourhoods and even regions, marks her as a uniquely pivotal figure.

The Noriko trilogy in this sense complies with Perkins and Verevis's assertion that intertextuality should be understood as 'the key condition of the form' in that 'a director can simply – perhaps inadvertently – cast new scenarios in terms of earlier concerns' (2012, 10). The idea of 'authorial remaking, with specific attention to the repetition of themes, settings, styles, characters, and actors' (Ibid., 12) obviously applies here. Leaving aside the important question of Ozu's recurring script collaboration with Noda Kōgo – *Late Spring* marked the resumption of their working relationship after a gap of fourteen years – I now wish to concentrate on the final value in this list, that of the actor, and link this to the naming as Noriko as the title bearer of the trilogy. By choosing to distinguish the idea of the trilogy in terms of its central character, Wood was also clearly drawing attention to the singular performance register of the films' leading female star, Hara Setsuko. Indeed, if we are to consider the trilogy in terms of intertextuality, the most obvious place to look, apart from Ozu and his camera operator Atsuta Yuhara's distinctive formal style, is of that of the agile nature of Hara's star image and the means by which her acting, in conjunction with Ozu's direction, enables a sense of internal repetition and progression.

Hara had started working for Nikkatsu at the age of fifteen and made about a dozen films there between 1935 and 1937, before moving to Tōhō where she appeared in several important war propaganda features, such as Yamamoto Kajiro's *The War at Sea from Hawaii to Malaya* (*Hawai mare oki kaisen*, 1942). By the time of her appearance in September 1949 as the youthful female lead in Shōchiku's *Late Spring*, she was already very well-known to Japanese audiences for such roles as her performance as the spirited professor's daughter, Yukie, in Kurosawa Akira's *No Regrets for Our Youth* (*Waga seishun ni kuinashi*, 1946).

Hara also starred as the charismatic schoolteacher, Yukiko, in Tōhō's highly successful two-part series, *Blue Mountains* (*Aoi sanmyaku*, 1949), directed by Imai Tadashi and released that same summer. The actor's contained – but also, when required, highly expressive – facial features were a central part of her recurring star image, which projected an idealised contemporary image of Japanese femininity that was palatable to a mass audience at an important time of transition within the Japanese film industry during the years of the American Occupation. In the films of the trilogy, her eyes are carefully illuminated by Atsuta Yuhara to register a full range of fleeting, non-verbal emotional expressions, very often seen in conjunction with a discreet movement of the head or aversion of the glance. Of equal importance was her voice, which possessed a particularly agile timbre, always hinting at suppressed depths of feeling beyond the commonplace vocabulary of domestic exchange. Some of the most affecting moments in each film are when nothing is being said and Noriko is either shown looking offscreen or has her face clasped in her hands. As I have argued elsewhere, it was specifically 'through the [wider] specific interaction of female stardom and the representation of female space that the contestation between the seemingly irreconcilable elements of tradition' and post-war modernity was actively discussed in Japanese film of the time (Phillips 2003, 155). Based on the recurring presentation of her star features on the cover of popular print publications such as *Eiga fan*, this had a profound resonance with the female filmgoing public. As Catherine Russell has also pointed out, Hara's own marriage prospects were a recurring matter of discussion in numerous Japanese women's magazines throughout the years leading up to and encompassing the 'Noriko Trilogy' (2003, 37). There is thus a fascinating degree of synergy between the intensified projection of Hara's star image within and across the three films that, taken in conjunction with the recurrent naming of Noriko as the core protagonist of at least the first two, invites a more fluid reading of a trilogy based around the projection of a female-centred constellation of acting, genre, narrative, studio practice and audience reception.

I want to continue reflecting on the notion of Noriko's fluidity by thinking more specifically about how she is pictured as a figure of mobility in each of the three films. I shall do this by focusing on the dynamic interaction that she has with other female figures within the narrative of each film. My argument is thus based in part on the assumption that the more politicised tenets of the trilogy, as initially defined by Wood, are rendered most visible by looking at how the figure of Noriko is activated both within and across each film by other women. Noriko's central female friendship in *Late Spring*, for example, is with the more sexually experienced character of Aya, performed with sly vivacity and humour by Tsukioka Yumeji. In another example of the numerous echoes and repetitions across the three films, a very similar version of Aya resurfaces in *Early Summer*, played by Awashima Chikage. In one sequence, quite early on in *Late Spring*, we have an opportunity to observe Ozu's particular orchestration of female space and movement in counterpart to the more static codified body language of the older father. Aya is visiting the family home after having just attended a school reunion without Noriko and interacted with several of both her and Noriko's female former classmates. In a typical low two shot, we see Aya to the right and the father to the left of the frame, both seated on the floor of the traditional living room on the ground floor of the house. Noriko's voice is heard offscreen and Aya's head turns to the left. As she rises, Ozu cuts 180 degrees to present a fuller shot of the pair from the reverse side of the room. Aya's legs have stiffened during her conversation with Somiya and, as she struggles to stand upright and regain her modern sense of self, Noriko is seen instead buoyantly entering the room in a broad, almost playful, stride that intersects the shared gaze of the pair. The manner with which Hara moves into both the centre of the frame and the apex of this newly established triangular composition, not to mention her self-conscious presentation of a handbag clutched in front of her lower waist and a carefully controlled pause under the bright illumination of the central ceiling light, all announce a performative synergy between Noriko's arrival and the movement into the limelight of the star actress playing the role. The now mutually upright bodies of the two women meet, in counterpart to the darkened stillness of the father to the left, and Noriko stretches out her hand to Aya, suggesting the pair move upstairs. Their arms start swinging girlishly in unison and they retreat, still holding hands, to Noriko's quarters on the floor above.

Figure 5.1 Performative synergy in *Late Spring* (*Banshun*, 1949).

If one of the ways that the trilogy operates is to extend, either bit-by-bit or significantly, Noriko's spatial co-ordinates in order to delineate a broader sense of social subjectivity within the material and ideological contours of post-war Japan, this process of differentiation begins in the home of *Late Spring*. The film now cuts to an empty shot of Noriko's room in darkness before a light is turned on offscreen – the stage is set for the arrival of the two women, who run in with arms linked and laughing from the left of the frame. Instead of sitting on the floor, they have the option of taking up position on two diagonally situated cane chairs that thus enable a greater degree of both intimacy and modern individuation. A floral tablecloth completes the conventional domestic feminisation of the mise-en-scène. This is the spirited sense of gendered friendship and separation that Noriko is forced to relinquish by the conclusion of the film, and it is the memory of such freedom in terms of space, time and movement that reinforces the fixity and oppression conveyed by the literal weighing down of her body in the final heartbreaking wedding headwear scene. In his suggestive analysis of the film, Woojeong Joo notes that 'Noriko's cheerful movement around the house ... enlivens the otherwise static and precisely framed domestic space' and that, most importantly, this 'element of movement ... [is] fundamentally related to the articulation of femininity in the film' (2017, 158–9). This is certainly true here and indeed elsewhere in the film when, as Joo goes on to argue, various objects are called back and forth not just within the house itself but between Kita Kamakura and the metropolitan centre of Tokyo. To extend Joo's point, however, as I have already begun to suggest, there is clearly a sort of stage-like musicality to this articulation that is especially prominent in this particular sequence. At this point of Noriko's progression within the trilogy, her social mobility only exists within the terrain of a certain kind of performance that is recognised by both the manner of Ozu's staging and the degree of complicity and allegiance between the two women as they converse in the relative privacy of their own world apart. It is thus telling that when Somiya reappears upstairs, he interrupts the intimate flow of rapid cutting within which each female character is seen speaking to the other in medium close-up by a camera positioned centrally between them. The necessary return to a proscenium shot marks Somiya's kindly hospitality in bringing some bread and tea, but also his manifest inability to know exactly how to manage these domestic arrangements. It also comes on the heels on a humorous but pressing exchange between the two women over Noriko's feelings about marriage. Within this conjugation of shared laughter at both themselves and the father's minor domestic ineptitude also lie the seeds of the apple that the father peels alone in the very final passage of the film.

As if to bridge the first and second parts of the trilogy, *Early Summer* begins with a similar shot of the same waves at Kamakura that end *Late Spring*. This continuity in terms of imagery, shooting style and location serves to intensify the logic of a sequel; whilst as Wood points out, the decisions made to cast the surviving son of the family as a doctor named Koichi, have him be the father of two boys called Minoru and Isamu, and have the older parents' son (who was killed in the war) named Shoji also link *Early Summer* to the final part of the trilogy, *Tokyo Story* (2008, 114). If Shoji in the former is Noriko's dead brother, he then crucially becomes Noriko's dead husband in the latter; someone only glimpsed in the photograph that the parents gaze at within Noriko's city apartment on their visit. Koichi, of course, in turn, is also played by Ryū Chishū, whose own appearance in all three films provides a further opportunity for Hara Setsuko's own performative intertextuality to rebound across time.

It is interesting that Noriko's presence in each film of the trilogy is also something that becomes increasingly defined by absence. A conventional way of considering this, much as each of the three films' protagonists do themselves, is to consider Noriko in terms of an absent husband; one who has yet to emerge or one who is now deceased. But another more ambivalent and perhaps more fruitful way of thinking about this same subject would be to consider the absence of men in general at specific moments of presence with other women. Ozu materialises this idea in *Early Summer* more broadly than in *Late Spring*, for here she not only has Aya again, but also her sister-in-law, Fumiko (Miyake Kuniko), played by the same actress cast as her previous father's potential love interest, Mrs Miwa. Importantly, the key scene that takes place toward the end of the film between Noriko and Fumiko is preceded by an intensified recognition of the separation that is occurring between Noriko and her other family members. Here, we see the conclusion to a worried family conversation between Noriko's parents and her brother and sister-in-law about the consequences of Noriko's decision to defy their recommendation of a husband (a middle-aged businessman who is never shown) and opt surprisingly for Kenkichi, the widower son of Mrs Yabe (Sugimura Haruko), who lives nearby. Fumiko is seated, head bowed, in separate shadow in the right-hand foreground of the frame. We hear the sound of the entrance door marking Noriko's return offscreen, and the group disperses with the parents moving upstairs. There is a shot of Noriko entering the corridor alone that signifies her nervous isolation as she prepares herself for re-entry into the emotional forcefield she has clearly decided to relinquish. Importantly, this image commences with an empty space that is then filled by Noriko's arrival to the right, but the next shot already contains Fumiko seated and alone at a floor table and thus Noriko's arrival here, to the left instead, becomes one of contrasting combination and performance. The awareness of being seen as she comes into the room forces Noriko to assume a brighter and more assertive air than we noticed before; a fact underscored by her decision to pause under the illumination of the ceiling light and address Fumiko by meeting her gaze whilst standing. As Noriko and Fumiko converse about the leftovers she can have, Ozu cuts to an image of the father seated at his desk from the rear. He listens to the two women but does not rise. This pattern continues as we move to a sequence of shots showing Noriko preparing and eating her meal alone in the kitchen. The spatial and the affective distance between father and daughter has now been finalised.

This sense of gendered absence and presence is developed in the succeeding scene in which we see Noriko and Fumiko alone for the first time outdoors, by the beach overlooking the sea where the film began. Throughout the trilogy, figures gaze at the ocean in different pairs to present an image of togetherness, but also of separation, and this is no exception. In one of the most extraordinary shots in the director's career, Ozu's camera cranes slowly above the sand dunes to show Noriko and Fumiko in an extended long shot walking forward towards the ocean in the distance. We cut closer to the two women as they continue their progression, backs turned to the camera and wearing near-identical clothing. The women's shared movement conveys not only a journey to the shore beyond, but a sense of their joint projection into the uncertain space and time of their future lives. The camera stops tracking the figures as they stand and then sit in unison; their movement temporarily suspended as they turn to contemplate the next stage for their family and their domestic and maternal arrangements. Importantly, the initial two shot that reframes the women from the front is more or less abandoned in the subsequent editing pattern as Ozu proceeds with a series of swiftly managed one shots that dissect the disparity in outlook between the characters. Noriko asserts a more optimistic outlook than her sister-in-law, thus hinting partially at some of the thinking that has governed her controversial decision to marry Yabe. At that moment Ozu cuts back to a rear view of the two, with Noriko rising spontaneously and running down to the shore. She disappears outside of the frame within the frame provided by the dune, thus initiating a broader pattern of abandonment that now begins to mark the concluding stages of the film. Crucially though, and in strong counterpart to the previous version of female friendship developed in the first film of the trilogy, Fumiko also rises to watch Noriko running freely to the water. Noriko's trail of footsteps on the sand, a mise-en-abyme of the broader trail of connections between the films in the trilogy, provides a material connection that is also reiterated by the more Ozu-esque gesture of a shared wave across a void of charged social space. The sequence concludes with Fumiko following the same path and the women meeting up again on the beach. It is a moment of shared female solidarity and connection that marks the most profound moment of progression so far from the isolation and suffering that the previous Noriko endures at the end of *Late Spring*.

If the governing question that underlies the plot construction of the first two Noriko films is the decision to marry and leave the family home, then the final Noriko film of the trilogy is markedly different from the outset. For in *Tokyo Story*, she lives alone as a widow and there is no mention of any other

Figure 5.2 A trail of connections in *Early Summer* (*Bakushū*, 1951).

blood relatives left in her life. Instead, Noriko's filial responsibilities rest in both nurturing her parents-in-law during their visit to Tokyo and how she also manages the death of Tomi (Higashiyama Chieko) and the subsequent emerging friendship with her sister-in-law Kyōko (Kagawa Kyōko) in Onomichi. One way of reading Noriko in this film is as a kind of contemporary bridge between the past of a family unit that now no longer exists and the emergence of a new female-centred relationship between two young women who, for different reasons, are living separately from each other without a husband in their lives. This configuration is underscored toward the end of the film following the decision of Shukichi (Ryū Chishū)'s other children to return to Tokyo immediately after their mother's funeral.

Ozu begins the sequence by showing the father apart from the two women tending his garden plants. He cuts to a long shot of Noriko cleaning dishes whilst framed by the doorway of the kitchen inside. In the third shot, Kyōko is preparing for her working day in the school, her finishing touch to this everyday routine being the watch she picks up from the floor just as Noriko enters the room. Noriko presents Kyōko with a wrapped bento lunch, the two meeting each other's gaze on an equal horizontal level in the centre of the frame. As they begin to converse, Noriko smartens Kyōko's dress in a gesture of care, but also affinity. She knows, more than most, the importance of the presentation of self. It is soon revealed that Noriko herself is now leaving for Tokyo and this moment of female camaraderie therefore also becomes a temporary one. As the conversation develops by turning to the subject of Kyōko's disappointment with the behaviour of her older siblings, Noriko moves closer to Kyōko by bending down on her knees on the floor; their spatial proximity now matching the intimacy of their communication. Noriko tells Kyōko that she should understand that older people naturally move away from their parents and that she, Noriko, might end up one day like the older daughter Shige (Sugimura Haruko) in spite of herself. 'Isn't life disappointing?' Kyōko asks, as if rhetorically summing up the general sentiment that looms over many of Ozu's films, including the 'Noriko trilogy'. 'Yes, nothing but disappointment' comes the devastating reply.

The two women rise and leave the room together, Kyōko turning offscreen right to say goodbye to her father for the day. Working with editor Hamamura Yoshiyasu, Ozu then cuts to a shot of Noriko and Kyōko arriving near the genkan by the doorway of the house. The horizontal line marking the relationship of equals is re-established, but this time Noriko reaches out and clasps Kyōko's hands in the kind of sisterly gesture so far unseen in the trilogy. Ozu's camera is positioned so that, after Kyōko exits screen left, Noriko is seen left suspended in the now empty space of the film frame, her body crumpling slightly into a stilled pause as if her solitude has now been reawakened after the bustle of separation. But this is, of course, a moment of two departures and two instances of female mobility. In one further moment of unison, now of space and of time – past, present and future – Ozu goes on to link the lives of the women with the absent figure of Tomi.

Kyōko gazes out of her classroom window, her watch visible in the right-hand corner of the frame. The film cuts to the object of her gaze: a long-distance view of the Onomichi townscape; the port and bay to the rear and the congregation of houses in the foreground intersected by a train track. A black steam locomotive enters and moves across the frame from screen right, the sound of its engine almost working in rhythm to the sound of absent singing children on the soundtrack. A cut to a ground-level shot of the tracks, the wheels and machinery now overwhelming the song, is followed by an image of Noriko alone again, seated centre frame in a railway carriage. It is now clear that this is the train taking her back to the present of Tokyo, away from the past of Onomichi and toward an unknown future of 'waiting', as she has recently put it to her father-in-law. She looks down, opens her handbag and brings out Tomi's watch that Shukichi has just given her. As she unfastens it, it is as if she simultaneously opens up the multiple layers of time that this moment signifies for both her and her now established affiliation with Kyōko, whose very knowledge of when to look down at the tracks for Noriko's train passing by has been determined precisely by her own watch she is wearing.[2]

Tokyo Story's more complex and perhaps more open-ended temporality is understandable in the context of the trilogy's wider social context. It is the only one of the three films made after the American Occupation and it is thus evident that Ozu's projection of Noriko's subjectivity is part of a wider concern with a society facing a shift in generational relations, especially when it comes to an imagined future that might contain a different place for women. The way that the Noriko of *Tokyo Story* is pictured in her solitary and affecting train journey would have been unimaginable in *Late Spring*. Here, the train ride to Tokyo that Noriko takes from Kita Kamakura is seen solely in relation to her daughterly relationship with her father to the extent that, as many critics and commentators, including Yoshida Kijū (aka Yoshida Yoshishige), have noticed, Ozu's priority is to instead establish a playful dialogue with the spectator around screen direction as the two converse (2003, 64–6).

Questions of direction and desire haunt all three films, and the various critical responses to the matter of Noriko's inner self have therefore also played a substantial role in thinking through the politics of the trilogy and how one might be tempted to read all three films as an episodic narrative of female becoming. In the case of the Noriko of *Late Spring*, her central female counterpart Aya provides both a role model and an alternative lifestyle that cannot be sustained and must therefore be discarded along with the remaining fan memories of Gary Cooper: the man that Noriko mistakenly thinks her invisible bridegroom most resembles. The Noriko of *Early Summer* assumes multiple personae and ultimately makes her own choice, albeit one that confirms a decision to map an unplanned future that resists the conformity of corporate masculinity. In one sense, the Noriko of *Tokyo Story* has already made her own decisions, albeit ones that have been forced upon her by the events of the war – a constant memory presence in all three films.

The matter of desire inevitably also raises questions about the nature of Noriko's subjectivity. A number of critics have recently sought to either resituate or displace a dominant narrative of heterosexual oppression. For example, Adam Mars-Jones argues, without much textual evidence, that the principal source of Noriko's malady in the film is down to her being a victim of sexual trauma during a period of forced labour rather than, as the script suggests, a matter of poor wartime nutrition (2011, 227–30). Robin Wood certainly acknowledges that the essence of the 'personal freedom' that Noriko seeks to preserve in *Late Spring* 'is that she remains undefined' (1998, 117). Interestingly, he points out that there is no suggestion, in fact, that Noriko is either sexually attracted to men or women. For Yuka Kanno, 'in addition to its focus on her reluctance to marry, the trilogy also [clearly] marks the virtual absence of Noriko's husbands, in the past, present, and future' (2011, 289). Noriko's attention to women, her fascination – offscreen – in *Early Summer* with the proto-lesbian film icon Katherine Hepburn, not to mention the way her boss in the same film notices how 'strange' she is, all therefore raise the possibility of what Kanno terms a form of 'queer spectatorship by "implication"' whereby we might imagine, retrospectively, a way of viewing the trilogy as a set of films about suppressed lesbian desire (Ibid., 288).

In one sense, these thoughts return us to the discursive conditions that define any notion of a trilogy, and especially one that was not significantly devised as such at the time of its tripartite history of production and circulation. What remains true, however, is that the mobile politics of the film trilogy form also informed the immediate context of the period. In his discussion of Ozu's work of the early 1950s, Woojeong Joo points out that the date of *Tokyo Story* coincided with the height of popularity of Shōchiku's take on the female-centred drama of everyday life with the success of the *What is Your Name?* (*Kimi no na wa*) trilogy starring Kishi Keiko and Sada Keiji (1953–1954), outstripping that of the previous record-holder in Japanese film culture, the *Love-Troth Tree (Aizen katsura)* trilogy starring Tanaka Kinuyo (1938–1939) (2017, 174). Ozu's unique contribution to global film culture, rightly or wrongly, has all too often been positioned within the context of a form of art-cinema production typically defined by a set of critical and material considerations that Perkins and Verevis, building on the work of Thomas Elsaesser, relate to a form of 'semantic and syntactic repetition' (2012, 13). This type of filmmaking practice has undeniably been bolstered by a wider set of discourses that circulate within the fluid international cultures of film criticism, film festival management and film museum curation.[3] Whilst these tendencies might certainly hold true in the case of world cinema directors such as Hou Hsiao-hsien and Wim Wenders, directors who have incidentally both venerated Ozu's own practice, this nonetheless displaces the equally important significance of the immensely popular studio, genre and star systems that the Noriko trilogy was originally conceived to be part of. Despite its retrospective formulation, the Noriko trilogy was named after a woman of the time, played by a woman of the time and very much addressed to women of the time. This is the most important aspect of its continuing historical significance not least because, as Robin Wood himself originally observed, so much of what it is speaking about – gendered social expectations and the matter of feminist self-definition – continues to resonate today.

NOTES

1. For more detailed discussion of Ozu's distinctive characteristics and attributes as a filmmaker, see Bordwell and Thompson (1976), Richie (1977), Bordwell (1988), Nornes (2007) and Desser (2010), amongst others.
2. My argument about the ending of *Tokyo Story* is taken from a longer discussion in Phillips (2022). There, I also remark on the disparity between the original Japanese and

the English language subtitles in the presentation of Noriko and Kyōko's exchange. For more on the conclusion of the film, see also Miyao (2021).
3. The genesis of this practice relates to the early institutionalisation of the director within the European and North American cinematheque circuit and the concurrent critical appropriation of Ozu within an art cinema discourse of alterity and national specificity. Even to this day, the 'Noriko' films are often packaged and disseminated outside Japan in trilogy form as a branded thread of cultural value.

REFERENCES

Bordwell, David. 1988. *Ozu and the Poetics of Cinema*. London: British Film Institute.
Bordwell, David and Kristin Thompson. 1976. 'Space and Narrative in the Films of Ozu.' *Screen* 17, no. 2: 41–73.
Choi, Jinhee. 2018. *Reorienting Ozu: A Master and His Influence*. New York: Oxford University Press.
Desser, David. 2010. 'Introduction: A Filmmaker for All Seasons.' In *Ozu's Tokyo Story*. Edited by David Desser, 1–24. Cambridge: Cambridge University Press.
Joo, Woojeong. 2017. *The Cinema of Ozu Yasujiro: Histories of the Everyday*. Edinburgh: Edinburgh University Press.
Kanno, Yuka. 2011. 'Implicational Spectatorship: Hara Setsuko and the Queer Joke.' *Mechademia* 6: 287–303.
Mars-Jones, Adam. 2011. *Noriko Smiling*. London: Notting Hill Press.
Miyao, Daisuke. 2021. 'The Melodrama of Ozu: *Tokyo Story* and Its Time.' *Journal of Japanese and Korean Cinema* 13, no. 2: 58–79.
Nornes, Abé Mark. 2007. 'The Riddle of the Vase. Ozu Yasujirō's *Late Spring*.' In *Japanese Cinema: Texts and Contexts*. Edited by Alastair Phillips and Julian Stringer. Abingdon: Routledge, 78–89.
Perkins, Claire and Constantine Verevis. 2012. 'Introduction: Three Times.' In *Film Trilogies: New Critical Approaches*. Edited by Claire Perkins and Constantine Verevis, 1–31. Basingstoke: Palgrave Macmillan.
Phillips, Alastair. 2003. 'Pictures of the Past in the Present: Modernity, Femininity and Stardom in the Postwar Films of Ozu Yasujiro.' *Screen* 44, no. 2: 154–66.
Phillips, Alastair. 2022. *Tokyo Story*. London: Bloomsbury Publishing.
Richie, Donald. 1977. *Ozu: His Life and Films*. Berkeley: University of California Press.
Russell, Catherine. 2003. 'Three Japanese Actresses of the 1930s: Modernity, Femininity and the Performance of Everyday Life.' *Cineaction*. no. 60: 34–44.
Wood, Robin. 1998. *Sexual Politics and Narrative Film: Hollywood and Beyond*. New York: Columbia University Press.
Yoshida, Kijū. 2003. *Ozu's Anti-Cinema*. Ann Arbor: University of Michigan Center for Japanese Studies.

CHAPTER 6

A Remake, But. . .: Media Infantility in Ozu's *Good Morning*

Rea Amit

Good Morning (*Ohayō*, 1959), Ozu Yasujirō's second production in colour, is generally recognised by historians as a loose remake of *I Was Born, But. . .* (*Otona no miru ehon: Umarete wa mita keredo*), his 1932 silent film. Both films showcase an interest in media, largely through the perspective of their two young protagonists. In *I Was Born, But. . .*, two children experience a rude awakening through the projection of a *kogata-eiga* (small-gauge film), and in *Good Morning* television prompts a process of mediation between the private and public spheres. In the former, notwithstanding class consciousness, a collective form of watching also gives rise to spectatorial awareness. Similarly, in the latter, despite the advent of a technology that allows media consumption in private spaces, it is public viewership that undergoes a process of domestication. Seen in this light, this chapter argues that the concept of the remake is not just a matter of underlining affinities between the films, but also of 'de-mediation'.[1] Although Ozu's films often defy Hollywood conventions (in terms of their formal, structural, and stylistic features), and do not follow the same commercial logic, this chapter nonetheless discusses them along the lines of Frank Kelleter's consideration of remakes and popular seriality. Rather than progressive ontological theorisation, however, I highlight aspects in the films that illustrate a devolving phenomenology. That is, instead of paying attention to technological improvements, I underscore features that demonstrate dysfunctional forms of communication and archaic modes of media consumption. This is neither a critique of Ozu or the films, nor is it an abstract statement on media as such that can be seen emerging from them. Indeed, the films equally employ nonsensical and even flat-out infantile humour that seem to lampoon critical thinking.

However, infantility does not mean insensitivity. In fact, it suggests hypersensitivity, even if to the extent of ludicrousness. In an influential article,

Thomas Elsaesser asks half-jokingly (and answers positively) whether Freud's discussion of the 'mystic writing pad' (what Elsasser calls 'essentially a child's toy' [2009, 102]) can be considered a theoretical deliberation of media. Following a similar line of thought (albeit in reverse), this chapter argues that Ozu's remaking of *I Was Born, But...* (the full title dubs it as an 'Adult's Picture Book') is indicative of a Freudian unconsciousness of Japanese viewership. The original film anticipated journalist Ōya Sōichi's famous concerns that television might transform post-war Japan into a nation of idiots, which the remake directly invokes. However, *I Was Born, But...* proves that Ōya was wrong, as it was film spectatorship that has already succeeded in doing so, whereas *Good Morning* simply resurfaces immature tendencies in Japanese media consumerism that belittle the purported significance of new communication technologies.

BIRTHMARKS

That *Good Morning* is a remake of *I Was Born, But...* is not an axiomatic proclamation. In several cases, critics and scholars acknowledged similarities among the director's other films, yet ultimately dismissed the label. Film historian Satō Tadao underscores such a reaction regarding the two films. He writes that despite being works that closely resemble each other (*yoku nita sakuhin*), the 'original' is recognised worldwide as a historically consequential masterpiece, whereas its post-war remake is considered a neglectable film. The reason for this, Satō speculates, is likely due to the appreciation of *I Was Born, But...* as featuring a serious moral discussion, whereas *Good Morning* is perceived simply as an absurdist coarse sketch (*tada no kokkei na fūzoku sukecchi ni suginai*) (2000, 468). It is unclear why Satō uses the loan word *sukecchi* (sketch) in this context. After all, strictly formally speaking, *Good Morning* is as meticulously stylised as, if not even more stylised than, any of his other films. This wording might therefore indicate a latent critique, as well as a preference for content over form.

One notable exception, which Satō does not mention, is the acclaimed film theorist Hasumi Shigehiko, who demands the affirmation of *Good Morning* as a post-war version of the 1932 film (Hasumi 1983, 51). This is not because of the films' apparent similarities or their shared focus on two juvenile characters, but due to their mutual engagement with space and the anomaly in Ozu's oeuvre in their depiction of eating. Hasumi observes that while sharing meals is a common feature in Ozu's works, in these two films it is the self-denial of food that is being emphasised. Moreover, in parallel scenes within the films, the protagonists defy Ozu's norm in the portrayal of the location where meals are shared. In the 1932 'original', Ryōichi (Sugawara Hideo) and Keiji (Aoki Tomio) enjoy their lunchboxes at an open field instead of at school; and in the 1959 version, Minoru

(Shitara Kōji) and Isamu (Shimazu Masahiko) eat rice with their bare hands by the riverbank instead of at home. Although this may not suffice as a validation of the 'remake' claim, it inexorably affirms their inherent relationship.

Even if kinship might seem an inappropriate analogy to make in delineating the affinity between the films, it is borne in the films themselves, both literally and visually. For one, *I Was Born, But. . .* directly refers to birth in its title. While such reference is absent in *Good Morning*, the latter does invoke the notion of human reproduction through the introduction of the character Haraguchi Mitsue (Miyoshi Eiko), who is a (likely retired) midwife. She mentions her occupation only once in the film, boasting that thanks to her training as an obstetrician she cannot be easily fooled. Although her job does not play a significant role in the film's narrative, the sign advertising her services anchors cinematic space as it appears at the centre of the frame from several angles throughout the diegesis. Although no similar character appears in *I Was Born, But. . .*, in this case, too, the centre of the imaginary space that the film occupies is marked by a midwife sign. It is placed by the railroad tracks that the children cross three times throughout the film on the way to school.

The Yoshii boys walk there with their father (Saitō Tatsuo), before straying away from the road that leads to their schools in two scenes, and in the last scene the father leaves them with their friend, the boss's son Tarō (Katō Sei'ichi) after he drives to work with the boss (Sakamoto Takeshi). Thus, given the attention to childbirth, *Good Morning* should neither be understood solely as sharing similarities with *I Was Born, But. . .*, nor even be considered as its post-war remake in the strictest sense, or according to the common meaning of the term. Rather, *Good Morning* signifies a rebirth. As such, it is not a replica of an original or an improved version. Instead, it is a re-emergence of the same film in a new media ecology, a resurgence that points to a redelivery conveyance.

Figure 6.1 On the left side, a sign at the centre advertises Haraguchi Mitsue's services as a midwife in Ozu's *Good Morning* (*Ohayō*, 1959), and on the right side, a midwife sign is visible in his earlier film *I Was Born, But . . .* (*Otona no miru ehon: Umarete wa mita keredo*, 1932).

LABOUR AND GROWING PAINS

Ozu entered the film business as a new hire at Shōchiku studios in 1926, the same year the 'father of Japanese television' Takayanagi Kenjirō conducted the first ever televisual experiment. The two simultaneous occurrences are no more than a coincidence, but they join a series of interactions between the director, the motion picture medium and other technologies of communication. Television as a mass medium was a long way from materialising in pre-war Japan, and Ozu cannot be credited for anticipating it. Indeed, the director is widely recognised for his uncompromising medium-specific formalism, and to some extent also for his reluctance to adjust to new technologies. For example, he directed his first talkie *The Only Son* (*Hitori musuko*) in 1936, about half a decade after the first Japanese sound production. Similarly, he completed his first film in colour *Equinox Flower* (*Higanbana*) in 1958, eight years after the release of the first Japanese colour film.

However, several aspects of Ozu's films indicate a more flexible approach to cinema as a growing medium, as well as an even greater awareness of filmgoing as a shared mode of experience. With regards to the latter, there is the direct reference to the pre-war film program as an exhibition practice in the 1933 film *Woman of Tokyo* (*Tokyo no onna*).[2] While cinephiles and film critics have lauded Ozu as an auteur, a singular filmmaker with a signature style whose motion pictures exhibit thematic consistency, he himself often likened his work to that of a tofu-maker (Satō 2000, 119). As hyperbolic and humoristic (if not even somewhat childish) an analogy as this may seem, the outright act of remaking films – a practice that might imply standardisation – can be seen as undermining the ostensible artistic integrity of both the original and the film produced in its mould. In a similar fashion, the serialisation of film, either by reintroducing characters and extending previously concluded plots – such as in the case of the famous post-war 'Noriko Trilogy' (1949–1953) discussed in the previous chapter by Alastair Phillips – might even conjure a notion more common in televisual programming than a singular cinematic experience. That is, by reviving key plotlines, characterisation tropes and diegetic worlds, Ozu implies predilection toward repetition and systemisation in place of originality and innovation.

I Was Born, But. . . and *Good Morning* illustrate the above-mentioned propensities. First, *I Was Born, But. . .* is branded as the third in what might be called the 'but' trilogy that encompasses *I Graduated, But. . .* (*Daigaku wa detakeredo*, 1929) and *I Flunked, But. . .* (*Rakudai wa shitakeredo*, 1930).[3] The three films mostly share what Alastair Phillips calls the wistful hanging participle 'but', which latently suggests a general conjecture concerning 'disappointments of life' (2007, 34). Even beyond textuality, their distinctive titles, in addition to common cast and staff, franchise them as a series. Granted, seriality is not necessarily a reference to mass media or an indication of film as a medium that subsumes the integrity of individual productions. However, popular seriality in Frank Kelleter's theorisation underscores first and foremost – apart from narrative similarities or other commonalities among works pertaining to a given series – the mere potential for a professedly perpetual reproduction (2012, 19–44). Whereas Kelleter illustrates the concept by referring to L. Frank Baum's *Wizard of Oz* franchise, the same logic can also be applied to the cinematic wizardry of Ozu.

To be sure, Kelleter limits the scope of his concept to a capitalistic framework that emphasises continuous revenue growth. Ozu's claim for popular seriality derives from a different source. It is not exigently an increase in profitability as much as a directorial or a cinematic brand that was interwoven into Shōchiku's own *shōshimin-eiga* line of production and its 'Kamata' style (Phillips 2007, 26).[4] In this sense, an Ozu picture is part of a franchise that brandishes a certain value trademark by the mere fact of being produced by the studio under the directorship of one of its leading filmmakers. Yet, the films themselves, as far as this chapter is concerned, showcase an appreciation for popular seriality in a more distinct fashion as well.

The most notable reference to film as a mode of reproducing moving images in *I Was Born, But...* is the scene mentioned above, wherein the boss projects footage from a small-gauge film at his house, where several of his employees and neighbourhood children have gathered. Characters and commentators alike misunderstand this sequence. First, the film's main protagonists, the young Yoshii siblings, fail to realise that their father's portrayal as a boorish stooge is not ignominious, but rather, in their friends' eyes, meritorious. The brothers' excessive awareness of socio-economic gaps ironically prevents them from realising that the boss's son Tarō believes that their father is indeed greater (*erai*) than his own father. Similarly, scholars tend to overemphasise the direct reference to the cinematic apparatus in the scene as a sign of Ozu's awareness of it as a theoretical mechanism. Markus Nornes, for instance, acknowledges the inept look of the footage, but moves on to associate the scene with experimental and avant-garde films (2003, 22). Yuki Takinami goes even further to compare the scene with Dziga Vertov's employment of seemingly analogous footage in *Man with a Movie Camera* (*Chelovek s kino-apparatom*, 1929). However, as Takinami himself ultimately recognises, the comparison is limited because 'Ozu's film lacks any ambition to organize viewer consciousness through cinematic operations' (2018, 150).

Rather than cinematic self-awareness, I argue that the scene is emblematic of a collective unconsciousness. Thomas Elsaesser sees, in Freud's early discussions of the unconsciousness, a deliberation on the potentiality for supplemental memory that anticipates future media as technology capable of input and output akin to film's function to store and project visual content.

In contrast, *I Was Born, But...* proposes a negative discourse that projects medial incompetence, misused or unused technological potential and the dysfunctionality, as well as the absurdity of communication systems. In other words, this is an articulation of the unconsciousness in the sense of unawareness and even ignorance of media functionality.

The notion of de-mediation that I employ in this chapter chiefly addresses inadequate vehicles of transmitting meaning, information or ideas. My main examples are the failure of communication technologies such as television and telephone to fulfil their intended design to deliver messages across distant locations. One feature in the two films that indirectly foreshadows transmission inefficiency – between individuals as well as the films in and of themselves – is transportation. *I was Born, But...* extensively displays fast-moving trains, presumably as a harbinger of the speed and progress that would become more conspicuous aspects of everyday life in Japan within a few years of its release. Yet, as Woojeong Joo points out, if the film had been a talkie that captures the location's live sound, 'the railway noise would have drowned out any other sounds including conversations' (2017, 43). Consequently, Joo infers that speeding trains in the film are indicative of a threat to modern society. In addition, trains are also a means of transportation, even though their functionality is never made clear in the film. They zigzag around houses, streets and characters, but never stop to drop off or pick up passengers. Transportation dysfunctionality is seen not only in the speciously moving trains. At the opening, the truck that helps the Yoshiis with their move to the suburbs is marooned in mud. Although neither trains nor other vehicles appear in *Good Morning*, it is telling that the second to last scene takes place at a train station, where Arita Setsuko (Kuga Yoshiko) and Fukui Heichirō (Sada Keiji) wait for a train that never arrives.[5] Thus, despite growing speed and technological advances, both films present development as non-foolproof in nature.

MEDIA ILLITERACY

More than mobility obstacles, the scene depicting passengers waiting at the platform to no avail toward the end of *Good Morning* denotes the core dysfunction both this film and its predecessor accentuate: that of incompetent forms of communication. Arita and Fukui, who appear to share deep feelings for one another, fail to express their emotions and resort instead to repeated banal exchanges about the weather. This failure adds to miscommunication problems between neighbours at the beginning of the film, and to the children's clamour against adults' speaking mannerisms that culminates in their refusal to talk. Despite being a silent film, *I was Born, But...* conveys a similar charge in opposition to verbal comprehensibility. Throughout the film, words lose their meaning and effect, especially in light of new technologies premised on the notion of improving communication. For instance, at Yoshii's workplace, employees are surrounded by telephones that are placed on their desks or attached to the walls, but they never fulfil their innate function of conversing with parties in faraway locations. This is a significant façade given that Yoshii's colleagues deride him behind his back for relocating only to be closer to the boss, despite the availability of a technology that should have made it possible to maintain good relationships from afar. Moreover, while the blasé workers uninterestedly attend to their duties using pencil and paper, on display in the manager's office is an idle typewriter. The scene is juxtaposed with the resounding anachronism of children at school attentive to calligraphy, an obsolete form of penmanship.

The consolidation of education, media and literacy plays a central role in both films, but *Good Morning* gives the matter new urgency with the introduction of television. As Jayson Makoto Chun points out, a debate took place in post-war Japan between those directly or indirectly following the footsteps of David Riesman's notion of 'new literacy', believing in the potential of visual communication; and those led by Ōya Sōichi who argued that television conditions viewers to 'crave visual stimulation' (Chun 2007, 170–1). Ozu's 1959 film participates in the debate, and as mentioned above, directly refers to Ōya's famous (or infamous) charge 'ichioku sō hakuchi ka', about television turning Japan into a nation of a hundred million idiots.

Good Morning seems to heed Ōya's brazen critique. Suggestive in this regard is one poignant scene where the younger brother, Isamu, attends class at school. The teacher leads a *shiritori* word game in which players are asked to pronounce a word that begins with the last syllable of a preceding word. However, rather than abiding by the rules, the first two students who volunteer to take part in the game utter random television show titles *Akdō Suzunosuke*[6] and *Gekkō kamen* (*Moonlight Mask*).[7] The new medium is also the main source of dispute between the protagonists and their parents, who initially refuse to purchase a television set and scold the children when they sneak into the neighbours' house to watch a sumo broadcast (under the pretence of going to study). It is this conflict that initiates the children's silent protest. Moreover, in one of their efforts to communicate after taking their facetious oath of silence, they engaged in pantomimed gesticulations while the rest of the family attempts to guess the meaning. The scene serves as an indirect point of reflection on the silent film era, and a reference to *Good Morning*'s own parental roots in that period. The scene also, and more directly, alludes to the popular television quiz show *Jesutā*,[8] and by so doing signifies a prevailing tendency in Japanese TV that continues to this day.

As media scholar Fan Kugion maintains, quiz shows are ubiquitous on Japanese television, and even shows that are not categorised as such often feature quiz sections. This leads Fan to characterise Japanese television as inherently boasting of quiz-like qualities (*kuizu teki seikaku*) (2014, 15). The proliferation of quiz shows in Japan might suggest an interest, at the national level, in expanding knowledge and promoting the country's education initiatives while strengthening the sense of viewer empowerment – presuming that TV audiences can take part in shows by guessing the right answer at home. Yet, as Koichi Iwabuchi demonstrates, Japanese quiz shows are different from those in other countries. He touches on the fact that, in Japan, contenders are usually professional *tarento* or celebrities (2004, 24). The absence of ordinary people who are not associated with the entertainment industry on television raises concerns about whether such shows are staged or scripted. Thus, although quiz shows appeared on Japanese television from the early days of broadcasting in the country, they share inherent similarities with the type of televisual content often credited as being responsible for the rise in popularity of the medium: namely, *puro resu*, or professional wrestling.

Media sociologist Ōta Shōichi argues that the introduction of television in post-war Japan transformed the nation into a televisual society (*terebi shakai*). Ōta singles out Matsutarō Shōriki, the founder of Japan's first commercial television station as most instrumental in this societal transformation by initiating a 'myth' (*shinwa*) surrounding pro-wrestling. Shōriki understood the widespread appeal of performative content that, while heavily regulated, is broadcast live; and he placed television sets in crowded locations throughout the country, in what became known as *gaitō terebi* or 'open air TV'. According to Ōta, Shōriki then prioritised the programming of pro-wrestling matches that subsequently became the content most associated with the medium. Ōta argues that, rather than participation in the sense promoted by quiz shows, television in Japan bolsters a notion of emancipation for the viewers (*shichōsha e no kaihō*). This is not a political or theoretical kind of liberation that coincided with the establishment of democracy in the country. Nor is it an act of defiance against commercialisation or Western ideals. Rather, Ōta contends that television empowered viewers to be liberated from their own selves, and from freedom (*jiyū*), the abstract term that has been enforced on them after the defeat Japan was dealt in the Second World War (2019, 9–13). By extension, television also detached viewership itself from the exclusive association with one medium, to further allow multifaceted manifestations of the term.

As prices of television sets rapidly declined in the latter half of the 1950s, open-air television gradually disappeared from the actual landscape as well as the broader mediascape. However, public television viewing is resurrected in *Good Morning*'s most emotionally charged sequence, when the children vanish from home following their failed attempts to communicate without words. Their private English teacher Fukui joins the search for them. Although he is poignantly advised to check the film theatre, he reports (after having returned the two home safely) finding them watching TV by the station. While unseen in the film itself, the episode alludes to the common practice in the early days of the medium.

As media sociologist Satō Takumi lays out in his extensive study on television and education in Japan, TV in the early post-war era evolved from and was influenced by other media. In addition to cinema was *kamishibai*, or what Sharalyn Orbaugh succinctly defines as something comprised of 'a set of pictures used by a performer to tell a story to an audience, usually of children aged four to twelve' (2012, 78). Television's first popular form, as was already mentioned, was in an 'open-air' version, between 1953 and 1955, with only a limited number of sets placed in crowded commercial areas of the most populated urban centres. The next phase, from 1955 to 1958, is marked by the spread of public television viewing into neighbourhoods, with 1958 signalling a transition into the average family's living room (*o cha no aida*) as well as a new recognition of the medium as home-cinema (*katei eigakan*). Satō also points out that children who did not have sets in their homes and watched television in their neighbours' houses were condescendingly labelled as 'TV gypsies', and in some places even *terebi kojiki* or 'TV beggars' (Satō 2019, 126–7). Minoru and Isamu are such children.

Despite the apparent social commentary the film projects concerning children who do not watch television at home, *Good Morning* appears to ridicule the phenomenon. In his analytical study of Ozu's cinematic poetics, David Bordwell pinpoints the visual gag presented in *Good Morning*, where Mitsue is seen as if praying for what he identifies as an electric tower (1988, 354). In fact, it is more likely to be a television tower, so the frivolous optical quip adjoins many verbal ones, as well as the frequent flatulence audio gag. Aural gags are obviously absent in the silent *I was Born, But. . .*, but the characterisation of sound in *Good Morning* by such coarse chords (regardless of how painstakingly harmonised and timed; see Masakiyo 2016) manifests the notion of evolving technology in tandem with devolving spectatorship. Despite the technological gaps between the films, they are firmly tied together; for example, visually, with images of electrical, television, telephone and (likely) telegraph wires stretched between poles, and also clotheslines that adorn scenes in both films. Moreover, miscommunication – albeit through different means – punctuates both films' comedic qualities.

Like the TV-deprived drifting children in *Good Morning*, the children in *I was Born, But. . .* appear to be roaming aimlessly in desolated spaces. In one such scene, on the back of a child is attached a handwritten note that asks readers not to feed the boy due to his sensitive stomach. Unsurprisingly, the boy is soon seen eating. Moreover, when the third grader Ryōichi needs a grade on the assignment he had completed while not attending school, the wandering boys turn to the apparently uneducated liquor delivery boy. He then mistakes the character *kō* (the best grade) for one that reads *saru* or *shin*, meaning monkey. Although not the sign commonly used to denote the mammal, the qualities associated with the animals, especially mimicking (seeing and doing), are inherent to the narrative of both films. Adults and children alike imitate one another in a repetitious mode that often defeats its original intention, mainly due to exorbitance. The behaviour of the younger brothers in both films is the clearest evidence of this feature, when they repeat their older brothers' rebellious acts, thereby turning them into farce. In this sense, *Good Morning*, too, is a more farcical version of *I Was Born, But. . .*

IN REALM OF THE SENSELESS

Both films evince illiteracy championed by ill-advised boys, but the context in which they misread the adults' coded communication, despite the excessive repetition, seems incommensurable. In *Good Morning*, consumerism and the literal production of air are tantamount to what Bernard Stiegler calls 'systemic stupidity'. This stupefying situation in Stiegler's theorisation is rooted in the experience of automatisation in capitalistic societies (2019, 34). Differently from Stiegler's disposition, *Good Morning*'s systematic stupefaction is fused with the precapitalistic society that *I was Born, But. . .* mediates. The 1932 film, too, fosters repetition as an offshoot of automatisation; but in lieu of Western capitalist ideology, it adheres to (even if somewhat latently) the outlook of imperial militarism.

I was Born, But. . .'s militaristic foreshadowing is evident at two moments. The first is during the film's second classroom session at the boys' school – a scene that parallels, or rather anticipates, the aforementioned one in *Good Morning*. Routines at the school already appear militaristic in their emphasis on uniformity and discipline, but the most direct reference to the militaristic system is marked by the inscribed message on the classroom wall: *bakudan-san'yūshi* ('three brave human bombs'). The banner celebrates an incident that occurred within the same year of the film's 1932 release, wherein three army engineers detonated themselves in the ensuing war against China. In addition to being a heightened patriotic event galvanised by the authorities, as Hanae Kurihara Kramer and Scott Kramer indicate, it was also used for commercial and entertainment purposes (2019, 164). Militarism is also conceived as an alternative to socioeconomic divides and the rules of the free market with the promise of glory in battle that is embraced by the protagonists toward the end of the film when they express a wish for a successful military career.

Good Morning seems to be a far cry from wartime politics and ideology. In fact, uniformity, arguably the most ostensible reminiscence of militarism, is mocked in the film. Examples of the changing tones in this regard are the two morning exercise scenes in the films. In *I was Born, But. . .*, Yoshii exercises by himself, using a stringed stretching device while appearing engulfed by electrical lines and clotheslines. In sharp contrast, in the parallel scene in *Good Morning*, a neighbour (Zenichi's father) is accompanied by two of the protagonists' friends as they exercise in synchronicity by following NHK (Nippon Hōsō Kyōkai, Japan's national broadcaster) morning *rajio taisō* or radio calisthenics. These morning broadcasts began in the late 1920s and continue to this day (Kuroda 1999, 11–6). In 1957, two years before *Good Morning*'s release, the program started airing on NHK's television channel. Unlike the silent black-and-white scene in *I Was Born, But. . .*, the post-war reincarnation of the scene does not only put on display an open blue sky, but most importantly, two additional participants.

The significance of the added players, however, is not necessarily a matter of projecting unison in an unbounded public sphere. Rather, their function is to provide infantile commentary on the elder character's ability to produce air at will. The contrast between the scenes appears and sounds as parodying the relicts of militarism in post-war Japan, despite the seemingly vulgar means. Yet, vulgarity here is not simply an off-colour comedic feature, nor can it be reduced to a crude political critique. Rather, it is more a reflection on the media. For one, the scene evokes pre-'open-air' televisual practices of communal 'open-air radio' listening practices. Moreover, and more crucially, the scene signifies a penchant toward communal consumption. The children's idiotic praises for breaking wind are not ironic, as they reflect the devolved spectatorship that *I was Born, But. . .* had already exposed. There, in the famous small-gauge film screening scene, rather than the projected images, is the excessive reaction to them that is emphasised. Specifically, beyond the adulated verbal

Figure 6.2 On the left side, Yoshii exercises by himself, using a stringed stretching device while appearing engulfed by electrical lines and clotheslines, and on the right side, the protagonists' neighbours are shown following the morning radio calisthenics, in these shots from *I Was Born, But . . .* (*Otona no miru ehon: Umarete wa mita keredo*, 1932).

responses between young and adult viewers, exaggerated reception is seen in the unnamed projectionist (played by Ryū Chishū, who also plays the father in *Good Morning*). Although the footage is amateurish and excessively immature, the grown man responds as if to a masterful comedic work.

Exchanging glances in the scene suggests acute awareness of who is watching as much as – if not even to a greater degree – what is being watched. The projectionist, whose role is literally to shed light, flashes out a dormant knee-jerk propensity to bolster collective amusement. In a way that is similar to the use and effect of a laugh track in television broadcasts, the manufactured laughter in the scene spurs viewers to collectively appreciate the otherwise crude images as being funnier than they really are. Gina Giotta convincingly dismisses notions of 'canned laughter' as superfluous, as well as either politically or emotionally flawed. Alternatively, she argues that the laugh track 'helped differentiate television from film' and even eased television's entrance into domestic spaces by diffusing anxiety about the medium, particularly among children (Giotta 2017, 332). While Giotta's analysis examines the televisual apparatus in North America, her discussion resonates with *I was Born, But. . .*'s visual equivalent, and by extension with that of *Good Morning*.

In the sense of added unconscionable reaction to only loosely conceived humorous acts, amplified laughter is akin to medial diffusion, as well as to the disintegration of domestic and public spheres. The visualisation of this mechanism in Ozu's silent film is premised on a social affect surrounding communal reception. Japanese television broadcasts implemented the laugh track much later than in North America, and even today it is used sparsely compared with other countries. One reason for this might be the type of shows popular on television in Japan. For example, in one Japanese study on the laugh track (*rokuon warai*), the author admits that the topic cannot be properly examined in Japan because of the lack of domestic sitcoms (Yoshimitsu 2021, 171).

In place of augmented sound, Japanese television shows often revert to amplifying excitement and soliciting the audience's emotional response by visual means. One such technique is inscribed in writing over images known as telop (*teroppu*), which as Aaron Gerow argues, can be utilised for 'making viewing an issue of collective agency' (2010, 146). Even if reading imposed texts while watching a show does not necessitate a unified disposition among viewers/readers, the second commonly used tool on Japanese television shows, the wipe (*waipu*), dramatically increases the probability of such outcomes. Similar to the case on Japanese quiz shows – where most participants are TV personnel who perform as competitors, and often hyperbolically express their feelings of joy or disappointment whenever they win and lose – many shows open small windows on the screen wherein a famous entertainer is seen responding to selected segments. Both techniques ultimately function to exaggerate already heightened emotional situations.

Neither *I Was Born, But...* nor *Good Morning* directly showcases analogous contemporary media technologies. Both do, however, provide insight into the mindset on which the predisposition toward hyperbolic reaction to innocuous phenomena is predicated. Innovative media are left largely unused in *I was Born, But...*, and the topic itself becomes a matter of social obsession in *Good Morning*. The remaking of the 'original' points to regressive tendencies in media consumption. In *I Was Born, But...*, despite militaristic collectivisation efforts, the protagonists strive to untangle themselves from the web that constrains them. Emblematic of their attempts is the disentanglement puzzle (*chie no wa* in Japanese, literally 'ring of wisdom'), which they manage to solve toward the end of the film. Unlike such disentanglement effort, in *Good Morning*, the protagonists appear to desire being boxed in. Despite the newly opened soundscapes, colour and perhaps even the contingency of other media fragrances, they remain myopic and narrow minded, interlaced in a system of idiocrasy.

CONCLUSION: REMAKING BACKWARDS FORESIGHTS

From an ontological perspective, *Good Morning* is an updated version of *I Was Born, But....* It is a newly mediated observation of technologies that purportedly bolster better media fluency. Yet, serial logic, which usually assumes progression, is reversed in this case. It presents two points on an imaginary axis that signify a regressive mode of appreciation.

Throughout 1956, media sociologist Katō Hidetoshi published a series of essays he later compiled into a book that traces Japanese media history until the arrival of television. In his study, the medium he marks as the beginning of mass media in Japan is *misemono*, the slideshow or what Aaron Gerow calls 'fairground entertainment' (2010, 44). Yet, as media scholar Iida Yuta studiously demonstrates, television itself was for an extensive period perceived similarly to the pre-cinematic entertainment apparatus, a visual attraction that lacked any formal specification. Iida cites one of Marshall McLuhan's aphorisms: 'We look at the present through a rear-view mirror. We march backwards into the future'; and points out that for some elderly people in Japan today, every screen is a TV, and that television in Japanese (*terebi*) has lost its original meaning of looking from afar (Iida 2016, 8–9). In other words, the medium's function has been adapted into a compromised social reality. In this discursive reconceptualisation of the medium, Iida explores a televisual media archaeology, and identifies several articulations of pre-war television along the lines of *katsudō shahshin denpa hōsō ki* or an electronically transmitting motion picture device. Yet, unlike similar studies in the West, such as Doron Galili's 'Seeing by Electricity', Iida reverts to *misemono*, which he ultimately theorises, following Daniel Dayan and Elihu Katz, as a 'media event'

(2016, 54–7). Although *I was Born, But...* first circulated during a time when public discourse was influenced by the proliferation of the radio and the plausibility of wireless transmission, the film exposes the absurdity of such unwiring. *Good Morning* further denotes the incongruity between wireless (*musen*) technology and a seemingly hardwired disposition toward social ties. In this sense, the films themselves are connected to one another as if by a medial umbilical cord. Yet, contrary to the common logic of the series, the remake exposes a backward-looking foresight of a regressive projection of a *misemono*-like media event.

As Hasumi aptly points out, the two films are connected by their approach to eating. Crucial in this context is children's consumption of questionable materials. In *Good Morning*, children imprudently consume pumice powder for the sake of breaking air by a telling nudge on the forehead. In *I was Born, But...* some children swallow the inside of sparrow eggs in order to achieve physical might. However, the protagonists sidestep health risks and feed their pet dog instead, who then requires veterinarian care. The dog's role in the film seems insignificant, but it is denotative of a certain compromised condition as it is seen tied to a box-like doghouse throughout the film. The dog's name is *Esu*, the Japanese translation for the Freudian term id proposed in *Jiga to esu* ('The Ego and the Id'), which appeared in Japanese as early as 1928. In this text, Freud characterises the id as the unconscious, as 'internal perceptions' that form the 'deepest strata of the mental apparatus' responsible for 'primordial' and 'elemental' sensations and feelings (1960, 14–5). In the sense of Elsasser's application of the term in the media context, *Esu* should mean suppressed input that could be made available for future output. However, unlike Elsasser's reading of the Freudian unconscious as a precursor to media theory, Ozu's films showcase a symptomatic manifestation of a sociopsychological unconscious. The condition represents an inclination toward infantilisation. Media in the films point to a descending phenomenology along with a basic desire for a presentational rather than a representational mode of participatory space. This is not a wish to be seen, but rather a desire to be part of a collective consuming body (us/we) with whom to peep on 'others', as if to join the panoptic 'big brother'. Given that new media and communication technologies enable more individuated forms of peer-to-peer exchanges, they are seen as being unused or misused in the films, not just by the characters, but also by the cinematic apparatus itself. It is therefore through the process of de-mediation that the 1932 film and its remake expose systematic stupidity.

Ozu's expositions are not necessarily limited to any Japanese media environment. As Bernard Stiegler writes, individuation and stupidity are intertwined with a 'psycho-social collective individual, and in so far as they must be thought in terms of a doubly epokhal redoubling over-determined by technical evolutions' (2013, 171). That is, each epoch represents itself as the highest in a serial process of accumulating knowledge; but given its infinitute, stupidity as an act or speech can only be perceived as performance. The mere presumption of an evolved or liberated media, therefore, is at best immature. *Good Morning* replicates its 1932-born sibling in a technologically more advanced media ecology. But rather than presenting an air of superiority, it gives an impression of an unconscionable sensation. Although unchained and free from ideological constraints, *Good Morning* seems to have internalised the system that cinema transmits, and from which *I Was Born, But. . .* tries to untangle itself. Thus, as a reproduction of a reproduction, *Good Morning* does not fall short of its predecessor but exceeds it in projecting foresights of a short-sighted spectatorial predicament.

NOTES

1. Garrett Stewart defines 'demediation' as the process by which a transmissible text or image is blocked by the obtruded fact of its own neutralized medium' (2010, 413). I loosely follow this definition, but intend to denote the misuse, or self-defeating use, of telecommunication.
2. For a detailed discussion of this aspect in the film, see Amit 2019.
3. Although not remakes, these films reveal direct influence from Harold Lloyd and Ernst Lubitsch's silent comedies, most strikingly, with posters appearing in the background of several scenes.
4. For more on Ozu as an international brand, see Bordwell (2018).
5. With Fukui the protagonists practice English/Japanese translation – another form of transferring meaning.
6. KRT (TBS today) and the Osaka channel aired live, nearly simultaneously, two different shows (each comprised fifty-five episodes) between 1957 and 1958.
7. The show was started by KRT in 1958 and became a long-running franchise.
8. An NHK broadcast, the show is one of the first of its kind on Japanese television, although not the very first. It aired from 1953 to 1968.

REFERENCES

Amit, Rea. 2019. 'Programming a Public Mediascape: Distribution and the Japanese Motion Pictures Experience.' *On Culture: The Open Journal for the Study of Culture*, 8.
Bordwell, David. 1988. *Ozu and the Poetics of Cinema*. Princeton: Princeton University Press.
Bordwell, David. 2018. 'Watch Again! Look Well! Look!' In *Reorienting Ozu: A Master and His Influence*. Edited by Jinhee Choi. New York: Oxford University Press, 21–32.
Chun, Jayson Makoto. 2007. *'A Nation of a Hundred Million Idiots'?: A Social History of Japanese Television, 1953–1973*. New York: Routledge.
Elsaesser, Thomas. 2009. 'Freud as Media Theorist: Mystic Writing-Pads and the Matter of Memory.' *Screen* 50, no. 1: 100–13.
Fan, Kugioin. 2014. *Kuizu ka suru terebi*. Tokyo: Seikyūsha.
Galili, Doron. 2020. *Seeing by Electricity: The Emergence of Television, 1878–1939*. Durham: Duke University Press.
Freud, Sigmund. 1960. *The Ego and the Id*. New York: W. W. Norton & Company.

Gerow, Aaron. 2010. 'Kind Participation: Postmodern Consumption and Capital with Japan's Telop TV.' In *Television, Japan, and Globalization*. Edited by Mitsuhiro Yoshimoto, Eva Tsai and JungBong Choi, 117–50. Ann Arbor: University of Michigan Press.

Gerow, Aaron. 2010. *Visions of Japanese Modernity: Articulations of Cinema, Nation and Spectatorship, 1895–1925*. Berkeley: University of California Press.

Giotta, Gina. 2017. 'Sounding Live: An Institutional History of the Television Laugh Track.' *Journal of Communication Inquiry* 41, no. 4: 331–48.

Hasumi, Shigehiko. 1983. *Kantoku Ozu Yasujirō*. Tokyo: Chikuma Shobō.

Iida, Yutaka. 2016. *Terebi ga misemono datta kro: Shoki terebijon no kōkogaku*. Tokyo: Seikyūsha.

Iwabuchi, Koichi. 2004. 'Feeling Glocal: Japan in the Global Television Format Business.' In *Television Across Asia: TV Industries, Programme Formats and Globalisation*. Edited by Albert Moran and Michael Keane. London: RoutledgeCurzon.

Joo, Woojeong. 2017. *The Cinema of Ozu Yasujiro: Histories of the Everyday*. Edinburgh: Edinburgh University Press.

Kelleter, Frank. 2012. '"Toto, I Think We're in Oz Again" (and Again and Again): Remakes and Popular Seriality.' In *Film Remakes, Adaptations and Fan Productions: Remake/Remodel*. Edited by Kathleen Loock and Constantine Verevis, 19–44. New York: Palgrave Macmillan.

Kramer, Hanae Kurihara and Scott Kramer. 2019. 'Japan's Most Beloved Suicide Bombers: The Nikudan-san'yūshi Phenomenon (1932–1945).' *War & Society* 38, no. 3: 163–84.

Kuroda, Isamu. 1999. *Rajio taisō no tanjō*. Tokyo: Seikyūsha.

Masakiyo, Kensuke. 2016. 'Ozu Yasujirō Ohayō ni okeru onara no oto.' *Hyōshō* 10: 259–77.

Nornes, Abé Mark. 2003. *Japanese Documentary Film: The Meiji Era through Hiroshima*. Minneapolis: University of Minnesota Press.

Orbaugh, Sharalyn. 2012. '*Kamishibai* and the Art of the Interval.' *Mechademia* 7: 77–100.

Ōta, Shōichi. 2019. *Terebi shakai Nippon: Jisaku jien to shichōsha*. Tokyo: Serica Shobō.

Phillips, Alastair. 2007. 'The Salaryman's Panic Time: Ozu Yasujirō's *I Was Born, But . . .* (1932)'. In *Japanese Cinema: Texts and Contexts*. Edited by Alastair Phillips and Julian Stringer, 25–36. New York: Routledge.

Satō, Tadao. 2000. *Ozu Yasujirō no geijutsu*. Tokyo: Asahi Shinbunsha.

Satō, Takumi. 2019. *Terebi teki kyōyō: Ichioku sō hakuchi ka e no keifu*. Tokyo: Iwanami Shoten.

Stewart, Garrett. 2010. 'Bookwork as Demediation.' *Critical Inquiry* 36, no. 3: 410–57.

Stiegler, Bernard. 2013. 'Doing and Saying Stupid Things in the Twentieth Century: Bêtise and Animality in Deleuze and Derrida.' *Angelaki* 18, no. 1: 159–74.

Stiegler, Bernard. 2019. 'For a Neganthropology of Automatic Society.' In *Machine*. Edited by Thomas Pringle, Gertrud Koch and Bernard Stiegler, 25–47. Lüneburg: Meson Press, 25–47.

Takinami, Yuki. 2018. 'Modernity, Shoshimin Films, and the Proletarian-Film Movement: Ozu in Dialogue with Vertov.' In *Reorienting Ozu: A Master and His Influence*. Edited by Jinhee Choi, 133–44. New York: Oxford University Press.

Yoshimitsu, Takashi. 2021. 'Mijuku to no gyappu ni yori hassei suru raffu torakku ni kan suru kōsatsu: Bei Chū shittokomu hikaku bunseki.' *Nihon Kansei Kōdaigakukai Ronbunshi* 20, no. 2: 171–8.

CHAPTER 7

The Cinema of Serial Vitality: Ozu Yasujirō and Yamada Yoji

Steve Choe

A *Japan Times* review of *Tokyo Family* (*Tōkyō kazoku*, 2013), director Yamada Yōji's remake of Ozu Yasujirō's classic *Tokyo Story* (*Tōkyō monogatari*, 1953), expresses a critical sentiment that was perhaps widely felt by audiences when the film was theatrically released: 'The standard critical compliment for a good remake (and yes, they do exist) is that it makes the audience want to revisit the original. *Tokyo Family* will have served its purpose if it encourages viewers to check out not only *Tokyo Story*, but Yamada's other, better films as well' (Schilling 2013). Upon its domestic and international release, Yamada's film, which hews to the original's basic plot and depiction of the transformations of modernity on the Japanese family, prompted more than a few critics to wonder why a remake of a motion picture that regularly appears on lists of the 'greatest' films ever made was necessary at all. According to the author of the aforementioned review, the 'purpose' of a film remake is apparently to draw the attention of viewers back to the original film on which it is based (Ibid.). This chapter takes into consideration the 'standard critical compliment' of the remake, particularly as a concept that, when deployed in journalistic reviews, typically privileges uniqueness and originality at the expense of reiteration and variation. In doing so, I seek to reconsider Yamada's work and career in general so that his status as an auteur creating films in the spirit of Ozu's cinema can be better appreciated as a vital link to Japan's cinematic past. As we shall see, this 'spirit' can be described somewhat specifically, in terms of story and casting, as a way to begin thinking about the serial nature of Yamada's filmmaking practice.

REMAKING A CLASSIC

Let me begin by briefly focusing on a series of key formal and narrative features in *Tokyo Family* so that we might consider how they rework Ozu's film. The stories of both are set mostly in Tokyo in the heat of summer. Both are put into motion by the same initial premise: an elderly couple, Shūkichi and Tomiko Hirayama (played by Ryū Chishū and Higashiyama Chieko, respectively, in the original film, and by Hashizume Isao and Yoshiyuki Kazuko in Yamada's remake), arrives from the countryside in Hiroshima prefecture (Onomichi in the earlier film and Osaki-kamijima Island in the later) to visit their grown children in Tokyo. Their oldest son Kōichi (Yamamura Sō in the original, Nishimura Masahiko in the remake) is a doctor and their daughter Shigeko (Sugimura Haruko in the original, Nakajima Tomoko in the remake) runs a hair salon. In both films, the young Noriko (Hara Setsuko in the original, Aoi Yū in the later film) is not related by blood to the Hirayama family. Kōichi's children, two boys, express some reluctance and even annoyance at the prospect of their grandparents' visit, a sentiment that perhaps the family members in Tokyo feel but do not verbally express. Unable to accommodate them in their homes, the two Tokyo families in both films shuffle their parents to a hotel in Yokohama so that they can control the time they spend with them. Shūkichi and Tomiko sense that they are interrupting their children's busy lives and, in one of *Tokyo Story*'s most famous scenes, decide to leave the next day and return to the comfort of their own home in Hiroshima.

The elderly couple's conversation takes place on a harbour and, as they rise to leave, Tomiko suddenly feels dizzy and faints. Her husband, visibly concerned, asks if she is alright. Tomiko smiles and assures Shūkichi that everything is fine. Because there is no room in Koishi and Shigeko's houses, even for one night, their parents are rendered 'homeless' and are forced to sleep apart from one another. Shūkichi will go drinking with an old friend and his wife will stay with a family member. The next day, however, Tomiko collapses and, following her gradual deterioration, passes away. With the mother gone, the families in Tokyo rush back to their hometown to attend to the business of her funeral service. After the service, the brothers and sisters sit around a table and bicker over who will claim some of their mother's belongings. Soon, however, they are called back to return to their busy lives. In a scene that is nearly identical in both films, Noriko receives Tomiko's watch from Shūkichi while sobbing in gratitude. Both Ozu's film and Yamada's film end on a melancholy note, with Shūkichi left alone at home.

Over the years, cultural critics and film scholars have drawn attention to the universal themes of this simple yet profound story of familial loss and generational division. 'The dissolution of this family', writes Donald Richie, 'the transience of this world, the disappointment of this life – this is the theme of *Tokyo Story*' (1974, 168). This statement about the theme of Ozu's film could very well apply to Yamada's, given *Tokyo Family*'s similar treatment of these existential themes and of the characters. While both works clearly revolve around the inability or unwillingness of the children to accommodate their elderly parents properly (that is, according to traditional notions of familial respect and filial conduct), Ozu and Yamada do not condemn or demonise Kōichi and Shige for their selfishness. Instead, they are portrayed as preoccupied, almost regardless of their intentions, because their work and family lives demand their constant attention. If *Tokyo Story* and *Tokyo Family* depict the dissolution of the traditional family, this process is not the fault of anyone in particular, but ostensibly can be attributed to the broad cultural, social and technological changes in modern and contemporary Japan, changes that may be diagnosed by reading the films symptomatically, as it were. Sixty years span the release of both films, reflecting broad cultural changes taking place at the time they were made but also the progress of this change. The treatment of the characters and the diegetic worlds of both films may remind one of an observation André Bazin made about Vittorio De Sica in his appreciation of the Italian director. Of the latter's *Bicycle Thieves* (*Ladri di biciclette*, 1948), Bazin writes that its merit lies 'in not betraying the essence of things, in allowing them first of all to exist for their own sakes, freely; it is in loving them in their singular individuality' (2005, 69). Ozu and Yamada also exhibit a kind of unconditional love for the characters in these and other films, one that finds the virtues in all of them even as they act in seemingly unvirtuous ways.

Many viewers familiar with *Tokyo Story* will recognise and even likely expect moments in *Tokyo Family* that reiterate shots and dialogue from the earlier film. A conversation outdoors between Tomiko and her grandson Isamu (Mori Mitsuhiro in the original, Ayumu Maruyama in the remake) occurs in both films. 'What do you want to be when you grow up?', she asks the boy, adding, 'A doctor, like your father?' Later in the film, when Shūkichi is sitting at a bar, his drunk friend insists that the female bartender resembles his late wife. In both films, they compare the accomplishments of their sons and daughters in identical ways. Shūkichi speaks to Noriko in one of the final scenes of both films and gives her Tomiko's watch. When she receives it and weeps, both films depict her crying in the same manner, with her hands covering the tears falling down her face. While the later film makes these and other specific references to Ozu's work, Yamada also features shots that reference aesthetic and formal features that have been associated with Ozu's style more generally. 'Pillow shots' – of an exterior of a building, a power line structure jutting into the sky or a train cutting through a landscape – establish locations but also provide some emotional respite following a narratively significant scene. *Tokyo Family* often does not obey the 180-degree rule while nevertheless maintaining clarity about the positions of the characters across cuts. Both Ozu and Yamada employ close-ups only sparingly. In interior settings, Yamada may position the camera at the height of a person seated on a tatami mat, as was Ozu's wont, while utilising shot-reverse shots that frame only one character at a time facing the camera directly. Continuing his humanist line of analysis, Richie comments that these shots allow a character to appear 'before us as a fellow human being with his dignity intact; he is not at all the laboratory animal found in some films' (1974, 158). Throughout the film, camera movement is kept to a minimum or is nonexistent. There are no flashbacks, thus lending the story a sense of urgency for the spectator as it unfolds continuously in the present moment. The image never fades in or out – there are no lap-dissolves from one shot to the next – and the film's montage is composed only of decisive cuts. The continuity of both Ozu's film and Yamada's film is construed through this series of stylistic features, but also through accompanying music that eases transitions between locations and emotions.

These and other 'Ozuisms' in *Tokyo Family* serve to pay homage to the aesthetics of one of the most celebrated films in Japanese film history, but also to entice us to reconsider the relationship between form and narrative in Ozu's cinema. In his study of the Japanese director's poetics, David Bordwell notes that *Tokyo Story* 'suggests how conventional narrative unity can pass over into a purely formal rigor' (1988, 56). Bordwell observes that Ozu's films, through their minimalistic style, create parallel structures that draw similarities and equivalences between characters, actions, objects, scenes and locations within a film – at times for their own sake. Montage and sound are the primary means by which these motivic parallelisms are constituted, such as that of travelling – between Onomichi, Tokyo and Atami – whereby space is traversed through editing. Continuity is dictated by cause-effect linearity but also the length of the shots and the rhythm of the editing, soliciting a rhythm of affective engagement of the spectator with the film text. Sometimes shots are held after an action has been completed, particularly following an emotionally demanding scene, allowing the viewer some release of tension following its build-up. In his analysis, Bordwell notes how sounds – the chugging of boats, the rumbling of a train and the buzzing of cicadas – establish a sense of place but also connect various moments of the film together through acoustic association. In the final shots of *Tokyo Story*, he writes, the boat horn exemplifies how 'an abstract rhythm of repetition and development... can punctuate or accompany narrative action and recall prior scenes without being reducible to exact meanings' (1988, 560). Indeed, Ozu's stylistic rigour gives rise to abstracted structures that do not emerge from or culminate with the aim of developing the narrative further. In this, images, sounds and sequences in *Tokyo Story* and in the director's other films could be read to construe a repertoire of purely formal elements that constitute a distinctive style, what might be referred to as 'Ozu's cinema'. The viewer of this cinema is called upon to recognise these elements, whether consciously or unconsciously, and link them to each other through logics of difference and repetition – the conceptual core, one might say, of remakes.

If Ozu's *Tokyo Story* can be seen to unify narrative through the implementation of formal rigour, clear differences and alterations emerge as we reflect on Yamada's remake. One can point to a number of key narrative details. Noriko is given a drastically reduced role while her boyfriend Shoji (Satoshi Tsumabuki), the youngest son of Shūkichi and Tomiko, and whose occupation is a theatre stagehand, plays a much more significant one. In Ozu's *Tokyo Story*, Shūkichi and Tomiko's youngest son is named Keizō (Ōsaka Shirō) and appears only briefly in the film, arriving too late to his mother's funeral service. Nevertheless, the experience of loss is integrated into the fabric of both films and treated as a trauma that has already been affirmed and lived with. Noriko's husband died during the Second World War in the earlier film, while the earthquake and the tsunami of March 2011 are referenced in the later one. Shūkichi is told that the husband of a friend was taken by the devastating tsunami and later Shoji tells his mother that he met Noriko while volunteering for the relief efforts following the Fukushima nuclear plant disaster. (The 3/11 tsunami in Japan delayed the filming and production of *Tokyo Family*.) Tomiko has her fatal collapse on the stairs in Koishi's house, while in Ozu's film she falls ill on the train. When Shūkichi reflects on his partner's death on top of a highrise building, it is Shoji that joins him and not Noriko. Here the father tells his son that his mother has passed, words that are perhaps profound in their mundanity yet serve ultimately to placate their strained relationship, if only momentarily. A host of other details mark small but crucial differences. Ozu's film opens in Onomichi while Yamada's starts in Tokyo. The Ferris wheel in Yokohama (it was Atami in *Tokyo Story*) reminds Shūkichi of a well-known scene from British director Carol Reed's *The Third Man* (1949), featuring Orson Welles. Shoji drives a dilapidated Fiat Cinequecento, about which family members repeatedly pester him – an element that has no corresponding equivalent in Ozu's film.

But aside from differences in narrative content, *Tokyo Family* seems ultimately to merely gesture toward Ozu's cinema. The relationship that Yamada establishes between form and narrative in his remake are at times forced and perhaps even awkward at moments. As it was his eighty-fifth film, it was perhaps difficult for the director to free himself fully from his own 'Yamadaisms' and long-standing stylistic habits. *Tokyo Family* does not frame space in parallel or perpendicular angles in relation to the camera. The shot-reverse shot sequences are constituted through typical over-the-shoulder two-shots and, for this reason, may seem to miss the sense that one is observing 'a fellow human being with his dignity intact', to recall Richie's observation of Ozu's cinema.

THE CINEMA OF SERIAL VITALITY   145

Figure 7.1 One of several over-the-shoulder, shot-reverse shot sequences in Yamada Yōji's *Tokyo Family* (*Tōkyō kazoku*, 2013), illustrating this remake's stylistic divergence from its source material (Ozu Yasujirō's *Tokyo Story* [*Tōkyō monogatari*, 1953]).

Many shots in the later film are not consistent with Ozu's systematic utilisation of the tatami shot. In *Tokyo Story*, the viewer quickly acclimates to the director's systematic positioning of the camera in forty-five-degree angle multiples in relation to the axis-of-action. And while Yamada may often adopt these geometric positions throughout his film, what is noticeable in his remake are the shots that do not conform to this principle, when the camera is placed in more diverse angles within the diegesis. Correspondingly, objects within the shot are not set with the same kind of geometric precision in relation to the camera. The patterns of sounds that establish the everyday fabric of life in urban Tokyo and more rural Onomichi in *Tokyo Story* do not function to underscore narrative parallels in *Tokyo Family*. Yamada creates parallels through editing, dialogue and mise-en-scène, not in order to create formal patterns, but more conventionally to establish character. In contrast to Ozu's quickly recognisable formal style, his editing and shot composition are constituted without seemingly any distinctive method and are rendered through 'invisible editing'. The movement from shot to shot is thus motivated, more predictably perhaps, by plot, characterisation and cause-effect linearity. In this, the narrational elements in *Tokyo Family* bring the viewer not into a system of signs that mark the unique style of an auteur but rather the sentimental and perhaps commercial expectations associated with the popular melodramatic mode.

Bordwell's interest in Ozu's cinema, like that of other film scholars, rests on the belief that it stands in ambivalent relation to classic Hollywood narration; he understands it as modernist in its delineation of an auteurist style. Perhaps with this thought in mind, critics will often perceive the stylistic differences in *Tokyo Family* as deficiencies that do not measure up to the original masterpiece while also charging that the remake delves into banal sappiness. While acknowledging that Yamada's film will 'vex Ozu devotees and bore mainstream audiences', a reviewer for *Variety* also notes that 'Yamada's characteristic sentimentality and the actors' uncharacteristically nuance-free performances run counter to Ozu's aesthetic of elegant understatement' (Lee 2013). The implication here is that Ozu's film belongs to the canon of art cinema while Yamada's remake is commercial, popular and participates in the open display of emotion. The reviewer here seems to suggest that that the 'elegant understatement' of the original work has devolved into mere sentimentality in the remake. Yet in insisting on these discursive categories in evaluating the film remake, we run the risk of subsuming and overlooking more fundamental issues.

THE GOD OF CINEMA IN-BETWEEN

Rather than see *Tokyo Family* for the film that it is not and deem it a debased rehashing of a putatively superior original, I would like to reconsider the metaphysics of difference and repetition that underpins the concept of the remake and propose an alternative framework that is much more capacious in its explanatory scope: serial vitality. This formulation can be defined in conjunction with a life that consists of continuous cinematic production and a cyclical working practice that is intimately connected to the unfolding of lived experience. While Yamada's remake of Ozu's most celebrated film has typically been subject to judgment that poses an original masterpiece over-against an unnecessary copy, reflection on a grouping of films will allow us to see the vitality of Yamada's style and the seriality that I believe serves as the driving impulse throughout his career. This vitality finds expression through the differences and repetitions that appear in the works that comprise Yamada's oeuvre, from one film to the next, but also in the return of themes, images, characters and actors from the distant past. This serial vitality may be most clearly detected in the films comprising his 'A Class to Remember' (*Gakkō*) series (1993–2000) and his 'What a Wonderful Family!' (*Kazoku wa tsurai yo*) series (2016–2018), featuring four and three works respectively, but especially the forty-eight instalments that make up the 'Tora-san' series of films (1969–1995).

Yamada began working as an assistant director for Shōchiku in 1954 and, although he never met Ozu formally (they had only merely crossed paths momentarily at the studio), he considers himself a disciple of the master. In 1969, Yamada made the first of fifty films featuring the comedic Tora-san character, named Torajiro Kuruma and played by Atsumi Kiyoshi, with *It's Tough Being a Man* (*Otoko wa Tsurai yo*). Always travelling and unlucky in love, Tora-san perpetually comes home in each film of the series to rejoin his sister, nephew and extended family. His arrival frequently instigates a ruckus between them. As Torajiro travels throughout Japan, the films showcase various sites of touristic interest while he encounters unusual characters along the way, including businessmen filled with wanderlust as well as famous scholars and artists. Two Tora-san films were released every year, during the summer and at New Year's, coordinating their arrival with the rhythm of the calendar. Yamada also wrote and directed several successful dramatic works not linked directly to the Tora-san films, such as *Home from the Sea* (*Furusato*, 1972) and *The Yellow Handkerchief* (*Shiawase no kiiroi hankachi*, 1977), which touch upon issues concerning lost romance and the modern Japanese family. When Atsumi passed in August 1996, it marked the end of the Tora-san series and compelled the director to work in other genres, including nonfiction and even more experimental forms. Outside of Japan, Yamada is perhaps best known for his 'Twilight Samurai' trilogy (2002–2006) which stars Sanada Hiroyuki in the title role and was the first pre-modern period production the director had made up to that time.

These different clusters of films suggest a filmmaking praxis characterised by reiteration, particularly in the way the productions repeatedly call attention to the tensions between journeying and the domesticity that is associated with the family melodrama. Expectations that are baked into the popular melodramatic mode are renewed, with each film wanting to begin and end in a space of innocence, where beset victims are made worthy of grief, and featuring narratives that work with the temporality of the 'too late' that solicits spectatorial sympathy and sentiment. Themes of responsibility, loyalty, friendship, hospitality and modern romance are raised through the repetitions of generic cues, dramatised by characters played by the same actors from one film to the next. Nishida Toshiyuki plays a teacher in two of the four films that make up the

'A Class to Remember' films, each of which characterises the student cohort as a kind of family. Members of the bonded families depicted in Yamada's films criticise and complain about each other, but these disputes somehow never jeopardise their cohesion. The repetition that is secured by the family unit assures all that its members, despite slights previously experienced and insults traded, will be seen again in the next film.

It is this spirit of iterability that underlies the casting of *Tokyo Family*. Actors that worked (or would continue to work) with the director play members of the Hirayama family, most of them widely known by Japanese audiences from other theatrically released features but from television programs and TV movies as well. In addition to the actors mentioned above, Aoi Yū, playing 'angelic' femininity in the Noriko character, would have been known to audiences from *All About Lily Chou-Chou* (*Riri Shushu no subete*, 2001) and *One Million Yen Girl* (*Hyakuman-en to nigamushi onna*, 2008). Yamada had already cast her in *About Her Brother* (*Ototo*, 2010). Natsukawa Yui, who plays the Hirayama daughter Fumiko, starred in *The Blind Swordsman: Zatoichi* (2003), directed by Kitano Takeshi, and in Koreeda Hirokazu's *Still Walking* (*Aruitemo aruitemo*, 2008). Nishimura Masahiko, the Hirayama son Kōichi in *Tokyo Family*, is best known from the many television series in which he appeared. Indeed, all of the actors in Yamada's *Tokyo Family* are familiar faces and performers from Japanese media and animation. More significantly, these actors would also continue to work with this director in his three 'What a Wonderful Family!' films, made back-to-back between 2016 and 2018. In this new trilogy, the unity of the family is tested as a key marriage relationship in each instalment is threatened with the prospect of divorce. The actors and characters are the same as in *Tokyo Family* except the clan is called Hirata while the architectural layout of the two-level house is different. *What a Wonderful Family!* could be considered a remake of his 2013 remake of Ozu's film, with both subsequent entries in the trilogy – *What a Wonderful Family! 2* (2017) and *What a Wonderful Family! 3* (2018) – emerging as a developing variation on the previous one.[1] Significantly, at the end of the first film, the grandfather played by Hashizume Isao watches *Tokyo Story* in his bedroom on television. The scene from Ozu's film that Shūzō Hirata is shown viewing is a familiar one. This is when Shūkichi gives the watch to Noriko and he remarks that she had done more for the Hirayama family than anyone who was related to them by blood. In Yamada's film, this is the corresponding moment when the grandfather and grandmother reconcile and decide not to divorce.

Yamada's seriality suggests an approach to filmmaking characterised by repetition and variation, where he is continuously remaking not only his own films, but himself as a filmmaker (albeit in subtle increments). These are discernible aspects of Ozu's practice as well. Across the filmographies of both prolific directors, actors reappear and change roles from one motion picture to the next, while never losing their connection to the Japanese family, and themes are reiterated and developed. Sugimura Haruko and Miyake Kuniko in *Tokyo Story* will be known to viewers of Ozu's cinema from *Brothers and Sisters of the Toda Family* (*Toda-ke no kyodai*, 1941), *Early Summer* (*Bakushū*, 1951), *Good Morning* (*Ohayō*, 1959) and *Floating Weeds* (*Ukigusa*, 1959). But it is Hara Setsuko and Ryū Chishū who will be immediately familiar to many audiences, for their portrayal of fathers, brothers, daughters and older sisters in key films by the Shōchiku auteur. Ryū performed in well over half of Ozu's fifty-four works and arguably his career cannot be considered separately from the films they made together. This partnership immediately recalls Atsumi's long relationship to Yamada, and this recollection is reiterated in the dozens of times when Ryū appeared in the Tora-san films as the local Buddhist monk. This is no mere cameo, but a role that is integral to the diegetic world in the 'It's Tough Being a Man' series. He would continue playing the 'Gozensama' role for Yamada until 1992, his last film appearance, before his death in 1993. Ryū's recurring appearance in the Tora-san films marks the passing of time, like the cyclical changing of the seasons, from late spring to early summer in Yamada's *Where Spring Comes Late* (*Kazoku*, 1970), which not coincidentally also stars Ryū. In the moving dramatic feature *A Distant Cry from Spring* (*Haruka naru yama no yobigoe*, 1980), the turning of the seasons signal the time it takes for the characters played by Baishō Chieko and Yoshioka Hidetaka to learn how to live with and then let go of a stranger to their farm. Notably, this film was remade as a TV movie in 2018 by director Asahara Yuzo, who was a co-writer on *Tora-san, Welcome Back* (*Otoko wa tsurai yo 50: Okaeri Tora-san*, 2019) and *It's a Flickering Life* (*Kinema no kamisama*, 2021). Watching Ryū and hearing his reedy voice again in Yamada's films, one perhaps cannot help but to remember the many sympathetic characters that he played in Ozu's, all of them embodied by this gentle face in particular. The familiarity of Ryū here is inseparable from the careers of both filmmakers, as they repeatedly make and remake him as a finite human being in their films.

Yet, this experience of familiarity is palpable as well when regarding the many key actors featured in Yamada's films since the beginning of his career. Baishō is best known for playing Tora-san's sister Sakura and Yoshioka her son Mitsuo. The latter actor started working with Yamada when he was a little boy and has appeared in dozens of the director's films since the 1981 production of *Tora-san's Love in Osaka* (*Otoko wa Tsurai yo: Naniwa no Koi no Torajirō*). Like seeing a beloved family member once more, each of their characters' gestures, facial expressions and manner of speech place the viewer in a state of comforting familiarity, while their inherent virtue is constituted through the accumulation of previous roles. Here I am reminded of a description Gilles Deleuze provided on the time-image and its foregrounding of perception as constituted through the co-existence of 'sheets of the past'. Childhood, youth, adulthood and old age converge in the image of a face; the temporalities of past, present and future in an image. Deleuze writes that 'the past which is preserved takes on all the virtues of beginning and beginning again: it is what holds in its depths or in its sides the surge of the new reality, the bursting forth of life' (1989, 92). Actors do not simply play characters from one film to the next; from Ozu to Yamada, they put into motion thoughtful reflection upon their lives, lived in the cinema. In turn, this serial vitality passes through discursive binaries that typically separate the actor and his or her role through the image of a human being who is bound by the experience of aging. The final moments of *Tora-san, Welcome Back* (*Otoko wa tsurai yo 50: Okaeri Tora-san*, 2019), a film that recalls Atsumi's Tora-san in spectral remembrances, give us close-up shots of Yoshioka's fifty-nine-year-old face, in tears, while he recalls memories of his uncle. This act of recall is doubled by the viewer's own as he or she reflects upon fifty years of Yamada's films starring Atsumi while also remembering past moments from their own lives that may be associated with his cinema.

Taking into consideration films such as *About Her Brother*, *Kyoto Story* (*Kyoto uzumasa monogatari*, 2010), *The Little House* (*Chisai ouchi*, 2014), which features Hashizume and Yoshiyuki, *Nagasaki: Memories of My Son* (*Haha to kuraseba*, 2015) and the *What a Wonderful Family!* trilogy, we can see how Yamada's productions reflect his preoccupation with the family and its changes in history that are the principal concern of his *Tokyo Family* from 2013. Some of these are period works that depict Japan during and after the Second World War, the time of *Tokyo Story*, or tell stories that recall Ozu's work in its everydayness and genial humour. The fictional romance depicted in *Kyoto Story* incorporates documentary interviews of people who worked in the Daiei Film Studios as they reflect on a part of Japanese film history that has all but disappeared. *It's a Flickering Life* recalls the nostalgic memories of obsessive gambler and deadbeat father Goh Maruyama (played by Sawada Kenji, a well-known singer since the 1960s who also appeared in Yamada's *Tora-san, The Expert* [*Otoko wa Tsurai yo: Hana mo Arashi mo Torajirō*, 1982]). Through flashbacks triggered by old movies, Goh remembers a moment in his youth when he worked in a film studio and almost became a director. While the film depicts professional and personal opportunities missed in the past, it also shows filming scenes with a director named Demizu that has more than a passing resemblance to Ozu. Another fictional director in the film's story is called 'Oda'. In Yamada's ode to the classic Japanese cinema of the 1930s, *Final Take: The Golden Age of Movies* (*Kinema no tenchi*, 1986), Yamada tells the story, set in 1934, of a young actress who stars in a film production called *Floating Weeds*. The title of this film-within-the-film clearly references Ozu's own production from the same year, while the filming scenes feature the director's routine of setting the camera low to the ground. *Final Take* features the familiar faces of Atsumi, Baishō, Yoshioka and even Ryū in a small role as the janitor of the

Shōchiku studios. One may also detect through this serial impulse a desire to remake *Tokyo Story* earlier in Yamada's career in *My Sons* (*Musuko*, 1991), which tells the story of a widowed father coming to visit his sons in Tokyo. The narrative to *My Sons* seems to follow what happens to the aged father in Ozu's film after becoming a widower. The diegeses of all these films are constituted by relations with familial and neighbourhood regulars, as if the boundary of the world were coterminous with the boundary of the family.

These connections encourage us to consider the notion of the remake diachronically, to think of film production as a serialised practice of remaking the life that sustains cinema itself. Beyond simply comparing and contrasting one work with another, this notion of the remake as serial vitality shows us that both Ozu and Yamada were constantly remaking their own films, recasting actors and retelling the story of the Japanese middle-class family melodrama while seemingly heedless to the metaphysics that reiterate conventional binaries between the original and copy. This 'flickering life', to cite the English-language title of Yamada's film *Kinema no kamisama* (which can be translated as 'God of Cinema'), underpins comparisons that might be made not only between human existence and cinema, or a life lived in tandem with those lights and shadows on the screen that assume the shapes of flesh-and-blood people, but also between an original film and its remake, regardless of whether we read the latter formally or symptomatically. Yet in identifying and drawing out similarities and differences, we would also do well to consider the metaphysical schematic that underpins this very process, the epistemological assumptions that make possible the operations of comparison and contrast, and that which ranks the text either as exemplary or derivative within these operations.

In his early philosophical work, *Difference and Repetition*, Deleuze aims precisely to launch a critique of this metaphysics. He begins his analysis by asserting that 'repetition is not generality' and through this assertion sets out to separate the concept of repetition from that of mere repeatability (1994, 1). Repetition, as Deleuze understands it, is unrelated to the generalisability of a specific trait, for it refuses the everyday notion of repetition as defined through a series of reciprocally determined elements, each of which disappear when ostensibly universal, timeless concepts are applied to them. Meaningful analytical concepts, such as narrative, character, history, the nature of the Japanese family and so on, may be traced consistently through their identification with a Platonic Idea. Deleuze understands these concepts as subsuming individual instantiations of life outside of philosophy into the language of metaphysics. Repeating this notion of identity to reproduce a dissimilarity, difference develops through an equal and opposite process, whereby one instantiation is set over-against another in a relation of negation. In both cases, that which is generalisable guarantees the belief that two traits (or singular elements) may be compared and contrasted at all. And in the cases of both similarity and dissimilarity, the underlying generalisability of the concept, that which grounds and legitimates the very notions of difference and repetition, is left unchanged. Traditional theories of the film remake impose these metaphysical generalities as they reiterate dichotomies between a celebrated original over-against a debased copy, a before and after that implicitly privileges the primary firstness of the former over against the derived secondariness of the latter. What we recognise as pillow shots and tatami shots, the violation of the 180-degree rule, the breakdown of the traditional Japanese family and other Ozuisms, are concepts that provide the means to play out differences and repetitions in Yamada's *Tokyo Family*, but they do so at the cost of subsuming instantiations of this director's serial vitality to these metaphysical models.

Underneath this schema of representation surges the continuous production of difference in itself. For Deleuze, the work of art and its production of simulacra is key for representing this non-representable vital force. 'It is a question', he writes, 'of producing within the work a movement capable of affecting the mind outside of all representation; it is a question of making movement itself a work, without interposition; of inventing vibrations, rotations, whirlings, gravitations, dances or leaps which thereby touch the mind' (1994, 8). Unmediated and without telos, these movements underlie but also surreptitiously inspire the very apparatus of representation while constituting its submerged interior. Not negation, not generality, but singular and without end, this phantasmatic form of repetition is shot through with radical difference and not simply opposed to it. Affirming its status as a copy without an original, Deleuze aligns this primordial movement with performativity and the production of 'real movement' – what I am calling 'serial vitality'. These forces are integral to the very means available to the moving image and the production that is inherent to its reproducibility.

Moments from *It's a Flickering Life* that refer explicitly to the film's Japanese title help us understand this continuous vitality, expressed through movement that unfolds, to quote Deleuze once more, 'outside of all representation'. Throughout the film, the 'god of cinema' refers to Goh's movie script, conceived when he was a young man. It tells the story of a movie star emerging from the screen and descending to meet a female fan sitting in the film theatre. At about the halfway point in *It's a Flickering Life*, in a flashback, the young Goh (Suda Masaki) is encouraged by his long-time friend Terashin (Noda Yōjirō) to bring his film to fruition in the studio's projection room. 'Only you could write "The God of Cinema"', he remarks, 'a star emerging from the screen, easily transcending fiction and reality'. This script will win him the Kido Prize and recognition for his lifelong dedication to the project. An earlier conversation in the same projection room reveals a different view of the film's title. Here Terashin explains to his friend that, 'Between each shot lives a divine spirit. The god of cinema.' His remark comes while loading the projector to screen the rushes from the day. This notion of a divine spirit that inhabits the space between each shot, and thus animates the film image, will be cited once more in Yamada's work. It recalls Bergson's observation that movement inheres, not in the shots, but 'in the apparatus' – that is, in the movement produced by the projector's electric motor and which animates the transitions from immobile shot to immobile shot (1998, 305). The film's conclusion brings these understandings of the god of cinema together, bestowing life onto the moving image, flickering in and out of existence, and without which the cinema would remain a mere series of still frames. Reality and script, actor and character: the god of cinema brings life and its simulacrum to fruition. I have tried to show how this principle of vital movement in the cinema could be carried over into the filmmaking practice of both Yamada and Ozu, a serial vitality that compels them to produce one film after the next. Each of them may be compared to an individual shot, a moment in history and memory framed by an individual film, but animated through their lived lives. These series of films – many of them direct or indirect remakes – constitute bodies of work, sustained by the underlying principle of the moving image itself.

NOTE

1. The reviewer for *The Hollywood Reporter* comments that *What a Wonderful Family! 2* is 'not Ozu, but it'll do' (Lowe 2017).

REFERENCES

Bazin, André. 2005. *What is Cinema? Vol. 2*. Translated by Hugh Gray. Berkeley: University of California Press.
Bergson, Henri. 1998. *Creative Evolution*. Translated by Arthur Mitchell, Mineola: Dover.
Bordwell, David. 1988. *Ozu and the Poetics of Cinema*. Princeton: Princeton University Press.
Deleuze, Gilles. 1989. *Cinema 2: The Time-Image*. Translated by Hugh Tomlinson and Robert Galeta. Minneapolis: University of Minnesota Press.
Deleuze, Gilles. 1994. *Difference and Repetition*. Translated by Paul Patton. New York: Columbia University Press.
Lee, Maggie. 2013. '*Tokyo Family*.' *Variety*, 13 February. https://variety.com/2013/film/reviews/tokyo-family-1117949249/. Accessed 28 April 2022.
Lowe, Justin. 2017. '*What a Wonderful Family! 2*: Film Review.' *The Hollywood Reporter*, 3 December. https://www.hollywoodreporter.com/movies/movie-reviews/what-a-wonderful-family-2-1066677/. Accessed 28 April 2022.
Richie, Donald. 1974. *Ozu*. Berkeley: University of California Press.
Schilling, Mark. 2013. '"*Tokyo Kazoku* (*Tokyo Family*)": Disaster Begets Repercussions in Yamada's Family Home.' *Japan Times*, 11 January. https://www.japantimes.co.jp/culture/2013/01/11/films/film-reviews/tokyo-kazoku-tokyo-family/. Accessed 28 April 2022.

Part III

Revisiting Personal/Political Traumas in East Asian Action Films, Gangster Films and Westerns

CHAPTER 8

Opting Out of History: Miike Takashi's *New Graveyard of Honor*

Earl Jackson

Young director Yoshimura Kōzaburō could hardly believe his good fortune when Shōchiku, one of Japan's 'Big Four' motion picture studios, offered to let him make his feature film directorial debut with the adaptation of Kishida Kunio's best-selling novel, *Warm Current* (*Danryū*, 1939). But there was one condition: Yoshimura could make this romantic melodrama only if he promised that his next film would be *The Legend of Tank Commander Nishizumi* (*Nishizumi Senshachō Den*, 1940), the story of an ordinary conscripted soldier from rural Kumamoto in Kyushu, Nishizumi Kojirō (1914–1938), who had recently been killed in battle in China (Jackson 2019, 4–5). Yoshimura kept his end of the bargain and made *The Legend of Tank Commander Nishizumi* in 1940 with superstar Uehara Ken in the title role (Yoshimura 1976, 61–3). The cinematic apparatus was deployed to construct a hero for specific imperialist purposes (Iida et al. 1940, 55–6).

Thirty-five years later, Fukasaku Kinji brought another real-life figure to the screen for a completely contrary agenda. *Graveyard of Honor* (*Jingi no hakaba*, 1975), based on the non-fiction novel of the same name by Fujita Gorō, tells the true story of Ishikawa Rikio (Watari Tatsuya), a self-made yakuza whose excesses included unsanctioned crime sprees, heroin addiction, murder and, eventually, suicide in prison. Fukasaku's narrative closely related Ishikawa's rise to the desperation of early post-war Japan. Although Ishikawa Rikio is considered an anomaly in Fukasaku's film, the ability of that anarchic, self-destructive subject to attain a powerful status within organised crime is intimately related to the aftermath of the Second World War. Both Ishikawa's sociopathy and its shocking success are indices of the physical and psychological devastation in which Ishikawa operates: the mass poverty and starvation immediately after the war; the cynicism of the police; the betrayal of a humanised emperor; and the contradictions of the compulsory democracy imposed by the US occupation that in itself had begun to sympathise with the right-wing politics of its war criminals.

Just after the turn of the twenty-first century, another iconoclastic Japanese filmmaker, Miike Takashi, attempted a thought experiment with *New Graveyard of Honor* (*Shin jingi no hakaba*, 2002), his tellingly titled remake of Fukasaku's film: what if there were an Ishikawa born a couple generations later, whose career began to peak at the end of the 1980s before careening into mayhem along with the post-bubble economy? While we would expect the answer to be complex, actually posing the question evinces its own complexities. This re-contextualisation of Ishikawa itself needs to be contextualised. While Miike's film sets Ishimatsu's life in the 1990s, he makes his film in 2002, a textual production fully conditioned and informed not only by the historical events of the 1990s but also by the new tendencies and contradictions within and new pressures on narratives of Japan in this era. For one thing, the old narrative of a homogeneous nation is no longer sustainable. Although Miike was one of the most active filmmakers of the 1990s to focus on the relation of 'others' within Japan, the nature of that inclusion has also come under scrutiny, most incisively by Mika Ko (whose work I will return to near the end of this chapter). Secondly, any account of post-bubble Japan must also take into consideration how the resulting malaise informs contemporary narratives of life thereafter, most succinctly and compellingly accomplished by Tomiko Yoda. Although Otsuka Eiji is deservedly one of the targets of Yoda's critique, Otsuka's revised theory of narrative consumption nevertheless seems promising in the present context, as it is articulated from within the zeitgeist it examines, in a feedback loop that also requires our attention, especially since an appreciation of Miike's film must distinguish the analytic gestures of the film from elements that seem more symptomatic of the millennial crisis in narrative and its relation to history.

FUKASAKU KINJI'S *GRAVEYARD OF HONOR* (1975)

In the late 1950s and early 1960s, Ishii Teruo made a series of lurid but engaging gangster films, first with Shintoho, then with Tōei, while Okamoto Kihachi made somewhat more elegant yakuza films for Tōhō and the older cross-town rival Nikkatsu supported the stylistic flourishes of Hasebe Yasuharu and Suzuki Seijun (most of which are set in contemporary Japan). In the mid-to-late 1960s, Tōei moved the yakuza back into the late nineteenth and early twentieth centuries with *ninkyo-eiga* or chivalry films that focused on the nobility of the yakuza, caught between obligation and human feeling (Watanabe 1993, 12–4). Another subgenre emerged in the 1970s, the *jitsuroku* or 'true record', that was much grittier and often based on actual criminal cases

(Fukuma 1993, 26–30). One principal figure of the *jitsuroku* was Ando Noboru (1926–2015), head of his own gang, the Ando Gumi, since 1952 (Oshita 2016, 12–24). In 1958 he was convicted of murder and served six years. Upon his release, he dissolved his gang and eventually became an actor in yakuza films, frequently in those that were based on his own life (Ando *Otoko* 89–93). He also wrote crime novels and served as producer and consultant for years. Ando figures prominently in Fukasaku's *Graveyard of Honor*, both for the role he plays and his extra-filmic persona. He also exerted significant influence on Miike's films from the period *New Graveyard of Honor* was made, most directly and dramatically by serving as a consultant on one of the director's most celebrated films, *True Account of the Life of Ando Noboru (Outlaw): Raging Fire* (*Jitsuroku: Andō Noboru Kyōdō-den - Rekka*), made in 2002, the same year as *New Graveyard of Honor*.

The second major moment in the rise of *jitsuroku* was Fukasaku Kinji's five-film series *Battles without Honor and Humanity* between 1973 and 1974. These films chronicled a fictionalised version of the gang wars in Hiroshima in the 1950s, following the work of Iiboshi Kōichi, who based his account on the memoirs of yakuza boss Kōzō Minō. *Graveyard of Honor* continued Fukasaku's *jitsuroku* explorations with its story of real-life sociopath Ishikawa Rikio. It is not surprising that Ando Noboru also appears in the film in a role that marks the dovetailing of national history and *jitsuroku* sensationalism. *Graveyard of Honor* is another major text in the *jitsuroku* canon, focusing on the inexplicable rise and catastrophic fall of a minor yakuza tough guy, and shaping the story into a prismatic look at the chaos of post-war Japan. Because Ishikawa is central to Fukasaku's film, and conversely, because that film has become the default version of Ishikawa's life, I would like to preface the reading of the film with a sketch of the life of the historical figure.

Ishikawa Rikio (1926–1956) was born into poverty in Mito prefecture. Even when very young he wanted to be a gangster and as a teenager he ran away to Tokyo to pursue that strange dream. Remarkably, he was accepted into the Wada-gumi at only sixteen and was personally guided by the *oyabun* Wada Kaoru (Fujita 1989, 16–18). Ishikawa's intense loyalty to Wada led him to acts of dangerous aggression against anyone he perceived to have disrespected his mentor. His first major act of violence got him sentenced to juvenile detention. After his release Ishikawa was also befriended by Imai Kōzaburō, who would eventually become *oyabun* of his own family. Although Wada admired Ishikawa's aggression and often sent him on missions because of it, he gradually began to phase Ishikawa out (Ibid., 68–74). Ishikawa became more erratic because of the perceived slight and was even jealous toward younger colleagues who seemed to have pulled Wada's favour away from him. One particularly extreme act led Wada to order Ishikawa to cut off his little finger, but instead the enraged Ishikawa stabbed Wada severely enough to require a month to recover (Ibid., 92–6). Ishikawa was sentenced to eighteen months in prison and he was banned from the Yakuza world of Tokyo for ten years for breaking the taboo. After his release Ishikawa went to Osaka, where he became addicted to heroin. He returned to Tokyo in 1949 in spite of the ban and sought protection from Imai, who initially helped him but also urged him to respect the ban and leave Tokyo. Again, Ishikawa felt betrayed and fatally shot Imai. He was sent to Fuchu Prison, where in 1956 he leapt off the roof. In his prison cell, his writings included one line that has become immortalised: 'What a big laugh – 30 years of lunatic antics!' (Ibid., 162–6).

Graveyard of Honor begins with a series of staged photographs representing Ishikawa's childhood, and the voiceovers are recreations of interviews with those who knew him as a child and a teenager. Ironically, the first statement of the film is erroneous, incorrectly giving 1924 as the year of his birth, when he was born in 1926. It is important to appreciate here both how young he was when he entered the yakuza world but also the symbolism involved in his being born in the first year of Shōwa – Ishikawa is intimately identified with the rise of Japanese nationalism and its particular horrors. The photo montage ends with poses of the actor Watari Tetsuya and the newsreel footage of immediate post-war Japan is replaced with the Tōei studio version of the black market.

Aaron Gerow has described Fukasaku's commitment to history in his films, citing the catastrophe that begins the first film in *Battles without Honor*:

> In Fukasaku Kinji's world, to begin a yakuza movie with the Bomb . . . is not only to create a symbol of the nihilistic, nearly apocalyptic realm of corrupt, internecine struggles that will ensue, but to fix a historical marker that delineates the core of much of his work and makes him one of cinema's unique historiographers (Gerow 2010).

While Hiroshima is the horizon against which the gang wars play out in *Battles*, in *Graveyard of Honor* the effects of the war are embodied in Ishikawa's sociopathy and the failure of even the criminal organisations to hold him in check.[1]

While the psychic desolation of early post-war Japan is focalised through Ishikawa's perspective for the most part, at times the character's actions can be read as a microhistory that parallel Japan's macro-historical changes. The first intersection of yakuza history and Japanese history comes when Japanese yakuza from at least two gang families raid a gambling club run by members of the minority population, known pejoratively as the *sangokujin* (people of three countries): Taiwan, China and Korea. In September 1945, the GHQ established certain conditions in Japan, based on the Morgenthau Plan that had been developed for Germany. Among them was a directive barring discrimination based on race or ethnicity (Cohen 1987, 29–30). In his study of the GHQ, Theodore Cohen makes the peculiar claim that this directive was misplaced, arguing that it made sense in Germany, given Nazi atrocities against 'Jews and Eastern Europeans', but 'the Chinese . . . Taiwanese and Korean residents who remained in Japan for the occupation needed no help' (Ibid., 30). Such a statement completely ignores the horrors visited upon them during the first half of the twentieth century, and the social disenfranchisement they continued to suffer. Fukasaku's film dramatises how the Japanese police relied on yakuza to act against these residents as proxies. The protection that the anti-discrimination policy provided also enabled immigrant control of black markets and gambling dens, such as the Taiwanese control of Shimbashi gambling in 1946 (Kaplan and Dubro 2003, 35–7), which is the model for the scene in question.

Significantly, the raid that is depicted in the film is prefaced by footage of a group of men on a jeep waving Taiwan flags and rousing the crowd around them as the voiceover explains that the Taiwanese, Chinese and Koreans who had been liberated by the allies were now free to express their anger at the decades of Japanese oppression. There is then a sudden cut to inside the gambling den, where a wild party is in progress with semi-naked women dancing and rolling around with their hosts as paper money rains down on them. These festivities are then violently interrupted when the Japanese gangs break in, fire shots into the air and around the people and scoop up gambling winnings from the floor under cover of the chaos. As the sound of the police sirens gets louder, the Japanese flee the scene, but they are eventually caught. All parties are initially placed in the same holding cell, where they immediately form two sides – the Japanese on the left and the foreigners on the right. The latter taunt the Japanese for losing the war and, hence, reaping the consequences of their imperialist aggression. The Japanese retort that the 'Japanese Empire' was not defeated by Asians but by the US. The argument is interesting for a variety of reasons: first, the '*sangokujin*' advance their protests in fluent Japanese, reflecting their polylingual fluency while the Japanese rely on the monolingualism of their former role as coloniser – a monolingual privilege now taken over by the Americans. Second, both sides are speaking from variations of imagined communities: the resident aliens who have been robbed of their homeland by being inducted into forced labour in Japan and in their respective homelands were not only distant but are only now beginning to recover the sovereignty Japan had taken from them. The Japanese, on the other hand, extol the fantasmatic glory of an Empire that no longer existed, and presumed an indigenous privilege as citizens of a nation still undergoing radical redefinition.

Battles without Honor also exposes the Japanese police favouring the yakuza in these fights in this scene. Once the two groups are given separate cells, the two leaders of the Imai gang are taken into the police chief's confidence, with the latter thanking them for giving the Japanese police an excuse to send the *sangokujin* to prison. He also shows gratitude by releasing the Japanese without charge.[2] Although Ishikawa is cast as one participant among others in that confrontation, Fukasaku's reconstruction of 1946 gives him a greater role in the failure of a political campaign, the candidacy of Nozu Kisaburo (Andō Noboru) for the Diet. Andō's appearance in the film elevates the 'reality effect', given that he was already a yakuza in the 1940s, based primarily in Shinjuku (Ando, *Shōwa*, 12–16; Oshita 2016, 22–7; Suzuki 2019, 36–7). Moreover, the dignity with which Ando plays the role, and his general gravity, contrasts markedly with Watari's Ishikawa, whose behaviour ranges from tasteless antics to unmotivated murderous assault. That difference gives another dimension to the distinction between the personal history of Ishikawa and the larger moments in the history of early post-war Japan: although the candidate is a criminal, the election is another step toward a new Japanese democracy.

This sequence also epitomises the coyness of Fukasaku's version: while Nozu Kisaburo is fictional, he is clearly modelled on the Shinjuku gang boss Ozu Kinosuke, who opened the first black market in Shinjuku on 20 August 1945, and named it 'A Light from Shinjuku' (*Hikari wa Shinjuku Yori*) (Whiting 1999, 7–8), which becomes the slogan for Nozu's fictional campaign, emblazoned on a banner on his headquarters. Ozu was the power behind the Shinjuku black market and his notoriety even reached the US media. Although he ran for the Diet in April 1947, apparently the general voting population was alienated by the violence involved in maintaining his hegemony because he lost to his Communist Party rival, Nosaka Sanzo (Kaplan and Dubro 2003, 38). Ozu's loss cleared the way for his arrest on 27 June; on 3 July he was indicted for 'violent crimes'. Eleven trials ensued until he was released to Tokyo University Hospital after suffering both physical and emotional illnesses from the stress. Detectives also discovered that Ozu did not own or have any legal claim to the land on which he rented out market stall space and on which his office building stood. Remarkably, arbitration resulted in allowing Ozu to remain in residence there and collect one half of all rents on that land until 1948 (Supreme 1949, 238).

In the film, Ishikawa causes a crisis when he sees an Ikebukuro-based Shinwa boss and his woman companion in a Shinjuku bar. He pulls the woman from a lavatory stall, rips off her dress and attempts to assault her sexually when the boss intervenes. Ishikawa then slashes the boss's face and stabs him. When the Shinwa group refuses the apology and gift, the Kawada and Shinwa gangs face off in Shinjuku, each waiting for the other to instigate violence. Although Nozu saves the day by persuading Kawada to get the US military to send everyone home, the threat of the violence costs Nozu the election.

The only direct contact between Nozu and Ishikawa exacerbates the latter's extreme behaviour to a point of no return. As Ishikawa is about to launch a temper tantrum at a Kawada gambling den when refused a large loan to keep playing, Nozu comes in and asserts his authority over Ishikawa, scolding him about his behaviour and then giving him some money to send him on his way. This enrages Ishikawa, who lights the money on fire and inserts it into the gas tank of Nozu's limousine, destroying the car and earning Ishikawa a brutal beating from Kawada. Later that night, Ishikawa breaks into Kawada's home and shoots him. Kawada survives but Ishikawa goes to prison. After his release he is banned from Tokyo for ten years. Suspending the question of historical accuracy, this scene is interesting in terms of representation. It is not only an encounter between the characters of Ishikawa and Nozu, but also between the acting styles of Watari and Ando, within a turbulent interface between two narrative planes: the relation to history and historical action (occupied by Nozu/Ando) and the sensational account of acting out (occupied by Ishikawa/Watari). Moreover, Ando's actual history with Ishikawa also gets invoked in texts that look back at that time. In a 2019 Mook ['magazine-book'] on the 'Yakuza Arts World', Suzuki Tomohiko opened his reflections on the gravestone that Ishikawa Rikio commissioned by claiming that Ando Noboru, when asked if he had known the real-life gangster, responded, 'I knew Ishikawa Rikio', and sighed with nostalgia (Suzuki 2019: 36). I do not doubt that Ando made that statement, but he definitely did not make it to Suzuki, since Ando had died in 2015. Suzuki must have pulled this from the culturally preserved memories of Ando. Ironically this move is reminiscent of the reconstructed memories of Ishikawa in the voiceovers at the beginning of *Graveyard of Honor*. Suzuki's narrative slight-of-hand, moreover, suggests that conjuring Ishikawa requires a witness of similarly enduring posthumous celebrity. It is between the exigencies of history and the lure of celebrity culture that Miike Takashi reworks the Ishikawa legend.

MIIKE TAKASHI'S *NEW GRAVEYARD OF HONOR* (2002)

The dynamic tensions in Miike Takashi's film begin with a contradictory relation to the original: a selective faithfulness to decisive events while reimagining the motivations behind them and resituating their sociohistorical contexts. The differences Gerow discerns between Fukasaku and Miike are suggestive. Gerow emphasises 'the centrality of writing history' to Fukasaku's film and, while seeing in Fukasaku a possible 'precursor of a Miike Takashi in his apocalyptic nihilism and sympathy for Japan's social marginals', Gerow contrasts Fukasaku's historiographic ethos with Miike's inclination toward 'an ahistorical postmodern mayhem' (Gerow 2010). While many of Miike's films, such as *Izo* (2004), substantiate Gerow's characterisation, I would argue that *New Graveyard of Honor* gestures toward a historical consciousness whose own failure nevertheless constitutes a historical record of the zeitgeist Miike both addresses and reflects.

It is also important to understand Miike's remake in terms of his lifelong respect for certain directors of the past. The first half of his career memoir,

Kantoku Chudoku [*Director Addiction*], focuses on his work as an assistant to filmmakers who shaped his future attitude toward their profession. In the preface, he mentions that there are many directors whom he has assisted who are no longer living but whose lives should remain in memory. The only filmmaker he mentions by name, however, is one he had never worked with: Fukasaku Kinji, director of *Graveyard of Honor*. He writes:

> I want to draw out from my memory the directors I have encountered. They are a breed entirely different from the staff one currently finds on a film set . . . Now such people are gone. It is an extinct breed. For example, even if we take Director Fukasaku Kinji who recently passed away, the period when the earlier Fukasaku shot films so fervently is utterly unlike the situation of his later years. The way of making films also changed, it had to conform to a kind of monumental work. Cinema is largely the practice of storytelling through film, and connecting the flow of humans' lives. But the surrounding circumstances have changed (Miike 2003, 7–8).

Two aspects of the above passage are particularly significant to the present inquiry. First, the division in Fukasaku's canon that Miike offers implies that in remaking *Graveyard of Honor*, he is bringing back the work typical of Fukasaku's first period, and resituating it in the changed conditions of the contemporary period. And second, there is a slippage in Miike's focus: the principal topic of the preface is the type of director that has been lost, but in turning to Fukasaku the focus shifts from loss of a type to a change in time. This tendency to vacillate between persona and history will be one of the peculiarities of the narrative in *New Graveyard of Honor*.

While Fukasaku's film begins with Ishikawa's personal history from his birth to his entry into the world of Tokyo yakuza, Miike's film begins with the protagonist's suicide, leaping from a prison tower. The main character of Fukasaku's film enters into history as the story opens onto the chaos and mass nihilism of post-war Japan. Miike's fictional Ishimatsu Rikuo (Kishitani Goro) is introduced through his final act, a dramatic last claim of free will that obviates all agency and ostensibly stabilises the meaning of the life it terminates. With that spectacular death, both Ishimatsu and the film opt out of history, albeit in different senses of the term.

In some ways, Miike's film is more conservative than Fukasaku's. In the latter's film, cinematographer Nakazawa Hanjiro's Dutch angles, swooping and lunging camera and frenetic *mise-en-scène* generate a turbulent, tremulous world on the verge of dissipation.[3] In contrast, Yamamoto Hideo's choreography is crisp and disciplined almost to the point of transparency. Miike foregoes vivacious cinematic representation, opting instead for conventionally framed spectacles, either of perversion or of mayhem.

In terms of the narrative, Miike rationalises elements in the protagonist's rise and fall that remain open questions in both Ishikawa's history and Fukasaku's account of it. It is unclear how Ishimatsu was able to be inducted into the Wada Gumi at such a young age, or why he earned the trust of the oyabun, who gave him the benefit of the doubt through all his rages until Ishikawa shot him. In Miike's version, the boss Sawada (Yamashiro Shingo) and his gang are in a Chinese restaurant when a killer (played by Miike himself, in an extended Hitchcockian cameo with a dash of John Woo-style ballistics) enters with two guns blazing. Just when the would-be assassin takes aim at Sawada, the dishwasher Ishimatsu (Kishitani Goro) calmly clobbers him over the head with a chair. For saving his life, Sawada makes Ishimatsu a full member in a formal ceremony in which senior yakuza, Yukawa (Ishibashi Renji) and Fukui (Sone Harumi), clearly resent this seventeen-year-old amateur being elevated above them.

Ishimatsu's most cataclysmic rages also are given a context absent in the original. One afternoon Ishimatsu walks into the Sawada offices where Yukawa and others are chatting. When Ishimatsu asks where the boss is, Yukawa's disdain is evident in the dismissive way he supposes that Sawada might be away at a hot spring. Ishimatsu becomes enraged and, wielding a heavy glass ashtray, wounds the two others and fractures Yukawa's skull. Sawada is actually at the dentist and has left a message for Ishimatsu to wait for him, intending to give the latter the ten million yen he had asked to borrow to set his girlfriend up in her own club. Ishimatsu thinks that Sawada is avoiding him because he has decided to refuse him the loan. Later that night, Ishimatsu breaks into Sawada's bedroom; and when Sawada reaches for the promised money, Ishimatsu misinterprets his action as reaching for a gun and shoots him. While this is an unforgivable breach of the yakuza code, it is unlike the actual crime in 1946 because Ishikawa actually stabbed Wada, and the assault in the film is premised on a fictionalised misunderstanding.

The temporal setting is explicitly introduced in a sequence that gestures toward an historical context that suggests an historical consciousness that is not ultimately sustained in the narrative. When Ishikawa has been released from his first prison sentence for stabbing a rival gangster, he arrives at his common-law wife Chieko's (Arimori Narimi) apartment late that evening. As she steps into the kitchen to get ice, he pins her against the refrigerator, forcibly removes her clothes and performs cunnilingus. She drops the ice cubes on an old newspaper with a photo of a government official proclaiming the beginning of the new Imperial Reign, Heisei (1989). Ishimatsu grotesquely embodies the Heisei era: the bravado of a bubble economy along with its catastrophic emptiness; a randomness of appetite that expresses itself in both sexuality and consumerism; a historical consciousness permanently deferred by a fixation on a volatile sense of the 'now'.

Figure 8.1 In this shot from Miike Takashi's *New Graveyard of Honor* (*Shin jingi no hakaba*, 2002), during a sex act ice cubes spill onto the proclamation of a new Imperial Reign.

The close-up on the ice cube-spangled proclamation triggers a montage and voiceover narration: 'Eight years went by. The economic bubble burst, causing hard times both to the daily lives of civilians and to organized crime.' Documentary images show people wandering in Kabuki-cho and drunks throwing punches at each other, interrupted by a photo of Asahara Shoko, the founder of the Aum Shinrikyo cult, and the mastermind behind the sarin gas attacks on Tokyo subways in 1995, killing fourteen people immediately, severely injuring fifty more and temporarily injuring over 1,000 people. The footage then includes seemingly more desperate people on the street and press reports of internal strife within the yakuza *gumi*. The montage cuts to a news magazine article of Diet members Katō Kōichi and Nonaka Hiromu locked in a power struggle, with the headline: 'Looking at Hell'. The magazine is held by Yukawa, who grimly jokes about the fate of then Prime Minister Mori Yoshirō. This is the conversation fatally interrupted by Ishimatsu demanding to know where Sawada is.

There are several peculiar aspects to this sequence. First, it begins in early 1989 (Heisei began on 8 January, but it is unclear how many days old the newspaper is in this scene), and the narrative claims to cover eight years, which would mean it ends in 1997. Mori was prime minister from April 2000 to April 2001. Conflicts between Katō and Nonaka were not infrequent, but those conflicts did not become intense enough to be newsworthy before May 2000, which means the historical period covered actually exceeds the temporal range designated in the voiceover. Furthermore, if it is 2000 when Ishimatsu first attacks Yukawa and then Sawada, the time span becomes even more peculiar. After the assault on Sawada, Ishimatsu's former prison buddy Imamura

(Miki Ryōsuke) hides him from both the gang and the police for at least several weeks if not more. When he is finally arrested, the trial must take some time (although it is not shown) and he is in prison for an unspecified amount of time when he starts hiding his daily milk ration in a Tupperware container. It takes several weeks for the concoction to become sufficiently toxic. When he drinks it, he becomes violently ill and is taken to a hospital, where he escapes and somehow finds his way to the villa of Imamura, now near death. It takes at least a week for him to recover enough to stab Imamura (falsely believing Imamura had given him up to the police) and then hide out with Chieko in various motels and other hovels until she dies of an overdose. Ishimatsu's final crime spree ends in the Sawada Gumi headquarters, where he is shot several times but not killed. When he recovers, he is returned to prison, and is there for an unspecified length of time before he climbs up the tower and leaps to his death. These events must have happened over a span of more than two years in total, which means Ishimatsu's life story also extends beyond the time of the film, since it was shot in early 2002 and released in June of that year.

The revelation of the boss's whereabouts when Ishimatsu came to see him is marked by a voiceover by one of the gang members: 'The Big Boss, suffering from a decayed tooth, went to the dentist. During his two-hour absence, a yakuza leapt into hell.' This kind of retrospective narrative intrusion is odd in itself, but this is actually the second time this voiceover occurred. The first time occurs at the very beginning of the film, while the screen is still black. All that can be heard, apart from the voice, are the jangling of the keys and the footsteps of the prison guard patrolling the cell block where Ishimatsu is incarcerated. Once the first image fills the screen, Ishimatsu persuades the guard to let him go up to the roof to dry his blanket. Thus, the voiceover seems to comment on the suicide. However, it is taken out of context from the far more banal misunderstanding because of an undelivered message. Several of Miike's films begin with a statement either voiced or inscribed on the screen from a character whose cryptic insights will be vindicated as the film unfolds. Films with such beginnings include *Bodyguard Kiba: Apocalypse of Carnage* (*Shura no mokushiroku: Bodigaado Kiba*, 1994), a sequel to *Bodyguard Kiba* (*Bodigaado Kiba*, 1993), a remake of a 1973 film with the same title directed by Takamori Ryuichi; *Shinjuku Triad Society* (*Shinjuku kuroshakai: Chaina mafia sensō*, 1995);[4] *Fudoh: The New Generation* (*Gokudō sengokushi: Fudō*, 1996); *Ambition without Honor* (*Jingi naki yabō Jingi naki yabō*, 1996) and *Dead or Alive 2: Birds* (*Deddōāraibu 2 tōbō-sha*, 2000). That *Graveyard* begins with a falsely contextualised statement only to correct it later in the film departs from Miike's established pattern, and here it succinctly demonstrates a pervasive practice within the film: exploiting an independence of narrative from history.

Although the sequence beginning with the Heisei proclamation suggests an intention to shape the new version of the Ishikawa story to a contemporary

Table 8.1 Similarities and differences between plot points in *Graveyard of Honor* (1975) and *New Graveyard of Honor* (2002)

Graveyard of Honor (1975)	*New Graveyard of Honor* (2002)
Childhood and early history of Ishikawa.	Suicide of Ishimatsu.
Violent defence of territory.	Violent defence of Godfather's name.
Ethnic crises with Taiwanese, Chinese and Korean residents flair up.	No ethnic/racial issues are addressed.
The main character rapes Chieko twice.	The main character rapes Chieko twice.
Chieko becomes devoted to Ishikawa, who forces her to overwork despite her TB. She eventually kills herself.	Chieko becomes devoted to Ishimatsu, who forces her to work in the bordello and deliberately addicts her to heroin. She dies from an overdose.
Ishikawa stabs Godfather, protected by Imai.	Ishimatsu shoots Godfather, protected by Imamura.*
Ishikawa is imprisoned and exiled for ten years – in Osaka he becomes addicted to heroin. He returns to Tokyo in spite of the ban. He is protected by Imai for a time and eventually stabs Imai.	Ishimatsu is imprisoned. He escapes but is extremely ill (Imamura provides medical care). He stabs Imamura and kills his assistant.
Ishikawa returns to Imai's house and fatally shoots him.	Ishimatsu returns to Imamura's house and fatally shoots him.
Ishikawa is shot several times in Kawada headquarters. He survives and is returned to prison.	Ishimatsu is seriously injured in an assassination attempt in a graveyard. He survives and is returned to prison.
Ishikawa leaps from a prison tower.	Ishimatsu leaps from a prison tower.
Last written words recovered: 'What a big laugh – thirty years of lunatic antics!'	Last written words recovered: 'What a big laugh – thirty years of lunatic antics!'

* Miike may have chosen the name 'Imamura' in honour of Imamura Shohei. Miike was his assistant director for the films *Zegen* (1987) and *Black Rain* (*Kuroi ame*,1989).

historical situation, the film's relative faithfulness to the 1975 story undermines such a project. The table above illustrates the correspondences between the plot points of the two films (from beginning to end).

Instead of focusing on contemporary history or reworking the actual biography of Ishikawa, Miike treats Fukasawa's film as the operative historical horizon. Let us consider specific points at which this process allows a slippage from both historical consciousness and responsible realism; in other words, an inattention to the actual situations of the 1990s in which Miike transferred his protagonist's life and crimes. The absence of the *sangokujin* in Miike's film is understandable since that particular configuration of outrage and black marketeering occurred in the 1940s. What is peculiar is the absence of the corresponding racial/ethnic realities in the 1990s. Beginning in the 1980s, recruitment in the major yakuza gangs showed a marked increase in *zainichi* Koreans (second or third generations). This was not so much a function of progressive politics among yakuza as the lack of options for this population (Hill 2003, 80–1). The absence of ethnic issues also departs radically from Miike's other films. *Shinjuku Triad Society* concerns Japanese of mixed-Chinese descent as well as relations with Taiwanese populations; *Fudoh: the New Generation* features resident Korean-Japanese people; *Ley Lines* (*Nihon Kuroshakai Rei Rainzu*, 1999) again deals with Chinese-Japanese people; *DOA* (*Hanzaisha*, 1999) tackles the question of 'returnees' from China and their descendants (*zanryū koji*);[5] and *The City of Lost Souls* (*Hyōryū-gai*, 2000) deals with Brazilian-Japanese. It is precisely Miike's earlier attention to race, nationality and ethnicity that makes its absence here more conspicuous. On the other hand, even in Fukusaku's film, Ishikawa's participation in the gambling den riot was depicted as him having been swept up in the crowd (he showed no particular animosity toward those he fought). In Miike's version, Ishimatsu's narcissism is too absolute to sustain a position regarding an abstracted Other, and his resentment too global to be localised in racial terms.

Even more baffling than the absence of the ethnic questions in *New Graveyard of Honor* is the preservation of the rapes and other violations of Chieko, and her absolute submission. Since the new film was supposed to reshape the narrative according to social changes that characterise the 1990s, Chieko's plight and response in 1946 do not provide a model for the late 1980s and the 1990s. In retaining this narrative, the rapes and domination of Chieko are elevated to an essential component of the update. Not only is there no amelioration or even critique of that behaviour, but Ishimatsu is even worse. While Ishikawa became addicted to heroin while in Osaka and kept it to himself, Ishimatsu deliberately addicts Chieko to strengthen his already absolute power over her. Nevertheless, the contrast between the mise-en-scène in which heroin is introduced to Ishikawa and the one in which Ishimatsu introduces heroin to Chieko illustrates the differences in the historical settings of the two films.

In Fukasawa's film, Ishikawa is destitute, exiled in Osaka and apparently has been seriously ill, when a prostitute servicing him in a flophouse offers him heroin. He has nothing to lose, and she was already a junkie. The image of the two of them in a drugged stupor while an elderly man in the next cubicle prays before an ancestral tablet becomes emblematic of the malaise of early post-war Japan. In *New Graveyard of Honor*, however, Ishimatsu has just finished beating four gang members unconscious (or worse) with a metal pipe. In rifling through their belongings for money, he happens upon a stash of heroin and hypodermics. He tries the drug as a fluke and later gives it to Chieko as they hide from both the Sawada gumi and the police by drifting from love hotel to love hotel. Addiction from an unmotivated hedonistic gesture and then deliberate manipulative indoctrination in a series of tacky commercial

Figure 8.2 Ishikawa (Watari Tetsuya) and prostitute (Seri Meika) are strung out on heroin while an old man in the next cubicle prays in this moment from Fukasaku Kinji's *Graveyard of Honor* (*Jingi no hakaba*, 1975) (top), and in a corresponding scene from Miike Takashi's *New Graveyard of Honor* (*Shin jingi no hakaba*, 2002) (bottom), Ishimatsu (Kishitani Goro) leads Chieko (Arimori Narimi) into heroin addiction in a love hotel.

sexual fantasy sites can also serve as a symptom of the post-bubble vacuum of the 1990s. The interanimation of the grotesque and the banal characterises not only the turbulence of the millennium but also the critical preoccupations of the intelligentsia at that time, epitomised by the manga writer, champion of otaku culture and social theorist, Otsuka Eiji.

In 2012 Otsuka Eiji published a revision of his monograph, *Theory of Narrative Consumption*. The first version of that important text focused on children's literature of the 1980s. Otsuka felt compelled to revise this work by including analyses of the changes brought about by digital communication, in particular web culture. His new model of narrative consumption begins with the provocative claim that post-web tendencies in one sense look backwards rather than forwards, evincing an affinity for the montage so popular in the 1920s. Otsuka points out that the practice of reorganising autonomous images into a new whole serves the goals of propaganda: with Sergei Eisenstein's *Battleship Potemkin* (1925) representing the Soviet historical consciousness and Leni Riefenstahl's *Olympia* (1938) advancing Nazi ideals (Otsuka 2012, 4–5). The image-stream narratives of the Japanese millennials, however, do not adhere to or even aim at any particular ideology. Otsuka's distinction, however, is only partially comforting, since such constructions without ideological aim can render the observed world as a series of acritical self-distractions. However, Otsuka also discerns a significant reordering of hierarchies. The process of turning fragments into narratives shifts the creative focus from the sender of the message to the receiver (Ibid., 6). I will return to another implication of this difference below.

Otsuka's vision of millennial narratives as fragments of uncompleted meaning succinctly describes how the capsule history of the 1990s in *New Graveyard* fails. The images of tense and despondent street life blended in with allusions to Aum Shinrikyo, and the crises in yakuza organisation and government institutions are offered as an oblique explanation for Ishimatsu, but the relation of the form to the content never coheres. Furthermore, the events such as the bursting of the economic bubble and the sarin gas attacks cannot be reduced to elements of an explanatory narrative since they are traumas in a national consciousness that disrupts any narrative rationalisation.

In her compelling intervention in discourses surrounding millennial Japan, Tomiko Yoda exposes another narrative woven from unrelated fragments, this one in the accounts of the compounding crises comprising the Japanese economic disasters of the 1990s. Yoda points out that the narratives of the bursting of the speculative bubble, the collapse of the banks and 'the meltdown of the Asian financial markets' resulted in 'a negative psychology . . . compounded by the association between the recession and a diverse set of ominous events and phenomena . . . not directly related to the recession' yet 'closely interwoven with the economic crisis in the popular imagination, underscoring the perception of national peril that encompasses virtually all aspects of Japanese contemporary society' (Yoda 2006, 20). These 'events and phenomena' included 'the Hanshin earthquake and the Aum Shinrikyō's sarin gas attack . . . both in 1995' (Ibid., 20–21). While the confluence of accounts Yoda records imagine 1990s Japan as a terrible yet coherent complex, the quasi-historical sequence in *New Graveyard* refuses to cohere, just as Ishimatsu defies explanation either from his sometime colleagues or from the history in which he finds himself embedded as a glitch in the system. As a 'glitch', however, Ishimatsu acts out within the system, not against the system that produced him. This distinction is significant both on the level of social phenomenon and on the level of critical analysis.

Yoda points out that the 'subculture' that Otsuka studies 'does not necessarily have countercultural or underground' alliances, and in fact 'seems to overlap with *popular (consumer/media) culture* in general' (Ibid., 36). Ironically, such an intermeshing also occurs between the yakuza film and its critical reception. One of the most influential collections of essays in Japanese on yakuza film, *Daiyakuza Eiga Tokuhon 1963–1993* [*The Great Specialist Book of Yakuza Eiga 1963–1993*], has emblazoned on its front cover and on the title page 'What a big laugh – 30 years of lunatic antics!', the final words of Ishikawa Rikio, left in his prison cell in 1956 and preserved in both *Graveyard of Honor* film finales.

Ishikawa left another writing that also yielded unexpected consequences. While Fukusaka used Ishikawa's real name, most of the names of other principal parties are changed: Wada Kaoru becomes Kawada Shuzo and Ozu Kinosuke becomes Nozu Kisaburo. But two others retain their real names: Ishikawa's long-suffering partner, Chieko, and Iwai Kōzaburō, the gang boss, whom Ishikawa fatally shot. Perhaps one reason for retaining their names is that Ishikawa had their names engraved in stone – he commissioned a tombstone with three names on it: his own, Chieko's and Iwai's. He also included the word *jingi*, which gives the film its title – *jingi no hakaba* – literally 'gravestone of honor'. And since the word's inscription in the tombstone implies that it no longer exists, the stone marks a *jingi naki jidai* – 'a period in which there is no honor' – in other words, Ishikawa obliquely anticipates the title (and critique) in the title *Jingi naki tatakai, Battle without Honor*: literally 'Battle in which honor does not exist'.

Battles without Honor has also left a living legacy in generations of narratives of the complex histories of the Hiroshima yakuza wars of the late 1940s and 50s, which gave rise to spin-off studies of specific gangs and gang leaders, as well as new fictional accounts of the Hiroshima crime world, most recently in the 2015 novel *Blood of the Lone Wolf* by Yuzuki Yuko, adapted into director Shiraishi Kazuya's highly successful film *Blood of the Wolves* (*Korō no Chi*, 2018) and the same filmmaker's sequel *Last of the Wolves* (*Korō no Chi Level 2*, 2021). In a *kaisetsu* (interpretative afterword) to a book on two notorious Hiroshima gangsters, Sakai Nobuo writes, 'The novel, *Battle without Honor* and the film of the same name succeeded in unfolding the infamous Hiroshima Gang War that spanned 25 years, an accomplishment unparalleled in yakuza history.' He goes on to extol how exhaustively these works detail the in-fighting among members of the same gang as well as inter-gang warfare. The works even explore the cultural specifics of the three regions involved: Hiroshima, Kure and Aga; and the ways in which immediately after the war, in Hiroshima the gambling-centred Oka-gumi and the stall-keeper Murakami-gumi came into conflict over the profits of their respective black markets (Sakai 2003, 357–8). Sakai's praise for the unique completeness of the history of this conflict more than suggests a kind of comfort in that 'full story' and implies that the Hiroshima gang war could lend itself to a consoling kind of narrative. Absent entirely in this *kaisetsu* is any acknowledgement of the atomic bombing of Hiroshima, and that silence is eloquent in the other function of the gang saga: it offers both a narrative fulfilment and a distraction – a story of Hiroshima that is rational and moves toward closure rather than the horrors of the bomb that cannot be rationalised and has no end for the victims, survivors, their descendants and a world continually threatened with obliteration.

The possibility of a complete narrative may be one of the attractions that draw readers and viewers to the *Battles without Honor* and the subsequent texts. Filmmakers also are clearly drawn to the storytelling gravity of Fukasaku's tour-de-force, but perhaps for differing reasons. Before making *New Graveyard of Honor*, Miike also tapped into the *Battle without Honor* legacy, partially borrowing some of its certainty but also to reinhabit it for meta-cinematic speculation in his films *Ambition without Honor* (*Jingi naki Yabō*, 1996) and *Ambition without Honor 2* (*Jingi naki Yabō 2*, 1997). Miike even visited Fukasaku to ask his permission to use the phrase, a gesture of respect and a declaration of a lineage. Such a 'lineage', however, is affected by changes in the relation between source and reception as Otsuka Eiji has described it. With the ascension of the internet, the writer has been displaced by the more egalitarian role of social media participant or 'content' provider. This also changes the relation of the source to the utterance. Rather than writing a text within the hierarchical structure of authorship, the new communications culture allows for 'making something public' by posting online (Otsuka 2012, 6–8). Such a revision of authorial control over the 'original text', and in turn the loosening of any form of responsibility between the new content provider and the utterance, could approximate Miike's relation both to the historical Ishikawa Rikio and Fukasaku's retelling of that life story. Furthermore, let us recall another of Otsuka's observations: the new focus on fragments and the need to fashion a narrative from them shifts a principle creative role to the receiver of those fragments (Ibid., 4–5). In the case of Miike's reworking of earlier material, this can be applied doubly to the resulting film: the subject that constructs the new narrative from select fragments (here the auteur/screenwriter/director) and the subject composed within that new narrative (the protagonist). The meta-cinematic dimension of the two *Ambition* films, moreover, make the process of 'becoming' the subject more complex than the narrative in which that process is attempted.

The first *Ambition* film tells the story of Kurashina Tetsuya (Sone Hideki), fledgling member of the Shiramatsu-gumi, who assassinates Kanezaki (Sone Harumi), head of the Tamazawa-gumi, and goes to prison for the crime, believing he will be handsomely rewarded with money and status by Shiramatsu after release. The narrative recalls the *Battles without Honor* series, in both the title and the plot, as that film also features a gang member who does the same thing for his godfather, and, like Kurashina, is essentially abandoned after the prison term. *Ambition* also recalls *Graveyard of Honor* in that Kurashina is only seventeen when he is given this task, just as Ishikawa was only sixteen when he was inducted into the Wada-gumi in 1942. And there is a link between *Ambition* and the future *New Graveyard of Honor*. The former film's action begins in a pachinko parlour. Words appear on the screen, giving the time as 'Seven years ago, the last year of Showa', which would be 1988. In *New Graveyard of Honor*, the historical montage begins with the newspaper photo of the sign announcing the first year of Heisei, 1989. (Let us also recall that Ishikawa was born in the first year of Showa.)

To borrow another analytic framework: Kurashina's singular 'ambition' to become a yakuza becomes the manifest content of the film that parallels its latent content, namely the ambition of actor Sone Hideki to become a recognised yakuza film actor. Sone had already had small roles in other Miike films, as had Hideki's father, Sone Harumi (1938–2016). The elder Sone had a long and distinguished career as a character actor, debuting in 1959 and appearing in over 100 films, including many by Ishii Teruo, Fukasaku Kinji, Kato Tai and Yamashita Kosaku. He was even in *Battles without Honor* and both Fukasaku's and Miike's *Graveyard* films. He debuted as a producer with *Ambition without Honor* and produced both the sequel and, in 2003, Miike's exquisitely delirious horror-gangster film, *Gozu*, also starring his son, Hideki.

All three of these films Harumi produced were intended to turbo-charge Hideki's acting career and raise his profile as a yakuza film actor in particular (Miike 2003, 252–3). Harumi also appears in both *Ambition* films, but they are small roles that serve as a kind of paternal psychodrama in the mythic creation of the son as yakuza in the plot and yakuza film actor in the representation and agenda. The parallels between the film fantasy and the promotional agenda are striking. Harumi's role as producer is responsible for Hideki's attempt at yakuza stardom in *Ambition*; Harumi's role in the film embodies Kurashina's supposed opportunity for advancement: Harumi plays Kanezaki, whom Kurashina assassinates within minutes of Kanezaki's appearance on screen. When Kurashina gets out of prison in 1995, he is disappointed there is no reception for him, and is utterly shocked when he visits the Shiramatsu headquarters and is essentially given the brush-off by middle-manager Kashira (Shimizu Kōjirō). While Kurashina was in prison, Shiramatsu and Tamazawa agreed on a truce, which would be threatened if they welcomed the killer of the former Tamazawa head back into the fold. Kurashina cannot accept this, and his attempts to beg and to force himself back into the fold become increasingly desperate.

In *Ambition without Honor 2*, Hideki now plays Iwasaki Tetsuya, son of the godfather of the Iwasaki syndicate (played by Sone Harumi) who has disowned him after Tetsuya had left suddenly for Osaka. When the father is hospitalised after an assassination attempt, Tetsuya returns (after a five-year absence), only to have his father send him away from the hospital room. Later when Tetsuya discovers his father's subsequent death was actually a murder arranged by the same gang that had commissioned the original hit, he assumes his father's role as godfather and undertakes a violent campaign against both the gang and the coterie of corrupt police.

Both Sone Harumi and Hideki also appear in *New Graveyard of Honor*. Harumi appears very early in the film, seated at the induction of young Ishimatsu into the Sawada group, his face twisted in profound but silent disapproval. Hideki plays a lower-ranking yakuza in the Imamura group, mostly in the background but with a couple of dialogue scenes until his lethal struggle with Ishimatsu at Imamura's country house. Ishimatsu has not yet recovered from his self-inflicted food poisoning when he stabs Imamura, mistakenly believing his host had betrayed him. As Imamura falls bleeding, Hideki's character tackles Ishimatsu, who stabs him, throws him outside and hacks him to death. In Ishimatsu's final invasion of the Sawada headquarters, when one of Sawada's men ventures into the room Ishimatsu has barricaded himself in, upon opening the door he finds Harumi's character with a bullet hole in the centre of his forehead. This film, therefore, kills off the multi-levelled father-and-son dyad of becoming so insistently developed in the two *Ambition* films.

The two deaths may seem too oblique to make a case for an intertextual relation between this film and two films produced six and seven years earlier, but during the period in which *New Graveyard* was made, Miike would also have been in negotiations with Sone Harumi regarding *Gozu*. Sone promised to fund the film provided that Miike make it a yakuza drama, set it in Nagoya (Sone's hometown) and cast his son Hideki as the star. Miike agreed to these terms, on the condition that it could be a hybrid yakuza-horror film, because Miike did not think Hideki had the screen presence to carry a typical yakuza film (Miike 270–2).

Miike was also involved at this time with another peculiar intervention in yakuza history. He was consulting with Ando Noboru in order to make a film purportedly based on Ando's life, and the former yakuza member remained a consultant through that process. *New Graveyard of Honor* was released in June of 2002, and *True Account of the Life of Ando Noboru (Outlaw): Raging Fire* was released in September of the same year. The film is a starring vehicle for Takeuchi Riki as Kunisada, whose rage, while slower burning and more elegant than Ishimatsu's, appears completely foreign to the medium-cool restraint associated with Ando's screen personae. Moreover, nothing resembling Kunisada's vengeance against his godfather's assassination can be found in Ando's copious autobiographical writings. Nevertheless, Miike stands by his characterisation when he writes: 'Although it is a side story, the blood of the true man, Ando Noboru, surges through this pure, incandescent film. . . . It is a film I want you to see, I want you to hear. When someone discards the analog heart, the man dies. Absolutely dies' (Miike et al. 2003, 106). By 'analog heart',

Figure 8.3 Sone Hideki as the figure of the would-be yakuza star, now murdered by the star of *New Graveyard of Honor* (top); Sone Harumi as Fukui, killed by Ishimatsu in *New Graveyard of Honor* (bottom).

Miike may be alluding to the soundtrack, composed and performed by the legendary actor/musician, Joe Yamanaka (1946–2011), who also plays a retired gangster in the film.

Moving from the musical aspect of the term, Miike's statement is both ironic and indicative of a dynamic contradiction. In this chapter, I have read the filmmaker's handling of history through Otsuka Eiji's conception of changes in the consumption of narrative, changes that suggest a shift from the continual flow of an analog representation of a life to a digital collection and arrangement of discreet fragments. In *New Graveyard of Honor*, Miike looks back on the analog life of Ishikawa Rikio through a digital environment whose fragments never restore a totality they commemorate. The contradictions within Miike's oeuvre inform even critical engagements with his films. For example, both Mika Ko's and Aaron Gerow's analyses on some levels defend the very excesses they critique. For example, Ko writes:

> [T]he presence of non-Japanese characters within the Japanese body politic of Miike's films, the breaking open of diegetic homogeneity and narrative integrity, and the constant emphasis on the transgression of body-boundaries are connected and echo each other.... [T]hese three aspects of his films ... constitute a kind of basic constellation, a matrix which organises important dimensions of his films and which, following the works of the anthropologist Mary Douglas, we may read as a preoccupation with the homogeneity of Japan – or its lack – as a social–political entity (Ko 2010, 55).

While Gerow responds to Ko's thesis, his cogent counterarguments discern and acknowledge the ambivalences within Miike's redemptive moves: 'Directly conjoining style with nation, Ko claims the violation of both narrative and body boundaries reflects the larger break-up of the national polity (*kokutai*) in recent Japan' (Gerow 2009, 25). Although Gerow summarises Ko's claim in order to offer alternative critical avenues, this summary – as it stands – is both a criticism of Miike and an argument for the value of his work. Gerow then undertakes a compelling meta-critical reflection on the 'general compulsion to locate a "deeper" meaning in Miike', on one hand, and the 'general assumption that stylistic excess is of lesser value ... politically because it perpetuates a reactionary and nihilistic cinematic postmodernism ... a cynical playfulness', on the other. Gerow warns such critical binaries are not only typical approaches to popular cinema but that they cannot accommodate a full appreciation of a filmmaker like Miike 'who himself seems nomadic in terms of style and politics, and less concerned with collapsing the divisions between surface and depth, or the image and reality than engaging in the more complex possibility of wandering between them' (Ibid., 25–6).

In examining the yakuza films of the 1970s, Kato Kenji distinguishes violence that moves the plot forward from violence whose flamboyance is more poetic than diegetically motivated. He suggests that the latter be considered a kind of 'urban *écriture*' taking the term from Roland Barthes and subsequent French theorists (Kato 1993, 93–5). I would like to take this suggestion but restrict it to the meanings it had for Barthes, and to apply it to the stylistic and epistemological excesses that characterise Miike's cinema. I will limit my scope to *Graveyard of Honor* and other films Miike made in 2002.

Barthes introduced his conception of *écriture* in *Writing Degree Zero*, drawing out the conception sporadically from readings of Camus and Flaubert. If we allow ourselves some license in repurposing Barthes's description of Camus's writing in *L'Étranger*, we discern a speculative model for Miike's displacement of history through style. According to Barthes, Camus reduced writing to a 'negative mood in which the social or mythical characters of a language are abolished in favour of a neutral . . . form', which allows 'thought' (or, in Miike's case, cinematic discourse) to '[remain] wholly responsible [to itself], without being overlaid by secondary commitment of form to a History not its own' (1968, 77). We see such a form both in Ishimatsu's digital plundering of fragments from Fukasaku's Ishikawa, without conforming to the lessons of post-war history, and in the *True Account of Ando Noboru*, which invokes the name of the man and actor who served as an anchoring point in Fukasaku's films, yet channels the 'idea' of the gangster/actor into a self-consuming artefact, in which Takeuchi Riki impersonates a subject foreclosed from this representational protocol. While the *True Account* film showcased Takeuchi as a simulacrum at an infinite distance from his model, *DOA: Final*, made the same year, features Takeuchi as a police officer who loses the authenticity of both his self and his history. At the end of the film, he discovers that he, his wife and his son are androids and that his family life was only a program. There is no loss of memory, but the memories are evacuated of their 'effect of the real' (Jackson 2018, 288–9).

In these exposures, Miike seems closest to what Barthes attributed to Flaubert, honing 'writing as craft' through a practice that exploited the bourgeois capacity for a delusion of a 'pure man' while exposing 'the bourgeois as a spectacle in no way commensurate with itself' (Barthes 1968, 64). In creating a cinema that allows a wandering 'between the image and reality', Miike may occasionally either achieve a subversion or allow a subversive reading similar to how Barthes' Flaubert undermined the novel from within through 'his ability to preserve an "ambiguity of a double object" . . . to put a mask in place and simultaneously point to it' (Just 2007, 392).

The determination of Fukasaku's Ishikawa to become a yakuza arguably came from his impoverished, motherless childhood. His heroin addiction began as self-medication when he was sick, penniless and in exile. Miike's Ishimatsu stumbled into yakuza elite status because of a lucky swing of a chair. He tried heroin as a fluke, a perk from a violent assault he committed. Ishikawa's story suggests the fatalism of historical determinism. Ishimatsu leaps into the vertigo of a random universe. In opting out of history, Miike's account does not indulge in the hedonistic myopia of the youth film; rather, he situates Ishimatsu in the aporia of multiple perspectives.

ACKNOWLEDGMENT

I gratefully acknowledge support for this research from a grant from the Ministry of Science and Technology, Taiwan. I would also like to thank Christophe Thouny, Nathan Stuart and Wu Ching-Hsieh for their invaluable assistance.

NOTES

1. Yamazaki Mikio has an interesting take on Fukasaku's *jitsuroku* films, arguing that they are motivated by both historical curiosity and a willingness to commit revenge against history (1993, 41–2).
2. Ando Noboru tells a story from that time that complicates the picture. He was a bodyguard for a Taiwanese gambling den owner, Xu Ke Lian. One evening Ando's 'younger brother' tells him that gangster Chen had invaded Xu's office with a gun. Ando rushed over and saw Chen threatening Xu with a revolver. He kicked it away and in doing so the gun went off, hitting Chen in the thigh, who crumpled to the floor in a convulsion. Ando thought they would have to kill him, but Xu wouldn't allow it. Instead, they stuffed Chen into Xu's Buick and hid him in a Shibuya apartment. The bullet had passed through, so they treated Chen with antibiotics and bandages. Chen says, 'It was my job to shoot Xu and you have promised to protect Xu, so you must do that after this too' (Ando 2012, 38–9).
3. Nakazawa was responsible for the look of Fukasaku's films in the 1970s – from *Sympathy for the Underdog* (*Bakuto Gaijin Butai*, 1971) to *Graveyard of Honor*. He also gave a nightmarish texture to Sato Jun'ya's *jitsuroku* from the same period. For a discussion of Nakazawa's contribution to the allegorical look of Uchida Tomu's *A Fugitive from the Past* (*Kiga kaikyō*, 1966) see Earl Jackson, 'Order and Chaos in *A Fugitive from the Past*', *A Fugitive from the Past*. Blu-ray. Arrow 2022. For a technical appreciation of the work of Nakazawa, see fellow cinematographer Ishizuka's discussion of his early work (Ishizuka 2017).
4. Mika Ko's reading of the young man Shu's opening narrative is incisive, brilliant and compelling. I would only like to correct one aspect. She writes that he speaks Mandarin. Actually, he speaks Taiwanese, also known as either Minnan or Hokkien. And he is clearly a native speaker. This difference is important to the cultural politics of the film itself as well as the issues in Taiwan the film obliquely addresses. It is also important in the contrast of this 'authentic language' to the attempted Mandarin by the Japanese actors playing Taiwanese policeman in the scenes set in Taipei (Ko 2010, 52–53).
5. Elsewhere I argue that Miike's backstory for the *zanryu koji* group in *DOA* articulates a melancholia on psychological, ethnic and macropolitical levels. See Jackson (2018, 282–5).

REFERENCES

Ando, Noboru. 2009. *Otoko no Kakugo*. Tokyo: Seishi Sha.
Ando, Noboru. 2012. *Shōwa fūun-roku. Ando Noboru no Sengo Yakuza Shi*. Tokyo: Best Book.
Barthes, Roland. 1968. *Writing Degree Zero*. Translated by Annette Lavers and Colin Smith. Boston: Beacon.

Cohen, Theodore. 1987. *Remaking Japan: The American Occupation as the New Deal*. New York: Free Press.
Fujita, Gorō. 1989. *Jingi naki Hakuba, Jitsuroku Sengo Yakuza Shi*. Tokyo: Aoki Sha.
Fukuma, Kenji. 1993. 'Yakuza Eiga no Jidai.' In *Daiyakuza Eiga Tokuhon 1963–1993*, edited by Fukuma Kenji and Yamazaki Mikio, 23–37. Tokyo: Yosensha.
Gerow, Aaron. 2009. 'The Homelessness of Style and the Problems of Studying Miike Takashi.' *Canadian Journal of Film Studies* 18, no. 1: 24–43.
Gerow, Aaron. 2010. 'Fukasaku Kinji, Underworld Historiographer.' *Tangemania: Aaron Gerow's Japanese Film Page* (4 October 2010). http://www.aarongerow.com/news/fukasaku-kinji-underworld-h.html. Accessed 8 June 2022.
Hill, Peter B. E. 2003. *The Japanese Mafia: Yakuza, Law, and the State*. Oxford: Oxford University Press.
Iiboshi, Koichi. 1980. *Jingi naki Tatakai-Mino Kozo no Shuki yori*. Tokyo: Kadokawa.
Ishizuka, Hiroshi. 2017. 'Nakazawa Hanjiro no *Oinaru Tabiji*.' *Eiga Satsuei*, no. 215: 60–1.
Jackson, Earl. 2018. 'Reframing Loss: Japanese Cinematic Melancholia in Inter-Asian Contexts.' In *The Palgrave Handbook of Asian Cinema*. Edited by Aaron Han Joon Magnan-Park, Gina Marchetti and See Kam Tan, 269–92. London: Palgrave.
Jackson, Earl. 2019. 'Passionate Agendas: Melodrama in the Work of Yoshimura Kōzaburō.' *Asian Cinema* 30, no.1: 3–16.
Jackson, Earl. 2022. 'Chaos and Order in *A Fugitive from the Past*.' Video Commentary, *Fugitive from the Past* (Uchida Tomu 1965). Blu-Ray. Arrow Video.
Just, Daniel. 2007. 'Against the Novel – Meaning and History in Roland Barthes's *Le degre zero de l'ecriture*.' *New Literary History* 38, no. 2: 389–403.
Kaplan, David E. and Alex Dubro. 2003. *Yakuza: Japan's Criminal Underworld*. Berkeley: University of California Press.
Kato, Kenji. 1993. 'Soshiki to Booryoku to [shimin] no ekurityuuru.' In *Daiyakuza Eiga Tokuhon 1963–1993*. Edited by Fukuma Kenji and Yamazaki Mikio, 92–101. Tokyo: Yosensha.
Ko, Mika. 2010. *Japanese Cinema and Otherness: Nationalism, Multiculturalism, and the Problem of Japaneseness*. London: Routledge.
Kokomi, Iida, Tomoda Junichiro, Uchida Kisao and Shimizu Chiyota. 1940. '*Nishizumi Senshacho Den* Gappyo.' *Kinema junpo* (1 December): 54–6.
Miike, Takashi. 2003. *Kantoku Chudoku*. Tokyo: Pia.
Miike, Takashi,T. D. C. Fujiki, Ginti Kobayashi and Todoroki Takio, eds. 2003. *Takashi Miike's Rushin' Works: Miike Takashi no Shigoto 1991–2003*. Tokyo: Ohta Shuppan.
Otsuka, Eiji. 2012. *Monogatari Shohi Ron*. Tokyo: Asuki Shinsho.
Oshita, Eiji. 2016. *Gekitō! Yami no Aeiō Andō Noboru*. Tokyo: Sakura sha.
Sakai, Nobuo. 2003. 'Kaisetsu.' In *Hiroshima Yakuza Den: Akuma no Kyuupii Onishi Masahiro to Satsujinki Yamagami Mitsuji*. Edited by Hondo Junichiro, 357–63. Tokyo: Gentosha.
Supreme Commander for the Allied Powers. 1949. *Political Reorientation of Japan, September 1945 to September 1948, Volume 1*. US Government Printing Office, Yokohama.
Suzuki, Tomohiko. 2019. 'Ishikawa Rikio – Oowarai Sanzyuunen no Baka Sawagi.' Yakuza to Geinookai. Special Issue of *Shōwa no Fushigi* (Autumn): 36–9.
Watanabe, Takenobu. 1993. 'Hiiroozoo no Tenkan – Yakuza Eiga wa ika ni shite tanzyoo shita ka.' In *Daiyakuza Eiga Tokuhon 1963–1993*. Edited by Fukuma Kenji and Yamazaki Mikio, 6–15. Tokyo: Yosensha.
Whiting, Robert. 1999. *Tokyo Underworld*. New York: Pantheon.
Yamazaki, Mikio. 1993. 'Fukasaku Kinji no Shoogeki: "Mada Dan wa nokotte iru n desu ze".' In *Daiyakuza Eiga Tokuhon 1963–1993*. Edited by Fukuma Kenji and Yamazaki Mikio, 38–45. Tokyo: Yosensha.

Yoda, Tomiko. 2006. 'A Roadmap to Millennial Japan.' In *Japan After Japan: Social and Cultural Life from the Recessionary 1990s to the Present*. Edited by Tomiko Yoda and Harry Harootunian, 16–53. Durham: Duke University Press.

Yoshimura, Kōzaburō. 1976. *Eiga no Inochi: Watashi no Sengoshi*. Tokyo: Tamakawa Daigaku Shuppan.

CHAPTER 9

The Promise of Hokkaidō: Trauma, Violence and the Legacy of the Imperial Frontier in Lee Sang-Il's *Unforgiven*

Lance Lomax

Histories of cinematic remakes arising between Japan and the United States have long captured the attention of both popular and scholarly audiences. Emphasis tends to rest upon the post-war reception of Japanese cinema via international film festivals and the resultant generic influences that manifested most readily between jidaigeki films (historical dramas often situated during Japan's pre-modern period prior to 1868) and Westerns. Discourses of cinematic remakes between the two nations reveal much about how their leaders and their cultural producers have addressed societal change in an increasingly transpacific context. After the Second World War, both nations converged in a manner that would mutually shape their geopolitical and ideological futures, resulting in extensive cultural crosspollination while also complicating and at times overriding regional, colonial and traumatic legacies in East Asia. In some ways, cinema was an ideal medium for both nations to engage with each other and explore new power dynamics and societal restructuring. Both Hollywood and Japan's film industry favoured genres well-suited to addressing the convergence of tradition and modernity. It is perhaps unsurprising, then, that the jidaigeki and the Western would develop a reciprocal relationship, particularly through cinematic remakes.

This is not to say that the genres of jidaigeki and the Western are simply interchangeable; rather, they are able to accommodate the increasingly transnational aspects of cinematic (co)production, distribution and reception that emerged after the Second World War, perhaps more adeptly than other popular genres (such as the comedy, the family melodrama and the musical, which are comparatively 'cloistered' in their spatial configurations). Most often, the heroes of jidaigeki films and Westerns are 'social outsiders who restore order or help people fighting against the villains while being fully aware that their virtuous action does not allow them to reintegrate themselves in a renewed social order' (Yoshimoto 2000, 231). As exemplified by Alan Ladd's titular gunslinger in *Shane* (1953) and Toshiro Mifune's titular swordslinger in *Sanjuro* (1962), the appeal of these characters arises from their mysterious pasts, mastery of weapons and a stoic concern for the wellbeing of the communities they briefly inhabit. A seemingly necessary violence follows these characters and what manifests through them goes beyond clearly defined morality and instead draws attention to the liminal worlds and wanderers that inhabit the spaces between periods of stability. This is not to say that every jidaigeki or Western challenges societal conventions or must be reflective of larger social issues, but that as genres they are certainly fit to undertake such tasks, especially through adaptation. Yet, cinematic histories about the reciprocal ties between Hollywood and Japan need not rest solely within a rigid transpacific hierarchy of iconic precursors and resultant remakes. As seen in Lee-Sang-il's *Unforgiven* (*Yurusarezaru mono*, 2013), a remake of Clint Eastwood's exemplary revisionist Western *Unforgiven* (1992), the process of remaking must often carry both the past and the present through a film's narrative and a generic horizon of expectations. The intersections of Lee's and Eastwood's films reveal the Japanese version of *Unforgiven* as a palimpsestic – or as Linda Hutcheon might deem, a 'palimpsestuous' – text that draws upon the familiarity or visibility of the American version's mythos as a vital component of a contextually sensitive remake (Hutcheon 2006, 21).

Set during Japan's Meiji-era imperial expansion into Hokkaidō (Japan's second largest island and northernmost prefecture), Lee Sang-il's *Unforgiven* encourages viewers who have seen its source material to draw parallels between William Munny (Clint Eastwood) and Kamata Jubei (Watanabe Ken), Ned Logan (Morgan Freeman) and Baba Kingo (Emoto Akira), The Schofield Kid (Jaimz Woolvett) and Sawada Goro (Yugira Yuya) and Delilah Fitzgerald (Anna Thomson) and Natsume (Kutsuna Shiori). Goro and Natsume take on much more significant roles in Lee's remake than their predecessors do in the American film. Goro, as half-Ainu, contributes to themes of imperial legacies, ethnicity and indigeneity that undergird much of the film and bear connections to Lee's experiences as a Zainichi Korean in Japan. So too does the lack of justice regarding Natsume's assault and disfigurement draw attention to the inequalities and social stratification that remained intact despite promises of a new and modern Japan under the Meiji Restoration.

As in Eastwood's film, much of the narrative is driven by themes of revenge and violence. However, while the American version situates a gruesome attack upon a prostitute at the forefront of the narrative, Lee's *Unforgiven* opens with a scene of imperial soldiers, later revealed as 'samurai hunters', pursuing a former Shogunate retainer across the frozen landscape of Hokkaidō. Moments later, a visceral bloodbath unfolds as the former samurai, cornered and frenzied, brutally dispatches his pursuers before falling face first into the snow from exhaustion. Rather than having a text crawl set against the backdrop of a meagre homestead, Lee introduces viewers to the protagonist Kamata Jubei in a scene that foregrounds both the landscape of Hokkaidō and the sociopolitical circumstances of the Meiji Restoration. As this scene plays out and Jubei eliminates his pursuers, a voiceover muses about wilderness and the indigenous Ainu population, the purpose and experience of fear and the role of Japan's emergent empire in 'civilising' the frontier of Hokkaidō. The voice is soon revealed to belong to Oishi Ichizo (Sato Koichi), a former samurai turned imperial peacekeeper in a frontier town in 1880 and a nuanced equivalent to Eastwood's antagonist Little Bill (Gene Hackman). Oishi is clearly established as a foil to Jubei as the scene ends by fading from Jubei's face to Oishi's and turns to the aftermath of a former samurai's assault of the prostitute Natsume. Oishi refuses to hold the man accountable beyond forcing him to compensate the brothel owner financially. Resultingly, Lee's narrative follows much of Eastwood's beyond this point. A bounty is offered, Kingo tracks down his former comrade Jubei and convinces him to participate, and the pair are eventually joined by an enthusiastic and overcompensating Goro. Yet as closely as Lee adheres to Eastwood's film, scenes of imperial soldiers humiliating and berating Ainu villagers, Goro's struggles and feelings of loss, and Jubei's desires to honour his late Ainu wife's wishes for a peaceful existence for their family all supplement themes of revenge and violence that appear as the primary concern in the original work.

Accordingly, Lee's unique take on the Western bears many of the generic hallmarks that have long informed aspects of cinematic exchange between the film industries of Japan and America. Yet, as a remake produced in East Asia and circulated internationally, the film draws attention to the 'complex workings of the latent tensions and contradictions within both the Western genre itself and its cross-cultural translation in Japanese cinema' (Vivian P. Y. Lee 2022, 281). Although many thematic and visual signifiers clearly place Lee's *Unforgiven* within the paradigm of Japan's national cinema, the film reinforces the 'notion [that] national cinemas must give way to transnational cultural industries' (Herbert 2008, ix). What makes this particular case study so illuminating are the myriad connections within an East Asian cultural sphere that it manifests, but which are often obscured under Hollywood's hegemonic shadow or by narratives of a homogenised national cinema. Thus, remakes produced in East Asia, such as *Unforgiven*, offer an ideal lens through which long-established narratives regarding the intersections of Hollywood and Japanese cinema might also account for what Yiman Wang deems a 'location-specific consciousness' (2013, 2). Such films also cast light upon legacies of imperialism, cultural trauma and identity, hence disrupting the centre-and-periphery dyad that often dominates conceptualisations of both cinematic remakes and national cinemas. Lost within early critiques of Lee's *Unforgiven* as being too beholden to Eastwood's vision or too reliant upon generic legacies are the sociohistorical and regional factors that continue to impact both Japan and East Asia. The film's diegesis is not merely a narrativised relic of Imperial Japan or a blind adherence to Eastwood's *Unforgiven*; instead, it reflects aspects of Japan's historical and contemporary sociopolitical policies and cultural imaginaries. This Japanese rendering of a film set in the 'Old West' (specifically Wyoming, but largely filmed in Alberta, Canada) exists as a chimera of Western and jidaigeki generic influences, yet also as part of a long domestic and transnational lineage of Meiji Restoration memory landscapes that have cyclically manifested within and across the East Asian nation's popular mediascapes, historical and traumatic discourses and modes of transnational exchange.

It is vital, then, to explore how a contemporary East Asian remake such as *Unforgiven* offers new points of entry into established histories of genre and cultural trauma while also focusing upon underexamined regional and cinematic histories within an East Asian cultural sphere. To consider these possibilities, this chapter attends to three primary concerns: understanding *Unforgiven* as an 'Asian Western'; delving into the process of remaking Eastwood's *Unforgiven*; and gesturing toward Japan's cinematic imaginary of Hokkaidō and the (re)writing of history. Essentially, this chapter explores how Lee's *Unforgiven* engages with Western and jidaigeki legacies, histories of wanderers and losers in Japan that maintain a hold on the country's cultural imaginary, and the 'remaking' that continues there and in East Asia more broadly regarding its former empire, frontier and national identity.

UNDERSTANDING *YURUSAREZARU MONO* AS AN 'ASIAN WESTERN'

Advocating for the contemporary cultural relevance of the Western, Charles Exley suggests that 'despite repeated claims of its demise', the genre 'continues to be remade, remixed, and revised' and that, while no longer produced in great numbers, it continues to serve a niche role within the American film industry (2018, 147). While it is traditionally viewed as an iconic Hollywood film genre, Vivian P. Y. Lee contends that the Western has nonetheless experienced a 'long history of intercultural dialogue that stretches far beyond its native soil' and carries significant historical and contemporary importance in discourses of transnational cinemas (2022, 267). Examples of the genre being reimagined around the world can be found in Italy ('Spaghetti Westerns' such as *A Fistful of Dollars* [*Per un pugno di dollari*, 1964] and *Django* [1966]), Germany ('Sauerkraut Westerns' such as *Apache Gold* [*Winnetou*, 1963]), Brazil ('Nordesterns' such as *O Cangaceiro* [1953]), the Soviet Union ('Osterns' such as *The Elusive Avengers* [*Neulovimye mstiteli*, 1967]), Australia ('Meat Pie Westerns' such as

Ned Kelly [1970]) and Angola ('Cowboiadas' films such as *Sambizanga* [1972]) among others (Koepnick 1995, 4).

In East Asia, a 'complex cluster of production interests and commercial imperatives' have seen Westerns 'establish their own generic pedigree through direct and indirect dialogues, so much so that localized genre labels such as "Asian Westerns" and "Easterns" have come to represent a homegrown genre in the region's film culture' (Lee 2022, 287). In the case of Japan, cinematic adaptations and remakes have played an integral role in these transnational exchanges. Lee argues:

> Since the 1960s, a two-way traffic between Japanese cinema and Hollywood has developed through mutual adaptations between the Western and the samurai film (or *chanbara*), a subgenre of the *jidaigeki* (period film) that went through a cycle of revisions in the post-World War II era in the hands of rising auteurs ... these new voices would redefine Japanese cinema to both domestic and international audiences in the 1960s and 1970s ... the reinvention of the samurai film coincided with the postwar effort of modern nation-building under the patronage of the US, who was eager to enlist Japan as an ally to consolidate its sphere of influence in Asia (2022, 287).

Lee addresses vital aspects of transnational cultural exchange that have undergirded established discourses of post-war Japanese cinema for decades. Studies of Japan's post-war period of exchange, which was facilitated through film festivals and an emphasis on auteurs such as Kurosawa Akira, Okamoto Kihachi, Gosha Hideo and Misumi Kenji, has long made clear the widespread impact of the Western across both scholarly and popular engagements with Japanese cinema.

Less studied, however, is the 'Asian Western'. Lee importantly contends that Japanese engagements with the genre must be understood as 'ideologically complex and self-consciously hybridised cinematic works that engage with the imperialist impulses of the West(tern) while maintaining a problematic relationship to their Japanese roots', regarding both the classics of 1960s samurai films and more recent works that 'explicitly pay tribute to the western film tradition in setting, visual motifs, and characterization' (2022, 268). In particular, the intersections of film genre and cinematic remaking have served Japan's efforts to bolster a domestic motion picture industry while also reinforcing conservative dimensions of national tendencies through transnational strategies. This was perhaps most obvious in 1950s Japan, where 'cinema was the palace for entertainment, the assembly-space for popular enlightenment, [and] an ideal medium with which to restore the cultural pride that the Japanese had long lost in the international arena' (Yomota 2019, 138). As a remake, *Unforgiven* exists within this history of cinematic exchange and remaking, but it also stands as a contemporary example of an 'Asian Western' that draws upon contextual influences from regional engagements within Japan and across East Asia. Often overshadowed by the historical two-way traffic between Hollywood and Japan regarding the Western and jidaigeki film genres are the legacies of imperialism and cultural trauma that have previously and presently shaped Japan's relationship with its regional neighbours. Dominant discourses of Hollywood and Japan's cinematic relationship tend to prioritise generic influence or cinematic adaptation from the post-war period onward, and largely within a transpacific context that at times obscures the complexities of East Asia as a cultural sphere, and especially elements of what is often considered Japan's 'history problem'.

At the risk of oversimplification, Japan's 'history problem' essentially concerns what Koyama Hitomi deems 'contentions over proper modes of history-writing [that] persist as a *rekishi mondai* (history problem) between the former empire and its victim states', or questions raised by Hashimoto Akiko regarding how 'national trauma remains relevant to culture and society' long after an event and 'why defeat has become an indelible part of national collective life, especially in recent decades' (Koyama 2015, ii; Hashimoto 2015, 3). Amidst these intersections of transnational cinemas, regional specificity and history problems, *Unforgiven* attends to Vivian P. Y. Lee's vital concerns of viewing Asian Westerns, and more specifically, Japanese Westerns, as ideologically complex and self-consciously hybridised cinematic works operating on multiple levels that extend beyond cinematic adaptation. Hybridisation is perhaps the hallmark of Japanese engagements with Asian Westerns and transnationalism has increasingly inflected the subgenre from at least the 1960s onward. Suzuki Seijun's *Man with a Shotgun* (*Shottogan no Otoko*, 1961), Sato Junya's *The Drifting Avenger* (*Koya no toseinin*, 1968), Okamoto Kihachi's *East Meets West* (1995) and Miike Takashi's *Sukiyaki Western Django* (*Sukiyaki Uesutan Jango*, 2007) are all examples of the generic and thematic hybridisation and transnationalism that undergird the paradigm of a Japanese Western. When considered within the context of Japan's 'history problem', the generic hybridisation seen in Japanese Westerns reflects the nation's 'hybridised' historical narratives that shift in perspective regarding complicity, guilt and transnational engagement within an East Asian context.

Lee's *Unforgiven* likely appears as the most conservative Japanese Western in this lineage due to its close adherence to Eastwood's film and its formal and stylistic fidelity concerning the Western and jidaigeki genres. However, despite its generic, thematic and aesthetic indebtedness to both the English-language *Unforgiven* and the post-war conventions of jidaigeki films, *Unforgiven* extends beyond influences of Golden Age Japanese cinema or Hollywood Westerns and subtly exemplifies the hybridisation of other examples of the genre produced in Japan. Lee's awareness of the challenges inherent in recasting histories most clearly arises when *Unforgiven*'s antagonist Oishi bluntly states, 'the survivors end up as the heroes and the dead end up as the villains . . . that's history, right?' More than a faithful adaptation of Eastwood's film, Lee's *Unforgiven* grapples with cinematic, ideological, sociopolitical and transnational legacies extant in Japan and across much of its former East Asian empire. If Eastwood's *Unforgiven* draws upon specific conventions of the Western genre, it does so while also 'inflecting them, adapting them, subverting them to refashion the genre into something viable for the modern age' (Buscombe 2004, 16). So too does Lee Sang-il do more than relocate iconography and themes of the Western or jidaigeki to the frontier of Hokkaidō. Rather, as a Japanese Western, *Unforgiven* tactfully recasts historical and contemporary narratives of nation, identity and the (cinematically mythologised) frontier, while contributing to the ongoing 'remaking' of Japan's cultural imaginary and rethinking of its history problem.

REMAKING *UNFORGIVEN*

On 3 September 2013, Kageyama Yuri interviewed Japanese film star Watanabe Ken in Tokyo to discuss his starring role in director Lee Sang-il's new release *Unforgiven*. While speaking with Kageyama and in service of promoting the work a few days before its premiere at the 70th Venice International Film Festival, Watanabe remarked that he 'was convinced from the start that [*Unforgiven*] will be an original Japanese movie in its own right' (quoted in Kageyama). Watanabe's claim could be written off as a last-minute marketing effort, or even an attempt to create a measure of distance between his previous collaboration with Eastwood in *Letters from Iwo Jima* (2006). Yet, Watanabe touched upon a deeper concern within histories of Japanese cinema. Unlike Sergio Leone's unofficial remake of Kurosawa Akira's *Yojimbo* (1961) and the resultant infringement case issued by Tōhō, Lee Sang-il had the full endorsement of Eastwood and the support of Warner Bros. in remaking *Unforgiven*. While many perceptions of Japanese cinema emphasise a unidirectional process of adaptation from Japan to the West, Lee's film draws attention to the role adaptation or remaking has long played within Japanese cinema's development. As Michael Raine argues, 'cinema in Japan was always adaptation . . . from other media, to particular contexts, and of a foreign form', and that 'we cannot understand films, or the debates around them without recognizing the dual orientation of Japanese film and film discourse toward the authority of Western cinema and toward the project of making it Japanese' (2013, 116–17). The dichotomy Raine reasserts emphasises the entanglements of artistry, industry, technology and transnational exchange that were manifested within Japan from the earliest introduction of modern motion picture technologies in the late nineteenth century.

Similar to Watanabe's remarks, when asked if he was directly attempting to engage in the symbiotic legacies of generic influence between jidaigeki films and Westerns, director Lee Sang-il claimed that 'the fact that the movie is going over the ocean is very interesting I would say' (Lee 2014a). Both Lee and Watanabe are acutely aware of the lineage to which their film is partially beholden, from its debut at the Venice International Film Festival, its transpacific generic influences and cinematographic stylings, and aspects of Watanabe's transnational stardom and popularity in Hollywood that in some ways echo that of Hayakawa Sessue in the 1910s. When asked about the motivations undergirding his adaptation of Eastwood's *Unforgiven*, Lee Sang-il noted that because he was 'aiming towards a Japanese audience initially' he sought to emphasise a balance of dark introspection and a commonplace emotional narrative concerning 'normal' people that attempted to close what he felt in Eastwood's film to be a 'cool and dry' sense of distance between the audience and a character such as Eastwood's Munny (Lee 2014). Yet, Lee's and Watanabe's motivations also support the idea that a remake, even one as faithful as *Unforgiven*, can nonetheless engage with and uncover historical, sociopolitical and industrial contexts that cast light upon the complexities of cinematic production and adaptation in the cultural sphere of East Asia.

Along with foregrounding a Japanese audience, Lee drew upon historical Japanese narratives of an expansively exploitable space that align with depictions of the frontier in American Westerns. Of his interest in frontier narratives, Lee claims:

> Prior to *Yurusarezaru mono*, I was already toying with the idea of depicting this era because we have the frontier in Japan as well. In Hokkaidō, there's a story about it. It's not very often that we get to see this work in terms of TV or films. Therefore, I wanted to show that era in Hokkaidō. I already started the research and going into Hokkaidō myself to study what's going on at the time. So that actually happened to match with the themes of *Unforgiven* (Lee 2014).

As Lee's research and desire to craft a period piece situated within Hokkaidō developed, the parallels and motivations between what Lee had envisioned and Eastwood's *Unforgiven* solidified. Charles Exley argues that as a remake, *Unforgiven* 'appropriates most of the narrative of Eastwood's film, and makes liberal use of the iconography, the familiar orchestral soundtrack, and the *mise*-en-*scène* in a way that underscores the ways in which a Japanese western interacts, overlaps, and interrelates with the classic western' (2018, 152). Lee's adherence to many of the formal and narrative aspects of Eastwood's film offer the pleasure of familiarity, but, as later sections of this chapter will address more specifically, Lee deftly builds upon this foundation to carry forward a regionally sensitive revisionist sentiment that moves his version of *Unforgiven* beyond mere replication.

Lee also recasts the ideological and thematic underpinnings of Eastwood's *Unforgiven*. Examples of a location-specific collective consciousness arise in the film through the shifts in characterisation Lee employs despite the quite obvious parallels that exist between his characters and those of Eastwood's film. Vivian P. Y. Lee notes that Lee Sang-il's remake 'reveals a perceptive grasp of Eastwood's original in terms of character psychology, moral conflicts and, most of all, its critique of the ideological ambivalences of the US-American western or what Allen Redmon calls the mechanisms of violence' (2022, 281). These thematic similarities are perhaps what inspired many reviewers from the West to proclaim Lee's film as being too beholden to Eastwood's *Unforgiven*. In fairness, this Japanese production is much more subtle in its adaptation of generic conventions of the American Western compared to other films such as *East Meets West* or *Sukiyaki Western Django*. Nonetheless, Lee's revisionist sentiment is what enables the foregrounding of concerns of indigeneity and oppression, the intersections and contradictions of state-sanctioned violence and justice and a Japanese frontier mythology that continues to shape aspects of Japan's cultural imaginary. These connections are only revealed, however, if efforts are made to see *Unforgiven* as a multivalent transnational and transhistorical engagement rather than a remake unilaterally engaged with Hollywood and tethered to entrenched perceptions of genre.

The ways in which Lee infuses his remake with a location-specific consciousness can be identified through a comparison of the opening scenes of both films. Eastwood's *Unforgiven* leads off by informing viewers through crawling text that Will Munny is a 'known thief and murderer and a man of notoriously vicious and intemperate disposition' and instantly complicates the notion of a western hero. This is not to say that the shift from an unquestionable paradigm of heroic endeavour to a morally complicated figure arose suddenly. As Edward Buscombe notes, 'even in the 1950s deep-seated faults in the bedrock of American society were causing cracks to appear in the previously impregnable carapace of the male hero' (2004, 10). Furthermore, Buscombe argues that Eastwood was sensitive to shifts in the Western as a genre over the latter half of the twentieth century and that if it was 'to continue to be viable, it would need to be adapted to contemporary sensibilities and show that it was aware of its own past and in touch with the present' (Ibid., 16). Similarly, Lee unveils a keen awareness of how to adapt the generic and cinematographic stylings of Westerns and jidaigeki films through his version of *Unforgiven*.

Lee's film also opens with textual information fading into black, but rather than setting the stage for the audience's understanding of the protagonist, Lee instead provides a brief historical background of the earliest moments of the Meiji Restoration (1868) and the resultant societal rifts. At various points across its modern history, Japan has turned to popular culture and various media to 'remake' the Meiji Restoration from the perspective of the losers – in particular, the former retainers of the Tokugawa shogunate who were hunted and often executed in the first years of the Meiji Restoration (Wert 2013, 109). Indeed, this is how viewers are introduced to Watanabe's character Kamata Jubei – a former samurai retainer fleeing to Hokkaidō as he is pursued by Meiji forces. Stories regarding Tokugawa retainers and political shifts arose through a 'hodgepodge of diaries, petitions, inflammatory statements, mocking rhymes, satirical cartoons, kabuki plays, popular literature, crude newspapers, broadsheets, handbills, and even graffiti' from the earliest moments of the Meiji Restoration and have cyclically appeared well into the present moment (Steele 1990, 140). From a cinematic perspective, Watanabe's character Jubei calls to mind the wandering ronin figures played by Mifune Toshiro in Kurosawa Akira's *Yojimbo* (1961) and Nakadai Tatsuya in Kobayashi Masaki's *Harakiri* (*Seppuku*, 1962). Yet, Watanabe's portrayal of Jubei casts a revisionist gaze upon a legacy that predates these cinematically mythicised characters by decades. Artists have long grappled with the Meiji Restoration in popular media and sociopolitical discourses as a process of constructing Japan as a modernising nation-state. As Michael Wert argues, 'whether in the call for greater political participation in the late nineteenth and early twentieth centuries, reaction to Japan's growing imperial aspiration in the 1920s and 30s, celebrating the economic boom of the 1960s, or expressing apprehension during the troubled 1990s', people have looked to the Meiji Restoration for models and solutions to contemporary problems (2009, 43). Embodied through Jubei, the 'restoration loser' is a motif that spans Japan's modern history and finds renewed purpose within specific discourses of a national and transnational imaginary alongside accounts surrounding Meiji-era figures such as Saigō Takamori – a figure Watanabe portrayed in Edward Zwick's epic action film *The Last Samurai* (2003).

Wert notes that, as losers, their 'stories embodied loss in, and of, Japan . . . the empire, its status in the world, and the Japanese who lost loved ones and any sense of well-being' (2013, 114). Oguri Tadamasa in particular was a Tokugawa bureaucrat who also became somewhat of a mythic figure owing to his staunch opposition to the emperor. While vilified in the ensuing decades following the Meiji Restoration, Oguri's legacy as a 'restoration loser' would find renewed purpose in a most unusual place and time – the 'lost decade' of the 1990s in Japan. While Oguri 'might not inspire a call to action as Saigo does, his portrayal as a tireless and honest samurai bureaucrat made him a hero in the 1990s' amidst a period of great economic and societal strife and the bursting of Japan's postwar cultural imaginary (Wert 2009, 48). Echoing localised historical efforts in Gunma Prefecture where Oguri was killed, many of the local citizens in Gunma Prefecture in the 1990s succeeded in promoting Oguri to a larger audience in a time when Japan was forced to reassess its national and cultural consciousness. Of these efforts, Wert argues:

> Historians wrote more books about Oguri, Gunma television stations produced documentaries and historical dramas about him, and anniversary celebrations of his life, held at the temple where Oguri lived, gave him greater exposure in the region. The Prefectural Governor and the mayors of Kurabuchi Village (where Oguri was killed) and Yokosuka City petitioned NHK to create a drama about him. In January of 2001, the first full treatment of his life appeared in the annual New Year historical drama. Since then, more books and his own manga series have come out, and he has even made it into a Japanese high school history textbook, sure signs of his rising status in Japanese historical consciousness (2009, 48).

Dominant histories of the Meiji Restoration place it as a foundational issue in explaining Japan's devolution into fascism, violence and warfare; yet, it has also led to the inverse in narratives of resistance that glorify the shogunate. *Unforgiven* tactfully addresses both of these oscillations by casting competing restoration narratives through individualised experiences of its characters. The most direct example occurs midway through the film when Jubei and Kingo are traveling to the frontier town of Washiro to pursue the bounty offered by the prostitutes. At this point, Kingo has convinced Jubei to accompany him and perform the acts of violence Jubei swore off after meeting his wife. Yet, Jubei still appears hesitant to engage in vigilantism. Kingo reminds Jubei that 'we've killed lots of men we had no quarrel with . . . that's how things were for men like us, the lowest of the samurai . . . the shogun and the emperor were two sides of the same coin . . . no difference'. Although Kingo has ulterior motives in convincing Jubei to accompany him, this moment exemplifies how localised violence and trauma in the frontier space of Hokkaidō has been filtered through grand narratives of socio-political upheaval and ideology. Lee challenges both the broad implications of imperialism and state-sanctioned violence, along with the violence and disruption that accompany frontier narratives of 'remaking' or opportunity. Although not depicted in the film, warfare and widespread conflict undergird the narrative, but Lee does not seek to elevate one side or the other in service of bolstering a national consciousness. Aaron Gerow notes that 'recourse to war is hardly a new tactic in the history of Japanese film; indeed, war has played a major role in shaping the industry throughout its history' (Gerow 2006, 2). Lee certainly had precedence to depict the fall of the shogunate or the large-scale conflict that in part contributed to Jubei's mythic status as a brutal enforcer of the shogunate prior to the events of the film. However, Lee offers no visual reference to these events, opting instead to emphasise Jubei's psychological trauma and contention through a series of flashbacks to the opening scene of the film where Jubei furiously kills his pursuers or through the questioning or recollection of stories by people Jubei encounters. In this sense, *Unforgiven* challenges the recourse to war present in aspects of Japan's film industry, but also recasts many domestic and transnational lineages of media, history and cultural trauma surrounding the Meiji Restoration.

Another way Lee infuses his remake with a location-specific consciousness attends to Eastwood's critique of violence while also recasting Japan's frontier narratives through an emphasis on weaponry. In particular, Lee juxtaposes swords and guns in ways that fit within the generic expectations of a Western or jidaigeki, but which also find historical parallels beyond their cinematic iconography. During the US military's post-war occupation of Japan, American censors in the country placed the cinematic gun against the sword – an instrument of ostensible justice against one of supposedly unwavering violence – and 'an American fear of the sword' led censors to argue that 'gunmen and sheriffs of the Wild West resorted to their weapons only to defend justice and to restore safety to their communities' (Hirano 1992, 67). Lee clearly engages with remnants of these ideas along with the generic legacy of the gun as a component of the redemptive violence that undergirds much of the Western and jidaigeki genres. Furthermore, a theme of displacement coincides with Lee's emphasis on weapons and their role in the frontier space of Hokkaidō. Charles Exley posits that Lee draws on the 'pre-existing association between the classic western and the wanderer in the Japanese film to highlight questions of displacement, especially as a consequence of the repression of political and ethnic others in the acquisition of Hokkaidō in the 1860s' (2018, 152). An example of these historical and cinematic intersections of weaponry, redemptive violence and displacement arose shortly after the defeat of the shogunate. In 1874, the Meiji government enacted a ban on swords in an effort to deconstruct further the image and symbolic power of the samurai class. This historical edict shapes the narrative and themes of loss in *Unforgiven* and draws out regional and sociopolitical legacies that extend beyond the generic or narrative influences of the Western and *Unforgiven* specifically.

The sword ban implemented by Oishi Ichizo in the frontier town of Washiro leads to a scene that mirrors the humiliation of English Bob (Richard Harris) in Eastwood's version of *Unforgiven*, but carries even greater meaning than establishing Little Bill's violent disposition masked by the trappings of his status as sheriff. Oishi, a former samurai turned Imperial police commander, humiliates and beats a former samurai and master swordsman named Masaharu Kitaoji (Kunimura Jun), who attempts to defy the ban upon his arrival in Washiro. Masaharu's arrival by wagon, accompanied by a skittish writer, offers a brief moment of levity in the film. Masaharu scoffs at the sign declaring a ban on carrying swords, provokes an inebriated bar patron to a duel and goes so far as to provide him a sword (conveniently stuck in its *saya*).

Figure 9.1 Officers aim their weapons at Masaharu Kitaoji (Kunimura Jun), in this scene from Lee Sang-il's *Unforgiven* (*Yurusarezaru mono*, 2013), a remake of Clint Eastwood's *Unforgiven* (1992).

He then masterfully embarrasses the drunken man by slicing his clothing in half but leaving him otherwise unharmed. The scene quickly shifts when Masaharu encounters Oishi upon returning to the bar. Oishi and his officers surround Masaharu, depriving him of his weapons. Oishi then mercilessly beats Masaharu, imprisons him overnight and sends him off battered and bruised the next morning. Oishi's rage is not merely a result of his authority being challenged; it is representative of his own legacy as a former samurai who now must justify an adherence to a nation-state that only values his continued presence as an enforcer of its imperial aspirations. Oishi's battering of Masaharu also reinforces Lee's hesitancy to present characters as admirable because of their mastery of weaponry and violence that often accompany heroes in the Western and jidaigeki genres.

Along with Oishi, Jubei is also a former samurai rather than the kind of outlaw character that Eastwood played in the original *Unforgiven*. Lee's framing of both the hero and villain as former agents of the previous government adds complexity to the film that situates it within its historical and cultural legacies, as well as the more abstract conceptualisations of individual experience and violence. While Jubei and Oishi are clearly set against one another, a less obvious parallel between Jubei and Masaharu exists through their respective swords. Before being destroyed by Oishi, Masaharu's sword is pristine, and he seems to have carried with him into Hokkaidō the pomp and privilege of his forbidden social status. Conversely, Jubei's rusted, haggard sword is made fun of – at one point, Oishi asks Jubei if he 'pulled it out of the garbage to kill bears'. Nevertheless, Jubei ultimately kills Oishi with the same sword and commits astounding acts of violence without the showmanship of Masaharu, proving that his widespread reputation as 'Jubei the Killer' is indeed warranted. By complicating the roles of his protagonist and antagonist as members of the same social class, and previously both in service of the same leader, Lee offers a more complex and culturally reflective portrayal of how violence often manifests as a means of state-sanctioned control rather than as a resultant circumstance of one's relation to the law or authority. Although he preserves the motif of the wanderer inherent to the Western and jidaigeki genres and engages with Eastwood's reflections upon an individual's capacity for violence, Lee situates these concepts within a wider framework of imperialism and cultural trauma. Simultaneously, the filmmaker presents a much more historically situated account of violence and sociopolitical instability that reveals *Unforgiven* as a Japanese Western concerned with specific tensions arising across Japan's modern history. In particular, the film attempts to reframe remnants of Japan's imperial frontier and attend to what Sara Spurgeon deems the 'stubborn survival and continual reimagining of myth in the face of an often-contradictory history' (2005: 5).

THE IMPERIAL FRONTIER AND THE 'CINEMATIC PROMISE' OF HOKKAIDŌ

On 9 April 2014, Yale University's Council on East Asian Studies held a symposium to discuss the significance of 'frontiers' across Japanese history. Contributors aimed to better understand the powerful hold upon popular imagination the frontier continues to carry even beyond the American West. Frontiers have played a recurring role in both the imaging and imagining of modern Japan from at least the time of the Meiji Restoration in 1868 and into the twentieth and twenty-first centuries. In the 1960s and 1970s, the historian Takahashi Tomio offered a frontier thesis in an attempt to 'transcend the limitations of Japanese history with a structural model recognizing the mutually constitutive nature of core and periphery, metropole and frontier' (Hopson 2014, 143). In 1946 the Japanese architect Ishikawa Hideaki drew upon frontier metaphors in viewing the destroyed urban space of Hiroshima as a site of opportunity for the physical and ideological construction of a new city and new society (Kovner 2017, 721). Alongside the construction of a post-war national imaginary or the process of urbanisation, the transnational circulation of Japanese cultural objects has long created influential sites of encounter that exist in some capacity as transnational frontiers. Perhaps the most obvious contemporary examples are the transmedial intersections of animation, fashion, ephemera and material culture that arose from the practices of 'Japan's media mix pioneers' in the late twentieth century and their 'total mobilization' toward a 'logistics of consumption' (Steinberg 2017, 244). The lineage of Japan's influential transnational image culture and media industries can also be traced through other cinematic frontier spaces: transnational encounters at post-war film festivals in part led to generic influences and exchanges between Hollywood and Japan's film industry; early forms of transnational stardom manifested through the work of actors such as Hayakawa Sessue in the 1910s and early 1920s; and the Russo-Japanese War (1904–1905) became an international spectacle, thanks in part to early motion picture technologies and media practices that cast light on the frontier spaces of East Asia and Japan's project of modernisation and the remaking of a national identity.

One of the most influential frontier spaces within Japan's modern history arose out of the annexation of Hokkaidō following the Boshin War during the Meiji Restoration in 1868–1869. Known today for its 'hot springs, ski resorts, seafood and magnificent scenery', in the late nineteenth-century Hokkaidō represented the ultimate frontier for the newly established Meiji government and Japan's modernisation (Nakamura 2008, 2). Before being renamed Hokkaidō by the Meiji government, the island was known to ethnic Japanese (*Wajin*) as Ezochi. Inhabited for centuries by the Ainu peoples, whose language, traditions and modes of existence were distinct from ethnic Japanese in Honshu, Ezochi was subsumed under Japanese control as Hokkaidō in 1869 and from that point forward played an integral role in Japan's national imaginary and regional sphere of influence. It is during this early period of expansion, modernisation and displacement that Lee situates the narrative of *Unforgiven*. In much of Japan's cultural imaginary and cinematic history, Hokkaidō has served as a perpetual frontier where Japan can reimage and reimagine a national or cultural identity against complex and at times conflicting histories. This process of remaking is traceable across a variety of Japanese cultural productions from the nineteenth century onwards that, despite utilising various genres, all hold onto the 'promise' of Hokkaidō as a space or idea of restoration, redemption or renewal.

However, contemporary scholarship questions such narratives, particularly those arising out of the early Meiji period, and posits that the casting of Hokkaidō as a space of opportunity was 'a process to quell domestic insecurity with out of work and discontent samurai left behind by the modern nation-state' (Mason and Lee 2012, 168). Evidence of this notion arises in *Unforgiven*. The perpetrator who disfigured the prostitute Natsume is a former samurai, and Oishi defends his lack of harsh punishment by claiming that the man is a hard worker simply trying to survive, but also that as a former samurai he has powerful friends. Furthermore, the colonisation of Hokkaidō 'played an integral part in the formation of the new Meiji nation-state, often using romantic and peaceful descriptions of scenery to cover up the violent suppression that was constitutive both of modern Hokkaidō and of the modern Japanese nation-state' (Ibid., 23). Kingo echoes this notion when he tells Jubei, 'without coal, trains and boats don't move . . . I know where there's coal, I just need money . . . come join in the dream . . . just once I want my place in the sun'. Kingo's claim turns out to be fabricated, much as the imaging of Hokkaidō as a space of limitless opportunity was in the early stages of the Meiji Restoration. Lee converses with romantic and idealised visions of the frontier through mise-en-scène and cinematography that emphasise the beauty and sublime landscapes of Hokkaidō and also invoke the frontier within the Western genre. However, much like Watanabe's character Jubei, *Unforgiven* approaches the frontier in a manner that extends beyond the transnational influence of the genre or the historical Japanese visions of Hokkaidō. Modern Japan has 'remade' Hokkaidō from the earliest moments of its colonial takeover and *Unforgiven* both engages in and challenges this cinematic and historical legacy of remaking facilitated through Hokkaidō with its contemporary concerns of indigeneity and marginalisation. Accordingly, Lee invokes and critiques what I would deem 'Hokkaidō's cinematic promise'.

Much like the historical and recurrent trope of the 'restoration loser', so too has Hokkaidō served various roles in the memory landscapes of Japanese histories and media. Yamada Yoji's *Where Spring Comes Late* (*Kazoku*, 1970), along with his radically different *Tora-san* films or Furuhata Yasuo's *Poppoya* (1999), Fukugawa Yoshihiro's *Dear My Love* (*60-sai no rabu reta*, 2009) and Sugawara Hiroshi's *Shashin Koshien Summer in 0.5 Seconds* (*Shashin oshien 0.5 byo no natsu*, 2017) are just a few examples of how Hokkaidō has offered a 'cinematic promise' of restoration, opportunity or redemption. *Unforgiven*, however, moves indigenous populations and issues of colonisation and assimilation to the forefront of the film to counter aspects of this cinematic promise. Although the Ainu were officially and legally recognised as Japan's indigenous population in 2019, without support from the Japanese government and education institutions the Ainu language is at risk of being lost. Early on, and as seen in *Unforgiven*, violence and aggression from the Meiji government threatened the indigenous population; but across the twentieth century, narratives of assimilation stymied the preservation or growth of Ainu culture.

Of his inclusion of the Ainu in *Unforgiven*, Lee, of Zainichi Korean descent, claimed 'I don't think it is a direct correlation between the film and the fact I am Korean, but at the time with Japan being both modernised and Westernised, they are trying to reclaim Hokkaidō . . . so what they did to the Ainu people was repeated further down the line with the Korean and Chinese people . . . this was the start' (Lee 2014a). While certainly not the first inclusion of the Ainu in a Japanese film, Lee's foregrounding of indigenous concerns speaks to the role that cinema and location-specific remakes in particular can play in shaping wider cultural discourses. Ukaji Shizue, an Ainu woman who travelled to Harvard University to speak at an event sponsored in part by the Cambridge-based human-rights organisation Cultural Survival, stated that 'language is the foundation of culture . . . it will be very difficult to maintain Ainu culture without a school, but when I talk about an Ainu school in Japan, no one pays attention . . . but the Japanese government is definitely influenced by the US government' (quoted in Schorow 2001, np). Ukaji's concerns speak to the complex relationships that constitute transpacific exchange between Japan and the United States. Along with political influence, so too do cultural texts and their reception shape contemporary discourses; by engaging with themes of cultural loss and forced assimilation in *Unforgiven*, Lee casts light on the potential loss of language via the international circulation of the film. While it certainly was not singularly responsible for the legal recognition of Ainu indigeneity, as a remake the film contributes to East Asian discourses of empire, cultural trauma and historical injustice, while utilising the transnational familiarity of the original *Unforgiven* and Eastwood's legacy (as an actor-filmmaker with more than six decades of experience under his gun belt) to amplify its reception. Recasting and demythologising one aspect of Japan's narrative of modernity, mono-ethnicity and empire – the Meiji Restoration – draws attention to the possibilities of remakes to influence and shape diverse aspects of an East Asian cultural sphere. In remaking an American Western, Lee repurposes the cinematic promise of Hokkaidō into a different sort of opportunity – one concerned with the remnants and spectres of an imperial frontier that continue to affect indigenous or marginalised populations within Japan and appear on screens that transform the landscape of Hokkaidō into an alluring shroud of concealment.

REFERENCES

Buscombe, Edward. 2004. *Unforgiven*. London: BFI.
Eastwood, Clint. 1992. *Unforgiven*, Malpaso Productions.
Exley, Charles. 2018. 'No Lands Man: On Remaking the Last Western in Japan and the Politics of Revision.' *Journal of Japanese and Korean Cinema* 10, no. 2: 147–62.
Gerow, Aaron. 2006. 'Fantasies of War and Nation in Recent Japanese Cinema.' *The Asia-Pacific Journal* 4, no. 2: 1–12.
Hashimoto, Akiko. 2015. *The Long Defeat: Cultural Trauma, Memory, and Identity in Japan*. Oxford: Oxford University Press.
Herbert, Daniel. 2008. *Transnational Film Remakes: Time, Space, Identity*. PhD diss., University of Southern California.
Hirano, Kyoko. 1992. *Mr. Smith Goes to Tokyo: The Japanese Cinema under the American Occupation, 1945–1952*. Washington: Smithsonian Institute.
Hopson, Nathan. 2014. 'Takahashi Tomio's "Henkyō": Eastern Easts and Western Wests.' *Japan Review* 27, no. 27: 141–70.
Hutcheon, Linda. 2006. *A Theory of Adaptation*. New York, NY: Routledge.
Kageyama, Yuri. 2013. 'Watanabe: New *Unforgiven* Honors Great Filmmaking.' *Associated Press* (4 September). https://apnews.com/article/687be053f3e94bba9a8ab705f3311de5. Accessed 11 March 2022.
Kitamura, Hiroshi. 2015., 'Paradox of Americanism: Kobayashi Akira and the "Japanese Western".' In *Transnational Asian Identities in Pan-Pacific Cinemas: The Reel Asian Exchange*. Edited by Philippa Gates and Lisa Funnell. New York: Routledge.
Koepnick, Lutz P. 1995. 'Unsettling America: German Westerns and Modernity.' *Modernism/Modernity* 2, no. 3: 1–22.

Kovner, Sarah. 2017. 'A War of Words: Allied Captivity and Swiss Neutrality in the Pacific, 1941–1945.' *Diplomatic History* 41, no. 4: 719–46.
Koyama, Hitomi. 2015. *Japan's History Problem: Agency, Violence, and the Limits of Decolonizing History*. Baltimore: The Johns Hopkins University Press.
Lee, Sang-il. 2013. *Yurusarezaru mono*. Nikkatsu & Warner Bros Pictures.
Lee, Sang-il. 2014a. '"People Around Me Often Say I Should Start Doing More Cheerful Movies" – In Conversation with Lee Sang-il.' Interview by Stephen Palmer. *Eastern Kicks* (27 February). https://www.easternkicks.com/features/people-around-me-often-say-i-should-start-doing-more-cheerful-movies-in-conversation-with-lee-sang-il. Accessed 19 February 2022.
Lee, Sang-il. 2014b. 'I Talk Remaking *Unforgiven* with Director Lee Sang-il.' Interview by Craig Grobler. *The Establishing Shot* (28 February). http://www.theestablishingshot.com/2014/02/i-talk-remaking-unforgiven-yurusarezaru.html. Accessed 19 February 2022.
Lee, Sang-il. 2014c. 'Interview: Sang-il Lee.' Interview by David Brake. *One Room with a View* (28 February). https://oneroomwithaview.wordpress.com/2014/02/28/interview-sang-il-lee/. Accessed 19 February 2022.
Lee, Vivian P. Y. 2022. 'Remaking the Western in Japanese Cinema: *East Meets West* (Kihachi Okamoto, 1995), *Sukiyaki Western Django* (Takashi Miike, 2007), and *Unforgiven* (Sang-il Lee, 2013).' In *Transnationalism and Imperialism: Endurance of the Global Western*. Edited by Hervé Mayer and David Roche., Bloomington: Indiana University Press.
Mason, Michele M. and Helen J. S. Lee. 2012. *Reading Colonial Japan: Text, Context, and Critique*. Redwood City: Stanford University Press.
Miller, Cynthia and A. Bowdoin Van Riper. 2013. *International Westerns*. Lanham: Scarecrow Press.
Nakamura, Akemi. 2008. 'Japan's Last Frontier Took Time to Tame, Cultivate Image.' *The Japan Times* (8 July). https://www.japantimes.co.jp/news/2008/07/08/reference/japans-last-frontier-took-time-to-tame-cultivate-image/. Accessed 11 March 2022.
Raine, Michael. 2013. 'Adaptation as Transcultural Mimesis in Japanese Cinema.' In *The Oxford Handbook of Japanese Cinema*. Edited by Daisuke Miyao. Oxford: Oxford University Press.
Schorow, Stephanie. 2001. 'Japan's Ainu Seek Help to Preserve Their Native Culture.' *Cultural Survival Quarterly Magazine* 25, no. 2. https://www.culturalsurvival.org/publications/cultural-survival-quarterly/japans-ainu-seek-help-preserve-their-native-culture. Accessed 11 March 2022.
Spurgeon, Sara. 2005. *Exploding the Western: Myths of Empire on the Postmodern Frontier*. College Station: Texas A&M University Press.
Steinberg, Marc. 2017. 'Media Mix Mobilization: Social Mobilization and Yo-Kai Watch.' *Animation: An Interdisciplinary Journal* 12, no. 3: 244–58.
Wang, Yiman. 2013. *Remaking Chinese Cinema: Through the Prism of Shanghai, Hong Kong, and Hollywood*. Honolulu: University of Hawai'i Press.
Wert, Michael. 2009. 'Remembering Restoration Heroes in Modern Japan.' *Education About Asia* 14, no. 1: 43–9.
Wert, Michael. 2013. *Meiji Restoration Losers: Memory and Tokugawa Supporters in Modern Japan*. Cambridge: Harvard University Asia Center.
Yomota, Inuhiko. 2019. *What is Japanese Cinema? A History*. New York: Columbia University Press.
Yoshimoto, Mitsuhiro. 2000. *Kurosawa: Film Studies and Japanese Cinema*. Durham: Duke University Press.

CHAPTER 10

Benny Chan's *Connected* and the Hollywoodisation of Hong Kong Cinema

Gary Bettinson

Film scholarship has generally ignored the cinema of Hong Kong director Benny Chan Muk-sing (1961–2020). An avowed 'commercial' filmmaker,[1] steeped in the traditions and trappings of popular genres, Chan could prima facie be dismissed as a slave to formula, beholden to the artistically suspect practices of filmic recycling and referentiality. His career encompasses sequels both legitimate (*Gen-Y Cops* [*Te jing xin ren lei 2*, 2000]) and nominal (*A Moment of Romance II* [*Tian ruo you qing II: Tian chang di jiu*, 1993]; *New Police Story* [*Xin jing cha gu shi*, 2004]). He braids his films with intertextual allusions and citations (for instance, *The White Storm* [*Sou Duk*, 2013] memorialises John Woo's heroic bloodshed sagas, and *Call of Heroes* [*Ngai sing*, 2016] pastiches Sergio Leone's Spaghetti Westerns). He plunders Johnnie To's *All About Ah-Long* (*A lang de gu shi*, 1989) in the male melodrama *Son on the Run* (*Dai zi hong lang*, 1991), while his historical drama *Shaolin* (*Xin shao lin si*, 2011) furnishes a loose reworking of the Shaw Brothers' martial arts classic *Shaolin Temple* (*Shao Lin si*, 1982). There are, as well, numerous borrowings from Hollywood staples: Michael Mann's *Heat* (1995) in the crime thrillers *Big Bullet* (*Chong feng dui nu huo jie tou*, 1996) and *Raging Fire* (*Nou fo*, 2021), *The Karate Kid* (1984) in the sports comedy *What a Hero!* (*Hua! Ying xiong*, 1992) and a welter of Marvel superhero movies in the high-concept blockbuster *City Under Siege* (*Chun sing gai bei*, 2010).[2] Not least, in *Connected* (*Bo chi tung wah*, 2008), there is that rare species of Hong Kong film: an authorised remake, co-produced by Hollywood, Hong Kong and Mainland Chinese companies, and modelled on David R. Ellis's American thriller *Cellular* (2004). In all, Chan's oeuvre might be seen to typify Hong Kong cinema's 'scavenger aesthetic' (Bordwell 2011, 7), so thoroughly does it rely on pre-existing source texts. For the critic attracted to filmic innovation and iconoclasm, Chan's cinema may seem too derivative, not to say too frankly profit-driven, to encourage scholarly attention.

Nor could a charitable critic easily posit Benny Chan as a case for auteur veneration. For one thing, Chan could not always lay claim to single authorship. He collaborated on directing the policier *Man Wanted* (*Wang Jiao de tian kong*, 1995) (with Steve Cheng Wai-man) and the spy caper *Who Am I?* (*Wo shi shui*, 1998) (with Jackie Chan). His mentor Johnnie To professed to having directed, sans credit, 'most' of *A Moment of Romance* (*Tin joek yau ching*, 1990), though the film was officially signed by Chan alone (Teo 2007, 228). Though celebrated as an action-genre specialist, Chan shared authorship of his exhilarating set pieces with an army of stunt co-ordinators and action choreographers. In addition, several of his films have been widely perceived – and in certain cases, explicitly promoted – less as auteurist ventures than as star vehicles, subordinating the primacy of the director to the popular appeal of a marquee player.[3] Similarly, critics construed *Gen-X Cops* (*Te jing xin ren lei*, 1999) and its 2000 sequel as manifesting not so much an authorial trademark as a house style, indicating that both films were assimilable to Media Asia's late-1990s blockbuster strategy. Even Chan's 'personal' themes – brotherhood, father-son relationships, the making of a hero – could be generalised to wider thematic preoccupations within Hong Kong cinema's phallocentric genres. That Chan is most closely identified with a disreputable genre – the high-concept action blockbuster – only reaffirms the impersonal nature of his filmmaking. For all such reasons, Chan's critical stock has remained low, while historical accounts of post-handover Hong Kong cinema typically accord him little importance.

My purpose in this chapter is not to espouse Benny Chan's auteur credentials, but I do aim to demonstrate:

1) that Chan's corpus of films is unified by a posse of signature themes, narrative tropes and stylistic techniques;
2) that Chan's significance springs, in part, from a sustained effort to impel and implement industrial change, particularly in the immediate post-handover years; and
3) that his habitual recycling, far from signifying creative bankruptcy, authorial stagnation or crass commercialism, served as a wellspring of artistic innovation and ingenuity.

Connected crystallises these concerns, exemplifying the ways Chan has innovated upon existing materials in ways both profit-making and personal.

It is useful to clarify this chapter's purview. It is not my purpose to show that *Connected* is superior to director David R. Ellis's *Cellular*, or to promote

Benny Chan as an auteur, or to extol the virtues of the Hollywood-style blockbuster as a mode of Hong Kong film production. Nor am I centrally concerned with the ideological motivations underlying *Connected* as a transnational joint venture. Rather, my principal locus of interest concerns Chan's effort to adapt *Cellular* in ways that accord with his authorial identity. Leo Braudy, reflecting upon filmic remakes, has neatly framed the key question that guides my analysis: 'How . . . does a filmmaker accomplish something personal that will attract an audience and assert the continuity of his . . . own career?' (1998, 332). In remaking *Cellular*, Chan's desire to 'attract an audience' is not to be downplayed; but I contend that his market-oriented concerns and artistic aspirations are not so much antithetical as thoroughly imbricated. For Chan, the practice of remaking is competitive in a creative as well as a commercial sense. *Connected* provides him an occasion not only to challenge the primacy of the source text (both in box office and creative terms), but also to push further – deepen, enrich, intensify – his own authorial proclivities and preoccupations. Perhaps paradoxically, the remaking process – far from being a cynical exercise in slavish mimicry or opportunistic 'scavenging' – is, for Chan, an opportunity to pursue aesthetic novelty and distinctiveness.

This chapter attempts to situate *Connected* historically, both in the context of the individual filmmaker's oeuvre and in relation to industrial changes taking place within post-handover Hong Kong cinema. I begin by tracing the broad trajectory of Benny Chan's 'middle period' (roughly 1998–2008), which, I argue, corresponded to a general industrial trend toward globalisation and new media. Critics have labelled this trend 'Hollywoodisation' – the strategy of remaking Hong Kong cinema in the Hollywood blockbuster mould – but it was equally a trend toward Mainlandisation, as local film producers courted mainland investors, tapped China's extensive production infrastructure and catered to the country's massive theatrical market. Benny Chan's post-handover cinema embodies these twin globalising forces. Sketching the historical background enables us to recognise how the late 1990s' surge toward Hollywoodisation and Mainlandisation – pursued by Chan and the local film industry alike – prepared the way for and culminated in *Connected*, a coproduced, transnational, authorised remake of a mainstream Hollywood property.

How does Benny Chan assimilate *Cellular* to his own authorial programme? To probe this question, we need first to characterise the aesthetic traits and tendencies established in his foregoing work. These signature features will, in turn, allow us to recognise that Chan was peculiarly qualified to remake a high-concept Hollywood action movie in the early 2000s. In the chapter's final sections, I pick out two of Chan's authorial traits for closer inspection. First, I examine the ways *Connected* elaborates its director's perennial fascination with heroic archetypes. I try to specify how the film reworks aspects of its US progenitor's story and characterisation in ways that reify personal themes. No account of Chan's cinema can ignore its scenes of physical action, and I go on to argue that *Connected*'s spectacular set pieces bear witness to the filmmaker's competitive quest for novelty. Hovering over this inquiry is a broader thesis. In the wake of 1997, critics prophesied the capitulation of local filmmaking traditions to Hollywood hegemony and mainland cultural imperialism. Though Chan actively blazed a path toward Hollywoodised co-productions, what he sought was a form of cultural synthesis, assimilating mainland resources and Hollywood technology to local storytelling traditions, rather than expunging those traditions altogether. In this respect, Chan epitomised the resilient and resourceful practices of Hong Kong filmmakers in the post-handover years, preserving local storytelling norms while adroitly navigating the joint pressures of Hollywoodisation and Mainlandisation.

THE ROAD TO *CONNECTED*

Benny Chan began his career as a television script supervisor and writer in the 1980s, hopscotching among rival stations Rediffusion, TVB and ATV. At TVB he worked as a production assistant to Johnnie To, before directing episodes of action dramas and martial arts series. He launched his film career in 1990, directing the To-produced *A Moment of Romance*. Chan's early films set the template for the rest of his career. He recognised the commercial logic of a presold property, turning out sequels (*A Moment of Romance II*) and adapting literary texts (*The Magic Crane* [*Xin xian he shen zhen*, 1993]). A passionate cinephile, he sprinkled his formative efforts with allusions to the Hollywood films he admired, including *Lethal Weapon* (1987) and *Die Hard* (1988). Though he experimented at first in different genres, he quickly gained a reputation as a skilful director of action sequences. *Big Bullet*, a gritty *policier* released in 1996, marked a personal breakthrough, earning him a Best Director nomination at the Hong Kong Film Awards. Thereafter, he would specialise almost exclusively in action genre filmmaking.

Just as Chan found his métier, the local industry fell into decline. A production boom at the start of the decade had begun to fizzle by the mid-1990s, as hyperproduction led to a slump in quality. Rampant video piracy undercut box-office profits. Triad infiltration of the film business frightened away legitimate investors, spooked local talent and tainted the industry's reputation (Curtin 2007, 74–5). By mid-decade, too, Hollywood imports had supplanted local films in popularity, attaining a stranglehold on the domestic box office, and steering audience tastes toward American-style entertainment. Competition sprang up from rival Asian cinemas as well – chiefly Hollywood-inflected blockbusters from South Korea, Thailand and Japan – while the popularity of Hong Kong films in regional markets plummeted. A virtual exodus to Hollywood, led by many of Hong Kong's major players (John Woo, Tsui Hark, Ringo Lam, Jackie Chan, Jet Li, Michelle Yeoh and others), depleted the industry's talent pool. In 1997 a crippling Asian economic crisis resulted in aborted productions, a drying-up of finance and a further drop in production output. Add to this tumult a swirl of instability attending the 1997 reunification, and the local industry's downturn was both precipitous and profound.

The major firms sought strategies of survival and recovery. If local audiences favoured Hollywood blockbusters, Hong Kong film producers – ever predisposed to imitation – would cultivate an indigenous variant, seeking to challenge Hollywood through direct competition. Adopting a 'blockbuster mentality', studios such as Golden Harvest strove to elevate production standards to the Hollywood benchmark. Now the local industry laboured to vanquish the technical crudity beloved by cult admirers of Hong Kong cinema. Mismatched postsynching of dialogue – for many decades a chronic technical flaw – had by the late 1990s been largely eliminated, thanks to an industry-wide uptake of direct sound recording.[4] Above all, the domestic shift toward a high-concept, Hollywoodised mode of production demanded substantial investment in visual-effects technology. 'The post-1995 crisis of the local industry coincided with the arrival of digital filmmaking', writes David Bordwell, who goes on to note that it was clear that 'any industry wanting to compete with Hollywood would need to upgrade' (2011, 236). In 1998 the Hong Kong government set aside $100 million 'to upgrade [the] special effects of local films' (Chung 1998, 5). A year later *The Hollywood Reporter* commented on Hong Kong cinema's recuperation strategy, namely 'the use of technology to pull the ailing Hong Kong film industry out of its malaise' (Chung 1999).

Not only did Benny Chan vigorously advocate these advances in technology, he also played a major role in implementing them, embracing the blockbuster mode of production, and eagerly modernising work practices, aesthetics and special effects. Here, then, is one facet of his importance: he stood at the vanguard of industry change at the turn of the century. Several interlocking impulses, I suggest, fuelled his support of Hollywoodisation (all but the first of which would later inform his *Cellular* remake). First, he held an earnest belief that high-concept 'event' movies, shot through with digitalised spectacle, could revitalise the waning industry. Chan believed that foregrounding 'technology and special effects [was] the only way forward for Hong Kong's then faltering movie industry' (Tsui 2004, 5). Second, he developed an unquenchable quest for novelty. This artistic urge buttressed Chan's entire career, and he spoke often of an ambition to plough a new furrow. With *Gen-Y Cops*, for instance, he was 'determined to create a new style of action film' and to create 'a new trend' (Lam 2001: 33). Here again CGI held the key to innovation: 'The computer effects [in *Gen-X Cops*] helped a lot and made it possible to bring in new perspectives for the action film', he stated (Chang and Lam 2000, 28).

Finally, Chan demonstrated a competitive streak – as much cultural as artistic, rooted in national pride – impelling his adoption of Hollywood techniques and technologies. Throughout his career, he measured both personal achievement and industry vitality by comparison to Hollywood. 'Special effects are a part of cinema', he remarked in 1999. 'If we don't experiment, we'll fall behind . . . In the field of computer effects, we're behind Hollywood by at least five years' (Chang and Lam 2000, 28).

Chan's desire to probe the possibilities of digital effects, and to preside over big-budget productions, could flourish in an atmosphere of industrial recovery and renewal. The 1998 Jackie Chan vehicle *Who Am I?* marked the director's first foray into mega-production territory, but his global ambitions found their most hospitable home at Media Asia, at that time a burgeoning local production and distribution outfit. Under the auspices of CEO Thomas Chung, the firm had pledged itself to Hollywoodising the Hong Kong film industry. Chung instructed the directors he hired 'to make [films] look more like the Hollywood movies that our audiences have embraced' (Curtin 2007, 260).[5] He boosted production values, invested heavily in digital special effects, and (several years before the Closer Economic Partnership Arrangement's [CEPA] script mandates) insisted on the value of a preproduction screenplay (Davis and Yeh 2008, 106). By the end of the 1990s, Media Asia had established an ethos of Hollywoodised entertainment, specialising in youth-oriented action blockbusters such as *Purple Storm* (*Zi yu feng bao*, 1999) and *2000 AD* (*Gong yuan 2000 AD*, 2000). The firm's brand identity would be distinguished by glossy production values, literate scripts, digitally composed spectacle and expensive publicity campaigns.

Into this milieu stepped Benny Chan, whose *Gen-X Cops* exemplified the new corporate strategy. Budgeted at HK$25 million, the film flaunted a high-gloss visual style and dazzling set piece attractions. Its bloated budget matched its swollen shooting schedule: filming consumed almost five months, a far cry from the 'quickies' of the early 1990s, and further demonstrating Media Asia's quest for quality. An aggressive and canny marketing campaign played up Chan's use of Hollywood-style computer graphics, positioning *Gen-X Cops* as a uniquely theatrical experience, not replicable on low-grade VCD. So much expenditure on digital effects and advertising replaced the hefty costs of star salaries; instead of major stars, *Gen-X Cops* showcased newcomers with no major name recognition. (Here we alight on another of Chan's notable contributions: he can be credited with ushering in a fresh generation of promising stars, from Nicholas Tse to Edison Chen, in pursuit of both novelty and industrial rejuvenation.) In addition, Media Asia's judicious strategy of the holiday-season release maximised *Gen-X Cops*' domestic box-office performance.[6] A theatrical hit in the summer of 1999, *Gen-X Cops* seemed to vindicate the 'survival strategy' championed by Chan and others – that is, a production mode driven by Hollywood-style digital effects.

Yet, by the Lunar New Year holiday of 2000, the studios' confidence in the Hong Kong 'mega-picture' had capsized. Why the volte-face? *Gen-X Cops* and Andrew Lau's *The Storm Riders* (*Fung wan: Hung ba tin ha*, 1998) had performed brightly, but a string of box-office misfires – including Golden Harvest's *A Man Called Hero* (*Jung wa ying hong*, 1999) and *Tokyo Raiders* (*Dong jing gong lue*, 2000), and Media Asia's *Purple Storm* and *2000 AD* – dampened the studios' ardour for Hong Kong's digital turn (Li 2000, 14; Curtin 2007, 69). Following the release of the 2000 sequel *Gen-Y Cops*, Benny Chan's amped-up CGI spectacle drew heavy criticism: the film's digital effects were derided by critics as being primitive and phony. Stung by failure, Chan re-evaluated the logic of challenging Hollywood directly. 'After *Gen-X Cops*, I thought special [digital] effects would help [the industry] enormously,' he reflected in 2004. 'We realised, however, that with our limited resources we were doomed to failure if we were to compare our work with productions elsewhere' (Tsui 2004). In the 2002 action thriller *Heroic Duo* (*Shuang xiong*) he resolved to employ 'more down-to-earth effects' (Wong 2003, 3).

Further, critics discerned in the new blockbusters a diminution of local flavour. Computer-generated spectacle, they forecast, would forever displace a rich and revered tradition of action cinema anchored in profilmic reality. Far from a survival tactic, Hollywoodisation would hasten Hong Kong cinema's extinction. The solution, Benny Chan now concluded, lay not in jettisoning CGI completely, and still less in abandoning the high-concept production model. Rather, Chan held that the local cinema could remain globally competitive, not to say culturally distinctive, by subordinating digital technology to practical effects, thus employing CGI to support (rather than supplant) traditional Hong Kong techniques. This attenuated approach to Hollywoodisation would govern Chan's remake of *Cellular*, and it held sway throughout the rest of his career.

Chan's newfound perspective was also emblematic of the way in which Hong Kong cinema as a whole altered its outlook in the fledgling 2000s. As one trade paper reported:

> There is now a definite trend in Hong Kong towards old-school martial arts and a limited use of wire-fu, which has become commonplace since *The Matrix*. The thinking goes that, as Hong Kong cannot compete with Hollywood budgets or effects, it makes sense to adopt a 'back-to-basics' approach (Shackleton 2004, 18).

Set against the global ubiquity of CGI, Hong Kong cinema's relative reduction of virtual imagery and its restored belief in the visceral tangibility of corporeal action could be grasped, variously, as a distinctive production value, a source of product differentiation and an ideological assertion of cultural autonomy.

By the time *Connected* was conceived, Hong Kong cinema's globalising strategies had wended through a process of experimentation, revision and entrenchment. The root-and-branch Hollywoodisation of Hong Kong aesthetics had given way to a delicate synthesis, as filmmakers calibrated the balance between local stylistic traditions and American techniques and technologies. This cultural synthesis obtained not only at the aesthetic level; it also pushed into the fibre of work routines. Here, as so often, Benny Chan typified his industrial milieu. Even before CEPA, he emulated Hollywood custom by carpentering a full-fledged screenplay in advance of shooting.[7] As per local practice, however, he employed the script less as an ironclad blueprint than as a tentative roadmap, apt to be reworked on the set.[8] Similarly, he adopted Hollywood's storyboarding methodology, painstakingly plotting out scenes of physical action in schematic fashion. Yet, here too, he counterposed the systematic rigour of Hollywood film practice with Hong Kong-style spontaneity and extemporisation. (Swerving from the storyboard devised for *Invisible Target* [*Nam yee boon sik*, 2007], he remarked, 'I think the most important thing was to improvise'.[9]) Chan's hybrid working methods reflected those of his peers. Hong Kong filmmakers are nothing if not adaptable, modifying their practices as production exigencies dictate, while, whenever possible, adverting to homegrown methods as a default heuristic. In short, Hong Kong cinema now bore the traces of Hollywoodisation and Mainlandisation (the latter visibly manifested in pan-Asian casting, mainland settings and grand narratives lionising Communist heroes), but the region's filmmakers endeavoured to preserve and prioritise local craft practices and aesthetic traditions. They also cleaved to personal themes, forms and styles.

CALLING THE SHOTS

Accordingly, Benny Chan adapted *Cellular* to a cluster of personal traits. These traits had already coalesced and crystallised in the preceding decade. Stylistically, Chan's beloved action genre inspired him to flaunt an arsenal of filmic devices. He declared: 'Action films are what I love – with them I can flex my directorial muscles' (Tsui 2007, 6). Consequently, he inclines toward extroverted devices: variable speeds, freeze frames, transitional wipes, zooms, split-screen effects, extreme shot scales and frantic camera movement. In his early work, Chan at times presented dialogue scenes as static sequence shots (for instance, one shot in *What a Hero!* runs nearly two minutes), the lengthy take supplying an oasis of stillness offset by a pervading kineticism; but Chan eventually shed the long-take device in favour of brisk analytical cutting, the better to maintain a lively momentum. His action scenes exploit rapid editing, but like those of his compatriots they display smooth spatial continuity, making their frame compositions instantly legible. More flagrant is Chan's selective use of discontinuity devices such as overlapping editing and serial repetition, a technique whereby 'an action is presented in its entirety two or more times in succession, either by means of looping a single take, or editing a number of different takes into a series' (Collier 1999, 73). As Joelle Collier points out, these flamboyant tactics had been widely adopted by local filmmakers since at least the 1960s, but Chan pushes them to extremes: at the climax of *What a Hero!* the antagonist drops to the ground six successive times, the single action shown from multiple vantage points. Such outré gestures push redundancy into the realm of excess, but it would be wrong to grasp these tactics as self-indulgently virtuosic. Rather, Chan adopts and redeploys – indeed, *remakes* – pre-existing stylistic techniques in order to galvanise the spectator, intensifying the sensory and emotional impact of his ecstatic scenes of spectacle.

Such scenes are further dynamised by outsized, concussive, habitual explosions. (To Western critics, this 'big bang' fetish is why designations of Chan as 'Hong Kong's Michael Bay' seem fitting; at home, he is known as 'Explosion Chan'.[10]) Much carnage and devastation is often staged against Hong Kong's most famous architectural icons: witness the demolition of the Convention Centre in *Gen-X Cops*, the chases down the Mid-Levels Escalator (*Invisible Target*) and the Causeway Bay flyover (*Divergence* [*Sam cha hau*, 2005]), the vertiginous dives off the Tsing Ma Bridge (*Heroic Duo*) and Sheung Wan's Harbour Building (*New Police Story*). If Chan's bombastic explosions betray signs of Hollywoodisation, they are nevertheless rooted in regional specificity. Indeed, this site-specific action serves as a localisation tactic, a touristic address to overseas markets and an expression of national (or regional) pride. Chan is explicit in his aims: 'I want the place to be instantly recognised as Hong Kong when the film is released overseas. I don't want to have a landmark which could be anywhere. I want my films to contain something of our culture. I want to introduce Hong Kong to an international audience.'[11]

Chan enlivens his action set pieces still further by means of exhilarating auto chases and vehicular stunts. Here he recruits fast cutting, interpolated close-ups of actors at the wheel, travelling views (from the dashboard, the fender, the hood) and tyre-screeching sound effects to conjure visceral, high-velocity pursuits. Judicious use of slow motion prolongs and italicises decisive phases in the chase, while serial repetition showcases a spectacular climax from an array of angles.

Narratively, Chan pursues a level of psychological change rare in Hong Kong cinema. He treats the character arc as a structural principle: the plot will reach its climax only once the protagonist's flaw is ameliorated or extinguished. More specifically, Chan's protagonists embark on the hero's journey, ruggedly surmounting obstacles, tests and trials en route to moral heroism. Often, the arc they trace is precipitously steep: the flawed and fallible protagonist, far from a paragon, might be a heartless crook (*Rob-B-Hood* [*Bao bei ji hua*, 2006]) or a merciless tyrant (*Shaolin*) before the 'call' to heroic action sets him on a righteous path (Campbell 2008). He is often a reluctant, unwilling or unlikely saviour, liable initially to refuse the call to adventure (as does Jackie Chan in *New Police Story* and Eddie Peng in *Call of Heroes*). Ultimately, he will chart a course toward Confucian virtue and heroic embodiment. The initial hesitancy of the hero allows Benny Chan to stretch his stars' heroic personas, seeking out new facets of familiar images. Lastly, the protagonist's trajectory involves profound personal sacrifice, throwing into jeopardy paternal relationships (fathers estranged from sons) and fraternal ones (blood brothers riven by betrayal). Chan is apt to depict these relationships in highly melodramatic fashion, mining scenes of reconciliation and separation for sentimental pathos.

Chan's authorial traits, his proven box office success, his proficiency in Hollywoodised storytelling and spectacle, his command of high-concept logistics, his penchant for filmic recycling – all these factors ideally positioned him to direct a HK$45 million Chinese-language Hollywood remake in the early 2000s. More specifically, his signature traits proved germane to *Cellular*'s chief attractions: explosions, gunfights, vehicular spectacle and pronounced character development. He was no less equipped to handle the remake's built-in marketing priorities, most saliently the 'product placement' of the branded cellphones integral to *Connected*'s plot. By now, Chan had mastered what we might call diegetically motivated product placement. When, in *A Moment of Romance*, the male hero must parry a party of hoodlums, he weaponises a pack of Carlsberg beer cans into a lethal bundle, smiting the crooks and facilitating a getaway. As we will see, Chan's facility for stitching branded products into the fabric of story action – and, moreover, binding them to authorial motifs – finds unique expression in *Connected*.

RINGING THE CHANGES

Few critics fail to describe *Connected* as the first authorised Hong Kong remake of a Hollywood film. Not surprisingly, given this cinema's notoriety for swiping, recycling and scavenging from Hollywood and other sources, the mounting of a legally sanctioned remake caught attention as a definite shift in industry policy.[12] The legal purchasing of Hollywood remake rights by Hong Kong and Chinese partners epitomised the Cantonese cinema's early-century push toward modernisation, and reflected the mainland's efforts to merge into the larger transnational film community. Media coverage and publicity, loudly proclaiming *Connected*'s official ties to Hollywood, ensured that the film did not constitute a 'disguised remake' – Michael B. Druxman's term for remaking-by-stealth, the retitled, updated film refusing to acknowledge its original source (1975, 13). This category better describes Hong Kong's furtively parasitic remakes of the 1980s and 1990s. By contrast, the promotional campaign for *Connected* strategically foregrounded *Cellular* as its source material. The singular status of 'official' remake, along with the financial backing of a Hollywood production arm (Warner Bros China), conferred legitimacy upon *Connected* as a US-approved transnational blockbuster. No mere rip-off, *Connected* flaunted the imprimatur and 'the added value of "Hollywood" as the biggest brand name for cinema' (Xu 2008, 197).

Not that *Connected* was to be a de facto Hollywood movie. Director and co-writer Benny Chan would need to localise the drama. Still, by the early 2000s he had thoroughly absorbed the norms of Hollywood script construction, including plausibly motivated action and cogent character development. In remaking *Cellular*, he found himself in the curious position of trying to Hollywoodise a Hollywood film. For David R. Ellis's thriller displays certain aesthetic features more typical of 1980s Hong Kong cinema than of Hollywood storytelling in the early 2000s: a tone that swings from fraught melodrama to ribald comedy; hair-raising stunts performed by the star actor; practical special effects; a saturated colour palette; 'mickey-mousing'; and a taut efficiency reminiscent of Hong Kong's lean 1980s genre films. The action, moreover, is 'expressively amplified' in the Hong Kong manner.[13] During a home invasion, the heroine Jessica (Kim Basinger) pivots from a dorsal position into frontal close-up, a gesture conveyed in pregnant slow motion and underscored by an exaggerated sonic whoosh – a cartoonish flourish commonplace in Hong Kong action cinema.[14] Then there is William H. Macy's gun-toting cop, Sergeant Mooney, who executes the sort of acrobatic, effortlessly graceful and decelerated mid-air leaps associated with Chow Yun-fat. These highly evocative gestures attest to the increasing cross-pollination between Hollywood and Hong Kong action cinema since the 1990s; they may also have indirectly positioned *Cellular* as ripe for Hong Kong remaking. If Ellis drew on Hong Kong stylistics, Benny Chan reworked *Cellular* in ways that restored the principles of Hollywood dramaturgy. He actively determined to amend 'plot holes' in the original screenplay, to make narrative causality more robust, and character motivation more 'convincing' and 'believable'.[15] As such, Chan mounted *Connected* as a Hollywoodised Chinese production conforming to international storytelling standards.

His remake adopts a distinctive twofold approach: it moulds the original material to authorial concerns; and it mobilises a strategy of intensification. An example of the former tactic can be found in Chan's decision to switch many of *Cellular*'s interior settings to outdoor locales, allowing his fondness for actual location shooting full play. The latter tactic – intensification – can be grasped in the context of Chan's aforementioned competitiveness. Thomas M. Leitch suggests that competition underpins any filmic remake – such a text more or less explicitly aims to surpass its progenitor – while Frank Kermode specifies the stakes of this competition as fundamentally economic in nature (Leitch 1990, 141–2). In Benny Chan's case, what is at stake is not only economic but also artistic (a desire to demonstrate creative ingenuity) and ideological (a culturally driven effort to prove that Hong Kong action cinema could outshine its American counterpart).[16] In *Connected*, Chan seeks to eclipse *Cellular* by raising story and style to a higher pitch of intensity. He ramps up violence, stating 'I felt that a Hong Kong action film needed to have a harder impact.'[17] This strategy of intensification suffuses the remake (as I will elaborate in greater detail below): the male protagonist is more flawed than in the original film, the time pressure more urgent, the emotional appeals more sentimental. *Cellular*'s climactic shootout unfolds in a subterranean boathouse, but Chan stages the scene far above ground, literally raising the stakes by jacking up the protagonist's peril – not only does our hero risk being shot and wounded (as in *Cellular*); he also might suffer a sickening fall to the death. In the rest of this chapter, we will see how Chan's two-pronged remaking strategy directly shapes two of his foremost authorial concerns: the hero's journey and the staging of physical spectacle.

CALL OF HEROES

Cellular introduces its teenage male protagonist, Ryan (Chris Evans), by highlighting his imperfections. 'You are irresponsible, self-centred, completely childish', bemoans Chloe (Jessica Biel), the girlfriend who has jilted him. 'I've changed', Ryan insists. But only the events of the narrative – which require him to rescue an abducted biology teacher (Kim Basinger) and her family from a cadre of depraved police officers, with only an erratic cellphone connection providing a lifeline between the heroine and hero – will engender authentic psychological change and eradicate Ryan's personal faults. Bob (Louis Koo), the male protagonist of *Connected*, is a flawed individual too, but Benny Chan deepens his defects. Several years Ryan's senior, Bob is down on his luck: his wife has left him, and his sister accuses him of lacking responsibility. Ryan is just a selfish idler, but Bob may be morally negligent: he habitually shirks time with his young son, Kit Kit (Tam Chun-ho), and he works a morally emasculating job as a debt collector.[18] Both Bob and Ryan, then, begin as improbable heroes. But whereas the jejune Ryan will trace an arc of maturation, Bob's transformation is one of moral rebirth and redemption, tacitly endowed with mythic significance. By elaborating the protagonist's shortcomings, Benny Chan gives Bob an arc of change more substantive and precipitous than that dramatised in *Cellular*.

At the levels of characterisation and casting, Chan bends *Connected* to one of his favourite manoeuvres: subverting star personas. Though portrayed by Hong Kong heartthrob Louis Koo, Bob is not presented as an embodiment of masculine spectacle. Contrast Chris Evans's Ryan, first shown striding down the Santa Monica pier alongside a bevy of bathers. Bare-chested, free-spirited, hedonistic and flirtatious, Ryan radiates sexual bravado and physical desirability. Director Ellis fully capitalises on his teen idol's athletic allure, while hinting at the superficiality of Ryan's carefree lifestyle. In contrast, Louis Koo's doleful, browbeaten Bob is hardly a sex object, nor does he display traditionally heroic attributes. Mostly he is diffident and flustered, fearful and dissembling. Omnipresent eyeglasses and a nervous stammer symbolise his lack of virility and heroic stature.[19] Note, too, that Benny Chan elects not to preserve the forename of *Cellular*'s protagonist, opting for an alternative that denotes ordinariness. In all, the two films utilise star personas in diametric ways. *Cellular* foregrounds Chris Evans's masculine star image from the outset, the better to both imply and prefigure Ryan's essential facility in the role of hero. No less strategically, *Connected* suppresses Louis Koo's masculine traits, deglamourising the matinee idol's persona in order to make Bob's eventual heroic potency all the more surprising and admirable.

Like its Hollywood ur-text, *Connected* literalises the 'call to adventure' of Joseph Campbell's hero monomyth: it is a desperate phone call from kidnapped heroine Grace (Barbie Hsu) that initiates Bob's mythological journey. In Campbell's morphology, Grace personifies 'the herald', the announcer of the adventure (2008, 44). The hero monomyth provides the broad structural underpinnings of *Cellular*'s plot, to which Benny Chan closely hews. But Chan amplifies both the personal stakes and the time pressure heaped upon the hero, thus ratcheting up the tension. Both Ryan and Bob initially 'refuse the call' to adventure – hence they are reluctant as well as unlikely heroes – but thereafter they must accept a string of tasks each of which constitutes a 'trial' in the heroic quest. Even by reluctant-hero standards, however, these protagonists prove startlingly ineffectual when pursuing localised goals. Their 'many failures attest to the difficulties' of heroic achievement (Ibid., 189).

In *Connected*, Grace's distraught phone call urgently enjoins Bob's aid. But Bob declines to help, partly out of scepticism (he suspects a prank) and partly in order to fulfil a prior task, established moments earlier. Here, *Connected* swerves from its source. Whereas the freewheeling Ryan is unburdened by family ties, Bob must travel to the airport to meet his son and sister, whose plane to Australia departs that afternoon. This time-bound goal harbours an emotional urgency of its own. For Bob's precarious relationship with his son, Kit Kit, hinges on an implicit ultimatum: if Bob breaks his pledge to attend the airport rendezvous, his rift from Kit Kit will be irreparable. 'A promise is a promise', the boy exhorts. By means of this wholly new subplot, Benny Chan intensifies the hero's dilemma. Can Bob rescue the damsel and, at the same time, salvage his relationship with his son? How is he to reconcile this clash of moral duties? Bob will soon become convinced of Grace's plight, but his efforts to help are periodically interrupted by cellphone entreaties from Kit Kit, en route to the airport. These frequent intrusions function not merely as redundancy, recapitulating deadlines and dramatic stakes; they also subject the protagonist to further stress and shift suspense into higher gear. Not least, they sustain an authorial fascination with father-son dynamics (absent from *Cellular*), to be paid off at the climax.

Throughout the film, Bob acquires new goals, each one bounded by a looming deadline. Dialogue frames these objectives in temporal terms ('Hurry – one more minute'; 'I'm giving you five more minutes'), the tyranny of the clock constantly palpable. Here again Benny Chan strives to intensify an aspect of the Hollywood version. He escalates the plot's relentless atmosphere of urgency and imminent jeopardy chiefly by shortening the deadlines for the hero's life-or-death tasks. (A ten-minute countdown in *Cellular* drops to five minutes in *Connected*.) The short-term goals themselves routinely end in failure, but with every renewed effort Bob moves closer to heroic competence. He also learns to stop making casual assurances – 'I can only try [to catch the kidnappers] – no promises', he tells Grace – thereby expelling a chronic flaw. For Benny Chan, Bob's faults are intrinsic to his gradual metamorphosis, and his failures are decisive phases in heroic consummation. 'Real heroes are not necessarily magnificent guys who save people and do great deeds', Chan asserts. 'It's only those who can brush themselves off and learn how to live after failure who deserve to be called heroes' (Tsui 2004: 5). Though Bob bungles many tasks, he pursues each new mission with a single-minded tenacity, heroically persevering in spite of short-term defeats.

At the film's midpoint, Grace assigns Bob a new goal, again driven by a deadline. The kidnappers have seized Grace's brother, Roy (Carlos Chan), whose portable video camera contains incriminating evidence against them. Now Bob must intercept the kidnappers and retrieve the object. At first, he blunders the task, but he is not to be defeated. He rallies, snatches the camera – which, in Campbell's morphology, instantiates 'the boon', an elixir that will restore order to the world – and escapes. With this triumph, Bob's heroic traits crystallise. Previously, he has been a figure 'acted upon' from without, his goals and actions steered by Grace's compelling petitions ('Please save my daughter'; 'Rescue my brother'; 'Retrieve the camera'). But now, with the boon firmly in his possession, Bob defiantly asserts agency, advising the kidnappers 'I'm calling the shots.' Henceforth, he will grow more causally influential upon the narrative events, befitting his burgeoning stature.

Shrewdly, he lures the kidnappers to the airport, thus advancing toward one of his primary goals (and enabling the plot's action lines to converge).

Director Chan treats the ensuing climax as an occasion to introduce another of his authorial traits: the staging of combat against a major regional landmark – in this case, the capacious Hong Kong International Airport, substituting for *Cellular*'s Santa Monica pier and boathouse. At the airport, Bob orchestrates the safe release of Grace and her kin, but still *Connected* keeps his proficiency in doubt. In the airport's cavernous warehouse, the chief antagonist, Fok (Liu Ye), traps Bob on a precariously exposed raised platform far above the ground. The ensuing physical struggle – repeatedly shown in dizzying aerial shots – culminates in both characters plummeting from the platform edge into the void below. In freefall, Bob's ankle becomes ensnared in a knotted bundle of dangling rope, which crucially breaks his fall. The sequence ultimately brings about Fok's demise, but not before the villain has roundly mocked Bob's credibility as a saviour ('What's next Mr Hero? . . . Want to be a hero, huh?'). In the climactic skirmish, Fok promises to deliver Bob 'the heroic death you're looking for', but Bob's dogged courage (aided by a dose of serendipity) finally prevails, and Fok plunges to his death from a stomach-turning height.

The resolution of the crime plot prepares the way for a sentimental coda, the purpose of which is to effectuate two emotive encounters. First, Bob and Grace finally meet in person. 'Bob, thank you for saving me and my family', says the heroine. 'I made a promise', Bob replies, reaffirming his victory over a habitual flaw. By banishing this defect, Bob proves himself worthy of the subsequent encounter: a melodramatic reunion with Kit Kit. This ending obliges us to reflect upon Benny Chan's major structural addition to *Cellular*'s narrative: the father-son plotline.[20] In *Cellular* it is the romance object (Ryan's ex-girlfriend, Chloe) that articulates and reiterates the hero's shortcomings.

Figure 10.1 Bob (Louis Koo), the protagonist of Benny Chan's *Connected* (*Bochi tungwah*, 2008), dangles from a platform seconds before falling in this Cantonese remake of the US action film *Cellular* (2004).

As per Hollywood convention, the hero transforms in ways that make the achievement of heterosexual romance possible. In *Connected*, by contrast, it is primarily the hero's son who precipitates psychological change. The child specifies the protagonist's flaws, serves as his moral conscience, and spurs him toward personal improvement and heroic fulfilment. Whereas *Cellular*'s closure foregrounds the relationship between male hero and female kidnap victim,[21] *Connected*'s ending prioritises the uniting of Bob and Kit Kit – for Chan, the film's most meaningful (and characteristically phallocentric) relationship. By reconfiguring *Cellular*'s central relationship, the Hong Kong director emphatically foregrounds one of his chief authorial concerns.

DIALLING IT UP

Midway through *Cellular*, Ryan's tenuous phone connection with the kidnapped Jessica abruptly falters. Ryan, driving a commandeered security car through teeming Los Angeles traffic, realises that a nearby driver, stalled at a traffic light, is the source of the crossline interference. He abandons the security car at a freeway junction and sprints toward the driver. As the pair remonstrates, a large cement truck suddenly hurtles into the idling car, which instantaneously explodes. Director Ellis presents this action across a flurry of rapidly edited shots, unfolding at normal speed. A long shot situates Ryan and the obdurate driver in the distant foreground, the security car visible farther in depth. The cement truck unexpectedly enters the shot from frame right, smashing into the car, which erupts into flames. This shot cuts to a closer ground-level view of the vehicles rushing toward the camera, the frame filling with advancing fire. A tight push-in registers Ryan's dumbstruck reaction. The narration cuts back to the initial wide shot, slightly reframing the spectacle as the blazing vehicles slow to a halt. The effect on the viewer is one of surprise and sensory stimulation. Ellis's restricted narration has not primed us for the arrival of the cement truck; and the sudden burst of movement into the frame, the inferno that ensues and the concussive blast pounding the soundtrack combine to trigger the startle effect. Ryan's shocked reaction mirrors our own.

For the director known as 'Explosion Chan,' this scene might present irresistible fodder for replication. Yet *Connected* omits this conflagration. Indeed, *Connected* is one of the very few Benny Chan films to exclude explosions altogether. Why? The answer, I suggest, lies in Chan's overarching strategies: competitive remaking, a quest for novelty, and aesthetic intensification. In interviews, he spoke frankly about his competitive effort to 'outdo' the American source. Evoking intensification, he claimed to have designed *Connected*'s action scenes to be 'more spectacular' than those of *Cellular*.[22] Consider the film's most spectacular set piece. Bob witnesses the kidnappers snatch Grace's daughter and spirit her

Figure 10.2 Bob's vehicle makes another type of 'connection' with a US cultural production – specifically, a truck full of Pepsi Max sodas – in this scene from *Connected* (*Bochi tungwah*, 2008).

away by car. Pursuing his quarry with a single-minded ferocity, he inadvertently crashes his car through the canvass-covered scaffolding of a building. As the vast bamboo framework collapses, a large sheet of canvass blankets Bob's speeding vehicle. His vision now obfuscated, Bob charges blindly ahead. An insert shot of his foot frantically pumping a pedal confirms a further setback: brake failure. Unable to stop or see, Bob is powerless to avert a head-on collision with a fish-tailing car. The ensuing crash forces his vehicle to rocket upward and soar through the air, plunging through myriad crates of soda heaped onto the belly of a large Pepsi truck. Crashing to the ground from the other side, Bob's car continues its forward surge. But the thick canvass sheet that envelops the vehicle is yanked taut against the truck, forcing Bob's car to violently flip backward before landing on its roof with a wallop.

The competitive and artistic desire for novelty, I suggest, spurs Chan to forfeit a generic explosion in favour of a more singular effect. *Connected*'s truck collision conjures an 'explosion' of a novel sort, discharging a fusillade of soft drink cans into the air with all the propulsive force of an actual blast. The dispersed Pepsi Max cans form a tsunami of projectiles, flung outward with fierce energy. Chan handles this combustive set piece in a way different from Ellis. The cutting is fairly brisk, but slow motion dilates the action: we are encouraged to savour the unfolding spectacle. A close view of Bob's car ploughing into the crates, an aerial long shot of its inexorable trajectory, a street-level view of the vehicle hitting the ground, and a string of wide shots capturing the car's backward flip – all of these images are afforded slow-motion treatment. Further intensifying the profilmic event is overlapping editing (here flirting with serial repetition), a favourite resource of Chan and his local contemporaries. Chan recapitulates key phases of the spectacle seriatim (the car's plunge into the truck; its vigorous somersault). Sound, too, amplifies the action. When Bob's car smashes into the truck, an ear-splitting 'boom' floods the soundscape. In sum, Chan imaginatively recasts an authorial motif (explosive spectacle) while preserving local techniques (overlapping editing), competitively innovating on *Cellular*'s rendering of physical action.

Ellis's explosive sequence elicits surprise, but Chan prioritises other effects and purposes. He tips us to the imminent crash by means of omniscient cutaways that show the Pepsi truck lurking up ahead, ominously drifting into Bob's path. If Chan thus dissipates surprise, he fosters suspense: Will Bob's runaway car avoid the monstrous truck? In addition, the sequence elicits what Ed Tan calls 'artefact emotions' (1996: 65) – that is, admiration for the technical feat and creative conceit of the auto stunt itself. This response hinges on the viewer's faith in the veracity of the action. In *Connected*, this faith is largely justified (the sequence at hand employs CGI enhancement minimally and photo-realistically). Further, the viewer's artefact emotions are explicitly facilitated and solicited by Chan's aesthetic devices: the decelerated motion and overlapping cuts force us to linger on the outrageous stunt work.[23] Chan's auto crash, then, engenders not only emotional and sensory arousal, but aesthetic contemplation too. Another purpose – less respectable, perhaps, but obligatory for commercial filmmakers – concerns product advertising, and here Chan puts the Pepsi brand on flagrant display.[24] Yet he embeds the product fully into the world of the fiction, confident that it will not obtrude against the decidedly more salient auto stunt – in other words, he melds artistic goals (imaginative remaking) and commercial imperatives (product endorsement) in relatively seamless fashion. By means of diegetically motivated product placement, Chan subordinates 'crude' commercialism to the uppermost priorities of story and spectacle.

In the final analysis, this deliriously outlandish action scene typifies *Connected* in toto. Adopting CGI yet pledged to the primacy of practical effects, furnishing global genre appeals yet foregrounding directorial traits, redolent of Hollywood yet steeped in local norms of style and story – this scene (and the film as a whole) reminds us that Hollywoodisation need not be synonymous with cultural erasure. Indeed, Chan's films, like those of many of his Hong Kong peers, embody a staunch effort to safeguard cultural heritage against globalising pressures. 'I don't want to see local action films vanish without a trace', Chan stated in 2007 (Tsui 2007: 6). But he was not content with mere survival. As his action sequences amply demonstrate, he strove not only to sustain but to evolve Hong Kong's purportedly endangered action cinema. Though he took seriously the norms and appeals of popular genre, he was not in thrall to received forms and formulas, and he prized originality. Not surprisingly, then, *Connected* epitomises cross-cultural 'remaking' in the purest sense of the term. It repudiates apish imitation in favour of competitive remaking, personal expression and cultural preservation.

NOTES

1. Chan describes himself as such in an interview published in *The Hollywood Reporter* (Anon. 2011).
2. Think also of *Gen-X Cops* (*Te jing xin ren lei*, 1999), which one producer describes as 'a remake of *The Dirty Dozen* with teenage pop idols and lots of explosions' (quoted in Curtin 2007: 260). This film also bears the influence of *Independence Day* (1996). Elsewhere, Chan's action caper *Rob-B-Hood* (*Bao bei ji hua*, 2006) riffs on *Three Men and a Baby* (1987), while *Big Bullet* cannibalises aspects of *Lethal Weapon* (1987).
3. Critic Clarence Tsui, for instance, noted 'how much *New Police Story* is seen as a Jackie Chan production' (2004).
4. For a historical account of the industry's sound practices, see Bettinson (2011).
5. Even Ann Hui, that most stalwart of indigenous filmmakers, was enjoined by Chung to make *Visible Secret* (*You ling ren jian*, 2001), 'a film that looked like it was made in the West, and [he] gave us HK$1 million just to spend on special effects' (Tsui et al. 2002: 105).
6. Still, foreign markets were essential (and planned for by Thomas Chung): despite its strong domestic takings (HK$15.6 million), the film would have posted a loss without overseas revenue. Media Asia distributed *Gen-X Cops* theatrically throughout East Asia. Market expansion, meanwhile, would be sought via home video distribution in Western territories.
7. Having begun as a writer of television series, Chan took an active involvement in script construction throughout his movie career, often co-authoring his films' screenplays.
8. As *Variety* reported on the production of *Heroic Duo*: 'Chan [came] up with a rough script, although in true Hong Kong style, the final scenes were written on the set' (Ghahremani 2003).
9. *Invisible Target* DVD (Dragon Dynasty edition, 2008).
10. See Sun (2001) and Bordwell (2011, 239).
11. Benny Chan interview, *New Police Story* DVD (Contender Entertainment Group, 2006).
12. For information on *Connected* and its copyright history, see He 2010.
13. For a discussion of expressive amplification, see Bordwell (2011, 146–54).
14. Look no further than Benny Chan's *Invisible Target* and *Rob-B-Hood* for displays of this device.
15. Benny Chan director's commentary, *Connected* DVD (Joy Sales [HK] edition, 2008). Several critics press the view that *Connected* more successfully motivates its protagonist's actions and psychological arc than does *Cellular*. For this perspective, see Wang (2013, 615), Williams (2011, 407–10) and Teo (2008).
16. In box-office terms, *Connected* could not compete with the distribution might of its Hollywood precursor: Chan's film grossed US$10.3 million worldwide, while *Cellular* attracted US$57.6 million internationally (*Box Office Mojo*).
17. Benny Chan director's commentary, *Connected* DVD (Joy Sales [HK] edition, 2008).
18. 'We made a conscious decision [to make Bob] more of a loser [than Ryan],' Chan declares. 'My hero is a much more flawed one.' Benny Chan interview, *Connected* DVD (CineAsia edition, 2010) and Benny Chan director's commentary, *Connected* DVD (Joy Sales [HK] edition, 2008).
19. In a Hollywood movie, Bob – having proven his heroic prowess – would shed the eyeglasses by the film's end, but Chan keeps the protagonist bespectacled throughout, reinforcing the notion that even an 'everyman' is capable of heroic action. Meanwhile, the ascription of a physical tic (in this case, a speech impediment) is a characteristic Chan touch, betraying a taste for vivid, instantaneous character delineation. Consider, for

example, the involuntary eye-twitch afflicting both Eric Tsang in *Gen-X Cops* and Louis Koo in *Meow* (*Miao xing ren*, 2017).
20. *Connected* can be loosely 'connected' to a tradition of Hong Kong films centred on father-son relationships. Contemporary examples include *My Father Is a Hero* (*Gei ba ba de xin*, 1995), *He Ain't Heavy, He's My Father* (*Xin nan xiong nan di*, 1993), and *All About Ah-Long* (1989). Critic Po Fung (1996, 31–3) identifies a trend within 1980s and 1990s Hong Kong cinema organised around 'prodigal sons' estranged from their fathers. These trends and traditions are pertinent contexts for *Connected*, to be sure, but a more proximate context is Benny Chan's oeuvre itself. If directors such as Johnnie To have alighted on father-son dynamics only occasionally or incidentally, Chan repeatedly returned to this theme throughout his career, in films including *Son on the Run*, *What a Hero!*, *A Moment of Romance II*, *New Police Story* and *Rob-B-Hood*. As such, the father-son topos is as much an authorial trait as a manifestation of generic themes circulating within Chan's immediate milieu.
21. A deleted scene reveals an alternative ending to favour a still more conventional romantic clinch between Ryan and Chloe. (*Cellular* DVD, New Line Home Entertainment, 2005.)
22. Benny Chan interview, *Connected* DVD (Joy Sales [HK] edition, 2008).
23. Chan's appeal to the artefact emotions, of course, fits within a tradition of Hong Kong action cinema. Local filmmakers, justifiably proud of their death-defying, 'corporeally authentic' action (Hunt 2003: 39), invite the viewer to take pleasure in serially repeated and frequently startling feats of physical dexterity.
24. That *Connected*'s brand strategy is organised around Pepsi is not incidental. As one of the earliest multinational organisations to forge an alliance with the mainland under Deng Xiaoping's Open Door Policy, Pepsi established its first bottling facilities just outside Hong Kong in 1982, growing into a 'beverage giant' by the 2000s (Lau 2013). Among the numerous celebrities to officially endorse Pepsi products in the early 2000s was Louis Koo. The makers of *Connected* exploited a blatant opportunity for cross-media synergy: while the film showcased the Pepsi brand by means of product integration, TV spots and viral ads featured a bespectacled Koo – evoking the distinctive look and appearance of his *Connected* protagonist – cheerfully swigging on cans of Pepsi soda.

REFERENCES

Anon. 2011. 'Fresh "Shaolin Temple" Goes for Drama Over Kung Fu.' *The Hollywood Reporter* (19 January). https://www.hollywoodreporter.com/movies/movie-news/fresh-shaolin-temple-drama-kung-73367/. Accessed 15 December 2021.

Bettinson, Gary. 2011. 'Sounds of Hong Kong Cinema: Johnnie To, Milkyway Image, and the Sound Track.' *Jump Cut: A Review of Contemporary Media*, no. 55. https://www.ejumpcut.org/archive/jc55.2013/BettinsonToAudio/index.html. Accessed 15 December 2021.

Bordwell, David. 2011. *Planet Hong Kong: Popular Cinema and the Art of Entertainment*, 2nd ed. Madison: Irvington Way Institute Press.

Braudy, Leo. 1998. 'Afterword.' In *Play It Again, Sam: Retakes on Remakes*. Edited by Andrew Horton and Stuart Y. McDougal, 324–7. Berkeley: University of California Press.

Campbell, Joseph. 2008. *The Hero with a Thousand Faces*. Novato: New World Library.

Chang, Bryan and June Lam. 2000. 'In Search of New Action: Benny Chan's *Gen-X Cops*.' In *Hong Kong Panorama 1999–2000*, 28–9. Hong Kong: Urban Council.

Chung, Winnie. 1998. 'Hong Kong Set for the Effects of Hollywood.' *South China Morning Post* (29 November), 5.

Chung, Winnie. 1999. 'Beyond Chopsocky.' *The Hollywood Reporter* (15 June), unpaginated.

Collier, Joelle. 1999. 'A Repetition Compulsion: Discontinuity Editing, Classical Chinese Aesthetics, and Hong Kong's Culture of Disappearance.' *Asian Cinema* 10, no. 2 (Spring/Summer): 67–79.
Curtin, Michael. 2007. *Playing to the World's Biggest Audience: The Globalization of Chinese Film and TV*. Berkeley: University of California Press.
Davis, Darrell William and Emilie Yueh-yu Yeh. 2008. *East Asian Screen Industries*. London: BFI.
Druxman, Michael B. 1975. *Make It Again, Sam: A Survey of Movie Remakes*. Cranbury: A. S. Barnes.
Frater, Patrick. 2008. 'WB, Emperor Keep "Connected".' *Variety* (7 February). https://variety.com/2008/film/asia/wb-emperor-keep-connected-1117980398/. Accessed 23 September 2021.
Fung, Po. 1996. 'The Prodigal Sons in Hong Kong Cinema.' In *The 20th Hong Kong International Film Festival Catalogue 1996*, 31–3. Hong Kong: Urban Council.
Ghahremani, Yasmin. 2003. 'Action Director Turns Spiritual for Latest Pic.' *Variety* (4 August), 13.
He, Hilary Hongjin. 2010. '*Connected* Through Remakes: Intercultural Dialogue Between Hollywood and Chinese Cinema Industries.' *Asian Cinema* 21, no. 1, (Spring/Summer): 179–92.
Hunt, Leon. 2003. *Kung Fu Cult Masters: From Bruce Lee to Crouching Tiger*. London: Wallflower Press.
Lam, Pierre. 2001. 'New Cast for New Action in Benny Chan's *Gen-Y Cops*.' In *Hong Kong Panorama 2000–2001*, 33–5. Hong Kong: Urban Council.
Lau, Adaline. 2013. 'Case Study: Pepsi China Leverages Web Video for CNY Campaign.' *ClickZ* (27 February). https://www.clickz.com/case-study-pepsi-china-leverages-web-video-for-cny-campaign/37747/. Accessed 1 March 2022.
Leitch, Thomas M. 1990. 'Twice-Told Tales: The Rhetoric of the Remake.' *Literature/Film Quarterly* 18, no. 3: 138–49.
Li, Cheuk-to. 2000. 'Asian Bearings and Post-97 Mentalities.' In *Hong Kong Panorama 1999–2000*, 13–15. Hong Kong: Urban Council.
Mak, Clara. 2008. 'Director Gets Connected to Hollywood via Cellular Bandwagon.' *South China Morning Post*, 18 February, 2.
Shackleton, Liz. 2004. 'The Year of the Hawk', *Screen International*, 16 January, 18.
Sun, Andrew. 2001. 'Cops and Models: "Y" Not?' *The Hollywood Reporter*, 9 January, unpaginated.
Tan, Ed S. 1996. *Emotion and the Structure of Narrative Film: Film as an Emotion Machine*. Mahwah: Lawrence Erlbaum.
Teo, Jasmine. 2008. 'Remake Outshines Original.' *The Straits Times*, 1 October, unpaginated.
Teo, Stephen. 2007. *Director in Action: Johnnie To and the Hong Kong Action Film*. Hong Kong: Hong Kong University Press.
Tsui, Athena, Li Cheuk-to, Rex Wong and Bono Lee. 2002. 'Ann Hui: Smooth Sailing through the Waves of Change.' In *Hong Kong Panorama 2001–2002* 103–10. Hong Kong: Urban Council.
Tsui, Clarence. 2004. 'Emotion Picture.' *South China Morning Post*, 22 September, 5.
Tsui, Clarence. 2007. 'Lights! Camera! Action Man.' *South China Morning Post*, 19 July, 6.
Wang, Yiman. 2013. 'Remade in China: Cinema with "Chinese Elements" in the *Dapian* Age.' In *The Oxford Handbook of Chinese Cinemas*. Edited by Carlos Rojas and Eileen Chang yin Chow, 610–25. Oxford: Oxford University Press.
Williams, Tony. 2011. 'From *Cellular* to *Connected*: Tracing a Global and Transcultural Odyssey.' *Asian Cinema* 22, no. 2, (Fall/Winter): 399–415.
Wong, Sharon. 2003. 'Hypnotic Charm of HK Stars.' *New Straits Times*, 5 August, 3.
Xu, Gary G. 2008. 'Remaking East Asia, Outsourcing Hollywood.' In *East Asian Cinemas: Exploring Transnational Connections on Film*. Edited by Leon Hunt and Leung Wing fai, 191–202. London: I. B. Tauris.

CHAPTER 11

Vessels and Cargos: Spaces of Inclusion and Exclusion in Johnnie To's *Drug War* and Lee Hae-young's Korean Remake *Believer*

Jinhee Choi

As Stephen Teo, Vivian Lee and other scholars have pointed out, Johnnie To's *The Mission* (*Qianghuo*, 1999) was a turning point in the Hong Kong filmmaker's directorial career, one in which he began to prioritise group ethics – of triads, of gangsters, of police squads – over acts of individual heroism. Concerning a motley crew of five bodyguards hired by a triad boss to protect him from assassination attempts, *The Mission* furthermore marks an aesthetic transition to 'stasis within motion' or 'stillness as a form of action', departing from hyperbolic action sequences that had previously characterised To's films in particular and Hong Kong cinema more generally (Teo 2007, 133; Lee 2009, 93). David Bordwell observes that another shift is discernible in the 2012 release of To's *Drug War* (*Du zhan*) – his production company Milkyway Image's first film shot entirely in Mainland China – in terms of its aesthetics and the denial of its protagonists' moral values (2013; see also Chu 2015, 192–205). In this nihilistic film, Timmy Choi (Louis Koo), a member of a drug cartel from Hong Kong, would risk anything, including trust and brotherhood, to save his own life. The group ethics endorsed by To in such films as *The Mission* and *PTU: Police Tactical Unit* (*Jidong budui*, 2003) are not to be found in *Drug War*, only the political and legal system that punishes characters whose actions deviate from it. As Sun Yi points out, survival is not only the primary concern for Timmy, but also an apt metaphor for the Hong Kong film industry as a whole (2018, 228).

The shifting moral, political purview manifest in *Drug War* provides a useful starting point for a comparison with its Korean-language remake, director Lee Hae-young's *Believer* (*Dokjeon*, 2018), which initially appears to be anchored in the individual rivalry between Won-ho (Cho Jin-woong), a detective, and Mr Lee (Ryu Jun-yeol), the secret mastermind behind a sprawling cocaine production network in South Korea. In this chapter, I focus on how the remake's restructuring of the earlier film's plot restricts characters' mobility. Despite the two films' diverging moral compasses and the spaces that are used, there remains an underlying similarity that allows us to uncover their respective sociopolitical systems, which deprive individuals of agency. As an adaptation, *Believer* self-consciously alludes to its source material while carefully weaving through the intricate layers of cultural exchanges and creativity in the East Asian region. In this light, it is significant that To is the director of the original film. As an enthusiast of adaptations and a frequent 'remaker' of previous works himself, the Hong Kong filmmaker embodies the kind of cross-cultural flows that have become increasingly apparent as a distinguishing regional feature, and he makes for a good illustration of how the past informs present-day filmmaking practices. For instance, he has repeatedly cited Kurosawa Akira as his major aesthetic influence, dedicating his 2004 judo film *Throw Down* (*Yau doh lung fu bong*) to the legendary Japanese director (Teo 2007, 118). Of course, Kurosawa also found inspiration in other cultures for his films, including *Throne of Blood* (*Kumomosu-jo*, 1957), an adaptation of William Shakespeare's *Macbeth* (1623); *The Lower Depths* (*Donzoko*, 1957) adapted from Maxim Gorky's play (1902); and *High and Low* (*Tengoku to jigoku*, 1963) based on Ewan McBain's *King's Ransom* (1959). A close analysis of the two main case studies of this chapter, *Drug War* and *Believer*, will highlight how the unending cycle of intertextual allusions and border-crossing conversations that links To to Kurosawa and the latter to his own forerunners continues to shape the output of filmmakers in the region, including Korean director Lee.

GROUP OR CORPORATE ETHICS?

Although not as popular or as prevalent as the many East Asian remakes that are based on romantic dramas, family melodramas and comedies, the region's motion pictures that have been inspired by previously produced crime/gangster films deserve attention, particularly for the way they engage the themes of masculinity, mobility and agency across national boundaries. Notable South Korean remakes of Hong Kong crime films and action films include such recent productions as Kim Dong-won's *City of Damnation* (*Yugamseureowun dosi*, 2009), based on Andrew Lau and Alan Mak's *Infernal Affairs* (2002); Song Hae-sung's *A Better Tomorrow* (*Mujeokja*, 2010) based on John Woo's *A Better Tomorrow* (*Yingxiong bense* 1986); Jo Ui-seok and Kim Byeong-seo's *Cold Eyes* (*Gamsijadeul*, 2013), based on Yau Nai-hoi's *Eye in the Sky* (*Gun Chung*, 2007), and Choi Dong-Hoon's *Wiretap* (*Docheong*, 2019), based on Alan Mak and Felix Chong's *Overheard* (*Sit ting fung wan*, 2009). Among these cross-cultural remakes of Hong Kong directors' works, *Believer* has proved the most successful at the domestic box office, attracting over five million admissions (26 June 2018, *Dong-a Daily*). In South Korea, To's *Drug War* was released as *Mayak jeonjaeng*, following its English title; whereas its remake *Believer* inherits the Chinese original title *Du zhan*, pronounced *Dokjeon* in Korean. At the time of its production, director Lee Hae-young was a novice of the crime genre, having debuted with the critically acclaimed coming-of-age comedy *Like a Virgin* (*Cheonhajangsa Madonna*, 2006), and then subsequently trying his hand at the horror genre, with the stylised period piece *The Silenced* (*Gyeongseonghakgyo: Sarajin sonyeodeul*, 2015). In the former film, a boy protagonist begins to practice Korean traditional wrestling (*ssireum*) with the hope of winning the competition prize to pay for gender-reassignment surgery.[1] *The Silenced* is set in a remote girls' boarding school in 1937, and its adolescent characters are not only subjected to strict conformity but are also expected to sacrifice themselves under Japanese colonial rule. They undergo medical experiments unbeknownst to them and are tested to see if they can rapidly improve their physical agility. Though steeped in different generic conventions, the two films underscore the institutional and ideological practices that allow only limited individual freedom or friendship. *Believer*, Lee's first foray into action-driven crime cinema, enables him to question how an individual may pursue professional goals or personal desires within a social arena largely defined by the status quo, and which operates under a very rigid, hierarchical system.

Believer focuses on the maverick chief of police narcotics division, Won-ho, who for years has obsessively been trying to track down the mysterious drug lord Mr Lee. In contrast to the original, where we see Timmy, who is unable to control his car on the road and eventually crashes it into a restaurant, *Believer* begins with shots of Won-ho driving down a snowy road in a foreign country. In *Drug War*, the focus is on Timmy, who is subsequently on death row and has no option other than to cooperate with the police to expose the illegal drug networks operated by the Hong Kong syndicate. In the final shootout against all parties involved – the police, the two deaf-mute employees at Timmy's amphetamine manufacturing factory, and the drug cartel that consists of seven members from Hong Kong – Timmy has no way out. The remake's plot turns the story into a male rivalry between Won-ho and Mr Lee.

After the opening credit sequence, the film quickly makes Won-ho's pursuit of Mr Lee even more personal by having his young female informant, Su-jeong (Keum Sae-rok), being brutally killed. Won-ho befriended her after she had served a sentence for drug use as a juvenile. As a favour to Won-ho, Su-jeong promises to be in touch with an insider who may help him to infiltrate the network run by Mr Lee. Won-ho is asked to meet up with Su-jeong after her meeting at Yongsan Train Station but instead finds her severely wounded in the station's parking lot. She dies shortly afterwards. For the final shootout, Won-ho returns to the same station to face Brian (Cha Seung-won), who presents himself as Mr Lee in hope of taking over the underworld network, while Won-ho himself impersonates Jin Ha-rim (late Kim Ju-hyuk), a Korean-Chinese, who provides him with Chinese raw materials to make cocaine and would then buy back the finished product from Mr Lee. After the finale at the station, the case is announced by the police to be 'closed', with Brian captured and identified as Mr Lee. Won-ho quits his job and the film cuts back to him driving the same vehicle seen in the pre-credit sequence, with yet another encounter that is awaiting the protagonist, this time with Seo Yeong-rak (Ryu Jun-yeol), who is the real Mr Lee and who has been helping Won-ho all this time to track down Brian. The film's narrative remains open-ended, with the sound of a gunshot fired inside the cottage audible from the outside. The two circular spatial trajectories of the main story and the framing story – Yongsan Station and the foreign country (shot in Norway) – in addition to the two different narrative outcomes underline the opposing forces that both restructure the characters' relationships and limit their places from within and without, following the Korean gangster/crime film convention that insists on the elimination of characters for their social transgressions.

As this Korean version of the story unfolds, Won-ho impersonates both the Korean Chinese drug lord Jin and Park Seon-chang (Park Hae-joon), who works for Brian, with Seo as a go-between, much as Captain Zhang (Sun Honglei) does in *Drug War* with the help of Timmy. Captain Zhang exploits the fact that Timmy is about to introduce Haha (Hao Ping), a distributor, and Li Shuchang (Tan Kai), a subordinate, to Uncle Bill (Li Zhenqi), a drug lord, but the two have never met in person. Zhang impersonates both in two subsequent meetings, a farcical one with Haha and a riskier one with Shuchang (Chang). Like Captain Zhang, who has to try two doses of cocaine to hide the fact that he is an undercover agent and to prove that he is serious in the deal, Won-ho in the Korean remake does the same and suffers severely from drug shock. But while his colleagues try to bring him back from the shock by submerging him in a bathtub filled with icy water, Won-ho has a hallucination of Su-jeong hovering over him: a sign of Won-ho's guilt for her death, as she passed away shortly after he had taken her to the hospital from Youngsan Station. Won-ho's relationship with Su-jeong, added as a backstory and brought to mind in this scene, turns his obsession with Mr Lee into a desperate determination to believe in Seo. Bordwell notes that *Drug War* 'humanizes the crooks more than the cops. Timmy mourns his family; we don't know Captain Zhang has one'; he continues, '*Drug War* gives no glimpse of the cops off duty. The result presents our officers as strictly business: no wives, kids, or civilian pals that distract them from their mission' (2013, 1). Unlike Zhang, Won-ho is portrayed as a character with depth in the sense that we have access to his interiority, and he shares with Seo a nemesis who is responsible for the death of women (Won-ho's female informant, Su-jeong, and Seo's mother, who died during the explosion at his drug factory).

In the original film, the drug cartel consists of seven characters, who are played by To's usual cast (a group of actors who also appear in his other Milkyway productions, including Lam Suet, Lam Ka-tung and Lo Hoi-pang, among others). These men collectively operate all the business deals, using Uncle Bill only as a cover-up. The most striking difference between the two films is that *Believer* foregrounds the corporate-like structure of the gang syndicate. Each member within that stricter hierarchy is always addressed with his 'work' title attached: Director Brian (Beuraieon-*isanim*), Associate Director Park (Bak-*sangmu*) and Assistant Manager Seo (Seo-*daeri*). Park even had a previous job experience at a large airlines company. The latter two characters' titles are often omitted in English subtitles, in which they are addressed only as 'Mr' or at times referred to by their last name ('Park' for Park Seon-chang) or abbreviated first name ('Rak' for Seo). As I have discussed elsewhere, Korean gangster films often feature a middleman as the protagonist, whose desire to go up the social ladder is eventually thwarted through his 'premature fall' due to social or sexual transgression. In such films as *Friend* (*Chingu*, 2001), *A Bittersweet Life* (*Dalcomhan insaeng*, 2005) and *A Dirty Carnival* (*Biyeolhan geori*, 2006), any such transgression results in a death (Choi 2010). Joseph Jonghyun Jeon further characterises such a narrative structure as one in which the gangster is a 'salaryman' embodying the post-IMF economic transformation that resulted in precarious job prospects and widespread anxieties around employability. With the collapse of the Asian market in the late 1990s, the patriarchal corporate model specific to South Korea, which guaranteed salarymen's lifetime employment and required their devotion in turn, was no longer sustainable and 'the massive layoffs represented not only a breakdown of the economy but also a breakdown of corporate paternalism' (Jeon 2019, 55–6). A gangster character such as *A Bittersweet Life*'s Seon-u (Lee Byung-hun) is quickly dismissed and punished once Seon-u is seen as disobeying Kang's order. Seon-u's 'residual image' or self-reflection on the glass wall of the restaurant at the beginning and in the epilogue of the film signals a feeble, unstable, fantasy-like status (Ibid., 53).

Believer both continues and subverts the aforementioned narrative trajectory in Korean gangster cinema that does not allow any social mobility of the male protagonist due to his social or sexual transgression. 'Assistant Manager' Seo seems to be able to successfully navigate the hierarchical structure as he is the only one who can liaise with the three parties involved in the large drug deal – the police, Jin and Brian. Despite his middleman status, Seo is an exception as he has more knowledge and thus more power; in that respect he appears to deviate from the middleman position and sidesteps the trajectory of Korean gangster films. But this is complicated by the final plot twist, which reveals that Seo is in fact Mr Lee; his 'salaryman' status is only a decoy. The final shootout at Yongsan Station is, then, Seo's personal revenge against, and punishment of, Brian, who has taken the lives of his family and attempted to replace him by disrupting the network system, if not hierarchy, that Seo as Mr Lee has built. We are not granted a residual image of Seo, like Seon-u in *A Bittersweet Life*, as a disposable salaryman; instead, we see that of Brian, an illusion of himself at the top of the hierarchy, controlling the criminal world.[2]

Unlike Seo, who escapes the final shootout safely, Timmy in *Drug War* is shown facing death row, babbling to save his life once again while he is receiving a lethal injection. To is said to have entertained the possibility of Timmy's escape in *Drug War* but suspected that such a plot development would not pass the mainland's censorship (Yi 2018, 229). Bordwell characterises the final shootout of *Drug War*, which takes place outside a primary school, as Timmy's act of vengeance: 'at the climax, he will take his revenge on both sides by halting the motorcade before it reaches the port, where cops are poised to arrest the gang' (2013, 11). What Bordwell refers to as the 'laconic' storytelling representative of To and his writing partner and co-founder of their production company Milkyway Image, Wa Ka-fei, however, obscures who is behind the factory's explosion from which Timmy is driving away at the beginning of the film, and thus the exact nature of Timmy's action. It appears that Timmy's setting up of the cops against the Hong Kong gang in the final sequence (or against his two deaf-mute employees) is part of his desperate ploy for survival rather than a form of revenge. In *Believer*, which abides by the 'redundant' storytelling characteristic of Hollywood (Bordwell 2006, 17), Seo verbally streamlines the cause and effect of events witnessed so far for both Brian and the spectator, explaining the motivation behind his punishing of Brian at Yongsan Station. Seo's identity as Mr Lee is reiterated twice more: in the conversation between Won-ho and his boss, and finally, when Won-ho visits Seo during the epilogue.

While some audiences might glean Seo's identity as Mr Lee faster than others are able to do, there are two occasions when the film's narrative seems to hint rather forcefully at his disguised identity. One is during Seo's first meeting with Jin, along with Won-ho impersonating Park. In the original, Captain Zhang and his team hide a secret camera in a cigarette case to record their deal with Haha to be used as evidence against the latter when he is charged. The scene pivots on a visual gag as well as building narrative suspense, as the secret camera's lens is repeatedly blocked by the dishes and saucers on the dining table, and the cigarette case is tossed between Zhang and Timmy, then passed even to Haha, who shows an interest in the box. In the remake, the small camera is pinned onto Seo's tie clasp. Marvelling at Seo's arrangement for her to sit next to Korean celebrity Lee Min-ho at a fashion show, Jin's partner Bo-ryeong (Jin Seo-yeon) (nicknamed as 'Bang-ul' by Jin in Korean, and subtitled as 'Kitty') teases Seo by asking 'Who the hell are you (*neo jeongchega meonya*)?' As a token of appreciation, she offers a new tie to Seo. As Bo-ryeong is about to replace Seo's tie herself with her gift, she blocks the camera. She inspects the pin closely and asks 'It's a fake (*jjaktung*), right?', pointing out that the pin is not from a genuine brand. The scene cleverly alludes to Seo's capability to arrange for what they desire and hints at his fake identity. Later in the film, when Bo-ryeong and Jin's thugs come to kidnap Seo and Won-ho for Seo's collaborating with an undercover agent, she again associates Seo's betrayal with the misinformation she has about Lee Min-ho: now she has learned that Lee has a girlfriend. Aubrey Tang underlines how Timmy's role in *Drug War* constantly changes from a criminal, an informant and a desperate and ruthless betrayer, who should negotiate and rediscover his identity whenever new opportunities arise (2019, 230); but not to the extent of Seo, whose whole identity was a sham.

The other occasion is when Seo is about to depart the factory to deliver the finished products to Park in Seoul, who then would meet Jin the next day. Here are even subtler visual cues that might lead audiences to suspect the truth behind Seo's disguised identity. As he walks toward the truck with a suitcase of cocaine, his reflected image, upside down, appears on the sea that fills the salt fields. The night before, the police also learned that Seo's legal identity is not real; that 'Seo Yeong-rak' was the deceased son of his Korean foster parents; and that his parents passed away in a cargo hold from an overdose of drugs while they were illegally immigrating to the country along with the smuggled goods. Seo's reflection invites doubt about his identity, thus far revealed, and marks his appearance and status within the corporate hierarchy as an illusion.

The upturned image of Seo is soon followed by the three-shot of Seo and the two deaf-mute siblings playing catch ball, very briefly. This image of the trio passing the ball to one another is reminiscent of To's geometrical staging in several of his films, but perhaps most brilliantly showcased in *The Mission* and *PTU*. Inspired by Kurosawa, To's static staging employed in both action and non-action sequences has replaced the balletic choreography of fight scenes associated with John Woo's gangster hero films, including the entries in his *Better Tomorrow* series (1986, 1987) and *The Killer* (*Dip huet seung hung*, 1989). But a more interesting genealogy can be traced from Kurosawa to To in their self-reflexive uses of striking geometric staging and symmetrical shot composition to signal or build tension among characters. To's *PTU*, for instance, not only shares with Kurosawa's *Stray Dog* (*Nora inu*, 1949) the narrative premise of a cop having lost his gun and following the processes of his retrieving it, but characters' conflicts of interest are manifest without disturbing the visual balance or symmetry of each shot.[3] Such an aesthetic in To's films further helps to signal the changing relationship among the members of a group. Both Stephen Teo and Vivian Lee pay particular attention to the paper ball soccer scene in *The Mission* as a sign of male camaraderie of the five bodyguards, who are hired to protect a gangster boss named Lung (Eddy Ko). It not only shows their boredom while they wait in the corridor for Lung to leave his office, but more importantly hints at their growing trust, which suggests how they will come to protect each other. As Lee states, 'it marks the completion of the team by showing an almost seamless integration and cooperation among the guards' (2009, 92) and leaves the spectator to question what their ultimate 'mission' was after the final plot twist occurs. Later, we witness Curtis (Anthony Wang), the leader of the group, betraying the boss's order to kill Shin (Jackie Lui), who has had an affair with the boss's wife. Teo makes a similar observation: for To, 'survival is dependent on the function of the group' – its 'unity' and 'integrity' as a homosocial grouping (2007, 121).

The scene involving catchball in *Believer* is comparable to, and functions like, the above-mentioned paper ball soccer scene. Earlier, the deaf-mute characters are shown organising a memorial for the death of Seo's mother, who passed away at the factory's explosion. But this short interlude further strengthens Seo's bond with the two as a form of play, not strictly as a facet of their business dealings. In To's original, even the relationship between Timmy and the two deaf-mute employees at Timmy's manufacturing factory in Erzhou

Figure 11.1 Seo Yeong-rak (Ryu Jun-yeol) and two deaf-mute drug factory workers are staged geometrically as they play catchball in Lee Hae-young's *Believer* (2018), a remake of Johnnie To's *Drug War* (*Du zhan*, 2012) (top), and in a re-establishing shot, the three continue to play while their image and the factory are reflected on the water's surface (bottom).

breaks down in the end, although the two men, as in the remake, arrange a little ritual to commemorate Timmy's wife, who died at another factory in Jinhai along with her two brothers. After the police's raid of their factory, the two attempt to exact revenge against their boss Timmy on the street during the final shootout, thinking that it is he who has set it up. Seo's bond with the siblings is extended beyond that of employer-employee, while the film suspends the revelation of Seo's true identity until the end. After the camera cuts to show each of the three characters in their respective one-shot, it reframes to show them in an extreme long shot, in which they are well integrated into the scenery along with the factory. Yet, with their reflection occupying a greater portion of the frame in the foreground, such a shot also reveals their peaceful moment to be illusory and transient, if not ghostly.

Characters' identities are closely tied to their respective spaces throughout the film. Both of the elaborate fight sequences – [1] Won-ho and Seo against Jin at his warehouse at the seaport and [2] Won-ho against Brian at Yongsan Station in Seoul – take place in interior spaces, which mirror one another; these are the spaces of their illegal activities and unrelenting desires. But a sense of both entrapment and mystery prevails. I will touch on the visual motif of Jin's warehouse shortly, but until we see Won-ho and Seo escape from it after having killed Jin, the spectator as well as the characters are kept in the dark with regard to where it is located or what it is. In the last shootout scene, which takes place in Yongsan Station, we see the cops' vans driving into the station for their final meeting with Brian, with the driveways to the station looking as though they are blood vessels that lead to the main body/building (Brian in fact uses the metaphor of 'blood rush' while looking at the trains passing). The station appears to be a larger scale version of the lab in the salt factory where the melted substances run and fall into lab flasks. Various hidden spaces and corridors inside the station are visually and spatially discontinuous; the metallic décor of the entry to Brian's lab and meeting space, both of which are allegedly located inside the station, do not allow any easy access or escape.

The interior spaces occupied by and associated with characters, as Teo puts it when he discusses the relationship between space and action in *The Mission*, 'evaporate once the action ends' (2007, 124). The exterior world outside character interiorities exists briefly only as a transition, to be absorbed into the space of one's own or another's interiority; such as outside the 'salt' factory where Seo can be seen playing catchball, and outside the cottage in the epilogue, where all four – Seo, the two deaf-mute siblings and his dog Leica – peacefully stay after they have escaped the final shootout. Regardless of whether Seo survives or not after Won-ho's final visit at the cottage, the two locations where the factory and the cottage are located mirror each other, offering a temporary, alternate space outside the system for these characters to disappear and escape. The wind turbines that surround the salt factory evoke a sense of the 'foreign' or even the exotic, although it was shot in a town called Yeonggwang, which is located in a southern province in South Korea (18 June 2018, *The Jungang*). Many fight sequences in *Believer* are staged using both depth and surface; the gun fights are staged in depth, as when Won-ho chases Jin from room to room in his containers, while extended fist fights are shown laterally. But while the two deaf-mute men fire ammunition at the two police officers in their factory, they walk laterally and disappear, sliding into their secret passageway inside the glass wall of their drug lab. Although the two deaf-mute characters in *Drug War* are shot similarly during the police's attack – they move laterally without a flinch – their existence is bodily, whereas their Korean counterparts are more ghostly in appearance. In the former, the two deaf-mute characters are in the middle of taking a shower and sitting on a toilet, respectively, when they see the alarm bells flashing as one of their spouses has pushed the button to inform them that the police entered the factory; they escape through a hole/tunnel dug under the factory floor.

None of the spaces in *Drug War*, be they the highway or the street in front of a primary school or the interiors of hotel rooms, offer an opportunity for escape; instead, they are under constant surveillance that aims to monitor and trace any outbreak of violence or practices of illegality. As Chu puts it, it is 'a [romantic] allusion to lack of freedom: ubiquitous surveillance in real life and censorship for the movie industry' (2015, 199). To's use of space in *Drug War* departs from his use of psychological space in *Exiled* (*Fong juk*, 2006) (Teo 2007; Choi 2017), and it does not restore a sense of order as it does in *Election* (*Hak se wooi*, 2005) or *PTU*. The latter film follows the squad headed by Mike (Simon Yam), which patrols the streets of Kowloon at night while they help a detective, Lo (Lam Suet, who plays a member of the Hong Kong gang in *Drug War*), retrieve his missing gun. The final shootout in *PTU* is staged on the street, similar to that of *Drug War*. The police squad led by Mike, Madame Cheung (Ruby Wong) of a special unit, the two gangster bosses Baldhead (Lo Hoi-pang, who also stars in *Drug War* as a Hong Kong gang member) and Eyeball (Eddy Ko), and the mainland gun dealers are all brought into the final scene, firing at each other with Lo bridging all four parties with his glances. But the narrative conflicts are dissolved in *PTU*, thanks to the 'group ethics' that have been built up prior to that point, the primary goal of which is the group's own 'survival and self-protection' at the expense of compromised moral integrity (Teo 2007, 133). Viewers are offered a brief glimpse at a similar geometric staging in *Drug War*, when the five members of the gang are caught between Timmy driving away on the bus and the police officers firing at them from behind. But they cannot survive due to Timmy's betrayal and the visual order quickly dissipates; and Captain Zhang and his team could capture Timmy only at the expense of many brutal deaths of police officers, including Yang (Huang Yi), the female officer and Zhang himself.

Figure 11.2 Hong Kong gang members are geometrically arranged as they fire at the police in the final shootout scene from Johnnie To's *Drug War* (*Du zhan*, 2012).

The spatial trajectory of *Drug War* – Jinhai, Erzhou, then back to Jinhai – underlies Timmy's constant move, reinforced by the vehicle motifs. He drives a sedan, a truck and even a school bus for the final shootout as well as using the train to move between places. However, his immobility or death is foreshadowed in the beginning when, chased by Captain Zhang and his crew, he ducks into a morgue in the hospital. The Korean remake draws the characters to the centre (central Seoul, Yongsan Station) and pushes them outside the mega city to manufacture and distribute drugs, overseen by Mr Lee. If Timmy's spatial displacement in *Drug War* – a Hong Kong citizen operating an illegal network in Mainland China – is the cause of his deprived agency and eventual death, in *Believer* both the centripetal and centrifugal forces drive the characters' movement as well as their desires. But the disappearance of Mr Lee/Seo and his spatial displacement are the result, not the driving force of the narrative or his actions.[4]

VESSELS OR CARGOS

In his anthropological study of migration into South Korea in the twenty-first century, Francis Collins notes the existence of migration 'regimes' and corresponding legal requirements that the South Korean government had adopted in order to manage and control the mobility of immigrants. As he states, 'migration is not governed by one but rather multiple intersecting regimes where criteria and conditions of entry vary considerably according to the perceived desirability and necessity of different migrants' (2018, 29). Collins's work is a fascinating study in and of itself, but what sheds light on my analysis of *Believer* is the South Korean government's immigration policies to 'contain' migrant workers who have entered the country through the Employment Permit System (EPS, introduced in 2003). These workers are also associated with illegality, as they often stay after their permits have expired, which could lead to both criminality and exploitation that require both 'restriction' and 'protection' (Collins 2018, 54, 56). What is worthy of note here is the disparity between government regulations and the movement of workers. The South Korean government's desire to manage and control is aptly illustrated by the idea of 'containing', both literally and figuratively. In one of Collins's interviews with an EPS worker, the latter reveals an initial, deplorable living condition offered by the company that hired him – a container which he had to share with six other people (2018, 71).

One of the major visual motifs apparent in *Believer* is that of containers, indicative of the way that flows of both people and commodities are controlled by the state. When Won-ho and Seo are blindfolded and taken to Jin as punishment for their betrayal, the two successfully fight their way out. But once they open the door, Jin's place is revealed to be part of a vast grouping of shipping cargos piled up at the pier. In a flashback, we also see Seo as a little boy inside a container, when he was illegally immigrating with his parents, along with the drugs smuggled from China. Both Jin and Seo are Korean-Chinese, and their presence and role are represented as a 'threat' to be contained or otherwise to be removed. As Collins notes, South Korea's self-perception as a 'territorially specific and contained homogeneous nation state' marks the border as 'a line between absolute inclusion and exclusion' (2018, 49).

Jin, a Korean counterpart of Haha in To's original, takes up considerably more narrative significance with the striking visual presence in the remake. In contrast to Haha, who boasts the number of his ships that could help quickly distribute cocaine from China to the rest of East Asia, Jin is the supplier who smuggles the raw materials from China to have them manufactured into cocaine in Korea and then have those finished products imported back. But Jin's eventual death inside his own cargo container further points to his 'foreign' status; his desire to profit through illegal means is constantly subject to the South Korean government's effort to have them 'contained' and be more strictly manageable. In contrast to such imagery in the remake, in To's original the desire to disseminate is foregrounded. A spectacular moment in the harbour scene in *Drug War* is showcased when the Hong Kong drug cartel remotely communicates to Uncle Bill through hidden microphones to test Haha's ownership of the vessels. Impersonated by Captain Zhang, Haha successfully demonstrates it by having ships designated by the gang be moved one by one. After a few ships start their engines, Haha/Zhang has all of them unleashed simultaneously. The inversed motifs of vessels and cargos in the two films deserve more scrutiny as, despite their visual contrasts, they also reveal a similar relationship between individual integrity or identity and the nation-state.

Tang analyses the visual threads of bodily rejection or abjection in *Drug War* — vomiting, defecating and hyperventilating – which run across the divide of the Hong Kong people and the mainlanders (2019, 213). Timmy is foaming at his mouth and almost vomiting toward the camera (Ibid., 222); Captain Zhang after his meeting with Shuchang must force himself to vomit the cocaine he inhaled. After his drug trafficking bust near the beginning of the film, Captain Zhang defecates behind the curtain along with some drug mules brought into the hospital. And in the final lethal injection scene, we see Timmy hyperventilating even prior to the injection of the first dose (Ibid., 217). (Let's not forget what one of the deaf-mute characters was doing when the police attacked their factory in Erzhou.) Tang suggests that the prevalence of abject forms of bodily expulsion throughout the film serves as a sign of physical resistance against the state's 'over-controlling sovereignty', when the human body has become 'both a state-owned property and a reified commodity in post-socialist Chinese judicial culture' (2019, 216, 229). Human bodies are constantly violated: 'a gest of intruded human bodies without personhood – a socially accepted attitude condoning the dissolution of the boundary between the exterior and interior of the body, between public and private space, and between the communal and personal integrity' (Ibid., 221).

The spatial and visual contrast between the two films in controlling the flows of both characters and commodities appears to underscore the two countries' diverging political systems or what Collins calls 'regimes' to manage and control them. Yet, the motifs of both ship/vessel in *Drug War* and container/cargo in *Believer* reveal a shared dynamic: individual desires and integrity are eventually tamed and 'contained' within their respective political system, or otherwise are eliminated. Jin's elaborate living space, made of several connected cargo containers, sharply externalises the conflicting aims of the state's control that would profit from their introduction to the country but limit unsatiable desires that move across borders. *Believer* does allow the possibility of Seo's escape and existence from without. Yet, Seo's residing in the foreign country or Won-ho's visit in the epilogue could be seen as both an escape and an illusion of such existence, similar to the reflection of the three – Seo and the two deaf-mute characters – on the salt fields that look like a mirage. As the camera pulls back after the gun shot is heard, their space shrinks even further and becomes one of isolation rather than integration.[5]

CONCLUSION

In this chapter, I have examined the contrasting plot structures and spatial trajectories manifest in To's *Drug War* and Lee's *Believer*. The initial contrast between the two films, however, betrays a similarity that only becomes apparent upon closer examination: that individual integrity or identity is denied under each sovereignty. Timmy literally faces death in *Drug War*, along with other characters in the film, including Captain Zhang. In the epilogue of *Believer*, Seo escapes, while the confrontation between the two male protagonists, Won-ho and Seo/Mr Lee, is suspended without any clear resolution. It is unclear whether there is any significant possibility for individual integrity and identity or merely their fractured identities and non-existence outside the system.

Believer's adaptation of *Drug War* adds an interesting layer to the film's allusion to, and self-reflexivity about, cultural and economic traffics in the region: exports of Korean media versus imports of foreign resources or goods into the country. Jin mockingly praises Korea's 'skills' to process or manufacture the materials from abroad into something more profitable with its advanced technology, be it computer chips or cocaine. Jin's partner, Bo-ryeong, is obsessed with the Korean actor/celebrity Lee Min-ho, who earned stardom in the broader region thanks to his performance in the Korean television remake of the regional mega-hit *Boys Over Flowers* (*Hana yori Dango*, comic books 1992–2003; the Taiwanese television adaptation of the comics, *Meteor Garden*, 2001; the Japanese TV series, 2005; the Korean remake *Kkotboda namja*, 2009) and *Heirs* (*Sangsokjadeul*, 2013). Seo exploits her fandom to earn her trust in the film. *Believer* adds an inverse stream to that flow, by making an adaptation of and 'replacing' the original *Du zhan* with To's film released in Korea as *Drug War*, as if Brian attempts to replace Mr Lee, which was welcomed by Korean audiences.

NOTES

1. Lee is a LGBT director, which he was compelled to reveal when he was falsely charged for sexual harassment (5 March 2018, *Hanguk kyungje*).
2. There might be a closer connection between the transformation of the Korean crime genre and the changing South Korea's socioeconomic conditions than I suggest in *Believer*, which I do not pursue. The 'salt' factory, run by two deaf-mute siblings in the film, could be seen as the large corporate's sub-contractor, which in turn exploits overseas employees, who appear to be illegal immigrants of foreign nationalities. Jeon notes that the Korean chaebols in fact grew stronger after the IMF crisis by trimming their practices; and the salt factory could be seen as operating at a cheaper cost, which recourses to exploitation.
3. In *PTU*, for instance, the hit of the character Ponytail (Chiu Chi-sing), a local hoodlum in Kowloon, is built through the scene's geometric, triangular staging as characters constantly need to change their seats in a restaurant due to the leaking from its ceiling and implicit hierarchy between Ponytail's gang and a cop, Lo (Lam Suet), who loses his gun shortly after. But this is done so without disrupting the balance of the initial shot composition; when there is created a space among the characters, even the restaurant owner fills that space. A comparable scene can be found in *Stray Dog*, where the protagonist Murakami (Mifune Toshiro) persistently urges the suspect Yusa's girlfriend,

Harumi (Awaji Keiko), to reveal Yusa's whereabouts. In the same film, To further adopts the aesthetics of Kurosawa's scope films, such as *High and Low*, in staging the police squad roaming the streets of Kowloon, with characters moving and filling each other's spaces and gaps to have shots remain balanced. In *High and Low*, viewers encounter a similar staging when Gondo (Mifune) answers a call from the kidnaper asking for ransom with the presence of cops in his mansion.
4. There is a way in which the spatial displacement of Seo as a young boy (he's Korean-Chinese, and illegally immigrated into South Korea), could be seen as the driving force; yet, the major premise has more to do with the visibility or invisibility of Mr Lee as the head of the criminal world, not his spatial displacement it seems. But the film's final spatial exclusion of him could be seen as the state's perception of the illegality as foreign, not internal to the territory.
5. In director Lee's previous film, *The Silenced*, the two girls dream of leaving the country and are temporarily able to escape the boarding school. But when they reach the cliff, where they believe Japan exists, there is nothing beyond, as if the external world outside the boarding school never existed. In the epilogue of *The Silenced*, we see the girls hanging out in their secret place only as an 'afterimage' of their death.

REFERENCES

Anon. 2018. 'Director Lee Hae-young comes out as a sexual minority, upon a charge against sexual harassment' [Yihaeyeong gamdok seongchuhang uihoke 'naneun seonsosuja' keomingaut]. *Hanguk kyungje*, 5 March, http://www.hankyung.com/print/201803052945H. Accessed 25 Mar 2022.

Anon. 2018. '*Believer*, the first Korean film of the year with its admissions over 5 million . . . its box office results surpassed that of *New World* and *Nameless Gangster*' [Dokjeon, olhae hangukyeonghwa cheoeum 500man dolpa . . . *Sinsege, Beomjeowaeui jeonjaeng* neomeotda]. *Dong-a Daily*, 26 June. https://www.donga.com/news/Entertainment/article/all/20180626/90774703/2. Accessed 25 March 2022.

Bordwell, David. 2006. *The Way Hollywood Tells It: Story and Style in Modern Movies*. Berkeley: University of California Press.

Bordwell, David. 2013. 'Mixing Business with Pleasure: Johnnie To's *Drug War*' (last updated 2019). http://www.davidbordwell.net/blog/2013/07/08/mixing-business-with-pleasure-johnnie-tos-drug-war/. Accessed 9 June 2021.

Choi, Jinhee. 2010. *The South Korean Film Renaissance: Local Hitmakers, Global Provocateurs*. Middletown: Wesleyan University Press.

Choi, Jinhee. 2016. 'Seoul, Busan and Somewhere Near: Korean Gangster Cinema and Urban Space.' In *Global Cinematic Cities: New Landscapes of Film and Media*. Edited by Johan Andersson and Lawrence X. Webb, 220–36. New York: Columbia University Press.

Choi, Jinhee. 2017. 'Exiled in Macau: Hong Kong Neo-noir and Paradoxical Lyricism.' In *Hong Kong Neo-Noir*. Edited by Esther Yau and Tony Williams 198–215. Edinburgh: Edinburgh University Press.

Chu, Yiu-wai. 2015. 'Johnnie's To's "Northern Expedition": From Milkyway Image to *Drug War*.' *Inter-Asia Cultural Studies* 16, no. 2: 192–205.

Collins, Francis L. 2018. *Global Asian City: Migration, Desire and The Politics of Encounter in 21st Century Seoul*. Hoboken: John Wiley and Sons, Ltd.

Jeon, Joseph Jonghyun. 2019. *Vicious Circuits: Korea's IMF Cinema and the End of American Century*. Stanford: Stanford University Press.

Kim, Ho. 2018. 'A Strange Reflection above the water . . . when you visit the salt factory in "Believer"' [Sumyeon wi myohan geurimja . . . 'Dokjeon' mayakgongjang yeomjeonmaeul gaboni]. *The Jungang*, 18 June. https://www.joongang.co.kr/article/22700568#home. Accessed 25 March 2022.

Lee, Vivian. 2009. *Hong Kong Cinema Since 1997: The Post-Nostalgic Imagination*. New York: Palgrave Macmillan.

Tang, Aubrey. 2019. 'Hong Kong's Cinema of Cruelty: Visceral Visuality in *Drug War*.' *antae* 6, no. 2–3: 213–33.

Teo, Stephen. 2007. *Director in Action: Johnnie To and the Hong Kong Action Film*. Hong Kong: Hong Kong University Press.

Yi, Sun. 2018. 'Renationalization and Resistance of Hong Kong Cinema: Milkyway Image's Journey to Mainland China.' *Inter-Asia Cultural Studies* 19, no. 2: 220–33.

Part IV

Local Flavours and Transcultural Flows in East Asian Comedies, Dramas and Fantasies

CHAPTER 12

The Power of Healing in *Little Forest*(s): Cross-Cultural Perspectives on Food, Friendship and Self-identity, from Japan to Korea

Nam Lee

Little Forest (*Liteul Poleseuteu*, 2018), director Yim Soon-rye's Korean remake of a Japanese film of the same title (directed by Mori Junichi, adapted from Igarashi Daisuke's manga series *Ritoru Foresuto* [2002–2005], and spread over two feature-length instalments: 'Summer/Autumn' [2014] and 'Winter/Spring' [2015]), offers a distinctive lens onto the various sociocultural and industrial factors involved in the reworking of a text across spatial and temporal boundaries. While it represents one of the most commercially successful examples of South Korean cinema's recent trend of remaking Japanese motion pictures (on the heels of Lee Gye-byeok's action-comedy *Luck-Key* [*Leokki*, 2016], which was based on the 2012 production of *Key of Life* [*Kagi Dorobō no Mesoddo*] and followed by Kim Jong-kwan's romantic drama *Josée* [2020], based on the 2003 production of *Josee, the Tiger and the Fish* [*Joze to Tora to Sakanatachi*]), the production was driven less by its box-office potential than by a desire to serve a particular social function. Namely, Yim's film provides a sense of 'healing' to a young generation of Koreans and a model of rural life as an alternative to a competitive and alienating existence in Seoul and other large metropolitan areas. This owes something to the evocations of rural life found in the original Japanese film, which was released in two parts (in 2014 and 2015) and was an adaptation of a manga about a young woman who retreats to her hometown in a remote village after a series of disheartening encounters. Through a self-reliant life of physical labour and food preparation, the female protagonist regains confidence and the deep sense of belonging she has pined for, but not found, in the city.

Both the original Japanese film and the Korean remake share this basic plot and setting; how each work portrays her rural life, cooking and search for identity, however, differs considerably. The fundamental difference between the two, which I will elaborate in this chapter, lies where the protagonist finds the 'power of healing'. Ichiko (Ai Hashimoto), the Japanese protagonist, finds it in regional traditions and the village community; Hye-won (Kim Tae-ri), the Korean protagonist, does so through renewed relationships with childhood friends and family (the mother in particular). The Japanese film foregrounds the regional characteristics and cultural heritage of the Tōhoku region where the story takes place; the Korean remake focuses more on Hye-won's interaction with her closest peers and the memory of her mother in the past through flashbacks. In both films, food plays a central role in the protagonist's cathartic quest for self-identity. Through cooking, she connects with the world around her, especially with nature.

This chapter offers a comparative analysis of the two films that sheds light on cross-cultural perspectives on food, friendship and self-identity. It focuses on the localisation process of the Korean remake that involved modifying and trimming elements that director Yim Soon-rye considered too 'distinctly Japanese', such as the film's slow rhythm, aspects of character and featured dishes. Thus, the key to the process was reinterpreting the original film according to Korean sensibilities.[1] In both films, the protagonist's self-healing process involves returning to her rural hometown, engaging in physical labour (agricultural work and picking wild fruits and vegetables) and coming to terms with her past; that is, healing the psychological wound caused by her mother. The latter character had left her without much explanation when she was still a teen.

Generally, the Korean remake adopts the themes, natural setting and character types from the original Japanese film; however, these same ingredients are reconstructed and transformed according to different cultural sensibilities and values, especially the sociocultural differences between Korea and Japan. For example, a young woman living alone in a remote rural house would not sit well with the Korean audience due to their security concerns. Also, as one blogger wrote, Ichiko's relationship with her mother 'did not fit our [Korean] sentiments', and the ending was 'wholly alien' (*Kkachi'irhanshiseon*); these elements were modified in the Korean remake. While Ichiko does not seem to miss her mother and becomes an independent person on her own, Hye-won constantly looks back to the past time with her mother. In the end, her face lights up as she sees the house's open door, which suggests that her mother might be back home.

Thus, each film parlays the cultural codes developed in their respective societies over time for the purpose of localising a story that could have broad, universal appeal (beyond East Asia). Since the Japanese manga and the film are deeply embedded in the local culture of the Tōhoku region in northeast Japan, it would seem almost imperative for the Korean remake to neutralise this element in some way. Compared to that of the Japanese film, the Korean remake's spatial locality is ambiguous. It could be any rural village in Korea. Instead, personal relationships – particularly with childhood friends and the mother – are foregrounded as an emotional zone where Hye-won might recover self-identity. These changes are especially illuminating of the differences between East Asian cultures, traditions and value systems in countries that, while geographically close neighbours under the influence of Confucianism, reflect distinct outlooks on community and self-identity.

In this light, the Korean version of *Little Forest* makes for a compelling case study through which to explore recent cross-cultural remakes, especially when we consider Constantine Verevis's argument that foreign films (or, in this case, Japanese films) 'are disposed of "local detail" and "political content" to exploit new markets' (2006, 3). The chapter thus highlights the underlying factors involved in localising a cinematic property and, more specifically, the fundamental changes that this Korean remake has brought to bear on an original film at the textual level (in terms of its erasure of specific regional history and culture) and at the contextual level (in terms of its expansion of an urban youth crisis into a broader sociopolitical issue). With those textual and contextual differences in mind, I look at how the films ultimately converge in the final meaning of their respective 'little forests'. While the title of the Japanese film is a literal translation of Komori, the fictional hometown of Ichiko in the film, in the Korean remake it is a metaphor for a place of self-realisation that Hye-won will build and keep in her heart.

Additionally, *Little Forest* represents an increasing number of film remakes that involve an inter-media adaptation from manga to film and an intra-medial (film to film) translation in a transnational context. In this case, the period of time between the publication of the manga, the production of the Japanese film adaptation and the production of the Korean remake should also be noted. The manga was first published in 2002, while the Japanese film adaptation was undertaken in 2014, with the Korean remake following four years later. The Japanese film is a faithful adaptation of the manga. It closely follows the manga's narrative, featuring all of its food recipes, and dialogue in the film is mostly straight from the pages of its source material. Conversely, the Korean remake has made substantial changes to its precursor texts. These changes exemplify Lucy Mazdon's claim that transnational remakes 'can be seen to cross both spatial (national) and temporal (historical) boundaries' (2000, 3). Comparing the two films reveals the dynamics of cultural politics that allow the more recent remake to address contemporary social issues different from, if not at odds with, the original story. In the Japanese manga and film, the history and tradition of the village in the Tōhoku region is a crucial part of the protagonist's self-identity. At the end of that film, Ichiko performs the village's traditional dance that symbolises the continuation and inheritance of village history. In Yim's version of *Little Forest*, Hye-won's self-identity is not rooted in the village history or traditional culture; rather, it lies in her ability to overcome personal trauma, specifically the pain resulting from her mother's sudden disappearance years ago. Thus, the flashback scenes showing mother and daughter occur more frequently than in the Japanese film.

In the Korean remake, acute attention to the broader social issue of the contemporary urban youth crisis replaces the regional history and specific locality in the Japanese film. Hye-won and her friends' workplace experiences in the city suggest the precarity and inhumane working conditions that today's younger generations face in contemporary Korea. Thus, the rural hometown functions as a place of mental recovery and spiritual healing for them. The rural retreat is also a recuperation site for Ichiko; however, the Japanese film focuses more on the female protagonist as an individual rather than as an overt stand-in for larger social or generational issues. In contrast, the Korean film allegorically expands Hye-won's experience to that of an entire generation. The portrayal of Hye-won's life in Seoul, the capital city of Korea, is more detailed than that of Ichiko's, and her friend's stories are newly added. In this way, the urban youth crisis is presented as a more urgent sociopolitical issue.

This chapter first examines the industrial context of the Korean remake (the commercial imperatives that shaped its production and release). It then explores the localisation process on the textual level (with its shift of focus from regional traditions and communal life to personal relationships and social issues). My analysis of the two films seeks to highlight the ways in which specific cultural codes and social relationship practices are embedded in their respective portrayals of food, friendship, maternal care, the rural village and its traditional culture. This comparative analysis reveals the cultural differences between the two societies and the specific values attached to food and social relations as they relate to self-identity. While the images and representations of food in the original Japanese film coalesce around the idea of 'self-sufficiency' or 'self-reliance', greater attention is given to the act of 'sharing' in the Korean remake.

FROM MANGA TO SCREEN ADAPTATION: SELF-SUFFICIENCY AND THE TOHŌKU REGION

The original two-part film exemplifies contemporary Japanese cinema's tendency to adapt popular manga on screen. The original manga *Little Forest* by Igarashi Daisuke was published from 2002 to 2005 as a series in the monthly comic magazine *Afternoon*. It came out as a two-part book and was translated into Korean and published in South Korea in 2008. The Korean-language translation was popular among manga fans.[2] Igarashi, a well-known artist, wrote and drew *Little Forest* based on his own experiences of living a self-sufficient life in Oushuu, Iwate Prefecture, in the Tohōku region, where his parents were born. Ichiko's rural hometown in the manga, Komori, is a fictional village modelled after Oushuu (Igarashi, 2009). The manga consists of thirty-four episodes, including thirty-two episodes titled after the food Ichiko cooks. Each episode introduces the food recipe in detail and the tools Ichiko uses to obtain the main ingredient by cultivating it herself in the field or picking it from the wild forest around her. Through cooking and intense physical labour, Ichiko overcomes her doubts and gains a sense of belonging, a profound connection to the land. The small community of Komori, its natural beauty and the physical toil of farming help Ichiko recover and rebuild her self-identity.

The manga's emphasis on self-sufficiency can be interpreted as addressing Japanese millennials, referred to as the 'yutori generation'. Born between 1987 and 1996, the yutori generation is defined by the public education reform implemented in 1978. The purpose of the reform was to make learning less intensive and less restrictive. However, it was reversed in 2010, as this new generation became increasingly stereotyped as 'overpraised, overprotected, and spoiled' (Hiam et al. 2017–2018, 5). They were considered lacking in independence and competence to compete economically on a global stage. Therefore, it is significant that twenty-something millennial Ichiko overcomes her uncertainty through hard, physical labour and independent, self-reliant life in the mountain village of Komori.

When the manga was adapted to screen six years later, a different social milieu informed the making of the film. In his interview with a Korean newspaper, the director Mori Junichi stated that he was making the film to give hope to the Tōhoku residents who lost their homes during the 2011 Great Tōhoku earthquake and tsunami that devastated the region. A photo of an older woman farming among the ruins inspired him (Mori 2015). In this intermedia move (from manga to film), a temporal/historical boundary is crossed to address a different issue from those featured in the original manga. The screen adaptation was shaped by the perceived public need and the filmmaker's desire to help rebuild society following the destruction caused by the earthquake, leaving the spatial boundary (that of the Tōhoku region) intact. Ichiko's intense and relentless labour represents the resilience of the Tōhoku residents.

With fastidious attention to detail, the film portrays Ichiko's various types of physical exertion, including farming, cutting firewood and other housekeeping chores. Also, to include all twenty-eight dishes Ichiko cooks in the manga, the adaptation is divided into four parts, one hour for each season. Then, the parts were paired into a duology: *Little Forest: Summer/Autumn*, released in 2014 and *Little Forest: Winter/Spring*, released in 2015. Each one-hour segment can stand independently, with separate opening and closing credit sequences. Each segment starts with Ichiko introducing the village of Komori through voiceover narration: 'Komori is a small settlement in a village somewhere in the Tōhoku region. There are no stores here, but if you have a little shopping to do, there is a small farmer's co-op supermarket . . . ', adding the seasonal descriptions and how long it takes her to go shopping to indicate how remotely her house is located from the village centre. This exact narration is introduced only once, at the beginning of the manga. Riding a bike, Ichiko narrates over Komori's seasonal landscape images: thick forests teeming with rich plants and wildlife, farmland and paddies at the mountain basin except during the cold, snowy winter.

As such, both the manga and Mori's film capture and foreground the regional characteristics of the setting. The Tohōku region is a remote area that has been historically marginalised within Japan. An area of primarily agricultural production across the northeast of Honshu Island, it was for a long time seen as '"backwards" in contrast to the more "advanced" southwestern part of the country' (Kawanishi 2006, xi). However, since 2001, the region's history has been given a spotlight for re-evaluation as a place that could 'provide a breakthrough model for creating a new kind of society' (Ibid., 6). In this respect, it is especially significant that Ichiko finds her sense of belonging and self-confidence in the village community of Komori, organising a community-based festival to showcase regional speciality products and traditional performances.

Ichiko's story is told in the Japanese manga and film through the various dishes she prepares and cooks using seasonal ingredients. A significant portion of the film's episodic narrative is spent in her kitchen as she prepares dishes while narrating the recipes in voiceover. Through her spoken narration and the filmmaker's use of flashbacks, the audience gradually learns about her childhood and her mother, who abandoned Ichiko seven years earlier, leaving her with a sense of loss and puzzlement. Through a 'slow and simple' mode of existence rooted in the vast, verdant nature surrounding her, Ichiko struggles but ultimately finds her place in the world, discovering what she wants to do with her life. Ichiko mainly cooks for herself except on a few occasions, such as Christmas, when she shares her food with her friends. In the above interview, director Mori states that he was attracted to the manga because of its 'spirit of self-sufficiency', something that 'has diminished in contemporary Japanese society' (2015). The Korean remake retains this basic scenario but differs substantially in the female protagonist's situations and social relations. Both temporal/historical and spatial boundaries are crossed in this transnational intra-media adaptation.

FROM SCREEN ADAPTATION TO CROSS-CULTURAL REMAKE: YOUTH CRISIS AND 'SMALL HAPPINESS'

Yim's *Little Forest* is indicative of South Korean cinema's recent trend of remaking Japanese films. The year 2018 alone also saw the release of Noh Dong-seok's *Golden Slumber* (*Koldeun seulleombeo*), Lee Jang-hoon and Lee

Seok-geun's *Be with You* (*Chigeum mannareo kamnida*) and Kim Jee-woon's *Illang: The Wolf Brigade* (*Illang*), the latter a live-action remake of Mamoru Oshii and Hiroyuki Okiura's animated film *Jin-Roh: The Wolf Brigade* (*Jinrō*, 1999). Considering the complex history of unofficial and official exchanges between the two cinemas,[3] it is worthwhile to explore this recent remake trend's cultural and industrial significance. Although a thorough study is beyond the scope of this chapter, it is noteworthy that the official remaking of Japanese films only began in 1998 due to the government's ban on pop culture from the former coloniser – a restriction that had been in place since Korea's liberation from Japanese rule in 1945. However, many Japanese cartoons were imported and broadcast on network television without being credited as Japanese. Moreover, as discussed by David Scott Diffrient in Chapter 2 of this volume, many unofficial remakes or poachings of Japanese films took place during the 1950s and 1960s.

Not until recently (over the past decade) have Korean remakes of Japanese films been commercially successful, a trend that the low-budget *Little Forest* further epitomises. *Little Forest* performed well at the box office, selling 825,027 tickets (Korean Film Council). It was an unexpectedly big hit for a relatively low-budget film (USD 1.4 million, including the marketing costs).[4] It is worth noting that when the Japanese duology was released in Korea in 2015 (*Little Forest: Summer/Autumn* on 12 February 2015, and *Little Forest: Winter/Spring* on 14 May 2015), it failed at the box office, with each selling only around 10,000 tickets. However, both halves of the original were met with a warm reception from fans of Japanese cinema. Many film bloggers described it as a 'healing movie' that gives viewers feelings of comfort through representations of food preparation, a life lived at a snail's pace, and Japanese cinema's unique sensibilities of calm and quiet.[5] Indeed, this 'healing' effect was at the heart of the remake's conceptualisation. Defying the conventional rule for film remakes, the Korean producer Shin Beom-soo did not select the original Japanese film for its proven box-office record but, instead, for its potential to respond to a particular social demand: the need for collective catharsis. He was so comforted by the Japanese original that he decided to remake it to convey a similar feeling for the young generation and to counter contemporary Korean cinema's strong tendency toward violent, adrenaline-pumping action films (Yim 2018).

Around the time of *Little Forest*'s release, there arose a distinct trend among the young generation of what is referred to as 'sohwakhaeng' (SCH: an acronym for 'Small but Certain Happiness'). Faced with a rising unemployment rate, increased competitiveness in the job market, steep home prices and general uncertainties about the future, young people in their twenties and thirties began to find solace in small forms of everyday happiness in lieu of pursuing bigger ambitions. Seoul National University's Consumer

Trend Analysis Center's research shows that the movement toward 'healing' and 'SCH' became prominent in 2013 due to economic stagnation (*Kookmin Ilbo*). The emphasis on creating a 'healing' film differentiates the Korean remake from the original. Nevertheless, it is significant that the concept 'sohwakhaeng' was borrowed from the Japanese writer Murakami Haruki's 1986 essay 'Afternoon in the Islets of Langerhans'. Here, he gives examples of 'small but certain pieces of happiness', such as eating a freshly baked loaf of bread with your hands and wearing a new shirt that smells clean and crisp, things one can easily find in daily life. Haruki suggests that all a person needs to enjoy beer is not a fancy glass or expensive import but hard physical labour or exercise. In order to feel proud of the folded underwear in the drawer, housework such as laundry, drying and organising is all that is needed. Also, self-control is necessary to avoid buying expensive vinyl records. We can read Murakami's essay as his comment on the 1980s Japanese society amid an economic boom that saw an attendant rise of materialism and hedonistic consumption. The fact that Murakami's idea of 'sohwakhaeng' is summoned into twenty-first-century South Korea, which saw the production of films and television shows built around that notion, is further evidence of Mazdon's argument on transnational remakes crossing 'temporal/historical boundaries'. In *Little Forest*'s case, each text can be read as a subtle commentary on something specific: the yutori generation (manga), Tōhoku residents after the 2011 earthquake (Japanese film) and the Korean youth crisis and the trend of 'sohwakhaeng' (Korean remake), respectively.

Alongside this 'sohwakhaeng' trend, the so-called 'mukbang', a Korean acronym for 'eating shows', became immensely popular in the years leading up to *Little Forest*'s 2018 release. In reality TV shows like *Three Meals a Day* (*Samsiseki*, 2014) and *Horyi's Homestay* (*Hyori-ne Minbak*, 2017), celebrities stay in rural villages and lead self-reliant lives – at least for a short time – farming and/or fishing before cooking their daily meals. This idea of a slow-paced mode of living appeals to audiences who have grown tired of the competitiveness and busy lifestyles associated with city living. Furthermore, South Korea has seen a 'return to the countryside phenomenon' since the early 2010s. Between 2013 and 2017, approximately 1,300 city dwellers born in rural areas returned to their hometowns to work in agriculture.[6] In the film, Hyewon's friend Jae-ha (Ryu Jun-yeol) is such an example. The Japanese *Little Forest* was released in this sociocultural climate in Korea and warmly received by fans of Japanese cinema. The audience rating was favourable on the Daum movie site, with 7.5/10 for part 1 and 8.0/10 for part 2. It satisfied the current trend of slow life, emphasising self-cooked food and addressing the nostalgia for rural life. In order to reach a wider audience, however, the film had to be remade and localised in the Korean language with familiar cultural codes, stars and sensibilities.

LOCALISING JAPANESENESS: MAJOR CHANGES

Any attempt to characterise a national cinema runs the risk of homogenising other cultures. However, as films are an integral part of the culture from whence they came, different national cinemas reflect and embed different cultural codes and attitudes. The success of transnational remakes depends on how well they transform these codes and attitudes for their local audience. When director Yim Soon-rye explains that the task of writing the script for the Korean remake was challenging because the original film was 'too Japanese' for the Korean audience, we can assume that there is a certain perceived notion of 'Japaneseness' in cinema. Not only the Japanese traditional culture and food depicted in the film but also the film's rhythm and narrative flow had to be transformed. According to Jung Wook-sung, a Korean scholar of Japanese cinema, one of the significant traits of the latter is a tendency toward 'calm and serene portrayals of everyday life or things that are easily found around us' (2014, 438). Yim also notes that her major concern in the remake was how to transform the slow and calm rhythm of the original. The remake had to have more drama driving the narrative forward at a faster pace (2018).

Since the original Japanese film was not considered commercially viable, many of the changes were for Korean box-office considerations. The first change was the length of the film. The four hours of the original film were cut to 103 minutes. It meant that all four seasons had to be included in one film. Because of the shorter length, the number of dishes Hye-won cooks for herself is drastically reduced from twenty-eight in the original film (seven dishes for each season) to twelve. In the original film, Ichiko narrates the step-by-step recipes for all dishes; however, in the Korean remake, the speed of making food and the static scenes of savouring nature are compressed. Instead, the proportions of the narrative devoted to the protagonist's childhood friends and mother are increased to add more drama.

The commercial imperative for the Korean remake led to a distinctly different film being produced, both in its narrative and style. The original work retains a manga-like sensibility by depicting imaginative and fantastical scenes; the Korean remake is more realistic and down-to-earth with conventional continuity editing that focuses on the character's transformation. In an early scene of the summer episode of the Japanese film, an amphibian web grows between Ichiko's fingers, and she jumps from her house to her rice field like a frog. Also, split screens are sparingly used for transitions during Ichiko's cooking and to juxtapose past and present, making the scenes reminiscent of the panels of the original manga. In contrast, there are no fantasy scenes or split screens in the Korean remake; instead, the emphasis is on using colour and sound to accentuate the tasty food and additional flashbacks to depict Hye-won's past with her mother. In addition, the Korean remake self-consciously expands Hye-won's

Figure 12.1 A scene of food preparation in Yim Soon-rye's *Little Forest* (*Liteul Poleseuteu*, 2018), a Korean version of a Japanese film and manga series of the same title.

worries to those of South Korea's generation of twenty-somethings and thirty-somethings. The decisive reason for her return is that she has failed the highly competitive teacher credential exam, which is a path to a stable career. (The average competition rate for the middle/high school teacher credential exam in 2021 was 12.04 for public schools and 32.21 for private schools.) (Korea Lecturer News, 2020).

RURAL LIFE AND VILLAGE COMMUNITY

Both films foreground slow-paced rural life and present the quiet but hard-working agricultural village as a place of recuperation, an alternative to the inhumane, cold city life from which Ichiko and Hye-won retreated. However, the reasons for those characters' returns diverge. For Ichiko, it is subtly suggested that she lacked a sense of belonging in the city. Neither her live-in boyfriend nor her male co-worker at a grocery store had shared the value she places on doing and making things independently. She refuses her boyfriend's help to pick a fruit hanging high on the tree and gets frustrated when she is not tall enough to reach it. Before she hands a homemade *bento* (lunchbox) to her co-worker, she overhears him talking with other co-workers, who say they do not appreciate handmade gifts. They prefer something readymade and mass-produced that is fancy. These incidents show her independent spirit. Therefore, her personal relationships and values mainly estrange her from living in the city. The city's name is not specified in the film; it is not the capital city of Tokyo but a city within the Tohōku region not far from Komori.

In the remake, Hye-won's experiences in the city of Seoul are mostly those commonly shared by fellow members of her generation. She has a part-time job at a convenience store and has to work many hours to make ends meet. On top of dealing with older customers looking down on her, she has no time to eat. One of the scenes shows her in her room about to consume the contents of a lunchbox, but finding their expiration date has already passed. The small refrigerator is almost empty, with some food already going bad. When she is back in her rural home, she tells her friends that she returned because she was 'hungry', literally and figuratively. Thus, her unfortunate experiences in Seoul are more due to social conditions than personal issues. Hye-won is mentally and physically exhausted, and she escapes to her hometown. As mentioned previously, she has failed the Teacher Credential exam and avoids calls from her boyfriend, who has passed it.

The depictions of rural life in the two films also differ in the protagonist's location within the village and the relationship with the neighbours. Ichiko lives alone in a secluded house in a remote forest. She is mostly by herself in the house, and the film's narrative is devoted to her cooking, eating and doing physical labour on her own. Hye-won also lives by herself, but she is often helped by her friends or her aunt, who live nearby. Her house is not as secluded as Ichiko's, and Hye-won often passes by the neighbours on her way to the downtown or the field. However, Ichiko has more positive interactions with the village community and neighbours than does Hye-won, who tries to avoid having lengthy conversations with older neighbours. They ask her about her mother, boyfriend and jobs – topics she wants to avoid. In contrast, the village elders of Komori are an inspiration for Ichiko. They play a crucial role in showing her the value of honest work and cultural heritage through their communal support and collaborations. One of the memorable scenes is when one member of the village shares his recipe for making braised chestnut, and other members follow with their own creative recipes using different spices and wines, thus making the braised chestnut a speciality food representing Komori. Braised chestnut reminds Ichiko of her most precious childhood memory about the village communal festival where she helped make the regional speciality food, the natto rice cake, with other kids.

At the film's end, Ichiko is back in Komori after five years. She had left the village again to find out where she truly belonged. She is now married with a child. She and her husband are part of Komori's traditional performance troupe. She performs and sings at the Komori communal festival, indicating that she has finally found her place within the village community. She is building a stronger community with her childhood friends by establishing a cooperative society that promotes and sells village specialities. In contrast, the Korean remake lacks such scenes of communal activity or collaboration. Instead, Hye-won's closest friends and memories of her mother help her decide to settle in the rural village.

FOOD, COOKING AND MOTHER

Both *Little Forest*s – the Japanese original and the Korean remake – are steeped in the iconography of their respective nations' culinary offerings. Ichiko's and Hye-won's rural lives consist of mainly agricultural labour and cooking (by themselves), using the ingredients they cultivated or picked in the wild. Food's crucial function in both films is strengthening the female protagonists' ties to their mothers. Both mothers were good cooks who came up with creative recipes that felt like magic to little Ichiko and Hye-won. Although Ichiko and Hye-won cook according to their own recipes, they are inspired by those handed down by their mothers. Many of the flashbacks containing their memories of their mothers are inserted in the kitchen scenes. Fathers are absent, thus accentuating the gendered space of the kitchen Ichiko and Hye-won inherit from their mothers. However, at the same time, the films challenge the traditional notion of motherhood by presenting unconventional mothers who leave their young daughters in pursuit of their dreams.

The reason for the father's absence is unclear in the Japanese film, but in the Korean remake, he died from an illness. Also, Hye-won's mother married him despite her family's strong objection, which demonstrates her independent subjectivity. Thus, the mother's influence on Hye-won's independence is more pronounced as her metaphor of the 'little forest' she will cultivate is inspired by her mother. When Hye-won comes to understand her mother's reason for leaving her, she says, 'I will find the little forest within me. Just like mom did.' Hye-won's mother had postponed her own desire to pursue a dream until her daughter graduated from high school and was ready to go to college in the city. In the Japanese manga and film, Ichiko regrets not helping her mother as she learns the hard work of farming and house chores and how difficult it is to live without a family to lend a hand. Cooking, traditionally a woman's domestic labour, binds the mother-daughter relationship; however, it is the independent spirit of the single mothers that is being succeeded by the next generation of women in both films.

However, the role of the mother in the young protagonist's 'healing' is significantly different in each film. In the original film, the circumstances of the mother's departure are not detailed. However, Hye-won's mother left her just before she graduated from high school, leaving a letter explaining why: she wanted to pursue what she had to put off while raising Hye-won. Nevertheless, Hye-won was too young to understand the letter at the time, and it becomes apparent that she has developed resentment toward her. Thus, for Hye-won, growth and healing are demonstrated by her ability to understand the meaning of the letter. In contrast, Ichiko's memories of her mother and her departure are not given such weight in her growth. She seems to accept the fact that her mother abandoned her. The reason is not given, but one of the flashback scenes alludes to the possibility that she has left to live with her lover. One of the flashback scenes shows a Caucasian man visiting them and Ichiko spending a little awkward but fun time with him. Throughout the film, Ichiko does not dwell upon the reason for her mother's departure except that she realises how difficult it must have been for her mother to do everything by herself without a family to help. (She forms her own family at the end, with whom she plans to build communal festivities in Komori).

Both Ichiko and Hye-won receive a letter from their mothers toward the end of their respective narratives. The central element in these letters is the hand-me-down recipe for the potato bread, a favourite of both Ichiko and Hye-won. When Ichiko asked for the recipe in the past, her mother replied that she would get it when she turned twenty. Hye-won's mother also informed her that she would share her secret recipe when the young woman becomes truly independent and mature enough to inherit it. The letter Ichiko receives does not include the recipe; Hye-won's does. Ichiko's recovery or 'healing' comes not from her mother's recognition of her maturity but from her labour and self-sufficient life. In contrast, for Hye-won, it is a symbolic endorsement from the mother of her maturity. At the end of the film, Hye-won is able to understand her mother by re-reading her mother's old letter. Hye-won's family had retreated to her father's hometown when he became ill. After her father's death, her mother decided to stay on so that Hye-won would always have a place to return to. Hye-won's embrace of her mother's wisdom and deep affection allows her to release her resentment finally.

This difference in the significance of the mothers' roles reflects a point of contrast between Japanese and Korean societies regarding the importance of the family in one's life. Kim Yongun, the author of the four-book series of comparative studies on Japanese and Korean societies, explains that Korean culture, traditionally, has placed greater emphasis on people's dependence on the family unit. Japanese society is based more on communal units. For example, every Japanese village has a shrine to the gods that protect residents; but in Korea, such a shrine does not exist or is reduced in significance. Instead, it is the family ancestors that each living member of that family pays tribute to in rituals. While Japanese villages have their communal festivals in the autumn, Koreans gather together in smaller family units on Chuseok ('Autumn Evening', popularly known as 'Thanksgiving'). Thus, Kim argues, Korean society reveals a commitment to blood relations and an individual's sense of belonging stems from the family rather than from more prominent communities (Kim 1994). The distinctive roles of the mothers in the films would appear to reflect these contrasting cultural traditions.

The two films differ in their food choices as well; each protagonist cooks for herself and consumes her food in her own way. Ichiko mainly works and cooks by and for herself. She has her friends come over to share the food occasionally, but only rarely. The film is documentary-like in its chronicle of the step-by-step recipes for each dish Ichiko cooks. The choice of dishes reflects the regional characteristics of the Tōhoku region, as Ichiko frequents the nearby forests to pick what nature has to offer. In the summer, she cooks pasta with tomatoes she cultivated and salsa with chrysanthemum; in the autumn, she makes rice balls with walnuts she gleaned from the forest. The film focuses on the physical work involved in cultivating and picking the ingredients. It shows the slow but healthy, self-reliant life Ichiko leads. It also includes scenes of Ichiko preparing living animals – fish and duck – for the nourishment they will provide, offering a moment of reflection on the law of nature and the human consumption of once-living creatures.

In contrast to the way that Ichiko's cooking serves as a crucial extension or facilitator of her self-sufficient life, Hye-won's food is more often shared with her friends. She also cooks with seasonal ingredients harvested from nearby fields. However, the choice of ingredients and dishes includes those that are generally popular among the young generation in Korea, such as tteokbokki (simmered spicy rice cake), pasta, crème brûlée and even makgeolli (raw rice wine). Thus, while food symbolises physical labour and the law of nature in the Japanese film, it is more about sharing in the Korean remake. For Hye-won, the dishes she prepares satisfy physical hunger and, more importantly, make it possible for her to treat a psychological void through intimate, laughter-filled conversations with friends. It is what accompanies the meals that give Hye-won self-reflection and renewed energy. While they bring to Hye-won childhood memories, including those of her mother, they also, as previously mentioned, share their experiences of the harsh realities of Korean society with Hye-won.

FRIENDSHIP AND SELF-IDENTITY

Both Ichiko and Hye-won have two close childhood friends; however, their presence is more pronounced in the Korean remake. Hye-won returns to her rural home and spends the first night on her own, but the very next morning, she is spotted by Jae-ha, who drives by her house. Not long after, she is visited by Eun-sook (Jin Ki-joo), another childhood friend. Hye-won also has an aunt who lives nearby, keeping an eye on her (Hye-won suspects her aunt is in touch with her mother).[7] Indeed, compared to Ichiko, Hye-won is rarely seen by herself, and there are many scenes in which these three friends share food, drinks, childhood memories, laughter and anxieties. These changes made in the Korean remake appear to have been motivated by commercial considerations and the urge to address an urban youth crisis in contemporary society. The friends add more drama to the narrative and make Hye-won's struggle a shared one among the young generation in South Korea.

The three friends commiserate over harrowing experiences they had in their workplaces. Jae-ha worked at a company in the city but quit the job after a humiliating treatment from his boss. With help from his father, he is now an owner of a small orchard. Eun-sook, who has never left her hometown, works as a teller at a local bank. She dreams of leaving to live in a city as she constantly complains about her boss. The friends also provide an element of romance not present in the original film. Eun-sook has a crush on Jae-ha and is teased by Hye-won; Jae-ha's ex-girlfriend visits him. The relational dynamics between the friends are similar to Yim Soon-rye's previous films; in particular, her debut feature, *Three Friends* (*Se chingu*, 1996) and the subsequent feature film *Waikiki Brothers* (*Waikiki beuradeoseu*, 2001), both of which portray the hardships the friends in the film (three high school graduates in *Three Friends* and four members of a music band in *Waikiki Brothers*) face within the Korean realities. Both films are portraits of youth that fell through the cracks in the materialist and competitive culture. While these films feature male protagonists played by relatively unknown actors, *Little Forest* is a women's story featuring popular stars Moon So-ri as the mother and Kim Tae-ri as Hye-won, with an uplifting ending. In this respect, the film is more reminiscent of Yim's 2007 film *Forever the Moment*, about Korea's women's national handball team winning a silver medal against all odds at the Olympic Games, also a commercial hit. Yim is well-known for her socially conscious depiction of the socially weak and the marginalised.

Although less prominently featured, friendship plays a significant role in Ichiko's self-reflection. In particular, Yuta (Miura Takahiro) throws her a tough question about whether she is living in Komori just as an escape and urges her to think about Komori as her permanent home actively. Like Jae-ha, Yuta had experience working in the city but is now settled in the village. He tells Ichiko that he realised how Komori residents live an honest life compared to city dwellers. He respects their hard work and has decided to follow their lifestyle. He came back from the city because he was tired of hearing shallow, empty words, and he respected and trusted people who had a way of life where they could say things with substance like the elders in Komori did. His thoughts inspire Ichiko to reflect on her life in Komori and decide to leave Komori again to find out her true home. Kikko (Mayu Matsuoka), another childhood friend of Ichiko, spends more time with the main character at her house, cooking and sharing food. At the end of the film, when Ichiko comes back to Komori for good, Yuta and Kikko are married with a child. They will work with Ichiko to build a cooperative society.

CONCLUSION

As I have shown, the two *Little Forest*s provide a rich ground for textual and contextual analysis that highlights how industrial and sociocultural factors shape the remaking process. Food and cooking are central in this story of self-sufficiency, healing and a woman's self-identity. Moreover, it is interesting to compare how similar ingredients or cooking methods produce different recipes in the two films. For example, Ichiko makes okonomiyaki with cabbage, while Hye-won makes cabbage sandwiches and cabbage rolls. Hye-won fries acacia flowers while Ichiko fries spring greens. Ichiko makes a sweet drink with rice and Hye-won raw rice wine makgeolli. Ichiko cooks hatto soup with flour dough in the winter, whereas Hye-won cooks spicy sujebi soup. Thus, in a way, the localisation in cross-cultural remakes resembles changing the proportions of certain ingredients, spices, flavours, etc. of a recipe to suit local tastes.

The promotional tagline for each film helps one to understand its production's intentions. The phrase 'To live is to take away another "life." Eat to live, make to eat', which is introduced in the Japanese film's trailer, emphasises self-sufficiency and physical labour while acknowledging that eating involves taking away another living creature's life. As Yuta says to Ichiko, 'we cannot trust words, but we can trust what our bodies feel'. This sums up the film's intended message of a self-sufficient life. The promotional discourse attached to the Korean remake (and printed on its poster), 'It is okay to take a break, to be a little different, and to be a little clumsy', clearly conveys the film's intended goal of providing a sense of comfort and healing to the young Korean audience struggling with fierce competition and social pressure to succeed.

The ending of each film also sheds light on the ways that specific sociocultural contexts affect the process of localisation. The Japanese *Little Forest* ends with a clear sense of resolution. Ichiko has finally found her sense of belonging and self-identity in the communal setting of Komori. She is 'healed' by opening herself to village traditions. Conversely, the Korean remake has a more open-ended, nonconclusive ending. After reconciling with her past, Hye-won leaves for the city again to prepare for a permanent return. The film ends with a scene similar to the beginning of the film, when Hye-won returns and enters the gate of her rural home. Her first return was on a cold winter day, but this time, it is a bright, sunny spring day; her steps are light. Upon arriving, she sees an open door in the house and her face beams with a smile, captured in a freeze frame. Has her mother returned home as well? Like Ichiko, Hye-won has decided to settle in her rural hometown, but how she will live there is not presented as concretely as the ending to Ichiko's story. It is enough to show her self-confidence in facing an uncertain future.

NOTES

1. In her interview with *Kookmin Ilbo*, Yim states, 'I had a hard time making the film in Korean style because the Japaneseness was so strong [in the original film]'. 'Rit'eul p'oreseut'eu' Imsullye kamdok "tangsinkke wiroga toeotkil', (*Little Forest* director Yim

Soon-rye, 'I hope the film gave you comfort'), *Kookmin Ilbo*, 2 March 2018. http://m. kmib.co.kr/view.asp?arcid=0923909882 [accessed 30 April 2022].
2. The twenty-second print of the first edition was published in 2020.
3. The first 'official' Korean remake of a Japanese film was Chang Kil-su's *Paradise Lost* (*Shilrakwon*, 1998), based on Morita Yoshimitsu's *Lost Paradise* (*Shitsurakuen*, 1997). However, it was not until 2016 that a steady production of Japanese film remakes began, with the success of such films as *Luck-Key* (*Leokki*, 2016).
4. The average budget for Korean commercial films is approximately five million USD. *Little Forest* broke even in just two weeks.
5. Reviews by bloggers Anunsaram <https://m.blog.naver.com/PostView.naver?isHttpsRedirect=true&blogId=wjdals5657&logNo=220588436319>, toki <https://m.blog.naver.com/toki_s/220487776909> and Daily Life Record <https://min7zz.tistory.com/439> are some examples, all written in 2015 [accessed 3 April 2022].
6. According to a survey conducted by South Korea's Ministry of Agriculture, Food and Rural Affairs, out of 2,507 households which returned to farming between 2013 and 2017, 53 per cent were born in rural towns, lived in urban cities and then decided to return to their hometown. 'Kwinong.kwich'on, yŏn'go itkŏna nongch'on ch'ulshin tudŭrŏjyŏ' ('Return to Rural Town Prominent among People with Rural Background'). *The Hankyoreh*, 11 March 2019. https://m.hani.co.kr/arti/area/area_general/885374. html#cb. Accessed 1 May 2022.
7. According to director Yim Soon-rye, these changes are related to the security concern that a young woman living by herself in a rural house would not sit well with Korean audiences. It is also the reason for Jaeha giving Hye-won a dog, whereas Ichiko has a cat, an iconic animal in Japanese culture.

REFERENCES

Ch'ae, Gyŏnghun. 2019. 'Ilboneui yeonghwa saneopkwa tongnibyeonghwa saengtaegye.' ('Japanese Film Industry and Independent Film Ecosystem.') *Ashiayeonghwayeon'gu (Asian Cinema Studies)* 12, no. 2: 265–96.
Hankyoreh, The, 'Kwinong kwichon, yeongo itkeona nongchon chulsin tudeureojyeo.' ('Return to Rural Town Prominent among People with Rural Background.') https://m. hani.co.kr/arti/area/area_general/885374.html#cb. Accessed 1 May 2022.
Hiam, Michael C., Paul D. Berger and Goli Eshghi. 2017–2018. 'Japan's Millennials: The Minimalist Consumer of the Yutori/Satori Generation.' *UBIT* 11, no. 1: 4–8.
Igarashi, Diasuke. 2009. *Riteul Porenneuteu* 1&2 (*Little Forest* 1&2). Translated by Kim Hee-jung. Seoul: Semicolon.
Jung, Wook-sung. 2014. 'Hilling chihyangjuŭi ilbon yŏnghwa.' *Journal of Japanese Language and Literature*, no. 64: 437–52.
Kawanishi, Hidemichi. 2006. *Tohōku: Japan's Constructed Outland*. Translated by Nanyan Guo and Raquel Hill. Boston: Brill.
Kim, Yongun. 1994. *Han'gugin'gwa ilbonin* (*Korean and Japanese*), vol. 1. Seoul: Hangilsa.
Kkachirhanshisŏn. 2019. 'Riteul poreseuteu ilbonpan lyom hangukpan.' (*Little Forest*, Japanese version vs. Korean version.) *Tstory*, 6 February. https://onion02.tistory.com/1454. Accessed 2 May 2022.
Kookmin. Ilbo. 2018. '[And t'eurendeu] "keurae, ige haengbogiji" sohwakhaenge wirobanneun 2030.' ([And Trend] 'Yes, this is happiness', 20s and 30s are comforted by sohwakhaeng), 30 March. http://news.kmib.co.kr/article/view.asp?arcid=0923925245. Accessed 2 May 2022.

Korea Lecturer News. 2020. 'Seoulsigyoyukch'eong, 2021 chungdeung imyonggosi kyeongjaengnyul teung eungsiweonseo cheopsu kyeolgwa palp'yo.' ('Seoul Metropolitan Office of Education announces the results of 2021 teacher credential exam applications including competition rate.' 29 October. http://www.lecturernews.com/news/articleView.html?idxno=54569. Accessed 2 May 2022.

Mazdon, Lucy. 2000. *Encore Hollywood: Remaking French Cinema*. London: British Film Institute.

Mori, Junichi. 2015. '[in-t'eo-pyu]to-si nam-cha-ka tchik-eun cha-keup-cha-chok la-i-p'eu.' ('[Interview] Self-Sufficient Life Shot by an Urban Man.') *JoongAng Ilbo*, 27 May. https://www.joongang.co.kr/article/17888847#home. Accessed 1 April 2022.

Verevis, Constantine. 2006. *Film Remakes*. Edinburgh: Edinburgh University Press.

Yim, Soon-rye. 2018. 'On the Remake of *Little Forest*.', Director's Masterclass at the Cinema Camp in Busan: Transcultural Student Networking, Im Kwon Taek College of Film and Media Arts, Dongseo University, 8 October.

CHAPTER 13

More than Blue and *Man in Love*: Transnational Korean-Taiwanese Film Remakes as a Facilitator for Taiwan Cinema

Ting-Ying Lin

Taiwan cinema, which remains widely acclaimed for its new wave (that is, the Taiwan New Cinema of the 1980s and the 1990s), has experienced a transition from arthouse sensibilities to popular tastes over the last two decades. Taiwan New Cinema – in particular, the work of internationally recognised auteurs such as Hou Hsiao-hsien, Edward Yang, Ang Lee and Tsai Ming-liang – has achieved tremendous success in global film festival circuits, though the milestones of that movement were not always welcomed by local audiences and failed to make a strong domestic box-office showing, a factor that partially explains the industrial downturn of the 1990s and the early 2000s. In contrast to that critically lauded yet financially underperforming output of previous generations, the most recent trend in Taiwan cinema – sparked by the commercial success of the locally produced crowd-pleaser *Cape No. 7* (*Hái-kak chhit-ho*, 2008) and sometimes referred to as the Post-New Wave – represents an industrial revival and a renewed interest in domestic productions among local moviegoers. The filmmakers associated with this Post-New Wave have also embarked on a potentially profitable journey of genre film production, offering spectators a steady line-up of several different types of narrative-based entertainment, including comedies, historical epics, romance and teen-romance films, horror films, thrillers and crime dramas (or triad films).

Despite the fact that this genre-focused trend marks the recent rise of Taiwan popular cinema, locally produced films have faced competition from other countries' imports, including Japanese anime and South Korean blockbusters, which have attracted local audiences. South Korean films in particular have demonstrated a capacity for broad appeal in various Asian countries and regions, as part of the Korean Wave or *Hallyu* phenomenon of the past two decades (Khoo 2021, 41). In fact, Korean popular culture was first introduced to Taiwan in a significantly large way beginning in the late 1990s, and it reached its peak in popularity around the time of the 2003 historical television drama *Jewel in the Palace* (*Dae Jang Geum*)'s airing in 2005 (Sung 2010; Huang 2018). In the years that followed, Korean popular culture has continued to exert trend-setting influence through the transnational dissemination of television dramas, pop music, idols, stars, fashions and consumer goods in Taiwan, and this phenomenon helps to shed light on the uneven, asymmetrical power relations of intra-Asian cultural flows (Iwabuchi 2008, 159–60). Yet, it should be noted that even though *Hallyu* has been a dominant force in Taiwan for more than a decade, Korean films did not begin occupying large parts of the country's domestic film market until 2016, around the time that director Kang Hyo-jin's *Wonderful Nightmare* (*Misseu waipeu*; literally 'Miss Wife'; 2015), a film perhaps inspired by another Korean hit, *Miss Granny* (*Susanghan geunyeo*, 2014), was released and subsequently remade as *Beautiful Accident* (*Mei hao de yi wai*, 2017). As a supernatural 'body-swap comedy' about a career-driven woman who is forced to take the place of a recently deceased mother, that latter film, directed by the Malaysia-born Taiwanese filmmaker Ho Wi-ding, gestures toward the idea of cross-cultural remaking as a means of substituting one set of bodies for another, a highly suggestive act of 'replacement' that makes this particular mode of commercially viable wish-fulfilment all the more relevant socially and politically.

With the transnational dissemination of the Korean Wave in Taiwan, genre productions such as *Train to Busan* (*Busanhaeng*, 2016) and *Along with the Gods: The Two Worlds* (*Singwa hamkke: Joewa beol*, 2017) have drawn local audiences to theatres in droves and soaked up a large proportion of the Taiwanese film market. To be more specific, *Train to Busan* and its sequel *Train to Busan Presents: Peninsula* (*Bando*, 2020) gained 376 million NT dollars (approximately $12.5 million in US currency) (Taiwan Film Institute 2017, 48) and 356 million NT dollars (approximately $11.9 million), respectively in Taiwan's film market (Taiwan Film and Audiovisual Institute 2020a). Meanwhile, *Along with the Gods: The Two Worlds* performed even better, raking in 513 million NT dollars (approximately $17.1 million) (Taiwan Film Institute 2019a, 88) and its sequel *Along with the Gods: The Last 49 Days* (*Singwa hamkke: Ingwa yeon*, 2018) doing nearly as well with 479 million NT dollars (approximately $15.9 million) (Taiwan Film Institute 2019a, 88) in box-office ticket sales in Taiwan. The Oscar-winning, Palme d'Or sensation *Parasite* (*Gisaengchung*, 2019), written and directed by Bong Joon-ho, also performed well in Taiwan, earning 151 million NT dollars (approximately $5 million) (Taiwan Film and Audiovisual Institute 2020b, 71).

Considering the box-office performance of Taiwan's locally produced films, in general a motion picture would be considered a blockbuster if it earns over 100 million NT dollars in the domestic market (approximately $3.3 million). In comparison with the overall box-office performance of Taiwanese blockbusters of recent years, the abovementioned Korean blockbusters far outperformed locally produced works in Taiwan's film market on average. Accordingly, Korean cinema presents something of a challenge or obstacle to Taiwan cinema, which has just experienced an industrial transition to genre film production. However, one could argue that Korean cinema not only plays the part of competitor but also that of facilitator for Taiwan cinema. Focusing on two Taiwanese remakes of Korean films – *More than Blue* (*Bi beishang geng beishang de gushi*, 2018) and *Man in Love* (*Dang nanren lianai shi*, 2021) – as case studies, this chapter explores how the cinema of Taiwan has gotten an industrial boost from earlier Korean productions. Moreover, I adopt a sociocultural perspective to explain how Taiwan's popular culture has been shaped and disseminated through these two remakes as a form of counter-flow within the context of *Hallyu*'s dominance in Taiwan and other Asian countries.

As mentioned above, contemporary Taiwan cinema has been experiencing a transitional period from the previous auteur-centred cinema to genre-focused productions. During the transition, lack of genre filmmaking experience and integrated industrial expertise has been looked upon as being problematic by local film industry practitioners. To be specific, Wei Te-sheng, considered by many to be one of the leading filmmakers of the Post-New Wave cinema who is best known for directing the blockbuster films *Cape No. 7* and *Warriors of the Rainbow: Seediq Bale* (*Saideke balai*, 2011), recently pointed out that, before the rise of Taiwan popular cinema, his nation's motion picture industry had not been 'mature and robust' enough to handle the production of genre films, and that it was necessary to turn to 'transnational cooperation in film production' in order to improve the state of the industry (Lin 2019, 201). As if following his lead, Taiwanese filmmakers have begun to seek opportunities for working with transnational teams, while soaking up the expertise of international filmmaking talents. Furthermore, as Ye Ru-fen, one of the leading producers in Taiwan's Post-New Wave film industry, indicates, given the rapid development of action-driven genre film productions in South Korea, the Korean experience in special effects and filmmaking technology is far ahead of Taiwan's film industry. In view of this, the filmmaking teams on Wei Te-sheng's *Seediq Bale* as well as on Noze Niu's *Monga* (*Báng-kah*, 2010) have learned special effects techniques and action staging know-how from South Korean teams. Noticeably, Ye further asserts that the exchanges of filmmaking expertise between Taiwan and South Korea can broaden the horizons of Taiwanese filmmakers (Wang 2013).

On the other hand, during the recent industrial transition to and rise of Taiwan popular cinema, government officials and local production companies also played pivotal roles in facilitating international cooperation and transnational filmmaking. In particular, attention to the need for talent in creating original content and scriptwriting has also been raised. Taiwan Creative Content

Agency (TAICCA), established in 2019 by Taiwan's Ministry of Culture, is a governmental organisation that aims to promote the country's original content and cultural industries. TAICCA also provides national funds to support local creative sectors, develop potential intellectual property (IP) and encourage international film co-productions (TAICCA 2022). However, support from the government still could not meet the domestic demand for original content and good quality scripts in the film industry. As a result, in addition to the top-down strategies provided by the governmental sectors, Taiwan's local production companies have also embarked on international cooperation and have sought South Korean original content and film scripts due to the popularity of motion pictures such as *Veteran* (*Beterang*, 2015) and *Forgotten* (*Gieokui bam*, 2017) in Taiwan. In other words, regarding the aforementioned industrialisation process of Taiwan cinema, which calls out for more talent specialising in scriptwriting and IP development, filmmakers have turned to South Korean original content.

Let us take a look, then, at how Taiwanese filmmakers employ and remake South Korean original content to facilitate their own local film culture, as demonstrated in the cases of the two remakes alluded to earlier: *More than Blue* and *Man in Love*. This chapter compares and contrasts the Korean original and the Taiwanese remake, while examining how these two Taiwanese remakes localise the previously produced films' content as a means of gaining popularity among audiences. Furthermore, this chapter argues that Korean-Taiwanese film remakes can function as transnational cultural flows, which are multilateral and multidirectional in their intra-Asian and even global contexts.

Drawing on Joseph S. Nye Jr's useful notion of 'soft power', which 'identified key resources as culture, political values, and foreign policies' (Nye 2004) in contrast to national 'hard powers' demonstrated in the economic and military forces, Song Hwee Lim proposes a framework that sees Taiwan cinema as a form of soft power (Lim 2013; Lim 2022: 2). Using Taiwan New Cinema and the recent Post-New Wave stage as examples, Lim focuses on three key ideas – authorship, transnationality and historiography – to foreground their triangulated relationship embedded in Taiwan cinema, which provides 'a case of a small nation with enormous soft power' potential (Lim 2022, 3). Moreover, Lim also emphasises that, as soft power 'operates on the level of the transnational', Taiwan cinema has to be examined in a way that goes 'beyond a national cinema framework' (Ibid., 2). Building upon Lim's concept, this chapter further argues that the localisation strategies of the two aforementioned Taiwanese film remakes function as a necessary cultural mechanism, wherein two forms of Taiwan's popular culture can be articulated and circulated as soft power – that is, the 'little freshness' imaginary constructed in *More than Blue* and the *Taike* culture reconfigured in *Man in Love* (which will be elaborated on later). More importantly, this chapter posits that with the regional (and global) spread of Korean original content and the localisation strategies that are part of the remaking process, the two cinematic remakes can facilitate Taiwan cinema by reshaping its brand, while also acting as vehicles of Taiwan's soft power in relation to its cultural-political (re)positioning vis-à-vis other East and Southeast Asian countries and eventually worldwide in accordance with twenty-first century geopolitical power dynamics.

MORE THAN BLUE: CROSS-REGIONAL AND TRANSCULTURAL FLOWS

More than Blue, directed by Gavin Lin (Lin Hsiao-chien), is a Taiwanese film based on a Korean romance of the same title (*Seulpeumboda deoseulpeun iyagi*, 2009). Produced by the leading Singapore media and content company mm2 Entertainment and Taiwan's local production company Good Movie Co., the Taiwanese version of *More than Blue* is aimed at both inter-Asian as well as global film markets. Regarding box-office performance, the film was first released in November 2018, gaining over 240 million NT dollars (approximately $8 million) (Taiwan Film Institute 2019b). Moreover, the Taiwanese remake not only gained blockbuster status in Taiwan, Hong Kong and China, but it was also released in Malaysia, Singapore, South Korea, United States, Canada, Australia and New Zealand, achieving a box-office record of nearly 143 million US dollars worldwide (Box Office Mojo 2018). As Steven Rawle points out, transnational circuits of film remakes 'problematize how capital and culture move across and between boundaries and how audiences consume products of culture' (2015, 101). On the one hand, the Taiwanese remake of *More than Blue* demonstrates one of the fundamental features of transnational film remakes as capitalist commodities, which can be seen in its cross-regional and international distribution and consumption alongside its massive box-office success. On the other hand, this particular case of a Taiwanese remake also sheds light on the multidirectional and multilateral flows not only of transnational capital but also of cross-regional cultures. Korean original content has played a pivotal role in the film remaking process, facilitating developments in Taiwanese cinema and enabling the latter to build its brand as a form of Taiwan's globally distributed soft power.

The original Korean romance drama tells the story of a young man, K (Kwon Sang-woo), who suffers from cancer and knows that he is about to die. He has lived with his beloved lady friend Cream (Lee Bo-young) since high school, because both of their families have left them – K's mother departed after his father died, and Cream's family died in a car accident. Even though the lonely couple loves one other, and they can each depend on their partner to the exclusion of nearly everyone else, K does not dare let Cream know about his illness, since he is afraid that she cannot live without him. Thus, K secretly arranges to find a good man who can marry and take care of Cream. One day, Cream meets a dentist, Joo-hwan (Lee Beom-soo), whose fiancée Jenna (Jung Ae-yeon) is a photographer; K knows about this and subsequently persuades the female photographer to break up with the dentist so that the latter might be compelled to marry his beloved lady. K successfully makes a deal with the photographer, on the condition that he needs to be photographed by her as the subject of her latest exhibition. As K wishes, Cream finally marries the dentist before K dies. However, without her best friend in her life, Cream cannot live long, and she also dies near the end of the film.

Compared with the Korean original, the Taiwanese remake of *More Than Blue* generally follows a similar narrative pattern and even features elements of the earlier film's mise-en-scène and the use of specific camera angles. Yet, the remake is rewritten to include more localised cultural elements in its appeal to Taiwanese audiences. For example, at the beginning of the original film, the story starts with a Korean male singer (Lee Seung-cheol) and his manager (Kim Jeong-seok) discovering a touching song written by K. They are curious about who the composer is and intend to use this song in the album. Subsequently, they meet a friend, Min-cheol (Shin Hyun-tak), in a café, who tells them the story of K and Cream. Notably, in the Taiwanese remake, the renowned female vocalist, A-lin (born Lisang Pacidal Koyouan), who is of Amis descent, plays the role of the singer. Moreover, the filmmaking team composed an original song, 'A Kind of Sorrow', specifically for this localised version, and director Lin himself wrote the lyrics for that number (performed by A-lin and the male lead Jasper Liu). Consequently, the localisation process of composing the original soundtrack was successful, resulting in more than eighty-four million views on YouTube and indicating its effectiveness as a film marketing strategy.

Figure 13.1 A well-known vocalist of Amis descent, A-lin (born Lisang Pacidal Koyouan), plays a singer in *More than Blue* (*Bi beishang geng beishang de gushi*, 2018), director Gavin Lin's Taiwanese remake of a South Korean film of the same title.

In comparison with a relatively minor character named Cat Girl (Nam Gyu-ri) in the Korean version, the Taiwanese Cat Girl Bonnie (Emma Wu) is imbued with greater importance in the remake, where she plays the role of the female protagonist Cream's close friend. The filmmaking team of the Taiwanese remake also wrote specific lines for Bonnie and chose to include nonsensical buzzwords from unique Taiwanese subcultures from recent times, such as 'dumbfounded cat' (*shayan maomi*) and 'scary to eat hands' (*xiadao chishoushou*). Such localisation enables the Taiwanese version to be more suitable for the local audience, while also creating more comedic effects within a narrative that embraces humour as a counterbalance to the story's underlying tragic elements. Moreover, it is interesting to note that these expressions are not only popular among the local audience but also widely used online in other Chinese-speaking countries and regions within East and Southeast Asia. Accordingly, the use of localised buzzwords can be regarded as a transnational marketing strategy targeting both domestic moviegoers as well as Chinese-speaking audiences in Asia and across the globe.

Furthermore, as Robert Ru-shou Chen explains, Taiwan cinema in the twenty-first century has been moving away from the sadness associated with the Taiwan New Cinema, which frequently touched upon the country's historical traumas. As such, today's local cinematic output seems far less 'tragic' than those national metanarratives of the recent past (Chen 2013, 10). This transition of Taiwan cinema is exemplified by the youth romance films that emerged around the beginning of the new millennium, such as Yi Chih-yen's *Blue Gate Crossing* (*Lanse damen*, 2002), Leste Chen's *Eternal Summer* (*Shengxia guangnian*, 2006) and Jay Chou's *Secret* (*Bunengshuo de mimi*, 2007). Subsequently, in the wake of the rise of Taiwan popular cinema, or this recent stage of Post-New Wave Taiwan Cinema, filmmakers have increasingly engaged in telling stories about teenagers and youth romance. Narratives about the pure love between young couples, abetted by the genre-focused directorial styles of the new generation Taiwanese filmmakers, have attracted local spectators, in contrast to the auteur-centred, arthouse stylings of previous generations. For example, in addition to Wei Te-sheng's *Cape No. 7*, Lin Shu-yu's *Winds of September* (*Jiu jiang feng*, 2008) played a significant role in the revival of the Taiwanese domestic film market. Giddens Ko's *You Are the Apple of My Eye* (*Naxienian women yiqi zhuide nühai*, 2011) and Chen Yu-Shan's *Our Times* (*Wode shaonü shidai*, 2015) have been extremely popular in Taiwan, and even performed strongly in the film markets of Hong Kong, China, Singapore and Malaysia (Lin 2019, 201). These Taiwanese youth-romance films have marked the cross-regional dissemination of Taiwan's popular culture through transnational film distribution and consumption in connection with the popularity of Taiwanese idol dramas and pop music in other East and Southeast Asian countries and regions in the last two decades.

As mentioned above, Song Hwee Lim's framework sees Taiwan's local filmic production as a form of transcultural and cross-regional soft power (2013). Drawing on Raymond Williams' concept of a 'structure of feeling' (Williams 1977), Lim further proposes an affect structure called 'little freshness' that 'describe[s] a range of cultural products and phenomena that mostly emanates from Taiwan that has captured the imagination of youths in China and Hong Kong' (2022, 122). As he posits, the imaginary of little freshness 'embodies an affective trait shared across the Taiwan Strait by youths whose engagement with a market of miniaturization as cultural producers and consumers is inflected by a sense of generational injustice in the face of neoliberal capitalism'. For Lim, the recent Post-New Wave stage of Taiwan cinema can be seen as a form of soft power activated by the specific cultural imaginary of little freshness represented by the cross-regional success of the aforementioned Taiwanese youth-romance films, including *Cape No. 7* and *You Are the Apple of My Eye* (Ibid., 122, 129). Furthermore, Lim also points out that this 'little freshness' has been shaped by indie music stars and their music videos, and especially by the image of Taiwanese female singer and songwriter Cheer Chen (Chen Qizhen) on the online media of the PRC (Ibid., 127). Chen embodies a perfect incarnation of the talented, clean and clever woman with a bright and positive image. In a sense, the optimistic image of little freshness stars can function well with bright and clean scenes or other visual elements mentioned by Lim such as 'blue skies, white clouds and green fields' alongside the 'school uniforms' and 'summertime settings' in the aforementioned films (Ibid., 128).

It should be noted that the Taiwanese remake of *More Than Blue* fits the categories of the Taiwanese youth-romance and the little freshness films discussed above. Considering the filmmakers' strategies in the aforementioned productions, in addition to the visual elements, costumes and settings, the use of Taiwanese young stars with bright, clean and positive images such as Lun-mei Gui and Bo-lin Chen (both from *Blue Gate Crossing*), as well as Kai Ko and Michelle Chen (both from *You Are the Apple of My Eye*), play a role in shaping the imaginary of little freshness. It should be noted that the new generation of young actors and actresses has been active in both cinema and television dramas, while also being popular not only in Taiwan but in other East and Southeast Asian countries and regions. Accordingly, the presence of the stars Ivy Yi-han Chen and Jasper Liu as the protagonists in the Taiwanese remake of *More Than Blue* can also enhance the imaginary of little freshness and enable the film to gain more popularity among a diverse cross-section of regional audiences. Hence, building upon the established framework of cinema as a form of soft power, we can see that the wave of little freshness prompted by Taiwan popular films (youth-romance films in particular) can function as a sign of Taiwan's cross-regional and transcultural spread (Lim 2022). Notably, filmmaker Gavin Lin effectively employs South Korean original content as a

Figure 13.2 Stars Ivy Yi-han Chen and Jasper Liu bring a 'little freshness' to this Taiwanese version (*Bi beishang geng beishang de gushi*, 2018) of the South Korean romantic drama *More Than Blue* (*Seulpeumboda deoseulpeun iyagi*, 2009).

facilitator while using the stars that have shaped the imaginary of little freshness as a strategy in the case of the transnational Korean-Taiwanese remake of *More Than Blue*. This can enable Taiwan cinema to construct a new image in the twenty-first century while foregrounding the dissemination of the country's popular culture through the transnational cinematic remake as both intra-Asian and global cultural flows.

LOCALISATION STRATEGIES AND THE *TAIKE* CULTURE IN *MAN IN LOVE*

Man in Love, released in 2021, presents another opportunity to explore the transnational entanglements of South Korean and Taiwanese cinemas. Directed by new-generation Taiwanese filmmaker Yin Chen-hao, this film is adapted from the romantic drama *Man in Love* (*Namjaga saranghal ddae*), released in South Korea in 2014. As a success in its home country's domestic market, the original film generated the equivalent of $13.1 million in revenue (Box office Mojo 2014). The Taiwanese remake is as popular as the original, but it also is acclaimed for its representations of authentic *Taike* culture as well as its visual style and aesthetic sophistication. It should be noted that in 2021, although the overall box-office performance was affected by the COVID-19 pandemic worldwide, the Taiwanese remake of *Man in Love* was still a hit and performed very well in Taiwan's domestic film market, earning 405 million NT dollars (approximately $13.5 million) (Taiwan Film and Audiovisual Institute 2021). This film is ranked sixth among the top ten local blockbusters in the history of Taiwan cinema within the last ten years, placed just after the two aforementioned youth-romance hits *You Are the Apple of My Eye* and *Our Times* (Hsiao 2021).

The original Korean version of *Man in Love* narrates a love story between a gang member named Tae-il (Hwang Jung-min) and a bank worker named Ho-jung (Han Hye-jin). The film begins by showing the male protagonist earning his keep in the gang as a debt collector. An early sequence shows Tae-il adopting a fierce attitude toward debtors, whom he forces to pay back loans. At the same time, he is personally considerate to these debtors and secretly helps them solve their financial problems in scenes that show his helpful, generous personality. One day, in a hospital he meets a beautiful young woman, who is the daughter of one of the debtors. The protagonist immediately falls in love with her, while starting to help her take care of her father, and eventually asks her out on a date in exchange for the debt payment. Subsequently, when the lady's father dies because of illness, the protagonist even helps her arrange the funeral, tugging at her heart in the process. Unfortunately, when they promise to live together, the protagonist loses all their money in an incident, and he finds out that he is suffering from cancer and will not live much longer. He is subsequently sent to jail and then released for treatment, and he finally returns to the arms of his beloved partner before he dies. In general, the Taiwanese remake of *Man in Love* follows the narrative developments of the Korean original, with minor alterations in the plot, characterisations and settings.

As Steven Rawle points out, cinematic remaking can be thought of as a 'process of localisation, part of a global strategy of appropriating cultural material, alongside translation, such as dubbing and subtitling, including producing local frames of reference of cultural signifiers, names, products, texts, or the wholesale reproduction of narratives, characters or culturally specific codes of identity, such as gender, sexuality, ethnicity and race' (2018, 180). In terms of the localisation strategies specific to *Man in Love*, the emerging director Yin Chen-hao plays a prominent role in undertaking a transnational, cross-cultural film remake and shaping Taiwanese *Taike* culture on screen. In post-war Taiwan, the term *Taike* was originally perceived as 'a pejorative term used by Mainlander Chinese to disparage *Holo* (or *Minnan*) Taiwanese who behaved, spoke, dressed, or otherwise bore the unsophisticated mannerisms of the Taiwanese countryside' (Ho 2009, 566). With Taiwan's ongoing process of democratisation and localisation over the past thirty years, the term *Taike* has no longer been used to demonstrate a social hierarchy between Mainlanders and local Taiwanese. Rather, it has been gradually appropriated by nativists to refer to grassroots Taiwanese culture and local identity. Subsequently, the *Taike* nomenclature has been associated with Taiwanese popular culture and came into a kind of heyday in 2005 'with heated media discussions and a proliferation of cultural products', including *Taike* rock music, films, performances and other various forms of artistic productions (Zemanek 2017).

Before making his cinematic debut with *Man in Love*, director Yin Chen-hao attracted attention for the unique narrative and visual styles of his music video series, a collaboration with Taiwanese language (*Taiyu*) rock band EggPlantEgg (*Qie zi dan*). Yin has produced three music videos for EggPlantEgg, and that output has been tremendously successful and popular, attracting more than a hundred million views on YouTube. The three videos are grouped together as a series under the 'Trilogy of *Langzi* (A Loafer)' banner, which includes *Langzi huitou* (*Return of the Loafer*, 2017), *Langliulian* (*The Loafer Goes Wild*, 2018) and *Zhekuan zizuoduoqing* (*This Kind of Unrequited Affection*, 2019). Notably, Yin Chen-hao's *Langzi* music video series is considered by local critics to represent an authentic manifestation of *Taike* culture through the presentation of touching stories about Taiwanese gangster layabouts and their affection for loved ones with the use of *Taike* costumes, styles and aesthetics.

In the Taiwanese remake of *Man in Love*, Yin continues to use his signature visual style to construct *Taike* culture on screen. First, considering the costume design, the protagonist A-cheng (Roy Chiu) wears stylish patterned shirts, suits and hairstyle as a typical Taiwanese gangster, while speaking authentic Taiwanese language (*Taiyu*) and biting a sugar cane rudely, with gusto, as a *Taike* – a figure far removed from the protagonist of the Korean original, a fairly typical gangster who wears a plain white shirt and suit trousers. Second, in the Taiwanese remake, audiences can see the subculture of Taiwanese youth in the scene where the protagonist A-cheng is singing a song for his beloved lady Hao-ting (Ann Hsu) in the bowling alley, which is also an alteration from the Korean one. Intriguingly, the director Yin Chen-hao asks the protagonist to sing like a rock star in a music video, combining the *Taike* recreational culture of karaoke and bowling games in Taiwan's localised context.

Figure 13.3 In this early scene of *Man in Love* (*Dang nanren lianai shi*, 2021), A-cheng (Roy Chiu) appears dressed like a typical Taiwanese gangster and speaks Taiyu, putting a decidedly 'local' spin on the Korean-language original of the same title.

Localisation can be further seen in the alteration of the plots in relation to the career ambitions and life goals of the protagonist couple: the female protagonist Ho-jung aims to open up a fried chicken store with her lover Tae-il in the Korean version, whereas the Taiwanese couple A-cheng and Hao-ting intends to open up a bubble tea shop in the Taiwanese remake – noticeably, this can be seen as a cross-cultural film remaking process by altering the cultural code from Korean fried chicken to Taiwanese bubble tea, both as the signifiers to the respective grassroots cultures. In doing so, from costumes, set designs to plots, director Yin employs abundant codes and references to Taiwanese grassroots cultures to forge *Taike* representations on screen, while also utilising this as an effective marketing strategy to gain more support from the domestic audience.

It should be noted that in the Taiwanese remake of *Man in Love*, most of the characters speak Taiwanese language (*Taiyu*). Furthermore, 'Siánn-khuán' ('what's up' in *Taiyu*), as one of the renowned lines created for the protagonist A-cheng in the Taiwanese version, has become a trendy slogan that is very popular among the younger generation. It has also created a new wave of *Taike* popular culture in connection with *Taiyu* rock music by the aforementioned *Taiyu* rock band EggPlantEgg. Considering cultural politics, Taiwanese *Taike* culture has been no longer despised and degraded by the Chinese Nationalists as in post-war Taiwan. Yet, it has become a trendy phenomenon and a significant vehicle of shaping collective memory and local identity in the wake of Taiwan's ongoing localisation process. Hence, regarding the localisation strategy in the cinematic remake process, with the benefit of South Korean original content, the Taiwanese remake of *Man in Love* effectively encompasses *Taiyu* popular music, *Taike* culture, styles and aesthetics, thereby acquiring popularity among the domestic audience, with tremendous success in its box-office performance, sustaining the Taiwan film industry during the pandemic era. This film has also opened up a possibility of contemporary *Taiyu* popular cinema for Taiwanese filmmakers in the process of Taiwan cinema's industrial transition, while bringing about the revival of *Taike* popular culture through film production, distribution and consumption.

CONCLUSION

Beyond the commercial success of the Taiwanese remake of *More Than Blue* in the global film market, alongside the excellent performance of the Taiwanese remake of *Man in Love* at the domestic box office, these two transnational works have also achieved popularity through their distribution and circulation on international streaming platforms. Noticeably, Olivia Khoo draws attention to the current changing media landscapes worldwide and addresses the significance of the new circuits of film distribution and exhibition of Asian cinema – that is, online streaming platforms (2021, 57). As Khoo posits, sites such as Netflix and Amazon Prime 'have significantly increased their catalogue of Asian films', and these 'alternative circuits of distribution respond to and in turn precipitate different audience consumption practices (including downloading and streaming) as filmmakers continue to seek ways of making films that will cross national markets' (2021, 58).

Regarding the popularity of the 2018 Taiwanese remake of *More Than Blue* in the international theatrical releases and on global streaming platforms, in 2021 Netflix launched a new television series version of *More Than Blue: The Series* (2021). Directed by the emerging Taiwanese director Hsieh Pei-ju and produced by Gavin Lin, the director of the Taiwanese film remake of *More Than Blue*, the television series adapts the 2018 Taiwanese cinematic remake, and is currently being distributed to more than 190 countries and regions worldwide exclusively on Netflix. In general, the narrative structure of the episodic drama primarily follows the storyline of the Taiwanese film remake, while the spectators can see more character details and elements of the plot added and altered in the television series version. For example, two new characters – the music producer Wang Po-han (Wang Po-chieh) and his assistant An Yi-chi (Shao Yu-wei) – become the main narrators who regale viewers in the love story between the protagonist couple Chang Che-kai (or K, played by Fandy Fan) and Sung Yuan-yuan (or Cream, played by Gingle Wang). Significantly, in the case of the intermedial adaptation of *More Than Blue* from the Korean-Taiwanese film remake to the Taiwanese television series, the global streaming platform has provided both financial support for the production as well as an alternative channel for Taiwan cinema and its related series to be distributed, exhibited and circulated globally.

To sum up, using two case studies, this chapter argues that with the dissemination of the Korean Wave (*Hallyu*) in Taiwan, Korean films can function not only as one of the competitors to Taiwan's locally produced films, but also as a facilitator for the development of Taiwan cinema both domestically and globally via the transnational and cross-cultural remakes. The two remakes discussed in this chapter have created a surge of interest in Taiwanese films as both transnational capital and cross-regional cultures, as seen in the case of *More than Blue*, while also reinforcing Taiwan's film industry with larger support from the domestic audience by the localised film production strategies deployed in *Man in Love*. In the cases of these two transnational film remakes, localisation strategies articulate two forms of Taiwan's popular culture: the affect of little freshness through the youth-romance film, as well as the configuration of the *Taike* culture through *Taiyu* popular music and *Taike* aesthetics. More importantly, despite the fact that the popularity of the Korean Wave in Taiwan hints at uneven and asymmetrical intra-Asian cultural flows, with the benefit from South Korean creative content, Taiwan cinema can reshape its brand through the success of these two transnational Korean-Taiwanese film remakes as an output of Taiwan's soft power, which has led to multidirectional cultural flows to other East and Southeast Asian countries and regions, and even worldwide.

REFERENCES

Box Office Mojo. 2014. '*Man in Love* (2014).' IMDbPro Website. https://www.boxofficemojo.com/release/rl4077683969/weekend/. Accessed 12 Feb 2022.

Box Office Mojo. 2018. '*More Than Blue* (2018).' IMDbPro Website. https://www.boxofficemojo.com/title/tt9081562/. Accessed 12 Feb 2022.

Chen, Ru-shou Robert. 2013. 'Walking Out of Sadness: The Other Side of Taiwan Cinema.' *The Journal of Literature and Film (Korea, the Association of East Asian Film Studies)* 14, no. 1: 61–79.

Ho, Tung-hung (2009), 'Taike Rock and its Discontent', *Inter-Asia Cultural Studies* 10, no. 4: 565–84.

Hsiao, Tsai-wei. 2021. 'There Have Been Three "Highest-grossing Domestic Films" by Wei Te-sheng in the Past Ten Years! *Man in Love* Entered the List in Half a Year' [Shinianlai piaofang zuigao guopian weidesheng jiuyou sanbu dangnanren bannian chongjinbang]. *ETtoday*, 16 December. https://star.ettoday.net/news/2147395. Accessed 12 Feb 2022.

Huang, Shuling. 2018. 'Japanese and Korean Popular Culture and Identity Politics in Taiwan.' In *Asian Cultural Flows*. Edited by Nobuko Kawashima and Hye-Kyung Lee, 215–32. Singapore: Springer.

Iwabuchi, Koichi. 2008. 'Cultures of Empire: Transnational Media Flows and Cultural (Dis)connections in East Asia.' In *Global Communications: Toward a Transcultural Political Economy*. Edited by Paula Chakravartty and Yuezhi Zhao, 143–61. Plymouth: Rowman & Littlefield Publishers.

Khoo, Olivia. 2021. *Asian Cinema: A Regional View*. Edinburgh: Edinburgh University Press.

Lim, Song Hwee. 2013. 'Taiwan New Cinema: Small Nation with Soft Power.' In *The Oxford Handbook of Chinese Cinemas*. Edited by Carlos Rojas and Eileen Cheng-ying Chow, 152–69. Oxford: Oxford University Press.

Lim, Song Hwee. 2022. *Taiwan Cinema as Soft Power: Authorship, Transnationality, Historiography*. Oxford: Oxford University Press.

Lin, Ting-ying. 2019. 'Charting the Transnational within the National: The Case of Contemporary Taiwan Popular Cinema.' In *Positioning Taiwan in a Global Context*. Edited by Bi-yu Chang and Pei-yin Lin, 196–210. London: Routledge.

Rawle, Steven. 2015. 'Ringing *One Missed Call*: Franchising, Transnational Flows and Genre Production.' *East Asian Journal of Popular Culture* 1, no. 1: 97–112.

Rawle, Steven. 2018. *Transnational Cinema: An Introduction*. London: Palgrave.

Sung, Sang-Yeon. 2010. 'Constructing a New Image: Hallyu in Taiwan.' *European Journal of East Asian Studies* 9, no. 1: 25–45.

TAICCA. 2022. 'About.' Taiwan Creative Content Agency Website. https://en.taicca.tw/#item-1. Accessed 12 Feb 2022.

Taiwan Film and Audiovisual Institute. 2020a. *National Film Box Office Statistics 14–20 September 2020*. Taipei: Taiwan Film and Audiovisual Institute.

Taiwan Film and Audiovisual Institute. 2020b. *Taiwan Cinema Yearbook 2020*. Taipei: Taiwan Film and Audiovisual Institute.

Taiwan Film and Audiovisual Institute. 2021. *National Film Box Office Statistics 16–22 August 2021*. Taipei: Taiwan Film and Audiovisual Institute.
Taiwan Film Institute. 2017. *Taiwan Cinema Yearbook 2017*. Taipei: Taiwan Film Institute.
Taiwan Film Institute. 2019a. *Taiwan Cinema Yearbook 2019*. Taipei: Taiwan Film Institute.
Taiwan Film Institute. 2019b. *National Film Box Office Statistics 29 April–5 May, 2019*. Taipei: Taiwan Film Institute.
Wang, Si-han. 2013. 'Bucheon International Fantastic Film Festival Ends, Taiwan-South Korea cooperation Starts' [Fuchuan qihuan yingzhan luomu taihan he zuo zhengqibu]. *Funscreen*, 5 July. http://www.funscreen.com.tw/feature.asp?FE_NO=84. Accessed 12 Feb 2022.
Zemanek, Adina Simona. 2017. 'Taiwaneseness Revisited: Lasting Themes and New Trends in Contemporary Popular Culture,' *East Asian Journal of Popular Culture* 3, no. 2: 139–52.

CHAPTER 14

The Pan-Asian 'Miss Granny' Phenomenon

Jennifer Coates, Hsin Hsieh, Sung-Ae Lee and Kate Taylor-Jones

Successful film remakes can become truly transnational phenomena, reaching across and beyond East Asia. This chapter explores the diverse and continued remaking of the 'Miss Granny' story, from its first iteration in South Korea to the multiple versions across East and Southeast Asia. The 'Miss Granny' story began as *Suspicious Girl* (*Susanghan geunyeo*, 2014), a romantic comedy, directed by Hwang Dong-hyuk, in which a difficult elderly woman struggling with her family relationships finds herself transported by a magic photobooth back into her twenty-year-old body, while retaining her knowledge and memories in the contemporary setting. After generating high box-office earnings of $51.7 million USD and significant critical acclaim, the story was quickly retold for Chinese-speaking audiences as *20 Once Again* (*Chóng fǎn èrshí suì*, 2015), directed by Leste Chan; for Vietnamese audiences as *Sweet 20*, aka *You Are My Grandmother* (*Em là bà nội của anh*, 2015), directed by Phan Gia Nhat Linh; and for Japanese audiences as *Suspicious Girl*, aka *Sing My Life* (*Ayashii Kanojo*, 2016), directed by Mizuta Nobuo. Spreading further, a Thai remake titled *Suddenly Twenty* (*Suddenly 20*, Araya Suriharn, 2016), an Indonesian remake titled *Sweet Twenty* (*Sweet 20*, Ody C. Harahap, 2017), a Philippine remake titled *Miss Granny* (Joyce E. Bernal, 2018) and a Telugu-language Indian version titled *Oh Baby!* (B. V. Nandini Reddy, 2019) are also part of this transnational phenomenon. The South Korean version's box-office success overtook that of *Frozen* (Jennifer Lee and Chris Buck, 2013), while the Chinese adaptation grossed $57.4 million and the Vietnamese version was the highest-grossing domestic film in Vietnam at the time of its release.

An examination of these 'Miss Granny' films, which have become a remarkable global phenomenon, is timely for many reasons. First, the director of the original, Hwang Dong-hyuk, has recently achieved global fame via his Netflix show *Squid Game* (*Ojingeo Geim*, 2021), and audiences who had not previously watched his earlier films such as *My Father* (*Mai Padeo*, 2007), *Silenced* (a.k.a *The Crucible*, *Dogani*, 2011) and *The Fortress* (*Namhan sanseong*, 2017) are now discovering them. By exploring some of the facets of *Miss Granny* that made it such an exportable, culturally appropriated production in neighbouring or nearby countries throughout the East and Southeast Asian regions, we might gain insight into the reasons for the director's recent success and *Squid Game*'s translatability as a pop culture text rooted in Korean modern history and memories of the past. Second, distribution of the remakes themselves has been heavily controlled by CJ Entertainment, which has partnered with local companies to ensure the remakes align thematically and stylistically with the original film, thereby engaging wider debates on the circulation of Korean products, a trend that continues apace at the time of this writing. Finally, all the films reveal the intricacies of ageing, gender and nationhood that operate in a variety of ways in the remakes, and this chapter will focus mostly on these elements while offering a multifaceted debate on the complexities of the 'Miss Granny' story. As the authors of this chapter, each of us has a keen interest in specific aspects of the film and, together, we wish to present a diverse but not exhaustive look at the various elements that spark interest in the East and Southeast Asian versions. Our respective expertise in Chinese, Japanese and Southeast Asian cinema in addition to South Korean cinema has allowed for a combination of perspectives deeply embedded in the cinema cultures of the 'remaking' countries as well as the home of the original film. We believe that this attention to the sociopolitical and historical backgrounds of the remakes' production – seen from the vantage of their 'receiving' countries as well as that of the 'sending' country – can reveal underlying aspirations and anxieties within a broader East Asian viewership that has made the 'Miss Granny' story legible and popular beyond its original South Korean context.

All the films maintain the same basic plot introduced in the original production. An elderly, rather cantankerous woman becomes estranged from her wider family. As she laments her loneliness, she is transported back to her youthful body via a magical photography studio. She becomes a singer in her grandson's band and manages a potential new relationship while maintaining her link to an old friend who has long harboured a romantic interest in her. In the end she sacrifices her youth to save her grandson's life after an accident. This may be an uncommon variant of the body-swap narrative trope, but it follows the expected structures of that script: a temporary change enables the character to reassess problematic aspects of her behaviour and, ironically, 'come of age' as someone with a newfound appreciation for things that she had once taken for granted. Her period of metamorphosis is both a chance to live a new life as a young person and an opportunity for her and her family to learn about what really matters in a family unit.

INTRODUCING 'MISS GRANNY': A COMPARATIVE ANALYSIS OF THE OPENING SEQUENCE

A crucial aspect of cinematic remaking is the handling of a film's beginning, which positions its audience by making incipient suggestions about genre, mode, setting and likely themes. Thus, how a particular remake engages in an implicit or overt dialogue with its pretext(s), whether an original film or a number of films within a genre, emerges during its opening movement.

The length of the opening sequence of each 'Miss Granny' film varies considerably, but always extends until the moment O Mal-soon (the main character in the original film, portrayed by Shim Eun-kyung and Na Moon-hee in her younger and older guises, respectively) or one of her iterations enters the magical photo studio. The remakes omit or shorten some segments, add new material, include more exposition or take longer to establish the deficiency or tension which motivates the action. *Miss Granny*'s beginning of 20:28 minutes becomes, at the extremes, 15 minutes in the Indonesian remake and 27 minutes in the Indian version. For example, the title screen in *Miss Granny* is immediately followed by a college seminar on ageism in which university students articulate negative attitudes toward the elderly, but both the Vietnamese and Indonesian remakes omit that scene. Presumably, the ageism seminar might be deemed to lack impact as an entry into the narrative in countries with large populations of young people and relatively low participation in tertiary education. Such modifications to the original film result in substantial disparity amongst the lengths of the opening sequence.

Because the beginning of a film is unlikely to coincide with the beginning of the film's story and furthermore entertains several thematic possibilities, a remake has numerous options for the kinds of establishing moves it makes and for the questions it prompts in the minds of viewers. The 'Miss Granny' films all make strategic use of a segment preceding the title screen to indicate a thematic direction for the film and to establish the distinctiveness of each film. The original *Miss Granny* begins with a rhetorical transaction between a female voiceover narrator and the viewing audience. This moment introduces the themes of sexism and ageism by drawing an analogy between women as objects of male attention and the different sorts of balls used in various sports, from a basketball to a dodge ball. That no woman appears in the segment only reinforces the assertion that a woman's life course is determined by male desire toward her, which diminishes in each decade of her adult life. None of the remakes retains this rhetorical gesture; instead, each of them steps away from the Korean pre-text and begins with a realistic establishing scene. The audience's immediate cognitive engagement with the beginning as an overt foregrounding of the themes of women's lives, gender and ageism is thus framed as an interface with a narrative mode from which those themes must be deduced.

In a clear thematic shift, three of the remakes (those from China, Vietnam and Indonesia) include a family portrait within the first two minutes of the film. Embracing three generations, the portrait is a schema of solidarity and continuity. When it first appears in the Chinese remake, the family portrait lacks a context. In contrast, viewers conclude that in the Vietnamese remake the photo is a part of the celebration of Mrs Dai (Minh Duc)'s seventieth birthday. The rest of the family is happy and playful, but she is steeped in misery. Her lack of a sense of wellbeing is thus indirectly introduced. In a further contrast, the Indonesian remake begins with a medium establishing shot which depicts a man and a woman on a motor scooter, who stop to exchange warm greetings with two women, presumably neighbours. The clothing of all four is characteristically Muslim, including hijab and abaya for women and a songkok cap for men, and the mise-en-scène indicates that it is the Lebaran festival (end of Eid al-Fitr). The scene then shifts to an extended family as they celebrate the festival. The occasion resembles the family meal that opens the Vietnamese remake, and which likewise establishes family togetherness as a central theme, but setting, clothing and purpose are very different. The Lebaran custom of asking forgiveness from one's parents and elders is enacted as the family form a line to kneel before Fatma (Niniek L. Karim), the grandmother, and say 'Forgive all my wrongdoings'. An element of instability is introduced when it is the turn of Salma (Cut Mini), the daughter-in-law, as instead of simply granting forgiveness Fatma remarks that she has been forgiving her for a long time already. Fatma's habit of privileging males and acting in a domineering manner toward females is extended to her grandchildren. This gender bias is evident in the original *Miss Granny* and is sustained across the remakes. Narratively, her bullying of her daughter-in-law (or daughter in the Japanese film) is the catalyst for her metamorphosis; thematically, her bias foregrounds gender inequality within cultures that were modernised during the twentieth century while still sustaining persistent inequalities in most aspects of women's lives. The granny's disruptive effect on the family appears consistently in her unconditional support for her grandson's apparently wayward desire to make a career in pop music. She is expressing her own thwarted desire (most overtly thematised in the opening minute of the Thai remake) and has no idea of how elusive success can be, or of the mediocrity of his band.

Variations within the opening sequences illustrate how the 'same' material can be handled quite differently to produce similar thematic effects. The cognitive principle enabling these variations becomes evident in the seminar about ageism, which is reworked in four of the remakes. The question put to the class – 'Give me one stereotype of elderly people that pops into your heads' – is a formulation of the concepts of schema and scripts, those cognitive structures that describe how knowledge and assumptions about life are organised, activated and modified within any individual human brain. In the original film, the seminar about ageism is a simple explication of an underlying schema for elderly people. In response to the lecturer's question, the students offer six components of a schema which expresses physical unattractiveness, physical incompetence and loss of social usefulness. The significance of the schema for this demographic is summed up by a conventionally beautiful young woman, who says, 'I'm going to kill myself before I hit my 30s. Why live till your 70s and have a sloppy life?' The scene then cuts to the first appearance of Mal-soon, who speaks as if she had heard the remark. This disruption of narrative realism, following the metaphorical opening movement, suggests that the film has a thesis to explore. In the Chinese and Thai versions, negative comments made by the students are interspersed with incidents in which the behaviour of the elderly protagonist confirms those prejudices, a strategy devised for, but not retained in, the original film. In *Oh Baby!* (the Indian remake), the lecturer mentions his own mother (the film's protagonist, known as 'Baby') as an example, and the scene then cuts to her as she performs the criticism that the elderly have the habit of telling the same stories over and over. The Filipino remake simply juxtaposes the seminar and the protagonist's confirming behaviour. However, none of the three remakes which retain the episode include the metacinematic segue whereby Mal-soon responds to the final student's comment (which she has not heard). Only retained in the Chinese remake, the female student's declaration that she will not grow old but will kill herself before turning thirty may seem comically absurd, but reflects a gender asymmetry embodied in a female obsession with personal beauty as a woman's major asset.

During the opening credits of the Chinese remake, the family portrait schema is followed by a schematic life narrative which, extending for a mere two minutes and twenty seconds, expands the portrait as if to summarise the male life trajectory of Xiang Guo Bin (Zhao Lixin) from boyhood to middle age. As he walks between visually interconnected spaces, he leaves his mother, meets a girlfriend, marries, becomes a father and then becomes the professor conducting the ageism seminar that comprises the next scene. The film's title appears on the screen as he enters the classroom. The curious insertion of this male script as an establishing scene reverses the thematic implications of the beginning of *Miss Granny* by suggesting that this is a family story with a male focus. The less obviously articulated female script about the granny protagonist does not emerge in any of the remakes until the film's beginning gives way to its middle section with her magical transformation.

In contrast, a recurrent theme of the Japanese remake *Sing My Life* is the challenge faced by women to lead an agentic life in the contemporary world. The film's title is preceded by a vignette from the blood transfusion scene near the close of the narrative so that in retrospect the temporariness of the protagonist's return to youth always overshadows the film. The substitution of a daughter, Yukie (Kobayashi Satomi), for the son of the original (and all other remakes) imparts a strong female focus, and a model script built into the beginning becomes a rendition of a common experience of female office workers in Japan, with its story of Yukie's demotion and her replacement by a younger, prettier woman. Yukie's change of circumstance also highlights one of the obvious failings of her mother, Katsu (Baisho Mitsuko), the 'granny' protagonist: because of her domineering personality and self-regard, Katsu does not engage in conversational turn-taking, and Yukie's attempt to explain her situation is swept aside by Katsu's inability to listen. The same situation occurs when Yukie's attempt to exert authority over her son, Tsubasa (Kitamura Takumi), is dismissed by Katsu. The human and familial consequences of the grandmother's overbearing personality is a feature of the beginning sequence of the original film and all the remakes, and in all except the Japanese version it is the primary cause of her daughter-in-law's stress-related collapse. In combination with her extreme preference for men, her oppressive behaviour further disrupts family harmony by provoking resentment and dislike from her granddaughter. This motif finds its epitome in *Oh Baby!*: following the collapse of Baby's daughter-in-law Madhavi (Pragathi Mahavadi), Divya (Aneesha Dama), Baby's granddaughter, assaults Baby verbally with a sharp analysis of her self-centredness and disregard for what others say or think.

As mentioned above, the Thai remake most overtly foregrounds the granny's unfulfilled desire for a singing career. This emphasis underlies the unique beginning to this film: for one minute preceding the title screen, the film, in perhaps a self-conscious contrast to the Chinese remake, presents a black-and-white and sepia-toned flashback with voiceover narrative which relates the story of the early years of granny protagonist Parn (Davika Hoorne as young Parn; Neeranuch Pattamasoot as old Parn). It depicts her passion for singing, her father's violent opposition and finally her foolish decision to elope in quest of a career. Following the title screen and transition to colour, the film depicts Parn working in a senior citizens' cafeteria, with her quality of life defined by moments interwoven with the seminar on ageing. The juxtaposition of past and present contrasts a youth oscillating between hope and lost opportunity with a present characterised by declining physical and social functions, by resentment and by ill temper. A sense of loss is more directly expressed in the Philippine version of *Miss Granny*. The film begins in a shopping complex, first with a children's party in a private room and then in the food hall as people affectionately greet one another. As a waiter leaves the children's party, a voice-over poses the question, 'How do you measure sadness? Is it being surrounded by happy people?' The voiceover is soon identified as the thoughts of granny protagonist Fely (Nova Villa) as she muses that love is seldom extended to an elderly woman like her. In this way, the film offers 'love' as its theme, but this love is not (only) romantic love – it encompasses the tenderness shared by parents and children and the caring between friends. Fely's moment of self-pity exposes a flaw in what will soon be identified as her self-centred conception of relationships.

Older women have long been depicted in films in stereotyped ways: as objects of sexism and ageism, they sacrifice for families, are rarely attributed with desires and ambitions of their own and are resentful about the lives they have led. The 'Miss Granny' films first affirm that such stereotypes endure across East Asian cinemas and then go some way toward challenging them by opening a space for a more transgressive representation of ageing Asian women. The carnivalesque 'time out' enabled by the body swap trope – an older life experience overlaid by a young body – envisages different possibilities, even though entrenched attitudes toward women require a sacrificial outcome and return to the status quo.

MOTHERING AND FAMILY RELATIONSHIPS IN *MISS GRANNY*

All the versions of *Miss Granny* surf the waves of what Susan Douglas and Meredith Michaels have dubbed the ideology of 'new momism' that has swelled since the 1980s (2004). 'New Momism' is an almost cult-like focus on motherhood as not just a woman's highest vocation but also the key to her own personal happiness. This section explores three main aspects of the original film and its remakes: first, the thematic focus on the self-sacrificial mother; second, the tension between the ideas of mothering and intergenerational conflict; and, last, the literal transformation of the elderly body and the narratives around a pre-maternal body that the many iterations of the main 'Miss Granny' story present.

This idealisation of the 'image' of the perfect mother over the realities of actual mothering practices has been well established in scholarship (see Thurer 1994; Hays 1996; Miller 2005; O'Reilly 2008), and popular culture and the media are instrumental in propagating images of selfless mothers who sacrifice their time, energy, careers and even their individuality in the name of raising the next generation of 'good citizens'. Feasey underlines the old-fashioned ideologies at play in these 'romanticised, idealised and indeed conservative images of selfless and satisfied "good" mothers who conform to the ideology of intensive mothering' (2012, 3). In all the nations where *Miss Granny* has been made and remade, the focus on motherhood as a key part of female identity has been emphasised across historical, political and cultural narratives (see Molony and Ochiai 2008; Song 2021; Liamputtong et al. 2004; Jolivent 1997; Francisco-Menchavez 2019; Uno 1999). From the Philippine Duterte Government's simultaneous promotion of motherhood as traditionally defined whilst heavily legislating against any motherhood seen as problematic, to the Vietnamese 'Heroic Mother award' (*Bà mẹ Việt Nam anh hùng*) that recognises any mother who makes a 'sacrifice' to the nation state, and the Mother's Day tributes given by the Film Development Council of the Philippines (FDCP) celebrating stars such as Lily Monteverde, Anitra Linda and Manay Ichui Maceda, a sense of motherhood as a heroic and vital force persists in cinematic ideas of nationhood.

The final scenes of the 'Miss Granny' films all conform to the same narrative, in which the repentant sons (and one daughter) confront their mother in hospital as she leaves to give blood to her grandson. They apologise for their actions, atone for their lack of filial piety and request her to enjoy her new youth. Without hesitation, the Granny protagonists respond that being a mother has been the foundational point in their lives and they would never choose to change that despite the hardships that it has brought. This idealised maternal self-sacrifice is enhanced by the various flashback sequences seen during her songs that show her becoming widowed and caring for a sick child while working long hours in poor conditions. These songs vary in position within the films, but all of them remain a core element. All the titular figures in Miss Granny, save for the Japanese version, are widowed and have never remarried, instead choosing to focus on her child. In each film, this focus has been repaid by a child who is both socially and financially successful.

Each remake has its own specific engagement with the idea of motherhood as positioned in the national narrative. In the Vietnamese version, after her physical transformation, the protagonist Mrs Dai takes on the name of Thanh Nga (Miu Le), a singer who died alongside her husband in 1978, ostensibly protecting her child from a kidnapping attempt – in short, the ultimate self-sacrificial mother. The Filipino version of *Miss Granny* was directed by Joyce E. Bernal, whose frequent work for President Rodrigo Duterte (she has directed three of his five State of the Nation Addresses) speaks to a political position in keeping with the sense of 'traditional' values that her film heavily stresses. The film stars Sara Geronimo, who gained fame in a television singing competition but has since gone on to become one of the most notable and successful modern Filipino singers. Her own public image is one that is wholesome, family-orientated and defined by traditional values; and the film ensures that this image is never disrupted. Recalled in the old OPM [Original Pilipino Music] hits from the 1970s such as 'Rain', 'Forbidden' and 'Kiss Me, Kiss Me', the 1970s was a highly turbulent decade for the Philippines for both man-made and natural disasters. The protagonist's sonic link to this period emphasises her ability to protect and nurture her child in highly complex circumstances.

Sharon Hays has focused on the concept of the 'intensive mother', which no other mother or woman can ever live up to, in her book *Cultural Contradictions of Motherhood*. The protagonist of the 'Miss Granny' story is the living embodiment of this role. She is expert at all matters related to the home, food and care, but she is also hard-working, self-sacrificing and child-focused (even if that child or grandchild is an adult). As Douglas and Michaels point out, this focus has not actually made any material or social gains for those undertaking the role of mother, but it certainly operates as a very powerful regulatory myth (2004, 24); and, as Valerie Heffernan and Gay Wilgus note, the 'homogenized, sanitized, media-fuelled images of motherhood bear little resemblance to the lived experiences of the majority of mothers' (2018, 5). Wider media discourses may 'idealize and glamorize motherhood as the one path to fulfilment for women' (Kinnick 2009, 3), but this idea of fulfilment is a curious one in the context of the pan-Asian 'Miss Granny' phenomenon. Parenthood for the most part is seen as a relentlessly negative experience. For the daughter-in-law, her child's refusal to listen or engage with her is echoed in the rejection of Granny by her wider family as she becomes more overbearing in her old age. As the narrative develops, and in every context, motherhood is marked in a negative way. In all the films, Granny in her younger format accosts another young woman and ends up directly, and publicly, insulting her parenting. Whilst initially, these scenes open with a sense of comradery, with her aiming to help the young mother by holding and admiring the child, she quickly reverts to the critical and harsh manner in which we had seen her treat her daughter-in-law – which, whilst possibly motivated by care, ultimately undermines and deeply hurts the other woman. Her father-in-law is triggered toward a breakdown and with these younger women, the mode of insult is very focused on the physical ability of the respective young woman to raise and care for her baby.

In Hwang Dong-hyuk's Korean version, the protagonist goes into detail about watery breast milk leading to diarrhoea and, while holding the baby, she loudly accuses the mother of substituting cow's milk for human breast milk to feed the child. In all the films, the admonishment is conducted publicly with no regard for the mother's privacy of feelings. In the Thai version, initially after admiring the baby, she criticises the woman for having breast implants, which have led to an inability to produce proper milk. In the Vietnamese version, young Miss Granny notes that the mother needs to wash her breasts – but also suggests that the mother is refusing to breastfeed due to the concern that her breasts will sag. The Telugu version has her criticise the mother for buying formula in a shop. In the Japanese version, the young mother gives in to tears and kneels wailing at the young Miss Granny's feet, as though she has become a child herself. In all the versions, the mothers are critiqued for dressing their children inappropriately and thus putting them at risk of illness. When compared to the protagonist and her generation, the maternal body of the modern woman is seen as lacking. Unable to manage as their forebears did with children strapped to their backs while working long hours, these women are shown as selfish and incapable. The modern woman seems unable to perform any role as proscribed by the patriarchal society in which she struggles to meet gendered expectations of motherhood.

Figure 14.1 The mother of a new-born baby reacts negatively to the title character's comments while riding a subway, in this scene from Hwang Dong-hyuk's *Miss Granny* (*Susanghan Geunyeo*, a.k.a., *Suspicious Girl*, 2014), the Korean-language basis for several cinematic remakes across the East and Southeast Asian region.

The role that youth plays is highlighted in all the versions as old age is defined by a loss of dignity, a loss of purpose and a lack of social value and space. The various old age centres are shown as sites of petty grievances and poor entertainment, neither a productive nor desirable space in which to thrive. As Jo Elfivng Hwang notes, 'Existing research on the ageing female body in South Korea has primarily focused on the so-called *noin munjae* ('the elderly issue') discourse' (2016, 6). Within this discourse, the ageing body is framed as passive, undesirable or out-of-control. While this is perhaps most notable in the Korean context and very much reflected in the original film, it is hardly out of keeping with global narratives about the ageing female body. Indeed, as Imelda Whelehan and Joel Gwynne describe, the place of post-menopausal women is usually 'on the scrapheap' (2014, 5). Frida Kerner Furman's ethnography of a New York beauty salon gave prominence to the relationship that older women have with their self-image and argued that they are 'twice-objectified' when they look in the mirror as 'a woman and as old woman' (1997: 109). In *Miss Granny* this is a literal experience of double objectification as both her gender and her age are reflected via screens in all the films. She initially desires a good photo for her funeral display – a moment that acknowledges her lack of place in her family unit. However, it is via the camera screen that the radical anti-ageing processes take place and it is also by literal reflection (windows and mirrored sunglasses) that she discovers her newly desirable image. All the films return Miss Granny to a clearly pre-maternal body. Nova Villa becomes Sarah Geronimo, Na Moon-hee becomes Shim Eun-kyung, Niniek L. Karim becomes Tatjana Saphira and Neeranuch Patamasood morphs into Davika

Hoorne. With this new body, the marks and trials of childbirth and rearing have been removed. All the versions stress that the maternal cannot be desirable. In the Korean original, the protagonist's ability to literally utilise this new body is emphasised far more highly than in the other versions. She faces down another woman in the bathhouse with impressive gymnastic feats and manages to humiliate her, once again stressing the power and the desirability of the youthful body. In the Thai, Indonesian and Vietnamese versions, the protagonist dances and does cartwheels behind older people doing their more sedate workouts, as she realises the capacity of her new body. In the Telugu version, she dances around an elderly rehabilitation centre, including jumping past a man struggling to learn to walk again after a stroke. Motherhood is not valued as a bodily mode of experience; however, at the same time, the films laud the idealised sacrificial mother figure.

MISS GRANNY TRANSFORMS . . . INTO AUDREY HEPBURN?

Mizuta Nobuo's Japanese language remake *Sing My Life* is perhaps the most faithful reworking of the South Korean original in terms of visual style. However, as noted above, the protagonist's son is replaced with a daughter, and a new focus on office life for ageing women is introduced. While the Chinese language version largely abandons the references to Audrey Hepburn and classic Hollywood which inform the transformation scenes, the Japanese version emphasises this connection. Indeed, the Japanese and South Korean versions of the story are linked through a shared experience of exposure to North American film culture against the historical background of US military activities in the Occupation of Japan (1945–1952) and the Korean War, respectively (the Philippine and Thai remakes also feature Hepburn-style visuals and references to the star in dialogue). This section of the chapter will focus on the use of the image of Audrey Hepburn and references to the William Wyler-directed film *Roman Holiday* (1953) in the Japanese remake in order to draw out the similarities and differences between the East Asian versions of the story and their approach to gender and ageing.

As alluded to in an earlier section of this chapter, the 'Miss Grannies' of the South Korean, Chinese and Japanese iterations are in their seventies in the contemporary settings of the films' release years (2014–2016), suggesting that the characters were born around the end of the Second World War, and more pertinently, the end of the Fifteen Years Asia-Pacific War, which ended Japan's colonisation and occupation of East Asia. The post-war popular culture boom in Hollywood imports is referenced in the Japanese and South Korean versions in the main characters' passion for Audrey Hepburn and *Roman Holiday*. Both women style their hair like the Hollywood star, adopt a similar mode of dress (despite the mid-2010s setting) and take new names that echo 'Audrey' – O Doo-ri for the South Korean 'Miss Granny' and Ōtori for the Japanese iteration.

Resonating with Hepburn's own star persona, singing and dancing are core plot points and aesthetic elements in all remakes of the 'Miss Granny' story, with karaoke playing a key role in the East Asian films, where 'Miss Granny' is discovered singing in public and is propelled to pop music stardom. The Japanese Ōtori Setsuko (the name chosen by protagonist Setayama Katsu for her youthful persona after transformation) even compares the full narrative arc of the film to Hepburn's *Roman Holiday* at peak moments of drama leading to resolution, aspiring to the life of a 'princess' and noting sadly at the conclusion of the story that even Hepburn's character had to leave her carefree 'holiday' as an everyday girl and return to her more restrictive life as a royal at the end of that movie. Setsuko/Katsu compares her own choice to undergo a medical procedure, risking a return to her aged body, to the ultimatum faced by Hepburn's character.

While Hepburn was twenty-four years old at the time of *Roman Holiday*'s production, it is clear that the protagonists of the Japanese and South Korean 'Miss Granny' stories are not attempting to channel the young adult Hepburn but rather a more youthful iteration of their own lives and experiences. Both protagonists are returned to a body visually similar to their twenty-year-old selves, but historical timelines suggest that these seventy-something women would have been closer to childhood when *Roman Holiday* introduced Hepburn to audiences in East Asia from 1954. The childlike glee with which the protagonists embark on the shopping trips that create their Hepburn makeovers recall the behaviour of younger teens or children, while the fusion of the language and behaviours the protagonists have used as older ladies with their now-youthful appearance creates an impression of childlike frankness and uninhibited expression.

Zen Yipu connects the image of Hepburn herself with an exuberant attitude to consumerism in Japan in an argument that suggests how the shopping spree of the transformation scene in the Japanese remake reflects the historical memory and aspirations of the protagonist. While Kanako Terasawa has noted the boom in women attempting to dress and style their hair like Hepburn in the wake of the distribution of *Roman Holiday* in Japan (2010, 250), Zen argues that Hepburn's impact on consumerism in Japan was reinvigorated in the 1990s in a series of advertisements and magazine articles featuring the 1950s-era image of the star. In 1998, the Kirin Beverages Co. produced a television commercial featuring Audrey Hepburn drinking tea, while *Asahi Graph* (Asahi Graph Extra 1999) published a special issue on Hepburn the following year in which twelve Japanese stars discussed their own fandom of the Hollywood icon (Zen 2004, 78). Such uses of the star's image brought her back into the popular consciousness in Japan in the late 1990s and, as Zen argues, 'provide an example of how imagery and its "aura" can be effectively commodified, and then either attached to goods or sold as a form of media content' (2004, 80).

Channelling Hepburn certainly fuels a consumer spending spree by the protagonist of the Japanese remake, who puzzles store owners in the slightly dingy covered market she frequents when she takes her newly youthful figure through a series of stores offering dated styles targeted at older customers. Waving the crisp 10,000 yen notes she has just accessed from her pension fund, she charms store owners into letting her walk out of their shops in her new items, dancing down the street in her 1950s-style ballet pumps. The commodification of the Hepburn aura does not stop there, as her new look attracts the attention of a series of record producers and musicians, who find her retro styling fresh and new in the contemporary pop music landscape. Teaming up with her own grandson, the protagonist turns his previously unsuccessful visual kei-style band into a hit, not only with her pleasant singing voice and sassy older lady dance moves, which become cute when performed by a young woman, but also by her unusual retro dress style. It is notable that when Ōtori Setsuko returns to her elderly body and life as Setsuyama Katsu, the replacement female singer in her grandson's band is newly costumed in retro dresses, suggesting the lasting commercial power of the Hepburn style.

Hepburn's image not only channelled a fantasy of grown-up Hollywood glamour for the generations born during the Second World War in Japan, but it also fit smoothly into a gendered understanding of the beauty ideals achievable for Japanese women, and those considered desirable within a Japanese imagination of femininity. Articles on Hepburn in the Japanese media, both in the 1950s and in the 1990s, noted her physical similarity to the ideal Japanese woman, with her dark hair, small stature and slim figure (*Dime* 1992). Several articles argue that this gave Hepburn's appearance 'a feeling of familiarity with that of the Japanese female', as well as channelling both feminine elegance and a 'child-like' impression (Zen 2004, 81, 83). These elements come together in the 'Miss Granny' narrative's use of the Hepburn image to lend both the Japanese and South Korean protagonists a presence that not only is aspirational but also speaks to their desire to recover their lost childhoods and young adult years, which the viewer implicitly understands to have been blighted by the aftermath of various wars, and which the films explicitly demonstrate to have been periods of heavy family responsibility and poverty. In this respect the narrative arc of the protagonist's backstory also mirrors Hepburn's, in that the star experienced the danger, poverty and restrictions of wartime and suffered the loss of her aspiration to a career as a ballet dancer due to this hardship.

In Japan, the Hollywood star lives on into the 2000s in a series of television narratives that may have shaped the representation of the Hepburn impersonation in the Japanese remake of the 'Miss Granny' story. From

October 2000 to March 2001, NHK broadcast a morning drama titled *Audrey* (*Ōtori*) set in 1953, the year that *Roman Holiday* was filmed but one year before it arrived in Japan. The story follows a Japanese translator in Kyoto, the 'Hollywood of Japan' (Lewis 2019), with a daughter named Audrey. In 2019 Hepburn's aura appeared again in the Japan edition of Netflix's popular makeover show *Queer Eye: Japanese Holiday* (S1E1), when the five American presenters intervened in the life of divorced fift-seven-year-old hospice nurse Yoko Sakuma. Yoko is introduced as having 'given up on being a woman' (*onna o suteru*) due to her commitment to her work and lack of attention to her physical appearance. As Eguchi and Kimura argue, this discourse suggests 'the logic of Japan's cisheteropatriarchy that assumes single women who are over 30 years old are no longer attractive and desirable' (2021, 227). Yoko channels the image of Audrey Hepburn as she goes through the makeover section, and Eguchi and Kimura argue that 'Yoko's admiration of Hepburn illustrates an embodied product of Japaneseness aspiring toward the U.S.' in an 'imbalanced power relation' (2021, 228). At the same time, however, we can see how the invocation of Audrey Hepburn's 'aura' is not only a mode of engaging with consumer culture and an identification considered particularly appropriate for Japanese or East Asian women, but also a common trope in the stereotyping of ageing as a loss of femininity. Perhaps the childlike and non-sexual aspects of Hepburn's physique and style discussed above mean that it is considered more appropriate for an elderly or ageing woman to mimic Hepburn than, for example, Marilyn Monroe. Hepburn's youthful star persona holds an aspirational place in the popular culture imaginary across much of East Asia even today, in tension with the issues of ageing and motherhood explored in the early parts of this chapter. In the next section, we will explore the replacement of Hepburn with the image of Teresa Teng in the Chinese language remake of the 'Miss Granny' story.

MISS GRANNY IN THE CHINESE-SPEAKING CONTEXT

While the shared or comparative historical experiences of Japan and South Korea are visible in the style and beauty ideals described above, the Chinese-language remake of the 'Miss Granny' story required considerable adaptation and localisation. The 2015 production of *20 Once Again*, directed by Taiwanese filmmaker Leste Chen (Chén Zhèngdào), is a collaboration between South Korea's CJ Entertainment, China's Tianjin Century Media and Catchplay Taiwan to remake the original *Miss Granny* for the Chinese film market. It stars Gua Ah-leh as granny Mengjun, Yang Zi-shan as her younger self, Lu Han as her grandson and Chen Bolin as the TV producer who becomes a love interest. Being a remake and produced by the same company as the original, the film tries to find a balance between how it connects with the original while finding its new identity within the Chinese-language film market. Lee Hyung-Sook argues that transnational remakes are simultaneously 'decontextualised' and 'recontextualised in the course of interpretation' and, therefore, meanings are 'constantly destabilized', creating 'multiple possibilities' (2019, 56). As such, *20 Once Again* demonstrates a tension between its status as a remake of a Korean box-office hit and its need to recontextualise the narrative's nostalgic themes to resonate with far-reaching Chinese-language audiences that include Mainland China, the wider East Asian Sinosphere and the Chinese-speaking diasporas. It does this, first, by making direct reference to the original film and, second, by including pop culture references that span various Chinese-speaking regions. This section of the chapter analyses the Chinese remake of *Miss Granny* to examine the tension whereby the multiple possibilities of interpretation are produced, with a special focus on two references: the iconic Chinese-language singer Teresa Teng (Teng Li-chun) as the image for the younger granny (replacing Audrey Hepburn), and the popular Chinese TV drama *My Fair Princess* (1998–1999) as another level of metatextual reference (replacing the fictional Korean drama show in the original). As *Miss Granny* is a film that conveniently provides opportunities for nostalgic displays, what do these culturally specific adaptations mean to audiences of the Chinese-language remake? Ultimately, it is clear that this particular remake adapts cultural references and history, which creates a mixed and imagined collective memory to accommodate the broader Chinese-language market.

Most of *20 Once Again* was shot on location in Tianjin City, but the narrative itself does not specify the actual setting of the story. The remake drops the Hollywood icon Audrey Hepburn, but inserts another American pop culture reference. When the grandson Xiang Qian-jin rides away from the concert, he encounters a scene that evokes Woodstock, as he passes a long queue of music festival participants, waving iconic anti-war slogans from 1960s America. However, this evocation is dropped when the camera cuts to a traditional-looking Chinese village with a herd of sheep occupying the main road. This blending of locations allows Chinese-language audiences from different regions to partake in a mediated form of collective nostalgia, as the references to American pop culture would doubtlessly work for a certain generation or region but possibly not others.

In a sequence leading up to the transformation scene in the photo studio, grandma Mengjun insists on going to Uncle Li's (Deshun Wang) place by herself after dining out with her family. The dinner provides an opportunity for Mengjun to reflect on her imposition on her family after her daughter-in-law Yang Qin (Yijuan Li) is hospitalised due to stress. Concluding that she must leave, Mengjun arrives at the bus stop. In the Korean version, the ageing granny is shown in profile next to a sunscreen advertisement featuring a smiling young woman, which is installed on the side panel of the bus stop. In this shot, granny looks relatively smaller than the young woman as the advertisement takes up half of the frame, with its reflection on the glass panel of the bus stop occupying the rest. The slogan of the advertisement reads 'strong against the sun, soft on your skin': a visual reminder of granny's ageing. However, in the Chinese-language version, the film cuts to Mengjun sitting at the bus stop, with the poster of the original *Miss Granny* shown prominently behind her, featuring actress Shim Eun-kyung as her Audrey Hepburn-inspired O Doo-ri. Juxtaposing Mengjun with the young O Doo-ri, this scene not only highlights the age discrimination issue at the heart of the film, but is both an intertextual reference to the Korean-language original and a self-reflexive nod to its status as a remake. However, when Mengjun receives a call from her grandson and walks away from O Doo-ri, the remake announces a rejection of the same nostalgic icon as used in the previous motion picture. On her way to meet her grandson, a depressed Mengjun enters the photo studio and decides to take a photo for her own funeral. Instead of referring to Audrey Hepburn as in the Korean and Japanese versions, she asks the photographer to make her look like Teresa Teng (or Teng Li-chun, hence the alias 'Meng Lijun', which Mengjun assumes for her younger self). The choice to use Teresa Teng over Hepburn is one of the ways we might answer the question 'whose memory is being recreated?' in the tellingly titled *20 Once Again*.

Historical events vary in different Chinese-language regions, as the 1960s marked a significant post-Second World War and post-Chinese Civil War (1927–1949) period, a contextual framework that is separate from, but not entirely unrelated to, life in Hong Kong under British colonial rule (1841–1997). From the late Qing dynasty onwards, Chinese/Mandarin speakers also have a long history of migration and diaspora, which 'serve as major subjects in Chinese modernity' (Yao 2020, 520). Pop culture references in *20 Once Again*, including allusions to Teng and *My Fair Princess*, connect these disparate histories. Teresa Teng began performing in Taiwan in 1967 and had albums released in Hong Kong by 1968, venturing into the Japanese market by 1973. Teng's pan-Asian fame demonstrates that her 'sociopolitical identity' is 'not static but fluid' and 'goes beyond that of [any other] Chinese popular singer' (Lee 2019, 521). While Teng's songs were officially banned in Mainland China during the early 1980s, people still found ways to hear them. As such, the popularity of Teng unveils 'a complex intercultural process of (re)production, exchange and circulation' (Yao 2020, 520) across the Sinosphere. Therefore, Teng's songs in *20 Once Again* are also a form of cultural 'remaking' as she often covered songs previously popularised by other artists. For example, 'Give Me a Kiss' (1954), the first song performed by the young Lijun in the film, was originally sung by Shanghai singer Chang Loo and later became one of Teng's biggest hits. After Teng's death in 1995, covers of her songs continue to generate revenue for their rights-holders, and *20 Once Again* also contributes to the maintenance of Teng's legacy.

Replacing Audrey Hepburn with Teresa Teng is one of the strategies the Chinese-language version uses both to differentiate itself from the original and to localise it for the Chinese-speaking audience. The other significant cultural insertion in *20 Once Again* is its reference to the Chinese TV drama *My Fair Princess*, echoing Hepburn's princess character in *Roman Holiday*. In the original *Miss Granny*, O Mal-soon and Mr Park (Park In-hwan) have been watching a long Korean drama together, and the way young Mal-soon reacts to the show leads him to suspect her real identity. The show used in this version is a fictional K-drama whose plotlines parody the conventions of TV melodramas. Its plot mirrors the central story of the film itself, which is to find out the identity of the main character (a princess). In *20 Once Again*, instead of creating a fictionalised Chinese TV show, clips from *My Fair Princess* are used to mirror the narrative of the film. Set in the Qing dynasty, one scene used from *My Fair Princess* involves the emperor trying to find out the identity of the princess, which plays on a TV in the background while other characters momentarily find Lijun suspicious. In addition to using the TV show to emphasise the theme of secret identities, another scene from *My Fair Princess*, with two women arguing, appears again in the background when Yumei (Qing Yang) from the senior centre is jealous of Uncle Li and Lijun's relationship. The use of this popular show demonstrates how the remake tries to maintain its relationship with the original version by undertaking a similar narrative strategy. But from a metatextual perspective, the show also recontextualises the film in relation to the original. *My Fair Princess* was written by Qiong Yao, a popular and prolific Taiwanese writer known for her romance novels and the numerous film adaptations of her work throughout the 1970s. Like *20 Once Again*, *My Fair Princess* was also a co-production between Taiwan (Yi Ren Communications Co.) and China (Hunan Broadcasting System). The popularity of *My Fair Princess* has also resulted in multiple pan-Asian remakes. These two strategic uses of intertextuality – Teresa Teng and *My Fair Princess* – demonstrate 'multiple possibilities' for the production of the remake, as its intended market spans several Chinese-speaking regions. The 'constantly destabilised' meaning that Lee Hyung-Sook discusses in her reading of the Korean Manchurian Western *The Good, the Bad, the Weird* (*Joeunnom nappeunnom isanghannom*, 2008) (2019, 56) applies here, with Meng Lijun's embodiment of Teresa Teng becoming a means for the Chinese remake to reach beyond the mainland and into the wider Sinosphere, as well as various Chinese-speaking diasporas. Therefore, through intertextual references between the Korean and the Chinese versions, *20 Once Again* embraces its identity as a remake and generates new meanings by incorporating contemporary cultural references for Chinese audiences around the world.

CONCLUSION

Whilst this chapter has explored some of the thematic and structural resonances across several 'Miss Granny' films, it is by no means exhaustive because we do not have the space to deal with the various remakes in the depth that they deserve as individual and interlinked texts. In particular, the various star bodies that are utilised inside the respective films, the use of physical violence as a mode of gendered communication, the role of diverse masculinities and the use of musical genres tropes – together with other topics – are worthy of further analysis. Charting a through-line from the complexities of ageism and gender bias, to the question of motherhood and the notion of female embodiment (as it especially relates to age), this chapter then analysed the use of the image of Audrey Hepburn as a youthful star persona, and finally considered the star persona and performance of Teresa Teng, the Chinese replacement of the Hepburn icon. This chapter has largely focused on East Asian remakes that, even in the relatively geographically close areas of South Korea, China and Japan, still require significant amendments to storylines, dialogues and performance style to make this 'universal' story intelligible to local audiences. Nonetheless, themes of family and questions of appropriate gendered and aged behaviour remain culturally relevant across the wide field of remakes.

NOTE

1. The section of this chapter titled 'Introducing "Miss Granny": A Comparative Analysis of the Opening Sequence' has been authored by Sung-Ae Lee. The section 'Mothering and Family Relationships in *Miss Granny*' is by Kate Taylor-Jones, 'Miss Granny Transforms . . . into Audrey Hepburn?' is by Jennifer Coates and '*Miss Granny* in the Chinese-Speaking Context' is by Hsin Hsieh.

REFERENCES

Dime. 1992. '"Audrey de manabu eikaiwa" made tōjō: A. Hepburn wa naze joseitachi no risō na no ka?' 3 December: 115.

Douglas, Susan J. and Meredith W. Michaels. 2004. *The Mommy Myth: The Idealization of Motherhood and How It Has Undermined All Women*. New York: Free Press.

Eguchi, Shinsuke and Keisuke Kimura. 2021. 'Racialized Im/possibilities: Intersectional Queer-of-Color Critique on Japaneseness in Netflix's *Queer Eye: We're in Japan!*' *Journal of International and Intercultural Communication* 14, no. 3: 221–39.

Elfving-Hwang, Joanna. 2016. 'Old, Down and Out? Appearance, Body Work and Positive Ageing among Elderly South Korean Women.' *Journal of Aging Studies* 38: 6–15.

Feasey, Rebecca. 2012. *From Happy Homemaker to Desperate Housewives: Motherhood and Popular Television*. London: Anthem Press.

Francisco-Menchavez, Valerie. 2019. 'A Mother who Leaves is a Mother who Loves: Labor Migration as Part of the Filipina Life Course and Motherhood.' *Journal of Asian American Studies* 22, no. 1: 85–102.

Furman, Frida Kerner. 1997. *Facing the Mirror: Older Women and Beauty Shop Culture*. New York: Routledge.

Hays, Sharon. 1996. *The Cultural Contradictions of Motherhood*. New Haven: Yale University Press.

Heffernan, Valerie and Gay Wilgus. 2018. 'Introduction: Imagining Motherhood in the Twenty-First Century – Images, Representations, Constructions.' *Women: A Cultural Review* 29, no. 1: 1–18.

Jolivet, Muriel. 2005. *Japan: The Childless Society? The Crisis of Motherhood*. London: Routledge.

Lee, Hyung-Sook. 2019. 'Transnational Film Remaking and Destabilized Meanings: Reading Kim Jee-woon's *The Good, the Bad, the Weird*.' *Korea Journal* 59, no. 3: 53–78.

Liamputtong, Pranee, Susanha Yimyam, Sukanya Parisunyakul, Chavee Baosoung and Nantaporn Sansiriphun. 2004. 'When I Become a Mother!: Discourses of Motherhood among Thai Women in Northern Thailand.' *Women's Studies International Forum* 27, no. 5: 589–601.

Miller, Tina. 2005. *Making Sense of Motherhood: A Narrative Approach*. Cambridge: Cambridge University Press.

Molony, Barbara and Emiko Ochiai, eds. 2008. *Asia's New Mothers: Crafting Gender Roles and Childcare Networks in East and Southeast Asian Societies*. Amsterdam: Brill.

O'Reilly, Andrea, ed. 2008. *Feminist Mothering*. Albany: State University of New York Press.

Song, Hojin. 2021. 'Baking Blogs: Negotiating Sacrificial and Postfeminist Neoliberal Motherhood in South Korea.' *Feminist Media Studies*: 1–16.

Terasawa, Kanako. 2010. 'Enduring Encounter: Hollywood Cinema and Japanese Women's Memory of the Post-war Experience.' PhD diss., University of London.

Thurer, Shari L. 1994. *The Myths of Motherhood: How Culture Reinvents the Good Mother*. New York: Houghton Mifflin.

Uno, Kathleen S. 1999. *Passages to Modernity: Motherhood, Childhood, and Social Reform in Early Twentieth Century Japan*. Honolulu: University of Hawai'i Press.

Whelehan, Imelda and Joel Gwynee. 2014. *Ageing, Popular Culture and Contemporary Feminism: Harleys and Hormones*. Basingstoke: Palgrave Macmillan.

Yao, Sijia. 2020. 'Teresa Teng in Diaspora: Affective Replacement in Chinese World-Making.' *Comparative Literature Studies* 57, no. 3: 520–9.

Ying, Li-hua and Jon Woronoff. 2009. *Historical Dictionary of Modern Chinese Literature*. Lanham: Scarecrow Press.

Yipu, Zen. 2004. 'Remade in Japan: The Case of Audrey Hepburn.' *Humanities Research* 11, no. 1: 78–105.

CHAPTER 15

Remaking in the Age of Chthulumedia: Stephen Chow's *The Mermaid*

Kenneth Chan

Stephen Chow's 2016 3D-fantasy extravaganza *The Mermaid* (*Meirenyu*) has reaffirmed the fact that Mainland Chinese-Hong Kong co-productions can continue to generate the kind of box-office largesse investors have been targeting. Outstripping director Raman Hui's mega-hit *Monster Hunt* (*Zhuoyao ji*, 2015), Chow's film crossed the US$419 million mark for Chinese ticket sales by 21 February 2016, two weeks after its Chinese New Year release date (Ehrlich 2016). The Internet Movie Database records its current global receipt at a staggering $553,810,228.[1] If the accuracy of the numbers is anything to go by, the film is obviously doing right by Chinese audiences,[2] since only one fifth of the box-office earnings seems to reflect international sales. However, it is probably not inaccurate to surmise that, like any major motion picture enterprise of this scale, *The Mermaid* must have had global aspirations, especially since Chow has chosen to rework a transnational fantasy subgenre, the mermaid film, which already occupies a prominent place in Hollywood history. One could potentially argue, as critics and scholars have done,[3] that Chow's remake is, in part, a contemporary reimagining of the romantic comedy *Splash* (Ron Howard, 1983) and Disney's animated fantasy *The Little Mermaid* (Ron Clements and John Musker, 1989). This postulation raises the question as to why the film's international theatrical run was less successful than its outsized Chinese reception. My brief attempt at answers, here in this chapter's introduction, is unscientific and speculative at best, but it does gesture toward an interpretive experiment on how to read this uneven reception of *The Mermaid*, which I see as an entertainingly quirky remake of aesthetic, intellectual and political significance.

Critical reviews of the film in mostly US newspapers and popular magazines may not be the perfect barometers of public sentiment, but they collectively provide a functional index of possible reasons for the film's uphill attempts at audience appeal in certain global markets, especially those in the West. While the US-based critics I have read were generally positive in their reception, it is how they express their appreciation that is symptomatic of the challenges at hand. First, a couple of reviewers lament the botching of the film's release in the US market, placing the onus on the Sony Corporation for not 'expect[ing] it to interest many people, outside of Chinese or Chinese-American film fans' (Abrams 2016).[4] If the reporting is correct, one of the hurdles Chinese filmmakers must apparently overcome is the perception that their work is too culturally specific and that transnational Chinese cinema must, therefore, inject more 'universal' elements into their films or, at least, conform to the genre typology that unfortunately pigeonholes Chinese cinema (for example, martial arts films as an 'ethnic' category) for it to have relevance in the Euro-American mass market. What needs to be problematised here is the notion of the 'transnational', which signifies the complex theoretical crosshatching of Hollywood global hegemony on the one hand, and the persistent global/local debates on the other. What usually gets translated as 'universal' or 'transnational' tends to be Hollywood/American conceptions and practices of cinema. Hence, Stephen Chow's appropriation/reimagining of the (Hollywood) mermaid film must have undergone a complicated and often conflictual process in working through these essentialisms to appeal to as many market sectors as possible.

Second, in celebrating its entertainment value, critics tend to focus mostly on the broad slapstick humour that characterises much of the film. Simon Abrams on www.rogerebert.com rather creatively labels the film 'a gag machine with gears that never stop turning', while generously celebrating the success of much of Chow's comedic set pieces (2016). In his review of *The Mermaid* for *Film Comment*, R. Emmet Sweeney 'wish[es] Hollywood blockbusters were half as unhinged and fearlessly creative' (2016). In an even more nuanced reading, David Ehrlich of *Slate* compares Chow's 'gauntlet of zaniness' to the comedies of the silent era, tapping into 'a primal wit that appeals to all audiences' (2016) – Hollywood slapstick being deployed, in this instance, as one of the 'universal' means/standards to achieve global cinematic legibility. In a less flattering review, Michael Nordine, from *The Village Voice*, concludes that the 'broad comedy eventually gives way to heavy-handed speechifying and graphic mermaid-slaying, little of which actually makes sense' (2016). While touting the film as 'pure enchantment', *Variety*'s Maggie Lee contends that the script 'is not wildly original', except for 'springing minor surprises and Chow's patented smart-alecky dialogue' (2016).

It is hard to disagree with the critics' underscoring of Chow's talent for comedic invention and the aesthetic unconventionality (at least in the eyes of those unacquainted or less acquainted with his oeuvre) of that comedy. But what many of them ignore or do not identify is the innovative and counter-intuitive ways with which this humour becomes entwined with and connected to the ethical and ideological core of the film and its message – hence leading to one reviewer's assessment that *The Mermaid*'s use of comedy and the ham-fisted environmental preaching appears contradictory, 'little of which actually makes sense' (Nordine 2016). It is this contradiction that I will address later in the chapter, to set forth methodologically Chow's playful auteurist tactics and to illustrate how they lend themselves to his stylised remaking of the mermaid film as a contemporary ecological text.

Also, the notion that Chow's remake 'is not wildly original' is a criticism that can be lodged against most remakes. In fact, any talk of 'originality', in an idealised sense of the word, undercuts the very concept of the remake itself, as many chapters in this book consistently demonstrate. In the next section, I take on this issue of originality to envision the remake as a transnational meme, thereby inscribing a much broader framework to think about the creative processes of cross-cultural filmic remaking and, of course, to immerse *The Mermaid* into this sea of cinematic citationality and appropriation as part of my hermeneutical experiment. Before analysing the opening segments of Chow's film, the mermaid-human romance, and the envisioning of interspecies community, I devote a short section of this chapter to the mermaid as a global cultural icon. Drawing on her presence in different national contexts – from oral traditions, folklore, mythology and literature to the latest artistic and media forms – the figure of the mermaid, as she has evolved in a hybrid transcultural/multicultural manner, resonates with consumers of cinema not only in an atavistic sense (as part of a nation's cultural mythology), but also in a form remade to appeal to modern/contemporary sensibilities. As global warming and the environmental crisis have become this generation's planetary rallying call, ecocinema – in both its documentary and its fictional narrative formats – is turning into a critical genre for global (including Chinese) audiences, while ecocinematic elements are permeating the narrational and the ideological spaces of film in general. As a hybrid eco-fairy tale, Stephen Chow's ambitious and ingenious work, with its mermaid assassin proverbially leading the way,[5] provides a formative illustration of cinematic remaking in an era of what some film scholars call 'chthulumedia', a nascent element in contemporary global mediascapes[6] that embodies in contradiction the conflicts and complicities between capital and ecological consciousness. This thesis is my way of proposing 'an act of interpretation'[7] to dislocate the reductive East-West model of examining global remakes, thereby allowing *The Mermaid* to be that planetary chthulumedia text it deserves to be.

REMAKING AS TRANSNATIONAL MEME

Over the last few decades, exciting critical work on film remakes has grown exponentially because scholars have successfully deconstructed the hierarchical and reductive linearity of the original-to-remake paradigm and, consequently, have unveiled the complicated and messy processes and intertextualities that constitute film remaking. Constantine Verevis sums this up perfectly by arguing that 'the construction of a particular intertextual relation between a remake and its presumed original is *an act of interpretation*' (2005, 29; original emphasis), thus bringing into view the extensive horizon of source material and industrial-cultural-ideological factors that energise and colour, often in interpenetrating ways, the hermeneutical method. The cross-cultural remake adds an extra layer of complexity to this interpretive/translational process that often renders visible the geopolitical power differentials between specific national film industries. Daniel Herbert observes that these 'transnational remakes . . . reveal tensions between national and transnational forces, between the local and the global, and between cultural specificity and abstraction', exposing the 'continuing disparities between Euro-American cultural exchanges and those between the US and the Pacific Rim' (2009, 144). This power dynamic plays itself out when filmmakers outside the United States remake Hollywood films, often with a strategy that is much more complicated and cunning than a straightforward appropriation of the Hollywood 'original' narrative, followed by a simplistic substitution of setting and characters with their localised counterparts. In this digital age of transnational cinematic (co)productions, the goal of the Hollywood-to-East Asian remake is double-edged in that, on one hand, it provides a means of reacting to, resisting and/or reducing Tinseltown's cultural and box-office dominance globally; while, on the other, it courts a global audience (including viewers in the United States) accustomed to cinematic plotlines, genre elements, character types and sophisticated digital visual effects popularised by Hollywood films. It is an ironic circularity of cultural exchange that deserves underscoring.[8] With the mermaid fantasy film having an established presence in Hollywood cinema, Stephen Chow's characteristically unique take on the subgenre embodies this double-edged approach with all its attendant contradictions and possibilities.

To plumb the culturally and cinematically heterogeneous and interactive depths that have spawned *The Mermaid*, I turn to Iain Robert Smith's elegant theoretical usage of the social media 'meme' as means of framing the multidirectional intersections and cross-pollinations that a more intricate envisioning of cinematic remakes is and could be. Smith examines the global reach of Hollywood's influence through a methodological 'structuring metaphor' he names 'the Hollywood Meme' (2017, 4). The concept of the meme disengages the binary paradigm of the authentic versus the culturally corrupt, allowing Smith to propose a distancing 'from models of cultural globalisation that rely upon notions of dominance and resistance to examine more closely the interstitial processes through which cultures borrow from and interact with each other' (Ibid., 6). What is especially useful in the meme is its reliance on genetics and its digital correlative as theoretical/figurative means of thinking about filmic appropriation and transformation. As Smith opines, 'Stories travel around the world and are adapted to their new environments through processes of mutation in ways analogous to genes, with some dying out and others flourishing' (Ibid., 31). In an online digital environment, easy-to-use software and applications allow users to create memes that appropriate, conjugate and/or manipulate disparate visual, textual and aural modalities to bring into being content of 'mimetic multiples and *variation*' (Shifman 2016, 199–201; original emphasis). There is also something usefully disjunctive about the meme in its suturing of disconnected cultural and temporal parts, forcing into view its stitching like Frankenstein's monster and, of course, the land/sea corporeal halves dividing the mermaid. This disjunction generates an estrangement aura that filmmakers like Chow use to great effect.

Extending from one metaphor (that of the human gene) to another (that of the internet meme), the remake as Hollywood meme – or more broadly, as a transnational cinematic meme – projects a three-dimensional spatiality to one's thinking about its (cross)cultural historicity, presence and futurity. In foregrounding the remake in terms of the multiplicity and heterogeneity of its 'originating' sources, enabling conditions, factors of influence, aesthetic (re)formulations (including adaptation, citation, appropriation, seriality), contemporaneous intertextualities and cultural impact, the meme as metaphor mobilises and effects a rhizomatic structure that Deleuze and Guattari have articulated in *A Thousand Plateaus*:

> Every rhizome contains lines of segmentarity according to which it is stratified, territorialized, organized, signified, attributed . . . as well as lines of deterritorialization down which it constantly flees. There is a rupture in the rhizome whenever segmentary lines explode into a line of flight, but the line of flight is part of the rhizome. These lines always tie back to one another (1987, 9).

While it 'ceaselessly establishes connections between semiotic chains, organizations of power, and circumstances relative to the arts, sciences, and social struggles', the rhizome is also paradoxically 'anti-genealogy' (Ibid., 7, 11). In inserting the rhizome into the metaphoric chain (meme-rhizome-remake), I seek to draw out the notions of cultural-political play and playfulness of which the remake is capable of effecting (in its multidirectional lines of extension in three-dimensional spacetime), including irony, parody and subversive mimicry. Further, I see the remake-meme as embodying the discursive potentialities of paradox and contradiction in its playful inventiveness. The twin concepts of play and paradox together produce a useful interpretive lens for one to view Stephen Chow's film, its place within the annals of the mermaid film and its engagement with contemporary ecological thinking, not just as Chinese ecocinema, but also as planetary chthulumedia in all its contradictory glory.

PLAYFULLY REMAKING THE MERMAID FILM

In their illuminating essay on the mermaid's presence in media and popular art in twenty-first-century China, Philip Hayward and Pan Wang identify contemporary representations of the mermaid as transplantations from the West, and further argue that China's capitalist makeover and rise in the global neoliberal economy figure metaphorically in the mermaid's hybridised human-fish embodiment and in her 'transformativity' as performed in Western narratives (2018, 129). It is within this cross-cultural framework that Hayward and Wang reasonably see in Chow's *The Mermaid* similarities to *Splash* and Disney's *The Little Mermaid* (Ibid., 137). Director Chow himself admits that he is 'actually a big fairy-tale addict' and considers his 'previous titles . . . as fairy tales', where 'the evil are punished and the good see a happy ending' (quoted in Fan 2016).[9] Chow's fanboy obsession with fairy tales as constitutive of his auteurist aesthetic is reminiscent of Mexican filmmaker Guillermo del Toro's own growing menagerie of monstrous figures in his cinematic oeuvre. One thinks of the idiosyncratic, quirky, bizarre, fantastical and mythological characters in Chow's films like in *Forbidden City Cop* (*Da nei mitan ling ling fa*, 1996), *The God of Cookery* (*Shishen*, 1996), *Shaolin Soccer* (*Shaolin zuqiu*, 2001), *Kung Fu Hustle* (*Gong fu*, 2004), *CJ7* (*Changjiang qi hao*, 2008), *Journey to the West: Conquering the Demons* (*Xiyou xiangmopian*, 2013) and, of course, *The Mermaid* (and not to mention the numerous films in which the director himself has appeared throughout his acting career). Akin to del Toro's approach to monstrosity, Chow's fantastical characters, and the narrative worlds they inhabit, are never what they seem to be on the surface. The deceptively uncomplicated notion that 'the evil are punished and the good see a happy ending' is his impishly playful way of turning to genre conventions that eventually fold in on themselves, deconstructing the cultural ideology that make these filmic typologies appealing in the first place.

One is prone to underestimate this apparent 'simplicity' that is Stephen Chow's mainstream cinema. Be it his deployment of *mo lei tau* (the Cantonese notion of nonsensical slapstick humour and wordplay) or his penchant for commercial genres, Chow underhandedly (and I mean this is the most complimentary sense) lulls his audiences into complacent expectations of genre formulae before pulling the rug from under them. He accomplishes this directorial sleight of hand by playfully redesigning the narrational, aesthetic and/or technical forms of popular cinema in ways that are both expected and unexpected, making them flip-sides of the same coin. This mode of complex and capacious remaking – to which Smith's theoretical metaphor of meme signals – not only surprises critics and audiences with its philosophical and political sophistication (which the cheeky silliness of *mo lei tau* seems to conceal), but also underscores how much Chow has his prescient finger on the pulse of contemporary cultural and social concerns.

At this juncture, it is also crucial to touch on, albeit very briefly, the cultural specificities of the mermaid in Chinese tradition. I am working on the assumption that discourses on and figurations of mer-people in oral storytelling, folklore, mythology and literature not only inflect the way filmmakers (like Chow) would portray them, but these culturally specific instances also appeal to Chinese-language audiences in a more focused and nuanced fashion. Furthermore, an intriguing question is how filmmakers bring these noncinematic and traditional resonances to bear when creating hybridised versions of the mermaid tale that suture (in both the cinematic and the ideological senses of the word) the Hollywood and the Chinese into the transnational remake, transforming the local into the global, so to speak.

In a short paragraph within their essay, Hayward and Wang gesture to the presence of mermaid-like entities in Chinese oral and literary traditions, referencing, for instance, the deification of China's Yangtze River as a merman-type immortal, and noting various sources that contain hybrid 'aquatic humanoids', including the popular ancient text *Shanhaijing* (2018, 130), commonly translated as *Guideways through Mountains and Seas*. Renowned sinologist Richard E. Strassberg hypothesises that *Shanhaijing*'s authorship dates back to the Xia or the Shang dynasties (2002, 3–6). In my reading of Strassberg's translation, I identify three different instances of the human-piscine hybrid.[10] First, the Di community is made up of denizens who 'have a human face and a fish's body, and they lack feet' (Ibid., 190). Second, in the section on Bingyi, Strassberg identifies him as 'the god of the Yellow River' and that according to 'some early accounts, he is described as having a white, human face and a fish's body' (Ibid., 201–2). Finally, '[t]he Hill-Fish has a human face, hands, feet, and a fish's body', though Strassberg notes that these creatures 'are all fish with human characteristics rather than mermen or mermaids' (Ibid., 204). My strategy here is not to draw a straight line of connection from *Shanhaijing* to Chow's version of the mermaid. Rather, my purpose is to tease out two critical lessons one can learn from ancient Chinese worldviews to help us appreciate Chow's remaking approach. The first and more obvious point is that the presence of these aquatic beings in Chinese legends and folktales constitutes elements of a cosmography – a word that Strassberg uses to describe *Shanhaijing* and other similar texts in ancient Chinese literary history (Ibid., 4) – serving as a foundational mythos for an 'imagined' community (see Anderson 1998), and as the basis for ideological instruction in communal ethical behaviour and relations, issues I see surfacing in Chow's film. The second and less obvious lesson of note is that these immortal-human-animal hybrid beings inhabiting the *Shanhaijing*, according to Strassberg, 'were almost never allegorically construed' like in European legends and myths, but 'were regarded as actual entities found throughout the landscape' of these cosmographies (2002, xiii). 'That is, fact and fantasy combined in works such as the *Guideways* to distribute a diverse population of strange creatures throughout a vast, sacred geography where they dwell in the eternal present of mythological time' and the texts 'were continually evolving as new intelligence about the world was gathered' (Ibid., 10). What I wish to accentuate in Strassberg's extended introduction to his translation is less an attribution of an orientalist primitivism and superstition than a form of humility when confronted by the fantastic, the strange, the nonhuman and the unknown in the natural and spiritual realms. In a way, *Shanhaijing*, with its mer-denizens, almost functions as a proto-ecological text, offering a zeitgeist that Chow's film potentially rearticulates and inhabits.

Before focusing on Chow's film in the remainder of this chapter, I make one final contextual turn to the mermaid in cinema. Because the filmic and televisual archive is substantive, and spatial constraints do not permit me to examine in any detail the various iterations and permutations of the mermaid on screen, I point readers to Philip Hayward's near-encyclopedic cataloguing of examples and references in Euro-American media in his book *Making a Splash* (2017) and the wide range of mermaid sightings in global screen cultures in his follow-up *Scaled for Success* (2018). In the latter edited volume, Hayward and Wang's chapter lists Chinese-language films featuring the aquatic wonder, including Norman Law's *Mermaid Got Married* (*Renyu chuanshuo*, 1994), Lou Ye's *Suzhou River* (*Suzhouhe*, 2000), Qiu Haoqiang's animated *The Little Mermaid: Attack of the Pirates* (*Meirenyu zhi haidao lai xi*, 2015), Lin Yunxiang and Ming Ye's *She's from Another Planet* (*Renyu xiaohua*, 2016) and Gao Weilun's *Goodbye Mermaid* (*Zaijian meirenyu*, 2016). Not included in that list is Kao Li's *The Mermaid* (*Yu meiren*, 1965), one of the Shaw Brothers' Huangmei operatic films. While it features a love affair between a magical carp spirit and a poor scholar, and is technically not a mermaid flick per se, Kao Li's work presents an early representation of interspecies sexual congress and cross-species transmogrification.[11] Together with the titles listed above, this film (with the gravitas of Chinese operatic tradition) expands the cinematic horizon of potential influences, beyond the Hollywood 'originals', out of which Chow's film emerged. Undoubtedly making its mark in this trend (like a meme), the overwhelming success of Chow's *The Mermaid* now has audiences waiting with bated breath for its sequel (the release of which has been delayed during the prolonged COVID-19 pandemic), though that desire might be temporarily sated by other productions released over the last three years from lesser-known Chinese directors.[12]

THE CHTHULUMEDIA REMAKE: STEPHEN CHOW'S *THE MERMAID*

In their ingeniously ludic and boundary-rupturing book on cephalopods and contemporary screen cultures, *The Squid Cinema from Hell*, William Brown and David H. Fleming bring together two ideologically opposing sources to invoke the concept of 'chthulumedia': H. P. Lovecraft's 'Cthulhu mythology' and Donna J. Haraway's theoretical neologism 'chthulucene' (Brown and Fleming 2020, 6, 32). To confront the apocalyptic crisis of the Anthropocene, Haraway makes the remarkable and influential philosophical argument that we need 'to make kin in lines of inventive connection as a practice of learning to live and die well with each other in a thick present'. 'Staying with the trouble', as she calls it, places an imperative on 'learning to be truly present, not as a vanishing pivot between awful or edenic pasts and apocalyptic or salvific futures, but as mortal critters entwined in myriad unfinished configurations of places, times, matters, meanings' (2016, 1). To conceive this spacetime materiality and discourse of ethical and relational entwinement, she coins the term 'chthulucene', etymologically derived in part from the Greek '*khthôn*', chthonic (2016, 2). But the critical fire that Haraway has since drawn, rather unfairly I might add, is that her terminology is seen as aligned with H. P. Lovecraft's fictional monstrous creation the Cthulhu (which appears in his famous short story 'The Call of Cthulhu') and, hence, indicating to some a kind of associative semantic complicity with Lovecraft's racist, sexist and anti-immigrant attitudes.[13]

Brown and Fleming suggest that Haraway, in her requisite rejection of Lovecraftian bigotry, should also not miss the opportunity of confronting 'the tentacular, cephalopod qualities of the [Cthulhu] creature' in order to assist our reflections on 'the chthulucene more clearly'. In so doing, 'chthulumedia' can 'deliver to us a vision of a radically other, nonhuman universe – even if human figures (whether racist and misogynist or not) remain central to these movies and media' (2020, 32–3). While rejecting and critiquing extreme reactionary and oppressive ideologies, Brown and Fleming's theorising of chthulumedia does not avoid the difficult route of acknowledging the interconnectivity of planetary life that 'pulls thought into dark, nonhuman realms, where many of the traditional boundaries, borders, and divisions no longer pertain' (Ibid., 33). Part of the paradox of chthulumedia is that the chthulucene's progressive idealism can still unwittingly risk inducing blind spots where the consequences of the Anthropocene and the failings of capital, including the cultural politics of hatred and alterity, are capable of reemerging. By underscoring this embodied paradox and contradiction in chthulumedia, readings of such texts will, hopefully, engender critical self-reflection of chthulumedia practices, both their potentialities and constraints/fault lines. As Brown and Fleming contend (and Chow demonstrates in *The Mermaid*):

> To create a paradox, or even a plain contradiction in terms . . . runs the risk of being at least weird, and at worst alienating and nonsensical, perhaps even controversial. However, the alienation and the nonsense are partially deliberate and also necessary if we are to grasp the weird world that chthulumedia bring to us (Ibid., 34).

To unpack this weird world of *The Mermaid* and the paradoxical and contradictory 'nonsense' that is Chow's cinematic construction, I have divided the film into four different realms for analytical purposes:

1) the opening credit sequence;
2) the 'Museum of World Exotic Animals' scene;
3) the mermaid-human love story scenario; and
4) the 'historical' worldbuilding of human-merfolk communal connectivity.

In the opening scene of Ron Howard's *Splash*, the boy Allen Bauer (Tom Hanks's character, played by David Kreps) is strangely mesmerised by the waters off Cape Cod, in the manner in which sailors were by siren songs in seafaring folklore. He unexpectedly jumps from the ferry into the water, only to be rescued by a child mermaid. This establishing sequence (which is also redeployed in Norman Law's Hong Kong remake *Mermaid Got Married*) not only foreshadows Bauer's eventual abandonment of terra firma to live with the mermaid Madison (Daryl Hannah) under the sea, it also reminds audiences of the film's geospatial framing that our planet is approximately 70 per cent aqueous, with a material boundary that the landbound Bauer crosses. This land-to-sea movement reverses its direction in Disney's *The Little Mermaid*, where Ariel (voiced by Jodi Benson) daydreams about the human realm, which she sings about so achingly in the song 'Part of Your World'. Ironically, Ariel finds the exotic mise-en-scène of the undersea kingdom pedestrian, though it does not stop the film from thrilling audiences with its (for that time) creative animation of luminous aquatic worldmaking. Both *Splash* and *The Little Mermaid*, in their fairy tale fashion, romanticise this land-sea interface, an intersection that Chow complicates in the opening credit sequence of *The Mermaid*.

The film's first image involves a zoom shot of what is clearly polluted water with a dirty greenish-blue tinge. The camera pulls back its focus to unveil an upside-down reflection of smokestacks. The land-sea interface is now de-romanticised, ruptured by the toxic output of the capitalist industrial complex. This initial unsavoury visual is expanded upon by a video montage featuring a wider shot of the intense fumes spewing from (what one assumes to be, as the filmic cut suggests) these very smokestacks, a low angle shot of trees being cut down, an aerial tracking shot of a swarth created by deforestation, a medium shot of black sludge gushing forth from industrial drains, another medium shot of oily trash floating on the watery habitat of birds, a close-up of a helpless bird covered in oil, a long shot of dolphins dying on a beach and a medium close-up of a shark's fin being sliced by a fisherman. That last image cuts a little too close to home, since shark fin soup is still considered by many in East Asian and Southeast Asian communities as a gourmet delicacy. The entire montage sequence stitches together documentary videos, many of which Chow has culled and collated from Getty Images. As Sheldon H. Lu observes about Chinese ecocinema, 'A concern with the environment has been a main preoccupation of such a documentary impulse' in the New Chinese Documentary movement, although 'Chinese ecocinema traverses feature films as well as documentaries' (2009, 3). Chow's choices are strategically heavy-handed in their vérité messaging; the over-the-top reality of the ecological crisis in documentary montage is matched, in ironic counterpoint, only by the over-the-top fairy tale that is about to unfold.

Two other observations about the geographical settings of these videos and the way this documentary segment segues to the fictive narrative deserve further mention. Even though the film's fictional setting is located along the Chinese coastline, the video clips that Chow uses capture pollution, animal cruelty and ecological irresponsibility from scattered locales around the world, including Japan, Laos, the Jänschwalde coal power station in Germany (the reflection of the smokestacks) and even Grand Canyon National Park in the United States. The globality of these images demarcates the planetary scope and impact of the Anthropocene, but it also places the film on a transnational footing, emphasising the relevance of this eco-fairy tale to an international audience. The documentary montage is also 'seamlessly' sutured to the fictional sequence where a submarine sphere is lowered into the waters to send a pulsing wave that violently scatters the marine life in its wake. The 'seams' are simultaneously invisible (in the way the submarine sequence is contiguous with real documentary footage) and visible (when what these scientists depicted in the control room are doing with the sphere is later revealed as an essential element in the fictional plot), a contradiction that allows Chow to heighten the political relevance of his filmic art in its connections to the environmental activism of the day, while pinpointing, in turn, the playful artifice that is *The Mermaid*. Or, as Fiona Yuk-wa Law puts it with a slightly different inflection, the sequence 'diverts the pleasure-seeking audience to the unpleasant reality, and prepares them to make the connection between the comic plot and the cruel reality of human destruction of nature' (2019, 187).[14]

With the documentary-fictional montage providing a sort of cinematic preface, the 'Museum of World Exotic Animals' sequence follows immediately, as the editors use the fleeing school of fish (as scattered by the sonic waves from the submarine sphere) as a fanciful transitional wipe, which plays to the spectacle of 3D technology. Thomas Elsaesser brilliantly locates the twenty-first century 3D trend as part of a larger trajectory of digitality by suggesting that 3D visuality reconfigures 'our sense of spatial and temporal orientation and our embodied relation to data-rich simulated environments' (2013, 221). While this fleeting moment of 3D inventiveness may just be one of the technology's multiple ploys, one cannot help but imagine this embodied 'stereoscopy'

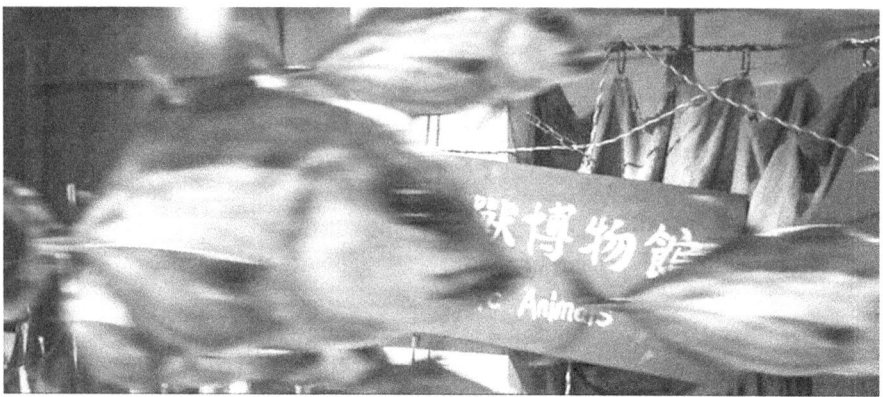

Figure 15.1 The school of fish functions as a playful 3D transitional wipe in Stephen Chow's *The Mermaid* (*Meirenyu*, 2016).

(Ibid., 228) as an opportune beginning for oceanic mediation – what Melody Jue terms, in her book *Wild Blue Media*, 'milieu-specific analysis' (2020, 3). Jue deploys 'conceptual displacement as a method of dislocating terrestrially nurtured thought into the ocean, a process that may involve physical immersion, technically mediated immersion, and speculative immersion through fiction, film, digital media, and the arts' (Ibid., 7). Whatever Chow's intentions may be, his film's 3D mimetic playfulness dips its audience, however briefly, into an aquatic stereoscopic sensorium that ultimately lends itself to chthulumedia's ludic potentiality of transcending anthropocentric perspectives on planetary life and existence.

This whimsical wipe editing further prepares audiences for the sheer absurdity that is the museum scene, which, at first glance, may seem unnecessary to the film's plot, apart from allowing Chow's *mo lei tau* to assume centre stage. In mock-scientific seriousness, the museum guide (Yeung Lun) gravely intones:

> Four billion years ago, the first marine life formed. First came the fish. Then, slowly, other life forms evolved. Therefore, our ancestors came from fish . . . Nature is truly wonderful. In order to adapt, creatures from land, sea and sky breed with each other. And humans are no exception.[15]

The dirty, dishevelled and sweaty tour guide leads an equally offbeat and idiosyncratic coterie of visitors, who are willing to shell out ten dollars for what is obviously a tourist trap (or an extreme parody of one). Each exhibit tops the other in its audacity to scam, which the visitors are quick to point out at every moment of the tour: a dried gecko simulates a Tyrannosaurus Rex, a pet dog tied to a chamber pot pretends to be '*Panthera tigris balica*' (or simply a

Balinese tiger), a medical mannequin is dressed as Batman with chicken wings for ears, and a mermaid made up of a Barbie doll stuck onto the lower half of a preserved fish. At this juncture, the audience is introduced to Shan (Jelly Lin, a.k.a. Lin Yun), the film's mermaid protagonist in human disguise, who proclaims that the mermaid exhibit is a staple Chinese ingredient called 'salted fish' in reality. 'I don't believe you! You're lying!' Shan decries (and she should know), thus egging the rest of the group to demand a refund. The angered and exasperated museum guide, in fake self-righteousness, proclaims 'Enough! I've worked damn hard to run this place! You idiots want to ruin me? It ain't happening! Open the door! Let them see it!' The *coup de grâce* alluded to abides in a bathroom. The point-of-view perspective assumed by the camera gaze suspensefully leads the visitors (and the film's audience) toward a green-tiled bathtub filled with seaweed-laced water that mimics the polluted water at the beginning of the film. Dramatically emerging out of the water is the museum guide in mermaid drag, as the strings soar climactically in the soundtrack. The faux mermaid adjusts his glasses as he lies prone on the edge of the tub like a model, nonchalantly proclaiming, 'I'm a mermaid.'

By adopting Timothy Morton's critical language, Law insightfully labels the props in this scene as 'eco-kitsch' (2019, 172); 'kitschy-comic elements [that] are strategically used to enforce a critical ecological message, as well as an implied critique of China's accelerated economic developments and its infrastructural projects in Hong Kong' (2019, 182–3).[16] While Law is on the mark with her analysis, I would like to build on this critique by mobilising a reading of this sequence that connects it more intimately to the film's broader mermaid love story. I describe this segment as a 'microcosmic prologue', working in tandem with the previous documentary montage 'preface' but effecting a slightly different inflection to the film at large. This microcosmic prologue not only encapsulates what the rest of the film is doing from a metanarrative perspective, but it also offers an ironic, self-reflective gloss on the film's paradoxes and contradictions. In her study of *Monster Hunt* and *The Mermaid*, Law argues that '[d]espite their comic representations of the nonhuman creatures and carnivalesque plots as features of eco-kitsch films', they 'investigate ecological issues by questioning their own defining features as profit-making cultural products' (2019, 173). Instead of 'despite', I contend that it is precisely 'through' these moments of comedic absurdity that *The Mermaid*'s complicity as capitalist commodity is exposed. The 'Museum of World Exotic Animals' is obviously a satirical take on tourist scams, but Chow goes to the extreme in the lampoon – making the faking so overt that the seams of the faking are exposed. Take the two mermaid spectacles in the museum as examples: the first instance is the ridiculous jamming of the top half of a Barbie doll to the bottom half of a piece of salted fish, the concatenation of the western ideal of feminine beauty in the human half to the epicurean commodification of Chinese seafood in the lower. What Chow has concocted here is also not new, as the fake 'Feejee Mermaid' was a carnival sensation at the hands of P. T. Barnum and his ilk in the nineteenth century – the top portion of the hoax came from an orangutan while the bottom was salmon (Hayward 2017, 182).[17] The thematisation of the mermaid on display at carnivals and 'freak shows' is common enough cinematic practice for Chow to appreciate its place in consumerist spectacles: Georges Méliès's 1904 short *La sirène* has a magician conjure a mermaid in his aquarium; a very young Dennis Hopper plays a sailor obsessed with a mermaid in a carnival sideshow in *Night Tide* (Curtis Harrington, 1961); Norman Law has the four villains in *Mermaid Got Married* capture the film's protagonist in order to embark on a world tour; and the sexual obsession with mermaids on display in night clubs, fake or real (ambiguity left intact), is depicted in Lou Ye's *Suzhou River*.

If the theme of displaying mermaids is problematic, isn't the simple diegetic presentation of the mermaid in cinema (film as a consumerist product) itself complicit, too, in this anthropocentric and ableist process of commodifying nonhuman lives and 'abnormal' bodies, respectively, as carnival spectacles? This particular paradox of chthulumedia Chow seems to be deeply cognisant. Not only does the museum guide's mermaid performance parody Disney theme parks and Sea World displays, but its greedy motivation also mirrors in microcosmic form the purchasing of the Green Gulf bay by the mega-rich businessman Liu Xuan (Deng Chao) for a supposedly 'ecologically friendly project'; the reality of which is a reclamation enterprise where, as Liu Xuan himself admits, 'the profits would be huge'.[18] One cannot disregard the fact that *The Mermaid* was also hugely profitable at the box office. When the museum guide performs his mermaid routine, one of the visitors melancholically asks him '*Guan zhang, ni zhe you shi heku?*', which is loosely translated as 'Curator, why are you going through all this trouble to do this to yourself and us?' To which the museum guide responds, 'Hey, I'm just trying to make a living, okay? Don't worry, be happy. Let's take a picture.' He inappropriately grins and flashes them a peace sign with his fingers.[19] The question asked is emotionally doubled-edged: why is he going to such ethical extremes to scam them just to make a profit? But it also connotes the absurdity of the spectacle in the context of one of the visitors dying from a heart attack after laughing so hard at the sight of the cross-dressed mermaid. It is the laughter of death, the paradoxical play of ecocinema as comedy; for the planet's environmental doom and species extinction are no laughing matter. Yet, ecocinema can risk becoming commoditised itself. In their rage at being cheated, the visitors kick the museum guide out of his own establishment, as he comically stumbles into the street in his mermaid suit. *The Mermaid* as chthulumedia finds itself entangled in a moebius-strip logic of laughter at its own predicament as both cultural critique and cinematic capital – laughing, stumbling, hurting, messaging and profiting all at the same time.

The moment when the museum owner and guide is thrown out into the streets is not the last time audiences see him. He returns at the end of the action-sequence finale on the pier, painting a picture in his mermaid suit and staring in shock at a bloodied and injured Shan. The fake mermaid quickly takes a photo of the real mermaid Shan in her battered state, a set-up that allows Chow to bring the film full circle: the museum guide continues his attempts to profit off the mermaid figure, this time at the expense of real lives at stake. Again, like the microcosmic prologue, the museum guide mirrors Liu Xuan in his pre-enlightened thinking about making money as the only goal worth pursuing, even if it means killing the dolphins and the merfolk (of which Liu Xuan maintains plausible deniability) in order to obtain a permit from the government to proceed with his reclamation project in Green Bay. This deeply fraught relationship between economic profit and ecological 'correctness' – Liu Xuan's company only 'abides' by conservation laws by surreptitiously using his sonar to scatter marine life, while ignoring the deadly fallout of the technology – becomes the motivating force in the mermaid love story.

In *Splash*, Madison's sexuality and her attraction to Allen Bauer provide the impetus for her adventures in Manhattan and the requisite Hollywood happy ending with Bauer joining her and leaving the life as he knows it. Disney's *The Little Mermaid* reverses the characters' final movement when Ariel's father King Triton (Kenneth Mars) learns the difficult parental lesson of letting go and magically transforms his daughter's tail into legs so that she can go and live with her prince. Both of these films ignore the violent and tragic story and ending of Hans Christian Andersen's version, where the motivation of the little mermaid is more complicated: she is not only in love with the prince but seeks 'the prize of an immortal soul' (Andersen 2008, 143). The merfolk in Andersen's story 'lack an immortal soul, and . . . shall never have another life' when they die (Ibid., 139). When the mermaid seeks out the Sea Witch for her help to become human, the latter warns her of the physical torments awaiting her: 'Your tail will then split in two and shrink into what human beings call pretty legs. But it will hurt. It will feel like a sharp sword passing through you.' The pain is compounded by the fact that 'every step you take will make you feel as if you were treading on a sharp knife, enough to make your feet bleed' (Ibid., 143). At the end of the story, instead of the Disney happy ending, the little mermaid could not make herself kill the prince, the only way she could return to her mermaid form and resume her previous life; instead, she sacrifices herself by jumping into the sea and drowning.

In looking at Chow's approach to the romance, I want to address the violence in the film as a route toward identifying the inciting chthulumedia elements that drive the love story. Critics have expressed their shock at the violence depicted in *The Mermaid*, despite the fact that Hans Christian Andersen's fairy tale is the gruesome literary source for the Hollywood films. I suppose the visualising of violence can foreground and force a needed reassessment of the discursive violence in Andersen's children's bedtime story, much of which is also only implied in the sanitised Disney adaptation. One reviewer describes the film as depicting 'graphic mermaid-slaying' (Nordine 2016), while another accuses Chow of 'the sadistic abuse he puts his sweet and innocent heroine through' as being consistent with 'the longstanding misogynist streak in his work' (Lee 2016). While I am in no way disputing the latter critic's claim of Chow's negative representation of women in his films (an issue that deserves analysis in a separate essay) nor am I endorsing the carnage depicted on screen (particularly when the violence is abusively directed at female characters – the bloodied Shan on the pier is especially hard to watch, a scene that the director could have toned down without detracting from his ultimate imagistic goal), it is also critical to see Chow's use of gore in the context of its sharp contrast to the absurdist comedy that precedes the jarring scenes of maiming and killing, hence inducing a jolt in the audience as its intended effect. Fiona Law reads the scene of the horribly injured Shan on the pier as akin to 'wartime photojournalism' by 'exposing the effects of human violence'. In alignment with my argument of the sharp contrast in tone, she further argues that this 'contrast between extreme violence and grotesque humor has resulted in a kitschy critique of the nonsensical extermination of marine creatures by humans' (2019, 190), while deploying an ecofeminist 'ethics of care' (Ibid., 168) to enact compassionate relationality toward nonhuman lives. Similarly, Hayward and Wang are on point when they compare the cruel attack on the merfolk in their waterfall-abandoned tanker ship hideaway to dolphin slaying: 'Ruolan's henchmen fire into the water, hitting various individuals and turning the water red with their blood (like the sea in Taiji Cove [in Japan] during dolphin hunting' (2018, 139). The violence, therefore, is metaphoric of the inhumane (for the lack of a less-anthropocentric term) practices directed at aquatic life in sectors of the fishing industry. The reaction to this violence and killing provides a new chthulumedia rationale for the mermaid love story to exist. Instead of sexuality (as in *Splash*), a coming-of-age identity crisis (in the Disney film) or the supposed spirituality (in Hans Christian Andersen's story), Chow's *The Mermaid* relies on a 'revenge plot with a seductive femme fatale', a fairy-tale film noir where 'nature strikes back' (Law 2019, 181). Before unexpectedly falling in love with her target, Shan's mission is to kill Liu Xuan for the havoc he and his company have wreaked on oceanic life, particularly the merfolk community. Remaking in the age of chthulumedia means for Chow deploying a storyline that not only has elements from the G- and PG-rated Hollywood mermaid films, but also spills over with the R-rated violence that is visualised in other examples of ecocinema, such as *The Cove* (Louie Psihoyos, 2009), clips from which Chow uses in the scene where Liu Xuan watches dolphin slaughter online (Law 2019, 189).

The blissful narrative conclusion of *The Mermaid* is surely a pragmatic compromise on Chow's part to ensure that his film appeals to mainstream audiences, and possibly even to get around the Chinese censors.[20] But the violence that I have traced out above has inevitably coloured the happy-ever-after ending of the fantasy rom-com aspect of the film, in a way that exposes the ideological complicities of Hollywood genre conventions in suppressing and 'resolving' thorny, controversial issues in a deus ex machina fashion. To extend further this form of critical self-reflection of the cinematic milieu in which he is working, Chow also tactically merges the endings of *Splash* and Disney's *The Little Mermaid* by having Shan and Liu Xuan live out amphibious existences. Shan does not need to sacrifice her aquatic community, as the final scene shows her and Liu Xuan diving into the deep; while Liu Xuan does not have to give up his life on land, as the interview scene with the student depicts Liu Xuan introducing Shan as his wife Lucy; a scene in which they 'live an ordinary [bourgeois] life'. Therefore, one should not be too hard on the director for choosing this terra-aqua happy ending, because he permits his film to expose and acknowledge its own fault lines, even in the worldbuilding and communal mythology on which the film's idealistic vision relies.

To conclude this chapter idealistically (in the spirit of Haraway's work), I want to return to the concept of community and its intersections with the cultural mythology that I discussed earlier in relation to *Shanhaijing*. In Chow's films, found community is not only a critical aspect of the diegetic worlds he builds, but it is also a way of invoking an ethics of planetary interconnection and interdependency.[21] *The Mermaid*'s fictional world mythmaking is channelled through the matriarchal mermaid (Fan Shuzhen) who, near the beginning of the film, starts telling her charges the human-merfolk joint history:

> In ancient times, both humans and our ancestors were apes. When the land changed, some apes were forced to live in the sea. Their legs were of no use and evolved into fishtails. Mermaids and humans should have coexisted side by side. But ever since ancient times, whenever humans spotted us, they hunted us down. Since then, we have stayed away from humans. However, the more advanced they get, the more violent they've become. So, humans are evil. But . . .

The matriarch drifts off to sleep, leaving her speech to Octopus (Show Lo), who in turn articulates his hatred of humans because of the harm they have inflicted on his community. But toward the end of the film, when Shan admits her love for Liu Xuan, the matriarch takes this opportunity to finish the speech she started earlier, filling in the final missing piece of the puzzle:

Love has no law. It is beyond any rules or boundaries. In the Ming Dynasty, over 600 years ago, we barely escaped from the seven attacks of the human navies. Without the generous help of Mr. Zheng, we would have been extinct. Human beings can be evil. But there are good ones, too. Love is all around. Love is patience. It can stand the test of time. Never-ending.

She concludes her sermon by suggesting that love is what is needed to bring humans and mer-people together.

The camera then immediately zeros in on an ancient Chinese painting of the aforementioned human Mr Zheng and his beloved, a mermaid in a traditional Chinese dress. One could conjecture that this prop is a convenient allusion, intentioned or otherwise, to the mythic tradition and 'history' implied in the human-fish hybrids of *Shanhaijing*, and to the Huangmei opera story of the scholar and the carp spirit in Kao Li's *The Mermaid*. Yeh and Chao also see this human figure as an 'anachronistic' comingling of 'unrelated historical figures Cheng He (1371–1433) and Cheng Chenggong (a.k.a. Koxinga, 1624–62) and contemporary Canto-pop [Hong Kong] star Adam Cheng (b. 1947)' (2020, 195), which alludes to the complicated entwining of Hong Kong's and China's political fates. From a local/national standpoint, the matriarchal mermaid's idealisation of community, humility and love presents a utopian philosophy that stands in stark contrast to the authoritarian politics of domination and force that Mainland China asserts over Hong Kong. But, more importantly, this community of love does not simplistically suggest acquiescence and submission; instead it proposes a tactic of loving resistance as represented by Shan's willingness to oppose the use of retributive violence as a sociopolitical tactic, and by Liu Xuan standing up for Shan (and her community) in the

Figure 15.2 An ancient painting depicts Mr Zheng and his mermaid lover in *The Mermaid* (*Meirenyu*, 2016).

end, as Ruolan vengefully and angrily shoots harpoons into his torso. Here, I would like to bridge the Hong Kong-China national politics to that of the planetary and ecological ethics of chthulumedia, where the notion of (global/local) community articulates the inspiration and aspiration of the chthulucene that Donna Haraway renders as staying with the trouble. For to love 'is to make kin in lines of inventive connection as a practice of learning to live and die well with each other in a thick present' (2016, 1). And in loving one another in this thick present, Shan and Liu Xuan are setting the example of staying with the trouble, 'to make trouble, to stir up potent response to devastating events, as well as to settle troubled waters and rebuild quiet places' (Ibid.). *The Mermaid* as chthulumedia remake-meme is that which troubles audiences with its contradictions and paradoxes, as witnessed in the integration of its nonsensical zaniness, the simplistic Hollywood-style romance and happy ending, the violent imagery and its overly gory turns, and the seemingly naïve idealism of the film's message of peaceful coexistence. And yet, it is these contradictions of chthulumedia,[22] like the unexpected contradictions of daily living, that inspire us to love and connect fearlessly with other planetary beings – human and nonhuman – even in the midst of our distinctiveness, distance and diversity.

NOTES

1. https://www.imdb.com/title/tt4701660/?ref_=fn_tt_tt_1. Accessed 24 March 2022.
2. An important caveat is that Chow has a well-established fanbase in China, hence the exceptional success of the film despite the generally declining national box-office receipts beginning in 2016. The film's appealing narrative and cultural connectivity, plus the Chinese New Year season, further contributed to its box-office earnings (Zhang 2017, 164–5).
3. See Chiarella (2016), Ebiri (2016) and Hayward and Wang (2018).
4. See also Ebiri (2016) and Ehrlich (2016).
5. Gracing the prow of Euro-American ships of yore were female figureheads, often of royal dignitaries, famous women from high society, deities and mythological characters, including the mermaid (Lewis 1996). Ironically, her association with the danger that sirens had supposedly presented to sailors and their ships did not deter shipbuilders from deploying her as a figurehead in the nineteenth century. To ward off calamitous storms, her presence assumed a totemic function on these vessels (Ibid., 838).
6. For a definitional discussion of 'mediascapes', see Appadurai (1996, 35–6).
7. I am proleptically using Constantine Verevis's terminology here, which I cite early in the next section of this chapter.
8. For more detailed discussions of the intricacies in Hollywood remaking and Hollywood remade, see some of the essays in Smith and Verevis (2017).
9. Hayward and Wang cite Chow's pronouncements in this source as evidence of what they surmise to be the director's thinking when making this film (2018, 137).
10. Strassberg counts seven instances (2002, 204) but I am only highlighting three that are more overtly material or significant in the text.
11. Some discussion of the film's sexual and gender politics is available in Tan See-Kam's essay on the Huangmei opera films (2007, 4).

12. Information about the films is hardly available in the West (much less access to viewing these movies) as these titles were released only in China with little to no fanfare, as far as I can gather from my limited online searches: *Legend of the Mermaid* (*Donghai renyu chuan*, Channel Choi, 2020), *Legend of the Mermaid 2* (*Donghai renyu chuan 2*, Channel Choi, Xun Lu and Ruan Fogo, 2021) and *The Legend of the Nanhai Mermaid* (*Sou shen ji: Nanhai meiren jiao*, Xiao-Hui Ma, 2020).
13. One such criticism can be found in the *London Review of Books* (Turner 2017), which was serious enough that Haraway took time to offer a detailed rebuttal in a response letter (which is available on the same website as Turner's piece). In the letter, Haraway reflects on how she should have 'used the term Chthonocene' instead. For a discussion of Lovecraft's overtly evident bigotry, see Leslie Klinger's forward to *The New Annotated H. P. Lovecraft* (2014, xxxvii–xli; lxvi–lxvii). A more trenchant critique of Lovecraft is available in Bruce Lord's online essay (2004).
14. Hayward and Wang rather creatively observe how '[t]hese two sequences set up polarities of the catastrophic-grotesque (of the environmental footage) and comic-grotesque (of the museum [sequence which follows])' (2018, 138).
15. For the film's dialogue, I have relied mostly on the subtitles from the US Blu-ray release but have, at times, either made minor changes or have incorporated my own translation of the original Mandarin for clarity, correctness and/or cultural nuance. (*The Mermaid*, dir. Stephen Chow, Blu-ray, Sony Pictures Home Entertainment, 2016).
16. Yeh and Chao also point to the China-Hong Kong tensions in these absurdist moments as the director's way of working round the Chinese censors and underscoring his Hong Kong identity, while still nimbly straddling the political divide within China-Hong Kong co-productions (2020, 193, 195).
17. See Jan Bondeson (1999, 36–63) for a fascinatingly baroque retelling of the Feejee Mermaid as carnival exploitation meets Victorian scientific inquiry. Of particular relevance is the notion that this fake creation is rumoured to have been retrieved from the Far East, an account enabled by the orientalist exoticism of the day.
18. Law presents some excellent historical context regarding Sha Lo Wan, 'a similar-looking bay area with traditional villages in the northwest Lantau Island in Hong Kong', and the political fights between environmental activists and government entities over capitalist intrusions and their impact on the China White Dolphins (2019, 184–5). For another Hong Kong-China intertextual reference, see Evans Chan's 2001 film *The Map of Sex and Love* (*Qingse ditu*), where one of the main protagonists depicts in his own sketches the mythic merfolk (as fish on the upper half and human on the bottom half) who 'rose up against their repressive Chinese rulers' in the eleventh century in what is purportedly a village on Lantau Island. This reversal of the fish-human corporeal structure is also deployed in the police station scene in *The Mermaid*, this time as part of the police officers' comical attempt at mocking Liu Xuan for reporting that he was just abducted by the merfolk. Echoing Evans Chan's political allegory, Yeh and Chao interpret the aquatic beings in Chow's film as metaphors for the Hong Kong citizenry (2020, 195).
19. It is most unfortunate and unacceptable that this set piece relies on transgender humour, which is sadly consistent with Chow's equally problematic use of effeminacy and gay sexuality in a few of his other films. But without exonerating the director on this score, one wonders if he might be developing some inkling of queer consciousness when he has what appears to be a transgender character (one of the visitors) be the one who asks the curator the crucial question I cited above.
20. Shiau and Yecies map out the labyrinthine pathways of the Chinese censorship system that Chow and his team had to navigate to get the film made and released (2018, 99–102). Shelly Kraicer's theory of *The Mermaid*'s success on this matter is rather ingenious: 'It hides a

controversial "political-social" allegory under the cover of another "political-social" but far more acceptable environmental parable' (2016). Of course, this tricky mise en abyme does not diminish the political efficacy of the film's ecological critique, nor are the two 'political-social' issues necessarily mutually exclusive and not intertwined in complicated ways.
21. Two intriguing instances are the residents of Pigsty Alley in *Kung Fu Hustle* and Tripitaka and his disciples in *Journey to the West: Conquering the Demons*.
22. In ascertaining a method to Chow's cinematic madness, as the director works within China's tight censorial regime, Kraicer concludes, as I do, that Chow 'always embraced contradiction and denied consistency', hence proving 'that even China's mainstream culture, allied to power as it is, can accommodate and even celebrate troublesome contradictions and unresolved difference' (2016).

REFERENCES

Abrams, Simon. 2016. 'The Mermaid.' *RogerEbert.com*, 20 February. https://www.rogerebert.com/reviews/the-mermaid-2016. Accessed 24 March 2022.
Andersen, Hans Christian. 2008. *The Annotated Hans Christian Andersen*. Edited by Maria Tatar. Translated by Maria Tatar and Julie K. Allen. New York: W. W. Norton & Company.
Anderson, Benedict. 1998. *Imagined Communities: Reflections on the Origin and Spread of Nationalism*. London: Verso.
Appadurai, Arjun. 1996. *Modernity at Large: Cultural Dimensions of Globalization*. Minneapolis: University of Minnesota Press.
Bondeson, Jan. 1999. *The Feejee Mermaid and Other Essays in Natural and Unnatural History*. Ithaca: Cornell University Press.
Brown, William and David H. Fleming. 2020. *The Squid Cinema from Hell:* Kinoteuthis Infernalis *and the Emergence of Chthulumedia*. Edinburgh: Edinburgh University Press.
Chiarella, Chris. 2016. 'The Mermaid.' *Sound & Vision*, 18 November. https://www.soundandvision.com/content/mermaid. Accessed 11 June 2022.
Deleuze, Gilles and Félix Guattari. 1987. *A Thousand Plateaus: Capitalism and Schizophrenia*. Translated by Brian Massumi. Minneapolis: University of Minnesota Press.
Ebiri, Bilge. 2016. 'The Overlooked *Mermaid* is a Hilarious Fantasy.' *Vulture*, 20 February https://www.vulture.com/2016/02/overlooked-mermaid-is-a-hilarious-fantasy.html. Accessed 24 March 2022.
Ehrlich, David. 2016. '*The Mermaid* Comes Ashore.' *Slate*, 26 February. https://slate.com/culture/2016/02/stephen-chows-the-mermaid-reviewed.html. Accessed 24 March 2022.
Elsaesser, Thomas. 2013. 'The "Return" of 3-D: On Some of the Logics and Genealogies of the Image in the Twenty-First Century.' *Critical Inquiry* 39, no. 2: 217–46.
Fan, Xu. 2016. 'Stephen Chow Gives Away Nothing – As Usual.' *China Daily*, 4 February. https://www.chinadaily.com.cn/culture/2016-02/04/content_23385646.htm. Accessed 23 February 2022.
Haraway, Donna J. 2016. *Staying with the Trouble: Making Kin in the Chthulucene*. Durham: Duke University Press.
Hayward, Philip. 2017. *Making a Splash: Mermaids (and Mermen) in 20th and 21st Century Audiovisual Media*. East Barnet: John Libbey Publishing.
Hayward, Philip, ed. 2018. *Scaled for Success: The Internationalisation of the Mermaid*. East Barnet: John Libbey Publishing.
Hayward, Philip and Pan Wang. 2018. 'Millennial Meirenyu: Mermaids in 21st Century Chinese Culture.' In *Scaled for Success: The Internationalisation of the Mermaid*. Edited by Philip Hayward, 129–47. East Barnet: John Libbey Publishing.

Herbert, Daniel. 2009. 'Trading Spaces: Transnational Dislocations in *Insomnia/Insomnia* and *Ju-On/The Grudge*.' In *Fear, Cultural Anxiety, and Transformation: Horror, Science Fiction, and Fantasy Films Remade*. Edited by Scott A. Lukas and John Marmysz, 143–64. Lanham: Lexington Books.

Jue, Melody. 2020. *Wild Blue Media: Thinking through Seawater*. Durham: Duke University Press.

Klinger, Leslie S. 2014. 'Foreword.' In Howard Phillips Lovecraft, *The New Annotated H. P. Lovecraft*. Edited by Leslie S. Klinger, xv–lxvii. New York: Liveright Publishing Corporation.

Kraicer, Shelly. 2016. 'Under the Sea, Under the Censors: The Mainland Success of Stephen Chow.' *Los Angeles Review of Books*, 6 May. https://lareviewofbooks.org/article/sea-censors-mainland-success-stephen-chow/. Accessed 23 February 2022.

Law, Fiona Yuk-wa. 2019. 'Fabulating Animals-Human Affinity: Towards an Ethics of Care in *Monster Hunt* and *Mermaid*.' In *Ecology and Chinese-Language Cinema: Reimagining a Field*. Edited by Sheldon H. Lu and Haomin Gong, 166–95. London: Routledge.

Lee, Maggie. 2016. 'Film Review: "The Mermaid".' *Variety*, 10 February. https://variety.com/2016/film/asia/the-mermaid-review-stephen-chow-1201701757/. Accessed 24 March 2022.

Lewis, Tony. 1996. 'Her Effigy in Wood: Figureheads with Feminine Subjects.' *The Magazine Antiques* 150, no. 6: 834–41.

Lord, Bruce. 2004. 'The Genetics of Horror: Sex and Racism in H. P. Lovecraft's Fiction.' https://web.archive.org/web/20150409062846/http://www.contrasoma.com/writing/lovecraft.html. Accessed 6 January 2022.

Lu, Sheldon H. 2009. 'Introduction: Cinema, Ecology, Modernity.' In *Chinese Ecocinema: In the Age of Environmental Challenge*. Edited by Sheldon H. Lu and Jiayan Mi, 1–14. Hong Kong: Hong Kong University Press.

Nordine, Michael. 2016. 'Stephen Chow's "The Mermaid" Returns – And Still Confounds.' *The Village Voice*, 6 July. https://www.villagevoice.com/2016/07/06/stephen-chows-the-mermaid-returns-and-still-confounds/. Accessed 24 March 2022.

Shiau, Hongchi and Brian Yecies. 2018. 'Producing Nuanced Chinese Fantasy: A Case Study of Stephen Chow's Box Office Hit *Mermaid*.' In *Willing Collaborators: Foreign Partners in Chinese Media*. Edited by Michael Keane, Brian Yecies and Terry Flew, 93–107. London: Rowman & Littlefield.

Shifman, Limor. 2016. 'Meme.' In *Digital Keywords: A Vocabulary of Information Society and Culture*. Edited by Benjamin Peters, 197–205. Princeton: Princeton University Press.

Smith, Iain Robert. 2017. *The Hollywood Meme: Transnational Adaptations in World Cinema*. Edinburgh: Edinburgh University Press.

Smith, Iain Robert and Constantine Verevis, eds. 2017. *Transnational Film Remakes*. Edinburgh: Edinburgh University Press.

Strassberg, Richard E., ed. and trans. 2002. *A Chinese Bestiary: Strange Creatures from the Guideways through Mountains and Seas*. Berkeley: University of California Press.

Sweeney, R. Emmet. 2016. 'Review: The Mermaid.' 22 February. https://www.filmcomment.com/blog/review-the-mermaid/. Accessed 24 March 2022.

Tan, See-Kam. 2007. 'Huangmei Opera Films, Shaw Brothers and Ling Bo: Chaste Love Stories, Genderless Cross-Dressers and Sexless Gender-Plays?' *Jump Cut: A Review of Contemporary Media* 49: 1–5. https://www.ejumpcut.org/archive/jc49.2007/TanSee-Kam/. Accessed 21 March 2022.

Turner, Jenny. 2017. 'Life with Ms Cayenne Pepper.' *London Review of Books* 39, no. 11, 1 June. https://www.lrb.co.uk/the-paper/v39/n11/jenny-turner/life-with-ms-cayenne-pepper. Accessed 1 April 2022.

Verevis, Constantine. 2005. *Film Remakes*. New York: Palgrave Macmillan.

Yeh, Emilie Yueh-yu and Shi-yan Chao. 2020. 'Policy and Creative Strategies: Hong Kong CEPA Films in the China Market.' *International Journal of Cultural Policy* 26, no. 2: 184–201.

Zhang, Rebecca Xiaomeng. 2017. 'In Light of China's New Film Industry Promotion Law: Implications for Cross-Border Transactions between China and the U.S. in the Film Industry.' *Northwestern Journal of International Law & Business* 38, no. 1: 161–85.

Index

Abbas, Ackbar, 17, 21
About Her Brother (film), 148, 150
adaptation, 6, 9, 21, 22n1, 27–8, 29, 30, 31, 32, 34, 36, 40, 45, 49, 157, 172, 183, 190, 203, 241, 242–4, 295, 306
   as criticism, 43
   cross-cultural, 17, 53, 65, 186, 187, 188–9, 222, 239, 241, 265, 269, 272, 285–6
   television, 18, 234
   theatrical, 43
Adventure of Denchu Kozo, The (film), 103
Adventure of the 13th Sister, The (film), 73
aesthetics, 11, 14, 17, 18, 21, 29, 37, 43, 44, 63, 66, 92, 101, 111, 142, 143, 146, 187, 202, 204, 207, 210, 217, 221, 235n3, 265, 267, 283, 296
   neorealist, 56
   Taike, 268, 269
   transgressive, 45
   see also 'scavenger aesthetic'
ageism, 19, 274–6, 278, 281
Ainu, 13, 183, 184, 196, 197–8
A-lin, 262
All About Ah-Long (film), 200, 219n20
All About Eve (film), 85
All About Lily Chou-Chou (film), 148
Along with the Gods: The Last 49 Days (film), 258
Along with the Gods: The Two Worlds (film), 258
Ambition without Honor (film), 167, 173, 174
Ambition without Honor 2 (film), 173, 174
Andersen, Hans Christian, 2, 305–6
Ando, Noboru, 159, 162, 163, 175, 178, 179n2
animation, 148, 195, 245, 291, 298, 300
   stop-motion, 94, 102, 104
Anno, Hideaki, 93, 96, 107n4
Anthropocene, 299, 301
anthropocentrism, 302, 304, 306

anticommunism, 68–9
anti-genealogy, 295
Apache Gold (film), 185
April Revolution (South Korea), 55
Arden, Toni, 63
Arimori, Narimi, 165, 170
Art Theatre Guild, 95, 101
Asian financial crisis of 1997, 14, 171
At Midnight I'll Take Your Soul (film), 64
atomic bomb, 34–5, 173
Aufderheide, Patricia, 14
Aum Shinrikyo cult, 13, 166, 171
aura, 9, 284–5
auteurism, 5, 10, 14, 39, 41, 55, 56, 70, 92, 127, 140, 146, 186, 201–2, 257, 259, 293, 296
authenticity, 10, 39, 46, 93, 99, 106, 107, 178
authorial remaking, 111, 113
authorship, 11, 37, 38, 43, 49, 112, 113, 173, 201–2, 209, 218n7, 260, 297

Baba, Masaru, 49
Bae, Chang-ho, 70
banality, 10, 129, 146, 167, 170
Bang! (film), 4
Barbie doll, 303
Barefoot Youth (film), 49–50, 51, 52
Barnum, P. T., 304
Barthes, Roland, 177–8
Basic Tsukamoto (film), 104
Basinger, Kim, 210, 211
Battles Without Honor and Humanity (film), 97, 159, 160, 161, 172, 173, 174
Battleship Potemkin (film), 171
Bay, Michael, 208
Be With You (film), 245
Beast, The (film), 15

Beat Girl (film), 53
Beautiful Accident (film), 258
Beijing, 21
Believer (film), 14, 15, 221, 222–3, 225–6, 228–34
Best Secret Agent, The (film), 3
Better Tomorrow, A (1986 film), 4, 15, 16–17, 90n2, 222, 227
Better Tomorrow, A (2010 film), 4, 15, 16–17, 222
Bettinson, Gary, 5, 21, 218n4
Bicycle Thieves (film), 142
Biel, Jessica, 211
Big Bird Cage, The (film), 7
Big Bullet (film), 200, 203, 218n2
Big Doll House, The (film), 7
Bittersweet Life, A (film), 15, 225, 226
black-and-white cinematography, 11, 16, 102, 103, 23n1, 49, 51, 277
Black Rain (film), 168
Blackboard Jungle (film), 53
Blind Swordsman: Zatoichi, The (film), 148
block-booking, 46n4
blockbuster, 107n4, 200, 201–2, 203, 204–5, 206, 210, 257, 258–9, 261, 265
Blood of the Lone Wolf (novel), 172
Blood of the Wolves (film), 172
Blue Gate Crossing (film), 263, 264
Blue Mountains (film), 114
Bodyguard Kiba (film), 167
Bodyguard Kiba: Apocalypse of Carnage (film), 167
Bong, Joon-ho, 258
bootleg videos, 2
border, 17, 22, 232, 299
-crossing, 2, 222, 233
Bordwell, David, 122n1, 132, 138n4, 143, 146, 200, 204, 218n10, 221, 224, 226
Boys Over Flowers (TV series), 234
Braudy, Leo, 202
bricolage, 3
brothel, 7, 75, 76, 77, 78, 83, 84, 85, 88, 184
brotherhood, 16–17, 128, 133, 201, 209, 221
Brothers, The (film), 16
Brothers and Sisters of the Toda Family (film), 149
Bu, Wancang, 8
Buddhism, 77, 80, 149
and karma, 77–8
and misogyny, 77
bullying, 275
Burmese Harp, The (1956 film), 92
Burmese Harp, The (1985 film), 92
Burst City (film), 101
Busan, 15
Buscombe, Edward, 190

Cabinet of Dr. Caligari, The (film), 51, 60
Call Girls, The (film), 88, 89
Call of Flesh (film), 34, 39
Call of Heroes (film), 200, 209

Campbell, Joseph, 209, 212, 213; *see also* hero monomyth
canon, 12, 55, 146, 159, 164
literary, 35, 38, 44
Cantonese, 4, 5, 20, 209, 296
'Comeback', 8–9
Cape No. 7 (film), 257, 259, 263, 264
capitalism, xi, 7, 76, 83–4, 86, 87, 90n2, 128, 133, 261, 264, 296, 300, 303, 310n18
cargo, 227, 231–3
Carnal Prayer Mat, The (novel), 76, 77, 79, 80
Cellular (film), 5, 14, 200, 201–2, 204, 206, 207, 209, 210–14, 215, 217, 218n15
censorship, 5, 6–7, 29, 30, 31, 32, 33, 37, 39, 50, 52, 53–4, 56–7, 68, 81, 193, 226, 230, 307, 310n16, 310n20, 311n22
Chan, Benny Muk-sing, 5, 14, 21, 200–19
Chan, Carlos, 213
Chan, Evans, 310n18
Chan, Gordan, 21
Chan, Jackie, 201, 204, 205, 209, 218n3
Chan, Peter, 21
chanbara, 186
Chang, Bryan, 204, 205
Chang, Cheh, 74
Chang, Kil-su, 255n3
Chang, Kuo-Chu, 83
Chang, Loo, 287
Chang, Myon, 55
Chang, Pei-pei, 74
Chen, Bolin, 285
Chen, Cheer, 264
Chen, Edison, 205
Chen, Ivy Yi-han, 264–5
Chen, Leste, 263, 272, 285
Chen, Michelle, 264
Chen, Robert Ru-shou, 263
Chen, Yu-Shan, 263
Cheng, Adam, 308
Cheng, He, 308
Cheng, Steve Wai-man, 201
Cheung, Leslie, 17
Chicken and Duck Talk (film), 90n2
childhood, 11, 60, 149, 160, 178, 249, 252
Choi, Jinhee, 10, 225, 230
Chor, Yuen (Chu Yuan), 7–8, 9, 73, 75–6, 80, 82, 85, 86, 87, 88
Chou, Jay, 263
Chow, Stephen, 2, 20–2, 291–307, 309–11
Chow, Yun-fat, 17, 210
chthulucene, 299, 309
chthulumedia, 291, 293, 295, 298–9, 302, 304, 305, 306, 309
Chun, Jayson Makoto, 130
Chung, Chonghwa, 49, 50, 65–6
Chung, Hye Seung, 57
Chung, Thomas, 205, 218n6
Chung, Winnie, 204

cinematography, 164, 197
  black-and-white, 23
citationality, 5, 64, 200, 293, 295
City of Damnation (film), 15, 222
City of Lost Souls, The (film), 169
City Under Siege (film), 200
CJ7 (film), 296
class difference, 4, 50, 87, 124
'Class to Remember' (film series), 12, 147–8
Classroom of Youth (film), 66, 70n1
Clements, Ron, 291
Closer Economic Partnership Arrangement (CEPA), 21, 205, 207
Cold Eyes (film), 15, 222
Collier, Joelle, 208
colonisation, 6, 13, 52, 64, 161, 182, 196, 197, 223, 245, 282, 287
comedy, 4, 18, 182, 210, 239, 292, 293, 304, 306
  'body-swap', 258
  coming-of-age, 223
  erotic, 77
  romantic, 272, 291
  slapstick, 2, 292, 296
  sports, 200
  see also humour
coming-of-age film, 19, 50, 51, 223, 306; *see also* teenpic; youth film
commercialism, 8, 76, 90n2, 93, 131, 201, 217, 247
Communist party, 162, 207
community, 22, 31, 99, 209, 240, 241, 243, 244, 248, 249, 293, 297, 306, 307–9
computer-generated imagery (CGI), 8, 204–6, 217
concubine, 7, 75–6, 78–80, 82, 83, 86–7, 89, 90n1
Confucianism, 73, 74, 209, 241
  and gender roles, 73
  and morality, 78, 84–5
Connected (film), 5, 14, 200–3, 207, 209–19
cooking, 18, 239, 240, 243, 246, 247, 249, 250–2, 254, 296; *see also* food
Cooper, Gary, 121
coproduction, 2, 14, 15, 18, 21, 202
copy, 1, 12, 50, 53, 57, 146, 151, 152; *see also* original
copyright, 38, 49–50, 218n12
'Copywood', 64; *see also* copy
Corman, Roger, 60, 76
costume drama, 7
Council on East Asian Studies (Yale University), 195
Count of Monte Cristo, The (film), 53
counterfeiting, 4, 17
Crazed Fruit (film), 7, 65
Crazy Family, The (film), 101
Crazy Thunder Road (film), 100, 101, 106
crime film, 10, 14, 15, 60, 222
Crimes of the Future (1970 film), 8
Crimes of the Future (2022 film), 8
criminal underworld, 4, 13, 223
Criterion Collection, 41

Cronenberg, David, 8, 102
cross-cultural remake, 2, 3, 5, 13, 14–17, 49–71, 182–3, 184–5, 200, 202, 208–10, 221–37, 239–55, 258, 260, 265, 266, 268, 269, 272–90, 291–310
cross-dressing, 74, 304
Cubism, 63
cultural anaesthesia, 52
cultural flows, 18, 222, 258, 260, 261, 265, 269, 270
cultural memory, 29, 46
cultural translatability, 184; *see also* translation
Curtin, Michael, 203, 205

Daiei (studio), 9, 93, 95, 150
daikaijū eiga (giant monster films), 96; *see also* *Godzilla* (film)
dance, 60, 66, 152, 161, 241, 282, 283, 284
Dancing Girl of Izu, The (film), 9
Dancing Girl of Izu, The (novel), 9
Dangerous Youth (film), 50
Daoism, 74, 76
Davis, Darrell William, 205
Davis, Michael, 86
Daydream (film), 6, 51–2, 54, 56, 60, 61, 62, 66, 67, 70
Dazai, Osamu, 27
Dead or Alive 2: Birds (film), 167
deafness, 223, 226, 228, 229, 230, 233, 234n2
Dear My Love (film), 197
defector, 4, 16
déjà disparu, 17
del Toro, Guillermo, 296
Deleuze, Gilles, 149–52, 295
de-mediation, 11, 124, 129, 137, 138n1
democracy, 55, 69, 131, 158, 162
Denis, Claire, 10
Denison, Rayna, 46n1
dentistry, 52, 55, 56, 57, 59, 60–3, 64, 65, 67, 165, 167, 262
derivativeness, 1, 4, 15, 57, 97, 151, 201
Desser, David, 65, 92, 122n1
Detour (film), 80
Diary of a Lady-Killer (film), 7
Die Hard (film), 203
Diffrient, David Scott, 245
Dirty Carnival, A (film), 15, 225
Dirty Harry (film), 96
disguised remake, 210
Disney, 2, 291, 296, 300, 304, 305–6, 307
Distant Cry from Spring (film), 149
Divergence (film), 208
Django (film), 185
'do-it-yourself' (DIY), 9, 93, 94, 96, 100, 101, 102, 105, 106
DOA (film), 169
Doane, Mary Ann, 81–2, 90n4
Double Indemnity (film), 80, 82
Dower, John, 31

Drifting Avenger, The (film), 187
Drug War (film), 14, 221–4, 226, 227, 228, 230, 231, 232–4
drug addiction and drug use, 13, 34, 157, 160, 168, 169, 170, 178, 223, 227,
drug dealing and trafficking, 15, 221, 223–5, 227, 231, 232, 233
Druxman, Michael B., 210
duology, 87, 88, 243, 245
DVD, 29, 41–2; *see also* home video

Early Summer (film), 10, 11, 111, 112, 114, 116, 117, 119, 121, 149
East Meets West (film), 187, 190
Eastwood, Clint, 2, 13, 183–4, 187, 188, 189–90, 193, 194, 195, 198
Easy Rider (film), 97
ecocinema, 293, 295, 301, 304, 306
8mm filmmaking, 9, 93, 94, 96, 97, 98, 99, 100, 101, 103, 104–5, 106; *see also* 16mm filmmaking
Ektasound, 94
Election (film), 230
Elfivng-Hwang, Jo, 281
Ellis, David R., 14, 200, 201, 210, 212, 215, 216, 217
Elsaesser, Thomas, 122, 125, 138, 301
Elusive Avengers, The (film), 185
empire, 161, 184, 185, 187–8, 191, 198
Empty Dream, An (film), 6, 49, 51, 52–70
episteme, 4, 17
Equinox Flower (film), 127
erotica, 37, 46n2, 76–7, 79; *see also* pornography
espionage, 3
Eternal Summer (film), 263
Evans, Chris, 211, 212
Evil Dead, The (film), 102
exclusion, 221, 232, 235n4
Exiled (film), 230
exploitation, 7, 22, 33, 37, 39, 40, 41, 43, 44, 54, 64, 75, 96, 232, 234n2, 310n17
Eye in the Sky (film), 222

family, 17, 19, 55, 57, 74, 112–13, 115, 117, 118, 119, 130, 132, 140–7, 149–53, 178, 184, 212, 226, 250, 251, 272, 273, 275–81, 284, 289
  breakdown, 152
  drama, 10, 66
Fan, Victor, 20
fantasy, 21, 34, 35, 41, 60, 174, 284, 291, 294, 297, 307
fatherhood, 112, 115, 117, 118, 121, 126, 128, 150, 151, 175, 201, 209, 213, 219n20, 250, 266
Female Prisoner 701: Scorpion (film), 96
femininity, 7, 45, 73–5, 81, 114, 116, 148, 284, 285; *see also* masculinity
feminism, 87–8, 122
femme fatale, 80–2, 85, 306
film festival, 3, 53, 70, 94, 102, 103, 122, 182, 186, 188, 189, 195, 257

film marketing, 101, 188, 105, 209, 245, 262, 263, 268
film stock, 92, 103
Fistful of Dollars, A (film), 185
flag, 35, 161
flashback, 17, 34, 84, 143, 150, 152, 192, 232, 240, 242, 244, 247, 250, 277, 279
flatulence, 11, 132
Floating Weeds (film), 92, 149, 150
Flowers of Shanghai (film), 75
Fly, The (film), 102
Flying Dagger, The (film), 74
food, 18, 31, 125–6, 239–55; poisoning, 175; *see also* cooking
Forbidden City Cop (film), 296
Forever with You (film), 60
Forgotten (film), 260
Fortress, The (film), 273
franchise, 5, 6, 27–30, 33, 34, 35, 37–9, 43–6, 127, 128
free speech, 51
freeze frame, 207, 254
French Connection, The (film), 97
Freud, Sigmund, 125, 128, 137; *see also* mystic writing pad; the unconscious
Friedkin, William, 97
Friend (film), 225
friendship, 112, 147, 223, 239–42, 247, 249, 252–3; female, 114, 116, 118, 119
From Beijing with Love (film), 20
frontier, 13, 95, 184–5, 188–9, 190, 192–3, 195–8
Frozen (film), 272
Fudoh: The New Generation (film), 167, 169
Fugitive from the Past, A (film), 179n3
Fujiwara, Kei, 102, 103, 104
Fujiwara, Shinji, 49
Fukai, Toshihiko, 30, 33
Fukasaku, Kinji, 12, 13, 157, 158, 159–65, 168, 169, 170, 173, 174, 178, 179n1, 179n3
Fukushima nuclear plant disaster, 144
Fung, Po, 219n20
Funny Games (1997 film), 8
Funny Games (2007 film), 8
Furukawa, Takumi, 65

gangs, 31, 32, 33, 36, 159, 160, 161, 162, 165, 167, 169, 172–3, 175, 225–6, 230–1, 266
gangster film, 10, 15, 86–7, 90n2, 158, 159, 174, 176, 178, 221, 222, 224, 225–7, 230, 267
Garbo, Greta, 10
Gate of Flesh (1948 film), 5, 27, 30, 32, 33, 36, 38, 39, 43, 44
Gate of Flesh (1964 film), 6, 30, 32, 33, 36, 38, 41, 43, 45
Gate of Flesh (1977 film), 30, 32, 33, 35, 36, 38, 43, 44
Gate of Flesh (1988 film), 30, 33, 34, 35, 36, 37, 38, 40, 41, 42

Gate of Flesh (2008 telefilm), 30, 32, 36, 38
Gate of Flesh (novel), 6, 27, 30, 31, 32, 37
gaze, 85, 112, 115, 118, 119, 303
  male, 7, 81
  scopophilic, 60
Gen-X Cops (film), 201, 204, 205, 206, 208, 218n2, 218n6, 219n19
Gen-Y Cops (film), 200, 204, 206
gender, 19, 27, 33, 45, 46, 73, 77–8, 86, 116, 118, 122, 223, 250, 266, 273, 274, 275, 276, 281, 282, 284, 289, 309n11
generational relationships, 10, 113, 121, 242, 245, 275, 278, 280
Genette, Gérard, 29
German Expressionism, 51, 60, 63
Geronimo, Sara, 279, 281
Gerow, Aaron, 135, 136, 160, 163, 177, 192
Ghahremani, Yasmin, 218n8
Girls without Tomorrow (film), 87
God of Cookery, The (film), 296
Godard, Jean-Luc, 96
Goddess, The (film), 8
Godzilla (film), 49, 96
Going by the Book (film), 4
Golden Harvest (production company), 204, 206
Golden Slumber (film), 244
Golden Sword, The (film), 74
Good Morning (film), 11, 124–6, 127, 129–38, 149
Good, the Bad, the Weird, The (film), 288
Goodbye Mermaid (film), 298
Gosha, Hideo, 30, 33, 34, 35, 36, 37, 38, 40, 41, 42, 186
Grant, Catherine, 29, 40
Graveyard of Honor (film), 12–13, 157–60, 163–4, 168, 169, 174, 178, 179n3
Gray, Jonathan, 28, 29
Gua, Ah-leh, 285
Guattari, Félix, 295

Hallyu, 257–9, 269
Hammer Studios, 7, 76
Haneke, Michael, 8
Hara, Setsuko, 10, 111, 113, 117, 141, 149
Harakiri (film), 191
Haraway, Donna J., 299, 307, 309, 310n13
Harrington, Curtis, 304
Harris, Jack H., 41
Harvard University, 197
Hashizume, Isao, 12, 141, 148, 150
Hasumi, Shigehiko, 125, 137
Hata, Toyokichi, 31, 39, 45
Hays Code, 82
Hayward, Philip, 296, 297, 298, 306, 309n3, 309n9, 310n14
He Ain't Heavy, He's My Father (film), 219n20
He, Hilary Hongjin, 218n12
healing, 239–40, 242, 245–6, 250–1, 254
Heat (film), 200

Heirs (TV series), 234
heist film, 4
Hepburn, Audrey, 282–5, 286, 287, 288, 289
Hepburn, Katherine, 121
Herbert, Daniel, 1, 3, 184, 294
hero monomyth, 212
heroic archetypes, 73, 77, 85, 202, 209, 212
Heroic Duo (film), 206, 208, 218n8
heroism, 73, 77–8, 85, 87, 202, 209, 212, 213, 214, 215, 218n19, 221
Higashiyama, Chieko, 12, 119, 141
High and Low (film), 222, 235n3
Hiroshima, 141, 159 160, 172–3, 195
Hitchcock, Alfred, 8, 16, 51, 165
Hokkaidō, 13, 183, 184, 185, 188, 189, 191, 193, 196–8
Hollywood, 8, 14, 53, 64, 73, 80, 81, 82, 87, 90n4, 90n5, 106, 124, 146, 182, 183, 184, 185, 186, 187, 189, 190, 196, 200, 202–7, 209–10, 213, 215, 217, 218n19, 226, 282–6, 291, 292, 294, 297, 298, 305, 306, 309n8
  -isation, 5, 14, 202–4, 206–8, 210, 217
  see also New Hollywood
Hollywood meme, 294–5
homage, 4, 10, 96, 143
Home from the Sea (film), 147
home video, 41, 95, 102, 218n6; *see also* DVD; VHS
Hong Kong Film Awards, 203
Hong Kong 'handover', 14, 16, 21, 201, 203, 204
Hong Kong, Hong Kong (film), 89
Hong Kong New Wave, 88, 90n2
Hopper, Dennis, 97, 304
horror, 8, 22n1, 60, 64, 102, 174, 175, 223, 257
Horyi's Homestay (TV series), 246
hotel, 141, 230
  love, 169, 170
Hou, Hsiao-Hsien, 10, 75, 122, 257
House of 72 Tenants, The (film), 9
Howard, Ron, 21, 291, 300
Hsu, Barbie, 212
Hu, Peng, 20
Hui, Ann, 218n5
Hui, Michael, 90n2
Hui, Raman, 291
humour, 4, 11, 20, 22, 114, 116, 135, 263, 292, 296
  infantile, 124, 137
  genial, 150
  grotesque, 306
  transgender, 310n19
  see also comedy
Hunt, Leon, 219n23
Hunter's Diary, The (film), 7
Hwang, Dong-hyuk, 18, 60, 272, 280, 281
Hwang, Jung-min, 266
hybridisation, 8, 20, 80, 186–7, 296, 297

I Graduated, But . . . (film), 127
I Flunked, But . . . (film), 127

I Was Born, But... (film), 11, 124–7, 128–9, 132–8
Ichikawa, Kon, 23, 92, 95, 107
Ichisei, Takashige, 96
identity, 13, 95, 151, 184, 188, 232, 239, 266, 268, 278, 286, 287, 288, 306
   brand, 205
   disguised, 226–7
   national, 185, 196
   self-, 240–2, 243, 252–4
Igarashi, Daisuke, 17, 239, 242, 243
Iida, Yuta, 136
Ikeda, Toshiharu, 22n1
Illang: The Wolf Brigade (film), 245
Illegal Immigrant, The (film), 89
illicitness, 6, 49, 51, 52, 56
Image Forum (Japan), 98
IMF Crisis, 15, 225, 234n2
imitation, 10, 14, 16, 50, 93, 96–7, 105–7, 204, 217
immigration, 169, 227, 231–2, 234n2, 235n4, 299
inclusion, 158, 232
Independence Day (film), 218n2
indigeneity, 13, 161, 183, 184, 190, 197, 198, 218n5
Indonesia, 19, 272, 274–5, 282
industrialisation, 3, 260
Infernal Affairs (film), 222
Inohara, Tatsuzō, 30, 32, 36
Inoue, Umetsugu, 9
'inter-networking connections', 28, 37
intermediality, xi, 28, 37, 45, 243, 269
intertextuality, xi, 1, 4–5, 22n1, 28, 33, 36, 37, 45, 46, 51, 60, 64, 93, 106, 113, 117, 175, 200, 222, 287, 288, 294, 295, 310n18
Intimate Confessions of a Chinese Courtesan (film), 7, 73, 75–6, 77–86, 88, 89
Inugami Family, The (film), 107n1
Inugamis, The (film), 107n1
Invisible Target (film), 207, 208, 218n14
irony, 89, 90, 295
Ishihama, Akira, 65
Ishii, Gakuryū (a.k.a. Ishii Sōgo), 9, 94, 95, 97–9, 100–4, 105, 106
Ishii, Teruo, 158, 174
Ishikawa, Hideaki, 195
Ishikawa, Rikio, 12, 13, 157–8, 159–60, 162–3, 164, 165, 167, 168, 169, 171, 172, 173, 174, 177, 178
Ishizaka, Yōjirō, 65
Itō, Shun'ya, 96
Itō, Toshiaki, 99
It's a Flickering Life (film), 149, 150, 152
It's Tough Being a Man (film), 147, 149
Iwabuchi, Koichi, 131, 258

James Bond, 3
Jang, Sun-woo, 70
Japan Institute of the Moving Image, 107n2
Jarmusch, Jim, 10
Jeong, Deok-hyeon, 16

Jewel in the Palace (TV series), 258
jidaigeki, 13, 14, 182–3, 185–9, 190, 193, 194, 195
Jin-Roh: The Wolf Brigade (film), 245
jishu-eiga (self-made film), 93, 94, 95
jitsuroku, 13, 158, 159, 179n1, 179n3
Jo, Chang-ho, 16
Joo, Woojeong, 10, 116, 122, 129
Josée (film), 239
Josee, the Tiger and the Fish (film), 239
Journey to the West: Conquering the Demons (film), 73, 296, 311n21
Ju, Jin-mo, 17
jump cut, 16, 17, 104
June 3 Resistance Movement, 50, 51
justice, 13, 36, 74, 75, 78, 79, 87, 89, 183, 190, 193

kabuki, 51, 191
Kageyama, Yuri, 188
Kaijū Shiatā (Sea Monster Theatre), 104
Kanaoka, Nobu, 105
Kang, Hyo-jin, 258
Kanno, Yuka, 121–2
Kao, Li, 21, 298, 308
karaoke, 267, 283
Karate Kid, The (film), 200
karma, 77, 79–83, 85–6, 87–90
Kasahara, Kazuo, 36
Kasai, Satoko, 34
Katō, Hidetoshi, 136
Kaurismaki, Aki, 10
Kawabata, Yasunari, 9
K-drama, 288
Kelleter, Frank, 124, 128
Kermode, Frank, 211
Key, The (1974 film), 22n1
Key, The (1997 film), 22n1
Key, The (novel), 22n1
Key of Life (film), 239
Kiarostami, Abbas, 10
Killer, The (film), 227
Kim, Dong-won, 222
Kim, Han-il, 54
Kim, Jin-kyu, 55
Kim, Ki-duk, 49, 66
Kim, Su-yong, 66
Kim, Tae-ri, 240, 253
kineticism, 207
King of Comedy, The (film), 20–1
King's Ransom (novel), 222
Kinoshita, Chika, 28, 37
Kirsch, Griseldis, 39, 46n1
Kishi, Keiko, 122
Kishitani, Goro, 12, 164, 165
Kitamura, Kyōhei, 41, 46n1
Kitamura, Takumi, 277
Ko, Giddens, 263
Ko, Mika, 158, 177, 179n4
Kobayashi, Masaki, 191

Kobayashi, Satomi, 276
Kodak, 94
Kōnami, Fumio, 99
Koo, Louis, 211, 212, 214, 219n19, 219n24, 221
Korean Central Intelligence Agency (KCIA), 57, 59, 68, 69
Korean Film Archive (KOFA), 53, 70
Korean Filmworker's Guild, 71n2
Koreeda, Hirokazu, 10, 148
Koyama, Hitomi, 187
Kratky, Daniel, 20–1
Kugion, Fan, 130
Kumashiro, Tatsumi, 23n1, 35
kung fu, 78; *see also* martial arts
Kung Fu Hustle (film), 296, 311n21
Kurosawa, Akira, 113, 186, 188, 191, 222, 227, 235n3
Kurosawa, Kiyoshi, 93, 96, 98
Kutsuna, Shiori, 13, 183
Kwan, Stanley, 10
Kyōeisha, 97–101
Kyoto Story (film), 150

Lam, June, 204, 205
Lam, Pierre, 204
Lam, Ringo, 204
Last of the Wolves (film), 172
Last Samurai, The (film), 191
Late Spring (film), 10, 11, 111, 112, 113, 114–17, 118, 121
Lau, Adaline, 219n24
Lau, Andrew, 206
Law, Fiona Yuk-wa, 301, 303, 306, 310n18
Law, Kar, 88
Law, Norman, 21, 298, 300, 304
Lee, Ang, 257
Lee, Hae-young, 14, 221, 222, 223, 228
Lee, Hyangjin, 55
Lee, Jang-ho, 70, 244
Lee, Man-hee, 68
Lee, Sang-il, 2, 13, 183, 188, 189, 190, 194
Legend of Tank Commander Nishizumi, The (film), 157
Legend of the Mermaid (film), 310n12
Legend of the Mermaid 2 (film), 310n12
Legend of the Nanhai Mermaid, The (film), 310n12
Legend of the Swordsmen of the Mountains of Shu (novel), 8
Legend of Zu (film), 8
Leitch, Thomas M., 1, 3, 211
Leone, Sergio, 188, 200
lesbianism, 7, 75, 76, 78–80, 81, 82, 88, 121–2
Lethal Weapon (film), 203, 218n2
Letters from Iwo Jima (film), 188
Ley Lines (film), 169
Li, Jet, 204
Li, Yu, 76, 77, 85
Like a Virgin (film), 223

Lin, Gavin, 261, 262, 264, 269
lip-syncing, 63
'literature of the flesh' (*nikutai bungaku*), 6, 27–8, 33, 38, 44–5
Little Forest (film), 17, 18, 239, 241, 242, 245, 246–54, 255n4
Little Forest (manga series), 17, 239, 241, 242, 243–4
Little Forest: Summer/Autumn (film), 17, 18, 239, 241, 243–4, 245, 246–54,
Little Forest: Winter/Spring (film), 17, 18, 239, 241, 243–4, 245, 246–54
'little freshness', 260, 264–5, 269
Little House, The (film), 150
Little Mermaid, The (film), 2, 296, 300, 305, 307
Little Mermaid: Attack of the Pirates, The (film), 298
Little Shop of Horrors, The (film), 60
Liu, James J. Y., 74, 78
Liu, Jasper, 262, 264–5
Liu, Ye, 214
Lo, Lieh, 74
Lo, Wei, 74
localisation, 3, 15, 16, 18, 169, 192, 208, 210, 240, 241, 242, 246–8, 254, 260, 261, 262, 263, 265, 266, 268, 269, 285, 288, 194
Lonely Fifteen (film), 87
Loock, Kathleen, 1, 3, 107n5
Lourant, Chico, 32, 41
Love and Duty (film), 8
Love without End (film), 20
Lovecraft, H. P., 299, 310n13
Lower Depths, The (film), 222
Luck-Key (film), 239, 255n3
Lung Kong, Patrick, 88, 89
Lust for Love of a Chinese Courtesan (film), 7, 73, 76–7, 80, 83–9

MacArthur, Douglas, 34
Macbeth (play), 222
Maceda, Manay Ichui, 279
McLuhan, Marshall, 136
Macy, William H., 210
Maeda's Young Up (TV series), 98
Magic Crane, The (film), 203
'Mainlandisation', 21, 202–3, 207
Mak, Alan, 222
Mak, Michael, 77
Makino, Masahiro, 30, 32, 38, 44
Malaysia, 9, 258, 261, 263
Man Called Hero, A (film), 206
Man in Love (2014 film), 265, 266
Man in Love (2021 film), 18, 259, 260, 265–8, 269
Man Wanted (film), 201
Man Who Knew Too Much, The (1934 film), 8
Man Who Knew Too Much, The (1956 film), 8
Man with a Movie Camera (film), 128
Man with a Shotgun (film), 187

manga, 17, 27, 170, 192, 239, 240, 241–4, 246, 247, 248, 250
Map of Sex and Love, The (film), 310n18
Marins, José Mojica, 64
martial arts, 74, 78, 84–5, 200, 203, 206, 292; *see also* kung fu; wuxia
martial law, 50
masculinity, 34, 36, 65, 73, 79, 80, 81, 82, 121, 212, 222, 307; *see also* femininity
Masumura, Yasuzō, 53
Matrix, The (film), 206
Matsui, Yoshihiko, 99, 100, 107n6
Matsutarō, Shōriki, 131
May 16 Coup (South Korea), 55, 56
Mazdon, Lucy, 1, 3, 241, 246
Media Asia, 201, 205, 206, 218n6
media literacy, 11, 129–30, 133
mediascape, 131, 185, 293, 309n6
Meiji Restoration, 13–14, 36, 183, 184, 190–3, 195–8
melancholia, 10, 141, 179n5, 304
Méliès, Georges, 22, 304
meme, 293–5, 296, 298, 309
Meow (film), 219n19
Mermaid, The (1965 film), 21, 298, 308
Mermaid, The (2016 film), 20, 21, 22, 291, 293–6, 298–311
mermaid film, 21–2, 291, 296–8
Mermaid Got Married (film), 21, 298, 300, 304
metaphysics, 12, 146, 151–2
metatextuality, 60, 83, 88, 276, 286, 288; *see also* reflexivity
Michi, Kanako, 63, 65
Midnight Girls (film), 87
Miike, Takashi, 12, 13, 158–9, 163–5, 166, 167, 168–9, 173–9
Miki, Ryōsuke, 167
militarism, 2, 27, 133–4, 136
military occupation, 29, 30, 32, 33, 35, 44, 45, 46, 114, 121, 158, 193, 282
mimicry, 67, 71n2, 133, 202, 285, 295, 303
Ming dynasty erotic literature, 7, 72, 75, 76–7, 85
minimalism, 10, 143
Ministry of Agriculture, Food and Rural Affairs (South Korea), 255n6
Ministry of Culture (Taiwan), 260
Ministry of Education (South Korea), 57, 58
Ministry of Justice (South Korea), 68
Ministry of Public Information (South Korea), 7, 53, 71, 72
mise-en-abyme, 22, 118
misogyny, 44, 77, 80–1, 82, 299, 306
Miss Granny (a.k.a. *Suspicious Girl*) (2014 film), 2, 18–19, 22, 258, 272–6, 278, 280–4, 287–9
Miss Granny (2018 film), 272
Mission, The (film), 221, 227, 229
Misumi, Kenji, 186
Miura, Rieko, 36
Miura, Takahiro, 253

Miyagawa, Kazuo, 23n1
Miyake, Kuniko, 117, 149
Mizoguchi, Kenji, 32
Mizuki, Arisa, 32, 36, 39, 40, 45
Mizuta, Nobuo, 272, 282
mo lei tau, 296, 302
modernity, 76, 113, 114, 140, 182, 198, 287
Moment of Romance, A (film), 201, 203, 209
Moment of Romance II, A (film), 200, 203, 219n20
Monga (film), 259
Monster Hunt (film), 291, 303
montage, 34, 35, 84, 143, 166, 171, 174, 300, 301, 303
dialectical, 63
Monteverde, Lily, 279
Moon, So-ri, 253
More than Blue (2009 film), 18, 261, 262, 268, 269
More than Blue (2018 film), 18, 257, 259, 260, 261–5, 268, 269
More Than Blue (TV series), 269
Mori, Junichi, 17, 239, 243, 244
Mori, Mitsuhiro, 142
Mori, Yoshirō, 166
motherhood and mothering, 18, 19, 40, 45, 144, 240–1, 242, 244, 250–3, 278–80, 282, 285
Motion Picture Law (South Korea), 6, 52
Mozi, 74
Mr. Primitive (film), 96
Mud-Spattered Purity (film), 49
Murakami, Haruki, 246
Murakami, Kenji, 97, 98, 100
Murder, My Sweet (film), 80
Musker, John, 291
My Fair Princess (TV series), 286–8
My Father (film), 273
My Father is a Hero (film), 219n20
My Sons (film), 151
mystic writing pad, 125

Na, Moon-hee, 19, 274, 281
Nagasaki: Memories of My Son (film), 150
Nagasaki, Shun'ichi, 93, 96, 97
Nagoya, 96, 175
Nakadai, Tatsuya, 191
Nakae, Ryusuke, 43
Nakahira, Kō, 7, 9, 49, 65
National Security Act, 68
Ned Kelly (film), 186
neo-noir, 16
Netflix, 60, 269, 272, 285
New Graveyard of Honor (film), 12–13, 158, 159, 163–79
New Hollywood, 97; *see also* Hollywood
New King of Comedy, The (film), 20–1
New Love without End (film), 20
New Police Story (film), 200, 208, 209, 218n3, 219n20
New Sister Flowers (film), 20
New White Golden Dragon (film), 20

Night Tide (film), 304
Nihon University College of Art (Nichigei), 97
Nikkatsu Film Company (studio), 9, 23n1, 30, 33, 35, 49, 65, 93, 94, 96, 98, 99, 100, 101, 113, 158
Nishikawa, Katsumi, 9
Nishikawa, Mineko, 36
Nishimura, Masahiko, 141, 148
Nishimura, Shōgorō, 30, 32, 33, 35, 36, 38, 43, 44
No Regrets for Our Youth (film), 113
Noda, Kōgo, 11, 113
Noda, Yōjirō, 152
Nogawa, Yumiko, 32, 36
Noh theatre, 27
Noma, Hiroshi, 27
'Noriko Trilogy', 11, 111, 114, 116–22, 127; *see also* Hara, Setsuko; Ozu, Yasujiro
Nornes, Markus, 122n1, 128
North Korea, 4, 16, 17
nostalgia, 1, 4, 34, 150, 163, 246, 286, 287
Noze, Niu, 259
nudity, 23n1, 31, 33, 54, 56, 58, 63, 69, 81

objectification, 65; double-, 281
obscenity, 7, 52, 54, 57, 59, 61, 68, 69; *see also* pornography
ocean, 22, 118, 189, 302
Odd Obsession (film), 23n1
Oh Baby! (film), 272, 276, 277
Okamoto, Kihachi, 158, 186, 187
Olympia (film), 171
Olympic Games, 33, 253
Ōmori, Kazuki, 93, 96
Onchi, Hideo, 30, 34, 39
One Million Yen Girl (film), 148
Only Son, The (film), 127
Onomichi, 112, 119, 120, 141, 143, 144, 146
Orientalism, 41, 298, 310n17
original, 1, 4, 8, 12, 15, 16, 19, 21, 28, 38, 43–4, 50, 57, 64, 83, 92–3, 100–1, 122n2, 125, 126, 127, 136, 140–1, 142, 146, 151, 152, 163, 165, 173, 188, 190, 198, 210, 210, 222, 232, 234, 239, 240, 241, 242, 243, 245–7, 250, 253, 261–2, 265, 266, 273, 274, 278, 281, 282, 286–8, 294, 298; *see also* copy
originality, 15, 127, 217, 293
Osaka, 30, 96, 160, 169, 174
Ōsaka, Shirō, 144
Oshikawa, Yoshiyuki, 43
Ōshima, Nagisa, 65
Otsuka, Eiji, 158, 170–1, 172, 173, 176
Our Times (film), 263, 266
Out of the Past (film), 80
Overheard (film), 222
Ōya, Ryūji, 97–8, 99
Ōya, Sōichi, 125, 130
Ozaki, Masafusa, 30, 31, 32, 33, 38, 39, 43, 44
Ozawa, Fujio, 31, 32, 43

Ozu, Kinosuke, 162, 172
Ozu, Yasujiro, 10–12, 92, 95, 111–23, 124–38, 140–53

palimpsest, 4, 183
Panic High School (1976 film), 9, 92, 94, 97–8, 99, 100, 101, 103, 104, 106
Panic High School (1978 film), 9, 92, 94, 99, 100, 101, 103, 106
panpan (streetwalkers), 31–5, 36, 39–40, 41, 44, 45
Parasite (film), 258
paratextuality, 6, 28–9, 35, 38–45
Park, Am, 61, 66
Park, Chung-hee, 50, 55, 56, 57
Park, Hae-joon, 224
Park, Su-hyeon, 54
Park, Su-jeong, 60, 61, 63, 69
parody, 4, 134, 288, 295, 302, 304
pastiche, 4, 200
Peach Blossom Fan, The (film), 90n1
Peckinpah, Sam, 97
Perfect Strangers (film), 18
Perkins, Claire, 1, 3, 111, 113, 122
Phantom of Regular Size, The (film), 94, 101, 102, 103
phenomenology, 124, 137
Philippines, 19, 272, 277, 278, 279, 282
'pillow shots', 11, 142, 152; *see also* Ozu, Yasujiro
'pink film' (*pinku-eiga*), 6, 22n1, 33, 35, 51, 61, 63, 95, 99; *see also* erotica; pornography
pixilation, 102, 104, 105
plagiarism, 7, 50, 53, 58, 70, 71n2
plot hole, 210
police, 4, 13, 15, 32, 35, 38, 55, 57, 87, 88, 98, 157, 161, 167, 169, 175, 178, 179n4, 211, 221, 223, 224, 227, 229, 230, 233, 310n18
Poppoya (film), 197
pornography, 30, 35, 38, 51, 59, 61, 70, 95, 99; *see also* erotica; obscenity
postmodernism, 4, 163, 177
Post-New Wave Taiwan cinema, 257, 259, 263–4
precarity, 225, 242
pre-tested material, 7
prison, 60, 69, 76, 157, 160, 161, 163, 164, 165, 167, 172, 174
Private Tutor (film), 66
progression, 11, 111–13, 116, 118, 124, 136; *see also* regression
prostitution, 36, 44, 55, 84, 87, 88, 89, 169–70, 183, 184, 192
protest, 50, 161
PTU: Police Tactical Unit (film), 221, 227, 230, 234n3
Purple Storm (film), 205, 206

Qing dynasty, 73, 78, 90n1, 287, 288
Queer Eye: Japanese Holiday (TV series), 285
quiz show, 11, 130–1, 135

radio, 27, 137; calisthenics, 134
Raging Fire (film), 159, 175, 200
Raimi, Sam, 102
Raise the Red Lantern (film), 75
rape-revenge plot, 7, 74, 78, 84–5
referentiality, 4, 36, 46, 92, 200; *see also* metatextuality
reflexivity, 95, 227, 234, 287; *see also* metatextuality
regression, 11, 50, 136; *see also* progression
relativism, 4
'remaking-by-stealth', 14
repertory cinemas, 95
repetition, 11, 27, 60, 76, 92, 93, 111, 113, 114, 122, 133, 143–4, 146, 148, 151–2, 208, 216
Return of Ultraman (film), 96
revenge film, 7, 22, 36, 75, 79, 87, 88, 183, 184, 226, 306
  rape- , 78, 84
  see also vengeance
revisionism, 3, 5, 13, 57, 183, 190, 191
Rhee, Syngman, 55, 56
rhizome, xi, 45, 295
Righting Wrongs (film), 88
Rob-B-Hood (film), 209, 218n2, 218n14, 219n20
Robinson, Edward G., 82
Rodin, Auguste, 56
Rollin, Jean, 7, 76
Roman Holiday (film), 282–3, 285, 288
romance, 49, 50, 95, 147, 150, 214, 215, 253, 257, 261, 263–4, 266, 269, 288, 293, 305, 309
Rouge Tears (film), 8
Royal Warriors (film), 88
Ruan, Lingyu, 8
Russo-Japanese War, 196
'ryoki culture', 31
Ryū, Chishū, 12, 112, 117, 119, 135, 149, 150
Ryu, Jun-yeol, 221, 224, 228, 246

Sada, Keiji, 122, 129
sadomasochism, 58
Saigō, Takamori, 191
Sakaguchi, Ango, 27
Sakai, Nobuo, 172
salaryman, 15, 102, 103, 105, 225–6
Sambizanga (film), 186
Samurai, 13, 183–4, 186, 191, 192, 193–4, 196
sangokujin, 13, 160–1, 168–9
Sanjuro (film), 183
satire, 11, 57, 303
Satō Junya, 187
Satō, Koichi, 184
Satō, Tadao, 125, 127
Satō, Takumi, 132
Sawada, Kenji, 150
Sawada, Yukihiro, 99, 100
scavenger aesthetic, 200
scopophilic gaze, 60

sculpture, 54, 56, 57
Season of the Sun (film), 65
Secret (film), 263
self-remake, 8, 9, 76, 92–4, 107n1, 124, 151
self-sufficiency, 242–4, 251, 252, 254
sensationalism, 8, 38, 39, 46n2, 54, 88, 159
Seo, Yoon-seong, 49
Seoul, 7, 15, 16, 50, 51, 55, 70, 227, 229, 231, 239, 242, 249
sequel, 20, 106, 117, 167, 172, 174, 200, 201, 203, 206, 258, 298
serial vitality, 12, 146, 151–3
seriality, 11, 12, 66, 124, 127–8, 136, 140, 146, 148, 150–1, 152, 153, 208, 216, 219n23, 295
Seven Female POWs (film), 68
sex and sexuality, 31–4, 36, 44, 51, 54, 60, 61, 66, 68, 69, 71n2, 74–5, 76–7, 79, 80, 81, 82, 83, 86–7, 88–9, 95, 162, 165, 212, 266, 298, 304, 305, 306, 310n19
Sex and Zen (film), 77
sexploitation, 39, 41, 63, 76, 80–1
Shackleton, Liz, 206
Shane (film), 183
Shanghai, 3, 8, 287
Shanhaijing, 297–8, 307–8
Shaolin (film), 200, 209
Shaolin Soccer (film), 20, 296
Shaolin Temple (film), 200
Sharp, Jasper, 64
Shashin Koshien Summer (film), 197
Shaw Brothers, 7, 74, 75, 80–1, 83, 89, 200, 298
She's from Another Planet (film), 298
Shiaishi, Kazuya, 172
Shim, Aegyung, 49, 52, 53, 68, 69, 70
Shim, Eun-kyung, 19, 274, 281, 287
Shin, Beom-soo, 245
Shin, Hyun-tak, 262
Shin, Seong-il, 50, 52, 61, 66, 70n1
Shin Ultraman (film), 107n4
Shinjuku Triad Society (film), 167, 169
Shintoho (studio), 158
Shishido, Joe, 34, 36
Shōchiku (studio), 9, 93, 113, 122, 127, 128, 147, 149, 151, 157
Shōichi, Ōta, 131
Shōriki, Matsutarō, 131
shōshimin-eiga, 10, 128
Silenced (film), 273
Silenced, The (film), 223, 235n5
silent cinema, 8, 11, 124, 129, 130, 135
simulacrum, 152, 153, 178
Sing My Life (film), 19, 272, 276, 282
Singapore, 9, 261, 263
Sinophone, 2, 9
Sirène, La (film), 304
16mm filmmaking, 101, 102, 104; *see also* 8mm filmmaking
Slope in the Sun, A (film), 65

slow-motion, 17, 216
Sluizer, George, 8
'Small but Certain Happiness', 245
'small happiness', 244
Smith, Iain Robert, 294–5, 296, 309n8
social problem film, 10, 38
'soft power', 260–1, 264, 270
Son on the Run (film), 200, 219n20
Sone, Harumi, 165, 173, 174, 175, 176
Sone, Hideki, 173, 174, 175, 176
Song, Hae-sung, 4, 15, 222
Song, Hwee Lim, 260, 264
special effects, 96, 105, 204, 205, 210, 218n5, 259
spectatorship, 2, 4, 34, 40, 54, 61, 66, 76, 80, 112, 124, 125, 132, 134, 143, 147
    queer, 122
Spellbound (film), 51
Splash (film), 21, 291, 296, 300, 305, 306, 307
spy thriller, 3, 201
Squid Game (TV series), 60, 273
staging, 20, 60, 116, 211, 214, 227, 230, 234n3, 259
Stam, Robert, 29
Stanwyck, Barbara, 82
star system, 8,
stardom, 8, 10, 29, 35, 36, 37, 50, 61, 66, 111, 113–14, 152, 174, 175, 176, 201, 205, 212, 234, 253, 265, 283–5, 289
    music, 264, 279, 208
    transnational, 189, 196, 258
stereotype, 82, 243, 275, 278, 285
Stevenson, Mark, 77
Stiegler, Bernard, 133, 137
Still Walking (film), 148
Storm Riders, The (film), 206
Story of a Discharged Prisoner, The (film), 16
Story of a Prostitute (film), 36
Story of Floating Weeds, A (film), 92
Strauss, Johann, 59–60
Stray Bullet, The (film), 55–7, 61, 62
Stray Dog (film), 227, 234n3
streaming platforms, 268–9
Street Mobster (film), 97
Street of Joy (film), 35
striptease, 30, 31–2, 66
'structure of feeling', 264
Student Couple (film), 50
stunt, 201, 208, 210, 217
subtitles, 123n2, 225, 226, 310n15
Suddenly Twenty (film), 272
suicide, 8, 12, 39, 45, 78, 88, 157, 164, 167, 168
Sukiyaki Western Django (film), 187, 190
Summer Heat (film), 7
sumo, 11, 130
Sun, Andrew, 218n10
Sun's Burial, The (film), 65
Suzhou River (film), 298, 304
Suzuki, Seijun, 6, 30, 32, 33–4, 35, 36, 38, 41, 43, 45, 158, 187

Suzuki, Tomohiko, 163
Sweet 20 (2015 film), 272
Sweet 20 (2017 film), 272
swordswomen, 73–4, 75, 86, 87
    as neo-femme fatale, 80
Sympathy for the Underdog (film), 179n3

Taguchi, Tomorowo, 102, 103, 104, 105
Taike culture, 260, 265–9
Taiwan Creative Content Agency (TAICCA), 259–60
Taiwan New Cinema, 257, 260, 263
taiyupian, 3
Takamori, Ryuichi, 167
Takechi, Tetsuji, 6, 51, 53, 56, 61, 62, 63, 70
Takeda, Akira, 61
Takeuchi, Riki, 175, 178
Takinami, Yuki, 128
Tale of a Foolish Woman, The (novel), 77
Tam, Chun-ho, 211
Tamura, Taijirō, 5–6, 27, 28, 29, 30, 31–2, 33, 34, 36, 37, 38, 40, 41, 43, 44–5, 47
Tan, Ed S., 217
Tanaka, Kinuyo, 122
Tanizaki, Jun'ichirō, 22n1, 35
Target, The (film), 15
Tasaka, Tomotaka, 65
'tatami-mat shots', 11, 143, 145, 152; *see also* Ozu, Yasujiro
Teacher of Violence: Massacre in Broad Daylight (film), 96, 98
Teddy Girls (film), 88
teenpic, 53; *see also* coming-of-age film; youth film
television, 11, 18, 27, 28, 39, 43, 45, 46n4, 52, 88, 89, 93, 95–6, 104–5, 127, 130–2, 135, 136, 246, 286, 288
temporality, 5, 12, 121, 147, 150, 165, 166, 213, 239, 241, 243, 246, 301
Teng, Teresa, 285–9
Teo, Jasmine, 218n15
Teo, Stephen, 221, 227
Terracotta Woman, The (novel), 34
territorial dispute, 2
Teshigahara, Hiroshi, 65
Tetsuo: The Bullet Man (film), 106
Tetsuo: The Iron Man (film), 9, 94, 101, 102–7
Tetsuo II: Body Hammer (film), 106
Thailand, 19, 203
That Guy and I (film), 65
Third Man, The (film), 144
3-D, 291, 301, 302
Three Friends (film), 253
Three Meals a Day (TV series), 246
Three Men and a Baby (film), 218n2
Throne of Blood (film), 222
Throw Down (film), 222
time-lapse, 105
To, Johnnie, 14, 200, 203, 219n20, 221–3, 225–8, 230–3, 235, 236

Todoroki, Yukiko, 38
Tōei (studio), 9, 30, 36, 40, 45, 93, 96, 97, 101, 158, 160
Tōhō (studio), 9, 30, 31, 32, 34, 93, 113, 114, 158, 188
Tohōku region, 240, 241, 242–4, 246, 248, 252
Tōjō, Hideki, 34
Tokyo, 11, 13, 31, 32, 44, 96, 97, 102, 105, 112, 116, 119–20, 121, 141, 143, 144, 145, 151, 159, 160, 162, 163, 164, 166, 188, 248
  bombings, 35
Tokyo Bordello (film), 36
Tokyo Family (film), 12, 140–6, 148, 150, 152
Tokyo Raiders (film), 206
Tokyo Story (film), 10, 11, 12, 111, 112, 113, 117, 118, 121–2, 140–5, 146, 147, 148, 149, 150, 151
Tone, Ichirō, 46n3
Tora-san, The Expert (film), 150
Tora-san, Welcome Back (film), 149, 150
Tora-san's Love in Osaka (film), 149
Train to Busan (film), 258
Train to Busan Presents: Peninsula (film), 258
trains, 113, 120, 121, 129, 142, 143, 144, 223, 229, 231
translation, 12, 18, 52, 84, 137, 241, 242, 266, 273, 292, 294, 297–8, 304; intra-medial; *see also* cultural translatability
transnational cinema, 22, 185, 187, 265, 294, 295
transnational meme, 293
transnationalism, 18, 19, 21, 22, 76, 182, 184–91, 193, 195–6, 197, 198, 202, 209, 210, 241, 244, 246, 247, 257–70, 272, 286, 291, 292, 293–5, 297, 301
trauma, 2, 3, 13, 55, 84, 121, 144, 171, 182, 184, 185, 187, 192–3, 195, 198, 242, 263
Treaty on Basic Relations (Japan and South Korea), 50, 58
triads, 203, 221, 257
trilogy, 11, 111, 112, 113–14, 116–18, 120–2, 127, 147, 148, 150, 267
True Account of the Life of Ando Noboru (Outlaw): Raging Fire (film), 159, 175, 178
Tsai, Ming-liang, 257
Tsang, Eric, 219n19
Tse, Nicholas, 205
Tsui, Clarence, 204, 206, 207, 213, 217, 218n3
Tsui, Hark, 8, 204
Tsukamoto, Shin'ya, 9, 94, 95, 96, 101–6
Tsukioka, Chiaki, 38
Tsukioka, Yumeji, 114
tsunami, 144, 243
20 Once Again (film), 19, 272, 285, 286, 287, 288
'Twilight Samurai' (film series), 147
2 or 3 Things I Know About Her (film), 96
2000 A.D. (film), 205, 206

Uehara, Ken, 157
Ultraman (TV series), 96, 107n4
Ultra Q (TV series), 96

Um, Aing-ran, 50, 66
uncanniness, 2, 19, 20
unconscious, the, 125, 128, 129, 137
Unforgiven (1992 film), 2, 13, 183, 185, 187–8, 189, 190, 193, 194, 198
Unforgiven (2013 film), 2, 13, 14, 182, 183–98
Universal Copyright Convention, 49; *see also* copyright

Vanishing, The (1988 film), 8
Vanishing, The (1993 film), 8
VCinema, 20
vengeance, 78, 85, 175, 226; *see also* revenge film
Verevis, Constantine, 1, 3, 28, 29, 35, 92, 93, 106, 107n5, 111, 113, 122, 241, 294, 309n7
Vertigo (film), 16
Vertov, Dziga, 128
Veteran (film), 260
VHS, 38, 41; *see also* home video
Videodrome (film), 102
Vietnam, 18, 19, 272, 274, 275, 279, 280
violence, 32, 36, 37, 38, 41, 45, 46, 51, 76, 80, 83, 87, 159, 162, 177, 183, 184, 194–5, 197, 211, 230, 289, 305–7
  redemptive, 193
  retributive, 308
  sexual, 33
  state-sanctioned, 190, 192
  woman-on-woman, 33
Visible Secret (film), 218n5
vulgarity, 53, 58, 88, 134

Wa, Ka-fei, 226
Wada, Kaoru, 159, 172
Waikiki Brothers (film), 253
Wakamatsu, Kōji, 23n1, 63
Wan, Chung-Shan, 78
Wang, Anthony, 228
Wang, Deshun, 286
Wang, Pan, 296, 297, 298, 306, 309n3, 309n9, 310n14
Wang, Yiman, 1–2, 8, 184, 218n15
war, 2, 3, 5, 10, 19, 27, 31, 34–5, 43, 112, 113, 117, 121, 131, 133, 144, 150, 157, 160–1, 182, 186, 192–3, 196, 282, 284, 287
  criminal, 158
  veteran, 31, 55
War at Sea from Hawaii to Malaya, The (film), 113
Warm Current (film), 157
Warner Bros., 188
Warner Bros. China, 210
Warriors of the Rainbow: Seediq Bale (film), 259
Watanabe, Ken, 13, 183, 188–9, 191, 197
Watari, Tetsuya, 12, 157, 160, 162, 163, 170
Wenders, Wim, 10, 122
Western, 2, 13, 182–98, 200, 288
  Asian, 14, 185–8, 190
  Manchurian, 288
What a Hero! (film), 200, 207, 208, 219n20

'What a Wonderful Family!' (film series), 12, 147, 148, 150
'What Is Your Name?' (film series), 122
Where Spring Comes Late (film), 149, 197
White Storm, The (film), 200
Who Am I? (film), 201, 205
Wiene, Robert, 51, 60
Wife Confesses, A (film), 53
Wife's Confession (film), 53
Wild Bunch, The (film), 97
Wilde, Oscar, 10
Williams, Raymond, 264
Williams, Tony, 218n15
Winds of September (film), 263
wire-fu, 206; *see also* kung fu; martial arts
Wiretap (film), 222
Woman in the Dunes (film), 65
Woman of Tokyo (film), 127
women-in-prison films, 7
Wonderful Nightmare (film), 258
Wong, Fei-hung, 74
Wong, Ruby, 230
Wong, Sharon, 206
Woo, John, 4, 15, 165, 200, 204, 222, 227
Wood, Robin, 111–13, 114, 117, 121
Woodland, Sarah, 1
Wu, Cuncun, 77
Wu, Gi-dong, 6, 51, 53–4, 56, 58, 61, 69, 70
Wu, Yonggang, 8
wuxia, 7, 8, 73–4, 75, 78, 79, 80, 82, 83, 85; *see also* martial arts

X
Xu, Gary G., 210

yakuza, 12, 13, 97, 157–62, 165, 166, 167, 169, 172, 174–5, 177–8

Yamamoto, Masashi, 101
Yamamoto, Hideo, 164
Yamazaki, Mikio, 179n1
Yang, Edward, 257
Yang, Gongliang, 20
Yau, Nai-hoi, 222
Yecies, Brian, 49, 52, 53, 68–9, 70, 310n20
Yeh, Emilie Yueh-yu, 205, 308, 310n16, 310n18
Yellow Handkerchief, The (film), 147
Yeoh, Michelle, 88, 204
Yes, Madam! (film), 88
Yim, Soon-rye, 17, 18, 239, 240, 247–8, 252, 254n1, 255n7
Yin, Chen-hao, 265, 266, 267
Yoda, Tomiko, 158, 171, 172
Yojimbo (film), 188, 191
Yongary, Monster from the Deep (film), 49
Yoshimura, Kōzaburō, 157
Yoshiyuki, Kazuko, 12, 141, 150
You Are the Apple of My Eye (film), 263, 264, 266
Youth Are Thirsty, The (film), 50
youth crisis, 241, 242, 244–6, 252
youth film, 9, 51, 65, 178; *see also* coming-of-age film; teenpic
Youth of the Beast (film), 36
Yu, Hyun-mok, 6, 51, 53–6, 60, 61, 63, 68–71
Yutori generation, 243, 246

Zahlten, Alexander, 53, 61, 69, 70, 71n2, 99
Zainichi, 13, 169, 183, 197
Zegen (film), 168
Zhang, Yimou, 75
Zhang, Yin, 3
Zhuhai, 21
zoom shot, 207, 300
Zu: Warriors from the Magic Mountain (film), 8
Zwick, Edward, 191

EU representative:
Easy Access System Europe
Mustamäe tee 50, 10621 Tallinn, Estonia
Gpsr.requests@easproject.com

www.ingramcontent.com/pod-product-compliance
Lightning Source LLC
Chambersburg PA
CBHW052050230426
43671CB00011B/1860